FRANKLIN PARK PUBLIC LIBRARY
FRANKLIN PARK, ILL.

Each borrower is held responsible for all library material drawn on his card and for fines accruing on the same. No material will be issued until such fine has been paid.

All injuries to library material beyond reasonable wear and all losses shall be made good to the satisfaction of the Librarian.

The 9/11 Encyclopedia

THE 9/11
ENCYCLOPEDIA

VOLUME 2

Stephen E. Atkins

Praeger Security International
Westport, Connecticut • London

Library of Congress Cataloging-in-Publication Data
Atkins, Stephen E.
  The 9/11 encyclopedia / Stephen E. Atkins.
    p. cm.
  Includes bibliographical references and index.
  ISBN-13: 978-0-275-99431-0 ((set) : alk. paper)
  ISBN-13: 978-0-275-99432-7 ((vol. 1) : alk. paper)
  ISBN-13: 978-0-275-99433-4 ((vol. 2) : alk. paper)
  1. September 11 Terrorist Attacks, 2001—Encyclopedias. 2. September 11 Terrorist
Attacks, 2001—Influence—Encyclopedias. I. Title: Nine eleven encyclopedia. II. Title.
  HV6432.7.A85 2008
  973.931—dc22   2008004185

British Library Cataloguing in Publication Data is available.

Library of Congress Catalog Card Number: 2008004185
ISBN-13: 978-0-275-99431-0 (set)
        978-0-275-99432-7 (vol. 1)
        978-0-275-99433-4 (vol. 2)

First published in 2008

Praeger Security International, 88 Post Road West, Westport, CT 06881
An imprint of Greenwood Publishing Group, Inc.
www.praeger.com

Printed in the United States of America

The paper used in this book complies with the
Permanent Paper Standard issued by the National
Information Standards Organization (Z39.48-1984).

10 9 8 7 6 5 4 3 2 1

Contents

List of Entries   vii

List of Primary Documents   xi

Guide to Related Topics   xv

Volume 1

Preface   xix

Encyclopedia   1

Volume 2

Chronology of Events Surrounding 9/11   xix

Primary Documents   327

Annotated Bibliography   547

Index   567

List of Entries

Abdel Rahman, Sheikh Omar
Able Danger
Abouhalima, Mahmud
African Embassy Bombings
Alec Station
American Airlines Flight 11
American Airlines Flight 77
American Society of Civil Engineers
   Report
Argenbright Security Company
Atef, Mohammad
Atta, Mohamed el-Amir Awad
   el-Sayed
Azzam, Sheikh Abdullah Yussuf

Bahaji, Said
Beamer, Todd Morgan
Biggart, William
Bingham, Mark Kendall
Bin Laden, Osama
Bin al-Shibh, Ramzi
Bucca, Ronald
Burlingame, Charles Frank "Chic" III
Burnett, Thomas Edward
Bush, George W.
Bush Administration

Cantor Fitzgerald
Casualties of September 11
Central Intelligence Agency
Chomsky, Noam
Churchill, Ward
Clarke, Richard A.
Cleanup Operations at Ground Zero
Clinton Administration
Conspiracy Theories
Counterterrorism Center

Dahl, Jason Matthew
DCA
Department of Design and
   Construction
Disaster Mortuary Operation
   Response Team
Dog Rescue and Recovery Teams
Downey, Ray Matthew

Economic Impact of September 11

Fadl, Jamal al-
Fahrenheit 9/11
Families of Victims of September 11
Family Assistance Center
Family Steering Committee

Federal Aviation Administration (FAA)
Federal Bureau of Investigation (FBI)
Federal Emergency Management
  Agency (FEMA)
Feehan, William M. "Bill"
Fetzer, James H.
Fire House 40/35
Firefighters at Ground Zero
Firefighter Riot on November 2,
  2001
Floyd, Nancy
Foreign Intelligence Surveillance
  Act of 1978
Freedom Tower
Freeh, Louis
Fresh Kills Landfill

Ganci, Peter J. "Pete"
Giuliani, Rudolph William Louis
  "Rudy" III
Giuliani Time (Documentary)
Glick, Jeremy
Goss, Porter J.
Graham, Daniel Robert "Bob"
Griffin, David Ray
Guantánamo Bay Detainment Camp

Hage, Wadih el-
Hamburg Cell
Hamburg Cell (TV Movie)
Hamdani, Mohammad Salman
Hamilton, Lee H.
Hanjour, Hani Saleh Husan
Hazmi, Nawaf bin Muhammad
  Salim al-
Homer, LeRoy Wilton Jr.

Ielpi, Lee
Immigration and Naturalization
  Services (INS)

Jarrah, Ziad Samir
Jersey Girls

Joint Terrorism Task Force
Jones, Steven E.
Judge, Mychal
Justification for the September 11
  Suicide Mission

Kean, Thomas Howard
Kerik, Bernard Bailey
Kifah Refugee Center, al-
Kuala Lumpur Meeting

Levin, Neil David
Lewin, Daniel M.

Marrs, Jim
Mazza, Kathy
Merino, Yamel
Meyssan, Thierry
Mihdhar, Khalid al-
Millennium Plots
Mohamed, Ali Abdel Saoud
Mohammed, Khalid Sheikh
Motassadeq, Mounir el-
Moussaoui, Zacarias
Murad, Abdul Hakim Ali Hashim

National Commission on Terrorist
  Attacks upon the United States
National Security Agency (NSA)
Naudet Documentary on 9/11
New York City Landmarks Bombing
  Conspiracy
New York City Police Department
  (NYPD)
Nineteen Martyrs
North American Aerospace Defense
  Command (NORAD)
Nosair, El Sayyid

Office of Emergency Management
  (OEM)
Ogonowski, John
Olson, Barbara

O'Neill, John
Ong, Betty Ann
Operation Bojinka
Occupational Safety and Heath
    Agency (OSHA)

The Path to 9/11 (TV Miniseries)
Pavel Hlava Video
Pentagon Attack
Phoenix Memo
Pilot Training for September 11
Port Authority of New York and
    New Jersey
Predator

Qaeda, al-
Quds Mosque, al-

Rendition
Rescorla, Cyril Richard (Rick)
Ressam, Ahmed
Rowley, Coleen

Samit, Harry
Saracini, Victor J.
Scheuer, Michael
Scholars for 9/11 Truth
Senate Select Committee on
    Intelligence and the House
    Permanent Select Committee on
    Intelligence Joint Inquiry into the
    Terrorist Attacks of September 11
Shehhi, Marwan Yousef Muhammed
    Rashid Lekrab al- (1978–2001)

Smith, Moira
Swift Project

Taliban
Tenet, George
TIPOFF
Transportation Security
    Administration

United Airlines Flight 93
United Airlines Flight 175
United 93 (Film)
USA PATRIOT Act

Victims' Compensation Fund
Von Essen, Thomas

Wag the Dog (Movie)
The Wall
Weldon, Curtis "Curt"
World Trade Center
World Trade Center, September 11
World Trade Center (Movie)
World Trade Center Bombing
    (1993)

Yousef, Ramzi Ahmed

Zadroga, James
Zammar, Muhammad Heydar
Zawahiri, Ayman al-
Zubaydah, Abu

List of Primary Documents

Document 1: Letter Justifying the Bombing of the World Trade Center (February 7, 1993)

Document 2: Osama bin Laden's Declaration of Jihad (August 23, 1996)

Document 3: Declaration of World Islamic Front (February 23, 1998)

Document 4: Communiqué of the World Islamic Front (1998)

Document 5: Al-Qaeda Training Camps in Afghanistan in 2000

Document 6: Al-Qaeda's Instructions on Living in the Western World While on a Mission

Document 7: Martyr's Blood

Document 8: Memorandum from Richard A. Clarke for Condoleezza Rice Informing Her about the al-Qaeda Network (January 25, 2001)

Document 9: Letter from Brian F. Sullivan, Retired FAA Special Agent, to U.S. Senator John Kerry (May 7, 2001)

Document 10: Letter from Michael Canavan, Associate Administrator for Civil Aviation Security, to FAA Security Managers (May 30, 2001)

Document 11: Presidential Daily Briefing (August 6, 2001)

Document 12: Brian Sullivan's E-mail to Michael Canavan, FAA Associate Administrator for Civil Aviation Security, about Aviation Security (August 16, 2001)

Document 13: Mohamed Atta's Letter of Advice for Hijackers (September 2001)

Document 14: Oral Testimony from Survivors of the World Trade Center

Document 15: Pentagon Attack

Document 16: United Airlines Flight 93

Document 17: Dog Handlers at Ground Zero

Document 18: President George W. Bush's Address to the Nation (September 11, 2001)

Document 19: Interview with Mullah Omar Muhammad (September 21, 2001)

Document 20: Environmental Protection Agency's Press Release (September 13, 2001)

Document 21: Statements by Federal Emergency Management Agency on

Its Response to the Terrorist Attacks on the World Trade Center in New York City and the Pentagon before the United States Senate's Committee on Environment and Public Works (October 16, 2001)

Document 22: *Dawn* Interview with Osama bin Laden (November 10, 2001)

Document 23: Bin Laden's Homage to the Nineteen Students (December 26, 2001)

Document 24: White House Declaration on the Humane Treatment of Al-Qaeda and Taliban Detainees (February 7, 2002)

Document 25: Testimony of Dr. W. Gene Corley on Behalf of the American Society of Civil Engineers before the Subcommittee on Environment, Technology and Standards and Subcommittee on Research of the U.S. House of Representatives Committee on Science (May 1, 2002)

Document 26: Report by Eleanor Hill from the Joint Inquiry Staff Statement on the Intelligence on the Possible Terrorist Use of Airplanes (September 18, 2002)

Document 27: Report by Eleanor Hill from the Joint Inquiry Staff on the Intelligence Community's Knowledge of the September 11 Hijackers Prior to September 11, 2001 (September 20, 2002)

Document 28: Statement of Special Agent of the Federal Bureau of Investigation (September 20, 2002)

Document 29: Report of the Joint Inquiry by Eleanor Hill on the FBI's Handling of the Phoenix Electronic Communication (September 23, 2002)

Document 30: Report of the Joint Inquiry Staff by Eleanor Hill on the FBI Investigation of Zacarias Moussaoui (September 24, 2002)

Document 31: Testimony of Richard A. Clark Before the National Commission on Terrorist Attacks Upon the United States (March 24, 2004)

Document 32: Testimony of Mary Fetchet, Founding Director, Voices of September 11th, on the Need for Reform in a Hearing of the Senate's Committee on Government Affairs (August 17, 2004)

Document 33: Assessment of the FBI on Pre-9/11 Intelligence (August 18, 2004)

Document 34: Testimony by Lee Hamilton, Vice Chairman of the 9/11 Commission, before the House of Representatives' Financial Services Committee (August 22, 2004)

Document 35: The Aviation Security System and the 9/11 Attacks (2004)

Document 36: Letter from Brian F. Sullivan to Thomas Kean, Chairman of the National Commission on Terrorist Attacks Upon the United States (2004)

Document 37: Comments of Representative Maxine Waters (D-CA) on Saudi Financial Support for Al-Qaeda before the House of Representatives' Financial Services Committee (August 22, 2004)

Document 38: Curt Weldon's Testimony about Able Danger (September 20, 2005)

Document 39: Essay by Ward Churchill (September 11, 2001)

Document 40: Selected Excerpts from the Testimony of FBI Agent Harry Samit in the Zacarias Moussaoui Trial (March 9, 2006)

Document 41: Testimony of the American Red Cross before the Management, Integration, and Oversight Subcommittee of the House Homeland Security Committee (July 12, 2006)

Document 42: Confession of Khalid Sheikh Mohammed at the Combatant Status Review Tribunal at Guantánamo Detention Camp (March 10, 2007)

Guide to Related Topics

Airline Flights
American Airlines Flight 11
American Airlines Flight 77
United Airlines Flight 93
United Airlines Flight 175

Airport Security
Argenbright Security Company
TIPOFF
Transportation Security
   Administration

American Intelligence Efforts
Able Danger
Central Intelligence Agency
Counterterrorism Center
National Security Agency (NSA)
Phoenix Memo
Scheuer, Michael
The Wall

American Political Leadership
Bush, George W.
Bush Administration
Clinton Administration
Clarke, Richard A.
Tenet, George
Weldon, Curtis

Centers of Terrorist Planning
Kifah Refugee Center, al-
Kuala Lumpur Meeting
Quds Mosque, al-

Counterterrorism
Foreign Intelligence Surveillance
   Act of 1978
Joint Terrorism Task Force
Predator
Rendition
USA PATRIOT Act

Critics of U.S. Policy before 9/11
Chomsky, Noam
Churchill, Ward

Economic Aftermath
Cantor Fitzgerald
Economic Impact of September 11
Swift Project

Families of 9/11
Families of Victims of
   September 11
Family Assistance Center
Family Steering Committee
Ielpi, Lee

Jersey Girls
Victims' Compensation Fund

FBI Agents
Floyd, Nancy
Freeh, Louis
Rowley, Coleen
Samit, Harry

Fighting Terrorism
Guantánamo Bay Detainment Camp

Firefighters
Fire House 40/35
Firefighters at Ground Zero
Firefighter Riot on November 2,
2001

Government Agencies
Federal Aviation Administration
(FAA)
Federal Bureau of Investigation
(FBI)
Federal Emergency Management
Agency (FEMA)
Immigration and Naturalization
Services (INS)
North American Aerospace Defense
Command (NORAD)
Occupational Safety and Heath
Agency (OSHA)

Ground Zero
Casualties of September 11
Cleanup Operations at Ground
Zero
Department of Design and
Construction
Disaster Mortuary Operation
Response Team
Dog Rescue and Recovery Teams
Fresh Kills Landfill
Zadroga, James

Jihad Supporters
Azzam, Sheikh Abdullah Yussuf

Joint Committee on Intelligence
Goss, Porter J.
Graham, Daniel Robert "Bob"
Senate Select Committee on
Intelligence and the House
Permanent Select Committee on
Intelligence Joint Inquiry into
the Terrorist Attacks of
September 11

Movies and Documentaries
Fahrenheit 9/11
Giuliani Time (Documentary)
Hamburg Cell (TV Movie)
Naudet Documentary on 9/11
Pavel Hlava Video
United 93
Wag the Dog
World Trade Center

**New York City Officials and
Agencies**
Giuliani, Rudolf William Louis
"Rudy" III
Kerik, Bernard Bailey
New York City Police Department
Office of Emergency Management
(OEM)
Port Authority of New York and
New Jersey
Von Essen, Thomas

9/11 Commission
Hamilton, Lee H.
Kean, Thomas Howard
National Commission on Terrorist
Attacks upon the United States

9/11 Conspiracy Theories
Conspiracy Theories

Fetzer, James H.
Griffin, David Ray
Jones, Steven E.
Marrs, Jim
Meyssan, Thierry
Scholars for 9/11 Truth

9/11 Hijackers

Atta, Mohamed el-Amir Awad
    el-Sayed
Hamburg Cell
Hanjour, Hani Saleh Husan
Hazmi, Nawaf bin Muhammad
    Salim al-
Jarrah, Ziad Samir
Justification for the September 11
    Suicide Mission
Mihdhar, Khalid, al-
Nineteen Martyrs
Pilot Training for September 11
Shehhi, Marwan Yousef
    Muhammed Rashid Lekrab al-

9/11 Hijacking Supporters

Bahaji, Said
Bin al-Shibh, Ramzi
Taliban

Al-Qaeda Leadership

Atef, Mohammad
Bin Laden, Osama
Mohammed, Khalid Sheikh
Qaeda, al-
Zawahiri, Ayman al-
Zubaydah, Abu

Al-Qaeda Operatives

Fadl, Jamal al-
Hage, Wadih el-
Mohamed, Ali Abdel Saoud
Motassadeq, Mounir
Moussaoui, Zacarias

Murad, Abdul Hakim Ali Hashim
Nosair, El Sayyid
Ressam, Ahmed
Zammar, Muhammad Heydar

Pentagon

Pentagon Attack

Reconstruction Efforts

Freedom Tower

Structural Reports

American Society of Civil Engineers
    Report

Support Efforts after 9/11

DCA

Terrorist Acts and Plans

African Embassy Bombings
Millennium Plots
New York City Landmarks
    Bombing Conspiracy
Operation Bojinka

**Victims of 9/11—American
Airlines Flight 11**

Lewin, Daniel M.
Ogonowski, John
Ong, Betty Ann

**Victims of 9/11—American
Airlines Flight 77**

Burlingame, Charles Frank "Chic"
    III
Olson, Barbara

**Victims of 9/11—United Airlines
Flight 93**

Beamer, Todd Morgan
Bingham, Mark Kendall
Burnett, Thomas Edward
Dahl, Jason Matthew

Glick, Jeremy
Homer, LeRoy Wilton Jr.

Victims of 9/11—United Airlines Flight 175
Saracini, Victor J.

Victims of 9/11—World Trade Center Complex
Biggart, William
Bucca, Ronald
Downey, Ray Matthew
Feehan, William M. "Bill"
Ganci, Peter J. "Pete"
Hamdani, Mohammad Salman
Judge, Mychal
Levin, Neil David

Mazza, Kathy
Merino, Yamel
Rescorla, Cyril Richard "Rick"
Smith, Moira

World Trade Center Bombing (1993)
Abdel Rahman, Sheikh Omar
Abouhalima, Mahmud
World Trade Center Bombing (1993)
Yousef, Ramzi Ahmed

World Trade Center Complex
World Trade Center
World Trade Center, September 11

Chronology of Events Surrounding 9/11

October 25, 1978	President Jimmy Carter signs the Foreign Intelligence Surveillance Act, which allowed investigations of foreign persons who are engaged in espionage or international terrorism.
December 26, 1979	Soviet forces invade Afghanistan, beginning the Afghan-Soviet War.
August 11, 1988	Osama bin Laden and Sheikh Abdullah Azzam start the al-Qaeda organization in Afghanistan.
November 24, 1988	Unknown group assassinates Islamist leader Sheikh Abdullah Azzam in Peshawar, Pakistan, with a car bomb, leaving Osama bin Laden in control of al-Qaeda.
February 15, 1989	Soviet forces withdraw from Afghanistan
November 5, 1990	El Sayyid Nosair assassinates Rabbi Meir Kahane in New York City.
July 24, 1992	Mohamed Atta arrives in Germany to begin graduate work.
September 1, 1992	Ramzi Yousef arrives in the United States at the request of Sheikh Abdel Rahman.
February 26, 1993	Bombing of the World Trade Center in New York City, by an Islamist terrorist team led by Ramzi Yousef, kills 6 and wounds 1,042.
March 4, 1993	FBI discovers the VIN number of the Ryder van that leads to the arrest of some of The World Trade bombers.

March 4, 1994	Three of the World Trade Center bombers convicted of bombing.
April 9, 1994	Saudi government revokes Osama bin Laden's Saudi citizenship.
December 11, 1994	Ramzi Ahmed Yousef plants bomb on Philippine Air Lines Flight 434 that kills Japanese engineer.
January 6, 1995	Ramzi Ahmed Yousef accidentally causes fire in a Manila apartment that exposes his plot to assassinate the Pope.
January 20, 1995	Abdul Hakim Murad confesses to a plot to fly a small plane into CIA headquarters in Langley, Virginia.
February 7, 1995	Pakistani authorities arrest Ramzi Ahmed Yousef, the head of the 1993 World Trade Center bombing, in Islamabad, Pakistan.
September 22, 1995	Ramzi Bin al-Shibh arrives in Germany.
January 17, 1996	Sheikh Abdel Rahman receives life sentence for his role in planning the bombing of New York City landmarks.
April 3, 1996	Zaid Jarrah arrives in Germany to continue his education.
April 28, 1996	Marwan al-Shehhi arrives in Germany with a military scholarship to further his studies.
May 18, 1996	Sudan expels Osama bin Laden, who leaves for Afghanistan.
June 25, 1996	Al-Qaeda operatives explode truck bomb at the al-Khobar in Dhahran, Saudi Arabia, killing 19 Americans and wounding hundreds of others.
July 17, 1996	Explosion downs TWA Flight 800 near Long Island, New York.
August 23, 1996	Osama bin Laden's Declaration of Jihad against the Western World.
May 26, 1997	Saudi government first to recognize the Taliban government in Afghanistan.
January 8, 1998	Ramzi Ahmed Yousef receives sentence of 240 years for his role in the World Trade Center bombing in 1993.
February 23, 1998	World Islam Front's Declaration of War against Jews and Crusaders by Osama bin Laden and others.

August 7, 1998	Bombing of U.S. embassies in Nairobi, Kenya, and Dar es Salaam, Tanzania, by al-Qaeda operatives.
August 20, 1998	U.S. Tomahawk cruise missiles strike al-Qaeda base camps in Afghanistan and Sudan.
October 8, 1998	FAA warns U.S. airports and airlines of al-Qaeda's threat to U.S. civil aviation.
November 1, 1998	Mohamed Atta, Said Bahaji, and Ramzi Bin al-Shibh move into 54 Marienstrasse in the Harburg area of Hamburg, beginning the Hamburg Cell.
June 7, 1999	FBI puts Osama bin Laden on its 10 Most Wanted list.
October 1999	Creation of the special intelligence unit Able Danger
December 1, 1998	U.S. intelligence makes the assessment that Osama bin Laden has been planning attacks inside the United States.
2000	Pentagon lawyers block Able Danger reporting to FBI three times during the year.
January–February 2000	Special intelligence unit Able Danger identifies Mohamed Atta and three associates as possible al-Qaeda agents.
January 5–8, 2000	Al-Qaeda holds summit conference in Kuala Lumpur, Malaysia, where plans for September 11 are discussed.
January 15, 2000	Logistical team of Khalid al-Mihdhar and Nawaf al-Hamzi arrive in Los Angeles to prepare for the September 11 operation.
June 3, 2000	Mohamed Atta arrives in the United States at Newark International Airport from Prague, Czech Republic.
July 2000	Mohamed Atta and Marwan al-Shehhi begin flying lessons at Huffman Aviation in Venice, Florida.
July–August 2000	Defense Intelligence Agency employees destroy evidence gathered by Able Danger.
August 12, 2000	Italian intelligence wiretaps al-Qaeda terrorist cell in Milan, Italy, whose members talk about a massive strike involving aircraft and the sky.
October 12, 2000	Al-Qaeda operatives place bomb next to the American destroyer USS *Cole*, killing 17 sailors and injuring 39 others.
October 24–26, 2000	Emergency drill at Pentagon on the possibility of a hijacked airliner crash into building.

December 20, 2000	Richard Clarke proposes plan to attack al-Qaeda, but it is postponed and later rejected by new Bush administration.
December 21, 2000	Mohamed Atta and Marwan al-Shehhi receive pilot licenses.
December 26, 2000	Mohamed Atta and Marwan al-Shehhi abandon rented plane on taxiway of Miami Airport after plane's engine fails during takeoff.
January 2001	Lt. Col. Anthony Shaffer, member of Able Danger, briefs General Hugh Shelton on the group's findings.
January 4, 2001	Mohamed Atta travels to Spain.
January 10, 2001	Mohamed Atta returns to the United States.
February 23, 2001	Zacarias Moussaoui arrives in the United States.
March 7, 2001	Government leaders discuss plan to fight al-Qaeda, but there is no urgency to proceed.
Spring 2001	Able Danger program terminated.
April 1, 2001	Oklahoma police give speeding ticket to Nawaf al-Hazmi.
April 16, 2001	Mohamed Atta receives traffic ticket for driving without a license.
April 18, 2001	FAA warns airlines about possible Middle Eastern hijackers.
April 18, 2001	Marwan al-Shehhi flies to Amsterdam.
April 30, 2001	Deputy Defense Secretary Paul Wolfowitz downplays emphasis on Osama bin Laden at a meeting on terrorism.
May 10, 2001	Attorney General John Ashcroft omits counterterrorism from list of goals of the Justice Department.
May 15, 2001	CIA refuses to share information with FBI about al-Qaeda meeting in Malaysia in January 2000.
June 10, 2001	CIA notifies all its station chiefs of a possible al-Qaeda suicide attack on United States targets over the next few days.
June 11, 2001	CIA analyst and FBI agents have shouting match over sharing information about terrorists' identification information.
June 20, 2001	FBI agent Robert Wright sends a memo that charges the FBI of not trying to catch known terrorists living in the United States.

June 21, 2001	Osama bin Laden tells Muslim journalist that an attack on the United States is imminent.
June 28, 2001	CIA Director Tenet issues warning of imminent al-Qaeda attack.
July 2, 2001	FBI warns of possible al-Qaeda attacks abroad but also possibly in the United States.
July 5, 2001	Richard Clarke briefs senior security officials on al-Qaeda threat at the White House and tells them al-Qaeda is planning a major attack.
July 8–19, 2001	Mohamed Atta, Ramzi bin al-Shibh, and Marwan al-Shehhi travel to Spain to finalize attack plans.
July 10, 2001	FBI agent Ken Williams sends memo about the large number of Middle Eastern men taking flight training lessons in Arizona.
July 10, 2001	Head of CIA, George Tenet, briefs Condoleezza Rice and warns of the possibility of an al-Qaeda attack in the United States.
July 17, 2001	Mohamed Atta and Marwan al-Shehhi meet with al-Qaeda leaders in Taragona, Spain, to make final plans for the September 11 attacks.
July 18, 2001	Both FBI and FAA issue warnings about possible terrorist activity.
August 6, 2001	President George W. Bush receives a briefing entitled "Bin Laden Determined to Strike in U.S." at Crawford ranch in Texas.
August 15, 2001	FBI agents in Minneapolis request a FISA search warrant for Zacarias Moussaoui.
August 16, 2001	Arrest of Zacarias Moussaoui by Harry Samit in Minneapolis for visa violation.
August 19, 2001	FBI's top al-Qaeda expert, John O'Neill, resigns from FBI under pressure.
August 20, 2001	Samit sends memo to FBI headquarters in Washington, D.C., citing Zacarias Moussaoui as a terrorist threat for an aircraft skyjacking.
August 23, 2001	FBI adds two of the September 11 conspirators, Nawaf al-Hazmi and Khalid al-Mihdhar, to the Terrorist Watch List.
August 23, 2001	Israel's Mossad gives CIA a list of terrorists living in United States on which four 9/11 hijackers are named.

August 23, 2001	John O'Neill begins work as head of the World Trade Center security.
August 24, 2001	Khalid al-Mihdhar buys his 9/11 ticket.
August 25, 2001	Nawaf al-Hazmi buys his 9/11 ticket.
August 28, 2001	FBI's New York office requests to open criminal investigation of Khalid al-Mihdhar, but FBI headquarters turns down request.
August 28, 2001	Mohamed Atta buys 9/11 ticket.
August 29, 2001	Khalid Sheikh Mohammed gives go-ahead for the September 11 attacks in a call from Afghanistan.
August 29, 2001	Mohamed Atta tells Ramzi bin al-Shibh date of attack in code.
September 4, 2001	Cabinet rank advisors approve of Richard Clarke's plan, proposed eight months earlier, to attack al-Qaeda.
September 9, 2001	Maryland police give Ziad Jarrah a ticket for speeding.
September 10, 2001	Attorney General John Ashcroft turns down an increase of $58 million for FBI counterterrorism budget.
September 10, 2001	At a dinner John O'Neill warns that there is distinct probability of an al-Qaeda attack on New York City in the near future.
September 10, 2001	Mohamed Atta and Abdulaziz al-Omari check in at a motel in Portland, Maine.
September 11, 2001	Assault on World Trade Center and the Pentagon.
12:45 a.m.	Willie Brown, the mayor of San Francisco, receives a call from security at San Francisco International Airport warning him about air travel on September 11.
6:45 a.m.	Two workers at the instant messaging company Odigo, an Israeli-owned company housed in the World Trade Center, receive messages warning of a possible attack on the World Trade Center.
6:50 a.m.	Mohamed Atta and Abdulaziz al-Omari's flight from Portland, Maine, arrives at Logan International Airport.
7:45 a.m.	Mohammed Atta and Abdulaziz al-Omari board American Airlines Flight 11.
7:59 a.m.	American Airlines Flight 11 leaves Boston Logan Airport with destination of Los Angeles.

8:13:31 a.m.	Last routine radio communication from American Airlines Flight 11; the aircraft begins climbing to 35,000 feet.
8:14 a.m.	United Airlines Flight 175 leaves Boston Logan Airport with destination of Los Angeles after 16-minute delay.
8:17 a.m.	Daniel Lewin, former member of the Israel Defense Force's counterterrorist unit Sayeret Matkal, is killed.
8:20 a.m.	American Airlines Flight 77 leaves Washington, D.C., with destination of Los Angeles.
8:21 a.m.	Transponder in American Airlines Flight 11 stops transmitting identification.
8:21 a.m.	Flight attendant Betty Ong, on American Airlines Flight 11, notifies American Airlines of hijacking.
8:25 a.m.	Boston air traffic control center becomes aware of skyjacking of American Airlines Flight 11 and notifies several air traffic control centers that a hijacking is in progress.
8:26 a.m.	American Airlines Flight 11 makes a 100-degree turn to the south, toward New York City.
8:37:08 a.m.	Boston flight control asks the pilots of United Airlines Flight 175 whether they can see American Airlines 11, and they answer in the affirmative.
8:38 a.m.	Boston air traffic control center notifies NORAD of hijacking of American Airlines Flight 11.
8:40 a.m.	FAA notifies NORAD of the American Airlines Flight 11 hijacking.
8:42 a.m.	Last radio communication from United Airlines Flight 175 with New York air traffic control; transponder is inactive.
8:43 a.m.	FAA notifies NORAD of the United Airlines Flight 175 hijacking.
8:43 a.m.	United Airlines Flight 93 takes off from Newark International Airport with its destination San Francisco after a 41-minute delay.
8:46 a.m.	NORAD scrambles Otis fighter jets in search of American Airlines Flight 11.
8:46 a.m.	Transponder signal from United Airlines Flight 175 stops transmitting.

8:46:40 a.m.	American Airline Flight 11 crashes into North Tower of the World Trade Center in New York City.
8:47 a.m.	NORAD learns about American Airlines Flight 11 striking the World Trade Center.
8:49 a.m.	United Airlines Flight 175 deviates from its assigned flight path.
8:50 a.m.	Female flight attendant from United Airlines Flight 175 reports to a San Francisco mechanic that the flight had been hijacked.
8:50:51 a.m.	Last radio communication from American Airlines Flight 77.
8:52 a.m.	Flight attendant on United Airlines Flight 175 notifies United Airlines of hijacking.
8:53 a.m.	Otis fighter jets become airborne.
8:54 a.m.	American Airlines Flight 77 makes unauthorized turn to south.
8:55 a.m.	Barbara Olson, a passenger on American Airlines Flight 77, notifies her husband, Solicitor General Theodore Olson, at the Justice Department that her aircraft has been hijacked.
8:56 a.m.	Transponder on American Airlines Flight 77 stops sending signals.
8:56 a.m.	American Airlines Flight 77 begins making a 180-degree turn over southern Ohio and heads back to the Washington, D.C., area.
8:57 a.m.	FAA formally informs the military about the crash of American Airlines Flight 11 into the World Trade Center.
9:00 a.m.	FAA starts contacting all airliners to warn them of the hijackings.
9:01 a.m.	Aide informs President George W. Bush of the crash of American Airlines Flight 11 into the World Trade Center at Emma E. Booker Elementary School in Sarasota, Florida.
9:02:54 a.m.	United Airlines Flight 175 crashes into the South Tower of the World Trade Center in New York City.
9:03 a.m.	Boston air traffic control center halts traffic from its airports to all New York area airspace.
9:05 a.m.	American Airlines becomes aware that American Airlines Flight 77 has been hijacked.

9:05 a.m.	Aide informs President George W. Bush about the second plane hitting the World Trade Center, and he understands that the United States is under attack.
9:06 a.m.	FAA formally informs the military that United Airlines Flight 175 has been hijacked.
9:08 a.m.	FAA orders all aircraft to leave New York airspace and orders all New York–bound aircraft nationwide to stay on the ground.
9:11 a.m.	Two F-15 Eagles from Otis Air National Guard arrive over New York City airspace.
9:15 a.m.	New York air traffic control center advises NORAD that United Airlines Flight 175 has also crashed into the World Trade Center.
9:16 a.m.	American Airlines aware that American Airlines Flight 11 has crashed into World Trade Center.
9:17 a.m.	FAA shuts down all New York City area airports.
9:20 a.m.	United Airlines headquarters becomes aware that United Airlines Flight 175 has crashed into the World Trade Center.
9:21 a.m.	Port Authority of New York and New Jersey orders all bridges and tunnels in the New York area closed.
9:24 a.m.	FAA informs NORAD that American Airlines Flight 77 has been hijacked.
9:24 a.m.	NORAD scrambles Langley fighter jets to search for American Airlines Flight 77.
9:24 a.m.	United Airlines Flight 93 receives warning from United Airlines about possible cockpit intrusion by terrorists.
9:25 a.m.	Herndon Command Center orders nationwide grounding of all commercial and civilian aircraft.
9:26 a.m.	Barbara Olson calls her husband again to give him details about the hijacking.
9:27 a.m.	Last routine radio communication from United Airlines Flight 93.
9:28 a.m.	Likely takeover of United Airlines Flight 93 by terrorists.
9:29 a.m.	Jeremy Glick, a passenger on United Airlines Flight 93, calls his wife, who informs him about the attacks in New York City.

9:30 a.m.	President Bush states in an informal address at the elementary school in Sarasota, Florida, that the country has suffered an apparent terrorist attack.
9:30 a.m.	Flight of F-16 Fighting Falcons takes off from Langley Air Force base and head toward New York City until redirected to Washington, D.C.
9:32 a.m.	Dulles tower observes the approach of a fast-moving aircraft on radar.
9:32 a.m.	Secret Service agents take Vice President Cheney to the underground bunker in the White House basement.
9:34 a.m.	Federal Aviation Administration (FAA) advises NORAD that American Airlines Flight 77's whereabouts is unknown.
9:34 a.m.	Herndon Command Center advises Federal Aviation Administration headquarters that United Airlines 93 has been hijacked.
9:35 a.m.	United Airlines Flight 93 begins making a 135-degree turn near Cleveland, Ohio, and heads for the Washington, D.C., area.
9:36 a.m.	Flight attendant on United Airlines Flight 93 notifies United Airlines of hijacking.
9:36 a.m.	Ronald Reagan Washington National Airport asks a military C130 aircraft that has just departed Andrews Air Force base to locate American Airlines Flight 77, and it answers that a 767 was moving low and very fast.
9:37:46 a.m.	American Airlines Flight 77 crashes into the Pentagon.
9:40 a.m.	Transportation Secretary Norman Y. Mineta orders the FAA to ground all 4,546 airplanes in the air at the time.
9:41 a.m.	Transponder no longer functions in United Airlines Flight 93.
9:42 a.m.	Mark Bingham, a passenger on United Airlines Flight 93, calls his mother and reports the hijacking.
9:45 a.m.	White House evacuates all personnel.
9:45 a.m.	President Bush leaves the elementary school in Sarasota to board Air Force One.
9:45 a.m.	Todd Beamer, a passenger on United Flight 93, tells a Verizon supervisor that the passengers have voted to storm the hijackers.

9:47 a.m.	Military commanders worldwide are ordered to raise their threat alert status to the highest level to defend the United States.
9:49 a.m.	Flight of F-16s arrives over the Washington, D.C., area.
9:58 a.m.	After receiving authorization from President Bush, Vice President Cheney gives instructions to engage United Airlines Flight 93 as it approaches the Washington, D.C., area.
9:57 a.m.	Passenger revolt begins in United Airlines Flight 93.
9:57 a.m.	President Bush departs from Florida.
10:03:11 a.m.	United Airlines Flight 93 crashes in field in Shanksville, Pennsylvania.
10:05 a.m.	South Tower of the World Trade Center collapses.
10:07 a.m.	Cleveland air traffic control center advises NORAD of United Airlines 93 skyjacking.
10:10 a.m.	Portion of Pentagon collapses.
10:15 a.m.	United Airlines headquarters aware that Flight 93 has crashed in Pennsylvania.
10:15 a.m.	Washington air traffic control center advises Northeast Air Defense Sector (NEADS) that Flight 93 has crashed in Pennsylvania.
10:24 a.m.	FAA orders that all inbound transatlantic aircraft flying into the United States be diverted to Canada.
10:28:31 a.m.	North Tower of the World Trade Center collapses.
10:30 a.m.	American Airlines headquarters confirms American Airlines Flight 77 has crashed into the Pentagon.
10:31 a.m.	Presidential authorization to shoot down hijacked aircraft reaches NORAD.
10:32 a.m.	Vice President Cheney tells President Bush that a threat against Air Force One has been received.
10:50 a.m.	Five stories of the Pentagon collapse due to the blast and fire.
11:02 a.m.	New York City Mayor Rudolph Giuliani asks New Yorkers to stay home and orders an evacuation of the area south of Canal Street.
11:40 a.m.	Air Force One lands at Barksdale Air Force Base in Louisiana.

12:04 p.m.	Los Angeles International Airport is evacuated and shut down.
12:15 p.m.	San Francisco International Airport is evacuated and shut down.
1:04 p.m.	President Bush, speaking from Barksdale Air Force Base in Louisiana, announces that all appropriate security measures are being taken and all U.S. military has been put on high alert worldwide.
1:48 p.m.	President Bush flies to Offutt Air Force Base in Nebraska.
2:00 p.m.	Senior FBI sources tell CNN that they are assuming that the aircraft hijackings are part of a terrorist attack.
4:10 p.m.	Reports surface that Building Seven of the World Trade Center complex is on fire.
4:30 p.m.	President Bush leaves Offutt Air Force Base to return to Washington, D.C.
5:20:33 p.m.	Building Seven (47 stories) of the World Trade Center collapses.
6:00 p.m.	Northern Alliance launches bombing campaign against the Taliban in Kabul, Afghanistan.
6:54 p.m.	President Bush arrives at the White House in Washington, D.C.
8:30 p.m.	President Bush addresses the nation about the events of the day.
October 21, 2001	Osama bin Laden gives his justification for the 9/11 attacks in an interview with an al-Jazeera journalist.
October 24, 2001	House of Representatives passes the USA PATRIOT Act.
October 25, 2001	Senate passes the USA PATRIOT Act
October 26, 2001	President George W. Bush signs the USA PATRIOT Act.
December 26, 2001	Osama bin Laden issues a statement of homage to the 19 martyrs of September 11.
November 15, 2002	National Commission on 9/11 is chartered over the objection of President George W. Bush.
December 20, 2002	Final Report of the Senate Select Committee on Intelligence and the House of Permanent Select Committee on Intelligence Joint Inquiry into the Terrorist Attacks of September 11 appears.

March 31–April 2003	First public hearings by the National Commission on 9/11.
July 22, 2004	Final report of the National Commission on 9/11.
June 2005	Representative Curt Weldon (R-PA) gives floor speech about Able Danger.
August 12, 2005	National Commission on 9/11 issues statement dismissing the Able Danger information as not "historically significant."
August 17, 2005	Lt. Col. Anthony Shaffer, a member of Able Danger, issues a public statement about the identification of Atta and others as al-Qaeda agents by Able Danger as early as 2000.
September 21, 2005	Senate Judiciary Committee holds hearing on Able Danger, but Defense Department prohibits Able Danger officers from participating in the hearings.
March 9, 2006	President Bush reauthorizes the USA PATRIOT Act.

Primary Documents

Document 1

Letter Justifying the Bombing of the World Trade Center (February 7, 1993)

This is the text of Ramzi Ahmed Yousef's letter justifying the bombing of the World Trade Center on February 7, 1993, which he had sent to the New York Times. *It was one of five such letters sent to five news organizations by one of Yousef's colleagues shortly after the bomb exploded. The "army" mentioned in the text was nonexistent, but the letter does express Yousef's hostile attitude toward the United States.*

We are, the fifth battalion in the LIBERATION ARMY, declare [*sic*] our responsibility for the explosion on the mentioned building. This action was done in response for the American political, economical, and military support to Israel the state of terrorism and to the rest of the dictator countries in the region.

Our demands:

1. Stop all military, economical, and political aids to Israel.
2. All diplomatic relations with Israel must stop.
3. Not to interfere with any of the Middle East countries interior affairs.

If our demands are not met, all of our functional groups in the army will continue to execute our missions against the military and civilian targets in and out of the United States. For your own information, our army has more than hundred and fifty suicidal soldiers ready to go ahead. The terrorism that Israel practices (which is supported by America) must be faced with a similar one. The dictatorship and terrorism (also supported by America) that some countries are practicing against their own people must also be faced with terrorism.

The American people must know, that their civilians who got killed are not better than those who are getting killed by the American weapons and support.

The American people are responsible for the actions of their government and they must question all of the crimes that their government is committing against other people or they—Americans—will be the targets of our operations that could diminish them. We invite all the people from all countries and all of the revolutionaries in the world to participate in this action with us to accomplish our just goals.

Liberation Army Fifth Battalion
AL-FARBEK AL-ROKN, Abu Bakr Al-Makee

Source: Simon Reeve, *The New Jackals, Ramzi Yousef, Osama Bin Laden and the Future of Terrorism* (Boston: Northeastern University Press, 1999), pp. 274–275.

Document 2

Osama bin Laden's Declaration of Jihad
(August 23, 1996)

Osama bin Laden had been disturbed by the Saudi government's granting of permission for American troops to be stationed on the holy soil of Saudi Arabia. He had gone to the Saudi government and volunteered his services, including those of Arabs that had fought in Afghanistan, to repulse Saddam Hussein's invasion of Kuwait. When the Saudis turned his offer down and invited the American troops, bin Laden was infuriated. Bin Laden is a Wahhabi Sunni, and the Wahhabi Sunnis believe that Christianity is a polytheistic religion because of the Christian belief in the Trinity. He subscribed to a saying in the hadith (sayings of the Prophet Mohammad) that reads, "Expel the Polytheists from the Arabian peninsula." Bin Laden issued this judicial edict of jihad, or holy war, on August 23, 1996, with the assistance of the religious council of al-Qaeda. It was an open declaration of war against the United States for their presence in the Kingdom of Saudi Arabia. The declaration is a lengthy document, so only the most pertinent parts have been included here.

It is no secret to you, my brothers, that the people of Islam have been afflicted with oppression, hostility, and injustice by the Judeo-Christian alliance and its supporters. This shows our enemies' belief that Muslims' blood is the cheapest and that their property and wealth are merely loot. Your blood has been spilt in Palestine and Iraq, and the horrific image of the massacre in Qana in Lebanon are [*sic*] still fresh in people's minds. The massacres that have taken place in Tajikistan, Burma, Kashmir, Assam, the Philippines, Fatani, Ogaden, Somalia, Eritrea, Chechnya, and Bosnia-Herzegovina send shivers down our spines and stir up our passions. All this happened before the eyes and ears of the world, but the blatant imperial arrogance of America, under the cover of the immoral United Nations, has prevented the dispossessed from arming themselves.

So the people of Islam realized that they were the fundamental target of the hostility of the Judeo-Crusader alliance. All the false propaganda about the supposed rights of Islam was abandoned in the face of the attacks and massacres committed against Muslims everywhere, the latest and most serious of which—the greatest disaster to befall the Muslims since the death of the prophet Muhammad—is the occupation of Saudi Arabia, which is cornerstone of the Islamic world, place of revelation, source of the Prophetic mission, and the home of the Noble Ka'ba where Muslims direct their prayers. Despite this, it was occupied by the armies of the Christians, the Americans, and their allies.

I meet you today in the midst of this gloomy scenario, but also in light of the tremendous, blessed awakening that has swept across the world, and particularly the Islamic world. After the scholars of Islam underwent an enforced absence—enforced due to the oppressive Crusader campaign led by America in the fear that these scholars will incite our Islamic *umma* against its enemies, in the same way as did the pious scholars of old (God bless their souls) such as ibn Taymiyya and al-Izz ibn Abd al-Salam—this Judeo-Crusader alliance undertook to kill and arrest the righteous scholars and hardworking preachers. May God sanctify who He wishes. They killed the *mujahid* Sheikh Abdallah Azzam, they arrested Sheikh Ahmed Yassin in Jerusalem, and they killed the *mujahid* Sheikh Omar Abd al-Rahman in America, as well as arresting—on the advice of America—a large number of scholars, preachers and youth in Saudi Arabia. The most prominent of these were Sheikh Salman al-Auda and Sheikh Safar al-Hawali and their brothers.

This injustice was inflicted on us, too, as we were prevented from talking to Muslims and were hounded out of Saudi Arabia to Pakistan, Sudan, and then Afghanistan. That is what led to this long absence of mine, but by the grace of God there became available a safe base in Khurasan, high in the peaks of the Hindu Kush, the very same peaks upon which were smashed, by the grace of God, the largest infidel military force in the world, and on which the myth of the great powers perished before the cries of the holy warriors: God is greatest!

And today, in the same peaks of Afghanistan, we work to do away with the injustice that has befallen our *umma* at the hands of the Judeo-Crusader alliance, especially after its occupation of Jerusalem and its appropriation of Saudi Arabia. We pray to god that He might bless us with victory—He is our protector and is well capable of doing so.

And so here we are today, working and discussing with each other to find ways of rectifying what has happened to the Islamic world generally and Saudi Arabia in particular. We need to study the appropriate paths to take in order to restore things to good order, and to restore to the people their rights after the considerable damage and harm inflected on their life and religion. This has afflicted every section of society, whether civilian or military or security personnel, whether employees or merchants, young or old, university students, graduates or the unemployed, who now represent a broad section of society numbering hundreds of thousands. The situation in Saudi Arabia has begun to resemble a huge volcano that is about to explode and destroy unbelief and corruption, wherever it comes from. The two explosions in Riyadh and Khobar are merely warning signs pointing to this destructive torrent which is produced by bitter repression, terrible injustice, and the humiliating poverty that we see today.

People are struggling even with the basics of everyday life, and everyone talks frankly about economic recession, price inflation, mounting debts, and prison overcrowding. Low-income government employees talk to you about their debts in the hundreds of thousands of riyals, whilst complaining that the riyal's value is declining dramatically. Domestic debts owed by the government to its citizens have reached 340 billion riyals, and are rising daily due to usurious interest, let alone all the foreign debt. People are wondering are we really the biggest source of oil in the world? They feel that God is bringing this torture on them because they have not spoken out against the regime's injustice and illegitimate behaviour, the most prominent aspects of which are its failure to rule in accordance with God's law, its depriving of legal rights to its servants, its permitting the American occupiers into Saudi Arabia, and its arresting of righteous scholars—inheritors of the Prophets' legacy—and unjustly throwing them in prison. The regime has desecrated its legitimacy through many of its own actions, the most important being:

1. Its suspension of the rulings of the Islamic law and replacement thereof with man-made laws, and its entering into a bloody confrontation with the righteous scholars and pious youth. May God sanctify whom He pleases.
2. Its inability to protect the land and its allowing the enemies of God to occupy it for years in the form of the American Crusaders, who have become the principal reason for all aspects of our land's disastrous predicament.

The voices of the shadows have spoken up, their eyes uncovering the veil of injustice and their noses smelling the stench of corruption. The voices of reform have spoken up, calling for the situation to be put right: they have sent petitions, testimonies, and requests for reform. In the year 1411 AH, at the time of the Gulf War, a petition was sent to the king with around 400 signatures calling for reform in the country, but he made a mockery of them by completely ignoring their advice, and the situation went from bad to worse.

Brother Muslims in Saudi Arabia, does it make any sense at all that our country is the biggest purchaser of weapons from America in the world and America's biggest trading partner in the region, while at the very same time the Americans are occupying Saudi Arabia and supporting—with money, arms, and manpower—their Jewish brothers in the occupation of Palestine and their murder and expulsion of Muslims there? Depriving these occupiers of the huge returns they receive form heir trade with us is a very important way of supporting the *jihad* against them, and we expect you to boycott all American goods.

Men of the radiant future of our *umma* of Muhammad, raise the banner of *jihad* up high against the Judea-American alliance has occupied the holy places of Islam. God told his Prophet: "He will not let the deeds of those who are killed for His cause come to nothing; He will guide them and put them in a good state; He will admit them into the Garden He has already made known to them." And the Prophet said: "There are one hundred levels in Heaven that God has prepared for the holy warriors who have died for Him, between two levels as between the earth and the sky." And the *al-Jami al-Sahih* notes that the Prophet said: "The best martyrs are those who stay in the battle line and do not turn their faces away until they are killed. They will achieve the highest level of Heaven, and their Lord will look kindly upon them. When your Lord looks kindly upon a slave in the world, He will not hold him to account." And he said: "The martyr has a guarantee from God: He forgives him at the first drop of blood and shows him his seat in Heaven. He decorates him with the jewels of faith, protects him from the torment of the grave, keeps him safe on the day of judgment, places a crown of dignity on his head with the finest rubies in the world, marries him to seventy-two of the pure virgins of paradise and intercedes on behalf of seventy of his relatives," as related by Ahmad al-Tirmidhi in an authoritative *hadith*.

I say to the youth of Islam who have waged *jihad* in Afghanistan and Bosnia-Herzegovina, with their financial, spiritual, linguistic, and scholarly resources, that the battle is not yet over. I remind them of what Gabriel said to the Prophet, after the battle of Ahzab: "When the Messenger of God, prayers and peace be upon him, departed to Medina and laid down his sword, Gabriel came to him and said: 'You have laid down your sword? By God, the angels have not yet laid down their swords. Get up and go with whoever is with you to the Bani Qurayza, and I will go ahead of you to shake their fortresses and strike fear into them.' So Gabriel went off, accompanies by his pageant of angels, the Prophet, and his holy warriors and helpers." This is as it was told by al-Bukhari.

I say to our Muslim brothers across the world: your brothers in Saudi Arabia and Palestine are calling for your help and asking you to share with them in the *jihad* against the enemies of God, your enemies the Israelis and Americans. They are asking you to defy them in whatever way you possibly can, so as to expel them in defeat and humiliation from the holy places of Islam. God Almighty has said: "If they seek help from you against persecution, it is your duty to assist them."

Cavalry of Islam be mounted! This is a difficult time, so you yourself must be tough. You should know that your coming-together and cooperation in order to liberate the holy places of Islam is the right step towards unification of the word of our *umma* under the banner of God's unity. At this point we can only raise our palms humbly to ask God Almighty to provide good fortune and success in this matter.

Source: Bruce Lawrence (ed.), *Messages to the World: The Statements of Osama Bin Laden* (London: Verso, 2005), pp. 23–30.

Document 3

Declaration of the World Islamic Front
(February 23, 1998)

If the 1996 Declaration of Jihad was Osama bin Laden's personal declaration of war against the West and Israel, the Declaration of the World Islamic Front in 1998 was a group declaration of war by al-Qaeda and its supporters. Signatories of the declaration included bin Laden; Ayman al-Zawahiri, amir, or head, of the Egyptian Islamic Jihad; Abu-Yasir Rif'ai Ahmad Taha, a leader of the Egyptian Islamic Group; Sheikh Mir Hamza, secretary of the Islamic Party of Religious Leaders in Pakistan; and Maulana Fazlur Rahman, a leader of the opposition in Pakistan's National Assembly. By having allies, bin Laden was able to answer criticism that he lacked the religious credentials to issue a judicial ruling, or fatwa. This document is an open declaration of hostilities by al-Qaeda and its allies that was to lead directly to the events of September 11, 2001.

Praise be to God, revealer of the Book, controller of the clouds, defeater of factionalism, who says in His Book: "When the forbidden months are over, wherever you find the polytheists, kill them, seize them, besiege them, ambush them." Prayers and peace be upon our Prophet Muhammad bin Abdallah, who said: "I have been sent with a sword in my hands so that only God may be worshipped, God who placed my livelihood under the shadow of my spear and who condemns those who disobey my orders to servility and humiliation."

Ever since God made the Arabian peninsula flat, created desert in it and surrounded it with seas, it has never suffered such a calamity as these Crusader hordes that have spread through it like locusts, consuming its wealth and destroying its fertility. All this at a time when nations have joined forces against the Muslims as if fighting over a bowl of food. When the matter is this grave and support is scarce, we must discuss current events and agree collectively on how best to settle the issue.

There is now no longer any debate about three well acknowledged and commonly agreed facts that require no further proof, but we will repeat them so that people remember them. They are as follows:

Firstly, for over seven years America has occupied the holiest parts of the Islamic lands, the Arabian peninsula, plundering its wealth, dictating to its leaders, humiliating its people, terrorizing its neighbours and turning its bases there into a spearhead with which to fight the neighbouring Muslim peoples.

Some might have disputed the reality of this occupation before, but all the people of the Arabian peninsula have now acknowledged it. There is no clearer proof than America's excessive aggression against the people of Iraq, using the Peninsula as a base. It is true that all its leaders have rejected such use of their lands, but they are powerless.

Secondly, despite the great devastation inflicted upon the Iraqi people at the hands of the Judeo-Crusader alliance, and despite the terrible number of deaths— over one million—despite all this, the Americans are trying to repeat these horrific massacres again, as if they are not satisfied with the long period of sanctions after the vicious war, or with the fragmentation and destruction.

Today they come to annihilate what is left of this people and humiliate their Muslim neighbours.

Thirdly while these wars are being waged by the Americans for religious and economic purposes, they also serve the interests of the petty Jewish state, diverting attention from its occupation of Jerusalem and its murder of Muslims there.

There is no better proof of this than their eagerness to destroy Iraq, the strongest neighbouring Arab state, and their efforts to fragment all the states in the region, like Iraq, Saudi Arabia, Egypt, and Sudan, into paper mini-states whose weakness and disunity will guarantee Israel's survival and the continuation of the brutal Crusader occupation of the Peninsula.

All these American crimes and sins are a clear proclamation of war against God, his messenger, and the Muslims. Religious scholars throughout Islamic history have agreed that *jihad* is an individual duty when an enemy attacks Muslim countries. This was related by the Iman ibn Qudama in "The Resource," by Iman al-Kisa'i in "The Marvels," by al-Qurtubi in his exegesis, and by the Sheikh of Islam when he states in his chronicles that "As for fighting to repel an enemy, which is the strongest way to defend freedom and religion, it is agreed that this is a duty. After faith, there is no greater duty than fighting an enemy who is corrupting religion and the world."

On this basis, and in accordance with God's will, we pronounce to all Muslims the following judgment:

To kill the American [*sic*] and their allies—civilians and military—is an individual duty incumbent upon every Muslim in all countries, in order to liberate the al-Aqsa Mosque and the Holy Mosque from their grip, so that their armies leave all the territory of Islam, defeated, broken, and unable to threaten any Muslim. This is in accordance with the words of god Almighty: "Fight the idolaters at a time, if they first fight you"; "Fight them until there is no more persecution and until worship is devoted to God"; "Why should you not fight in God's cause and for those oppressed men, women, and children who cry out: 'Lord, rescue us from this town whose people are oppressors! By Your grace, give us a protector and a helper!'?"

With God's permission we call on everyone who believes in God and wants reward to comply with His will to kill the Americans and seize their money wherever and whenever they find them. We also call on the religious scholars, their leaders, their youth, and their soldiers, to launch the raid on the soldiers of Satan, the Americans, and whichever devil's supporters are allied with them, to rout those behind them so that they will not forget it.

God Almighty said: "Believers, respond to God and His Messenger when he calls you to that which gives you life. Know that God comes between a man and his heart, and that you will be gathered to Him."

God almighty said: "Believers, why, when it is said to you, 'Go and fight in God's way,' do you dig your heels into the earth? Do you prefer this world to the life to come? How small the enjoyment of this world is, compared with the life to come! If you do not go out and fight, God will punish you severely and put others in your place, but you cannot harm Him in any way: God has power over all things."

God Almighty also said: "Do not lose heart or despair—if you are true believers you will have the upper hand."

Source: Bruce Lawrence (ed.), *Messages to the World: The Statements of Osama Bin Laden* (London: Verso, 2005), pp. 59–62.

Document 4

Communiqué of the World Islamic Front

Following the formal declaration of the formation of the World Islamic Front in 1998, there was a need to rally potential supporters. The following communiqué was one such effort. It appeared shortly after the Clinton administration retaliated for the embassy bombings in Africa with Tomahawk missiles directed against targets in Afghanistan and the Sudan. The tone of the communiqué is much more strident than the almost scholarly language of the Declaration of the World Islamic Front.

Communiqué of the World Islamic Front

Clinton Scorns More Than a Billion Muslims.

Kill the infidels where they are, drive them out of the places from which they have driven you. America is the leader of the infidel countries. The aggression against Sudan and Afghanistan is an aggression against the Muslims of the entire world. To fight the infidel countries, American and Israel, is a duty for all Muslims. These two aggressions are the height of world terrorism, worthy of pirates or cowboys. . . . This aggression proves the Americans' lack of strategy, which brought Clinton to power. This attack demonstrates American cretinism and its contempt for Muslims. It proves the ineptitude of the CIA, for there was no connection with Sheikh Mujahed Osama bin Laden. . . . These attacks prove the hostility of the 'black dogs and swine, vile beings against men full of pride.' Let us fight in the jihad for our pride and our lands. It is a duty imposed by Sharia to answer aggression from American and its allies.

We must close all their embassies in Muslim countries, boycott their economy. withdraw all our money from their banks and companies, prohibit their use of our air space, and block their means of communication.

Muslims, awake!

Return to your religion, stop supporting your corrupt leaders so that they can stop humiliating you, terrorizing you, and making you into a consumer product.

Source: Roland Jacquard, *In the Name of Osama Bid Laden: Global Terrorism & the Bin Laden Brotherhood* (Durham, NC: Duke University Press, 2002), p. 184.

Document 5

Al-Qaeda Training Camps in Afghanistan in 2000

British intelligence presented an assessment of al-Qaeda training camps in Afghanistan in 2000. This report shows the variety and specialties of al-Qaeda's training camps. It also showed that the Pakistani intelligence service, Interservices Intelligence (ISI), played an active role in some of the camps. There is also a suggestive report that al-Qaeda was building a command and control center in a natural cave system in Kunduz province near the border with Tajikistan. It was in one of the al-Qaeda camps in Afghanistan that Mohamed Atta and the members of his team trained in the years before September 11.

Training camps for militants involved in Kashmir, in battlefields around the world and in international terrorism are located in Taliban-controlled Nangarhar, Pakhita, Logar and Kunar provinces of Afghanistan, bordering Pakistan and in several cases it is not clear which side of the Pak-Afghan border they are on. Pakistanis, Kashmiries and Arabs from Saudi Arabia, Algeria, Tunisia, Iraq, Egypt, Jordan and Palestinians were among those trained in these camps.

Camps in Khost Area

(i) Al Badr-I and Al Badr-II camps in Khost area of Pakhtia province are two major militant training camps in the country. Soon after Taliban captured Kabul, these camps were reported to have been handed over to the Harkat-ul-Ansar (HuA) for its use, after initial reports that Taliban had closed these camps. Al Badr-I was holding among others, about 200 Pakistani recruits being trained to fight against the Indian Forces in Kashmir and for Harkat-ul-Ansar. Al Badr-II had around 160 trainees, mostly Arabs and Sudanese Muslims for the fight in Chechnya and Bosnia They were being given lessons in bomb making, use of automatic weapons, rocket launchers and antiaircraft guns. These camps, which were being used by the followers of Osama Bin

Laden were however, destroyed in August 1998 by the US Tomahawk (cruise) missiles fired from the Arabian Sea with the aim of killing Osama, for his alleged involvement in the bomb blasts in the US Missions in Nairobi and Tanzania. These, as well as those camps located in Khost (Paktia province) at Khawaja Mastoon Gundai, Sati Kundo on Pak-Afghan border and Tora-Bora base near Jalalabad (Nangarhar) and Julrez town (Wardak) 30 miles west of Kabul were however, reportedly rebuilt by Osama. A Command and Control Centre for AI [sic] Qaida outfit of Osama is also learnt to be under construction in a natural cave system in Kunduz province (near Tajik border).

(ii) Besides Al Badr I and II camps, other camps in Khost area are Omar, Al Khuldan and Farooq camps along the Pak-Afghan border and known to be involved in training of Arab-Afghan mercenaries for fighting in Chechnya. A training centre called Abdullah Azzam Training Centre for training of Arabs and Tajiks also exists here. Camps affiliated to Osama Bin Laden for training terrorists for Kashmir operations under the leadership of Egyptians and Algerians are also functioning in Khost area. Mine warfare training is reportedly carried out by the Egyptian militant group Al-Jehad at the Abu Bakr camps on the outskirts of Khost.

(iii) Some of the camps previously located in Peshawar have been shifted to Khost area. Qaida camp is one such example.

(iv) Khost camp—Essentially, Yemeni extremists are trained here, though some Algerian militants have also been trained in the past.

(v) Nearly 700 fundamentalists from Chechyna, Indian Kashmir, Laskar-e-Toiba, Harkat-ul-Mujahideen, Somalia etc had undergone 9 month military training at a place locally known as Jarangiya in Khost since 15.01.2000. Col. Latif of ISI is the Incharge of this training centre. Of the 700 fundamentalists, nearly 90 each belong to Kashmir and POK, which includes activists of Lashkar-e-Toiba. 26 Uighur activists from Xinjiang province of China had also undergone training in this camp.

(vi) Two training camps for Kashmiri militants are currently operating in Khost province. These are at Sarobi village in Nadir Shah district and in the premises of a technical school near the Governor's house in Khost.

Other Camps in Pakhtia Provinces

(i) Jaji camp—Known for training Kashmiri militants and earlier linked to Ittehad-e-Isalami (Sayyaf) group. The camp is also known to train Arab mercenaries for the fighting in Kashmir who are linked to Harkat-ul-Ansar. A Syrian is currently believed to be leading the group of Arabs in this camp and was reported to be the main instigator behind the kidnapping of the four western hostages by the Al-Faran group.

(ii) Spin Shaga—A camp for Kashmiri militants.

(iii) Shepuli—A camp for Kashmiri located here.

(iv) Al-Jehad—It is near Zambar (Lz-3223). About 650 militants of LeT from J&K and POK under the supervision of Col. Saifullah Akhtar are being trained there.

(v) Khaldoon camp—It is controlled by OBL and is used for training 1800-2000 militants from Egypt, Sudan, Algeria, Saudi Arabia and Philippines.

They are prepared to be deployed in Chechyna, J&K, Sudan, and Lebanon etc. This camps [*sic*] had been directed by an Algerian extremist named Kheddar Abden Nasser (Abu Banane, or Commander Abd-El-Nasser), who died recently following a booby-trap explosion.

(vi) Gurbaz—It is about 4 kms. East of Khaldoon camp. About 150 Uighurs from CAS and Xinjiang province of China are undergoing training there.

Camps in Nangharar Provinces

(i) Teraki Tangi—Kashmiri militants are known to be trained in a camp located here.

(ii) Nazian Shinwar—Known for training Kashmiri militants and earlier linked to Ittehad-e-Islami (Sayyaf) group. The camp is also known to train Arab mercenaries linked to Harkat-ul-Ansar for fighting in Kashmir.

(iii) Muzaffarabad (Distt. [*sic*] Shinwari)—A camp for Kashmiri militants.

(iv) Dehbala—A camp for Kashmiri militants.

(v) Jalalabad camp—A leader of Egyptian militant group Al Gama'a Al Islamiya Shawki Al-Islambuli, was known to have run a training camp for Arab mercenaries in Jalalabad for the Afghan Jehad. Arabs, especially Egyptians, belonging to the Al Gama'a are known to be undergoing training here for terrorist activities abroad. The area between Jalalabad and Torkham along the Pak-Afghan border is known to be a base of Arabs undergoing training.

(vi) Darunta—It is situated at a distance of 20 kms from Jalalabad close to a dam at its western exit. A camp run by Abu Abdullah, an Egyptian, is located here. Approximately 300 mercenaries from Philippines, Pakistan, POK, Kashmir, Malaysia, Turkey, Egypt, Algeria and Sudan are known to be receiving training in this camp. Militants from here have been involved in fighting in Bosnia and Azerbaijan while a large number are currently in Chechnya and Kashmir. An Algerian here reportedly conducted a training course on explosives for Arab terrorists in early 1996. The camp is financed by Islamic terrorist organizations. Pak ISI officers are learnt to be frequently visiting this camp.

(vii) Moroccans were undergoing training at Darunta camp during early 2000. The training of Moroccans included handling of weapons and preparation of IEDs.

Camps in Logar Province

Kanjak Camp

Camps in Kunar Province

(i) Camps for training of Kashmiri militants exist in Barikot, Pir Qala, Sarkana and Pench.

(ii) Toshi camp—Located near Asadabad, the camp is a training centre for large numbers of Kashmiri fighters and is under control of Pak ISI.

(iii) A militant Arab group called Khalifa Group, led by Jordanian-Palestinian national Abu Abdullah Al Refaee, is based in Kunar. It recently threatened to raise an Islamic army to wage war against the West. The group is reportedly in league with Takfiris, yet another militant Arab militant group.

(iv) The Ikhwan ul Muslimeen (Muslim Brotherhood) is also active in Kunar province for consolidating their basis in the region bordering the Central Asian States, especially Tajikistan.

(v) Another Egyptian militant group Al-Jehad led by Islambuli, has training bases in Kunar and Nangarhar province of Afghanistan and also a camp in Jalozai region in NWFP, Pakistan. The group receives financial assistance from private individuals in Saudi Arabia through the 'Human Concern International' Organisation registered in Canada. This organization undertakes social projects in Afghanistan.

(vi) Azad Abbas—It is located in the Taliban-controlled Kunar province. Its armed unit is Hizbal-Mujahideen. It [*sic*] prominent leaders are Vat Ziad (Pakistani). It is supported by Pak JI, ISI and is know [*sic*] to be imparting training to Pakistanis and Arabs.

Camps in Kabul Province

(i) The Muslim Brotherhood is known to provide training to Kashmiri militants in camps located in Paghman area of Kabul province. There are also reports of camp being run by Taliban some 15 kilometers outside Kabul city.

(ii) Lava Raking—It is located near Panhuman in Kabul province and is under the Taliban control.

(iii) Sarobi—It is located near Kabul, Makah Al Adam and Pak ISI support it. Its trainees constitute members from Arab, [*sic*] Algerian, [*sic*] Tunisia and Kashmir.

(iv) A Services Bureau, a branch of the Peshawar Services Bureau, is in existence in Kabul and provides support to mercenaries, especially Arabs.

Camps in Jawzjan Province

A training camp for imparting training in light weapons exists in Jawzjan. After training, the mercenaries are sent to Kashmir as well as to the battlefront to fight alongside the Taliban against NA.

Camps in Balkh (Mazar-e-Sharif)

(i) Saidabad—300 families of Uzbek fighters are housed here. 50 Chechen families have also been accommodated in Mazar-e-Sharif. Further, there is a military camp at one end of Saidabad, in an area called Dasht-e-shor where 200 Uzbek receive military training.

(ii) Base-e-Sokhta—located between Mazar town and air base. It is a large place and provides training for Chechens.

Camps in Bamyan Province

The Taliban are reported to have established two new militant training camps in Bamyan besides the existing camp in Bagram, run by the Lashkar-e-Jhangvi (military Wing of the Sipah-e-Sahaba). The Bagram (Bamyan) camp, under one ABDUL JABBAR, is currently imparting training to 50 Pak mercenaries.

Camps in Ghor Province

An Osama-run camp is reported to be in existence in Ghor province, where the pace of training activities has been increased.

Camps in Kandhar Province

A training camp for imparting training in light weapons exists in Kandhar. After training, the mercenaries are sent to Kashmir as well as to the battlefront to fight alongside the Taliban against NA.

Source: Roland Jacquard, *In the Name of Osama Bin Laden: Global Terrorism and the Bin Laden Brotherhood* (Durham, NC: Duke University Press, 2002), pp. 263–267.

Document 6

Al-Qaeda's Instruction on Living in the Western World While on a Mission

All al-Qaeda operatives received training on how to be inconspicuous while on a mission. Trainers identified the most intelligent trainees with the most potential to pass unnoticed in the Western World. Language expertise and personal appearance were of the utmost importance. To insure that the training would last, a manual of behavior was prepared and given to those on operations in the Western world. Here is an excerpt from a lengthy document that gives an insight into this training.

MEMBER SAFETY

Defining Members' Safety:

This is a set of measures taken by members who perform undercover missions in order to prevent the enemies from getting to them.

It is necessary for any party that adopts Jihad work and has many members to subdivide its members into three groups, each of which has its own security measures. The three groups are: 1. The overt members; 2. The covert members; 3. The commander.

Measures that Should be Taken by the Overt Member:

1. He should not be curious and inquisitive about matters that do not concern him.
2. He should not be chatty and talkative about everything he knows or hears.
3. He should not carry on him the names and addresses of those members he knows. If he has to, he should keep them safe.

4. During times of security concerns and arrest campaigns and especially if his appearance is Islamic, he should reduce his visits to the areas of trouble and remain at home instead.

5. When conversing on the telephone he should not talk about any information that might be of use to the enemy.

6. When sending letters, he should not mention any information that might be of use to the enemy. When receiving letters, he should burn them immediately after reading them and pour water on them to prevent the enemy from reading them. Further, he should destroy any traces of the fire so the enemy would not find out that something was burned.

Measures that Should be Taken by the Undercover Member:

In addition to the above measures, the member should . . .

1. Not reveal his true name to the Organization's members who are working with him, nor to the [Islamic] Da'wa [Call].

2. Have a general appearance that does not indicate Islamic orientation [beard, toothpick, book, (long) shirt, small Koran).

3. Be careful not to mention the bothers' common expressions or show their behaviors (special praying appearance, "may Allah reward you," "peace be on you" while arriving and departing, etc.)

4. Avoid visiting famous Islamic places (mosques, libraries, Islamic fairs, etc.)

5. Carry falsified personal documents and know all the information they contain.

6. Have protection preceding his visit to any place while moving about (apartment, province, means of transportation, etc.).

7. Have complete and accurate knowledge of the security status related to those around him in his place of work and residence, so that no danger or harm would catch him unaware.

8. Maintain his family and neighborhood relationships and should not show any changes towards them so that they would not attempt to bring him back [from the Organization] for security reasons.

9. Not resort to utilizing letters and messengers except in an emergency.

10. Not speak loudly.

11. Not get involved in advocating good and denouncing evil in order not to attract attention to himself.

12. Break the daily routine, especially when performing an undercover mission. For example, changing the departure and return routes, arrival and departure times, and the store where he buys his goods.

13. Not causing any trouble in the neighborhood where he lives or at the place of work.

14. Converse on the telephone using special code so that he does not attract attention.

15. Not contracting the overt members except when necessary. Such contacts should be brief.

16. Not fall into the enemy's excitement trap either through praising or criticizing his Organization.

17. Performing the exercises to detect surveillance whenever a task is to be performed.

18. Not park in no-parking zones and not take photographs where it is forbidden.
19. Closing all that should be closed before departing the place, whether at home or his place of undercover work.
20. Not undergo a sudden change in his daily routine or any relationships that precede his Jihad involvement. For example, there should not be an obvious change in his habits of conversing, movement, presence, or disappearance. Likewise, he should not be hasty to sever his previous relationships.
21. Not meet in places where there are informers, such as coffee shops, and not live in areas close to the residences of important personalities, government establishments, and police stations.
22. Not write down on any media, specially [sic] on paper, that could show the traces and words of the pen by rubbing the paper with lead powder.

Measures that Should be Taken by the Commander:

- The commander, whether in overt or covert work, has special importance for the following reasons.
  1. The large amount of information that he possesses.
  2. The difficulty of the command in replacing the commander.
  3. Therefore, all previously mentioned security precautions regarding members should be heightened for the commander.
- Important Note: Married brothers should observe the following:
  1. Not talking with their wives about Jihad work.
  2. The members with security risks should not travel with their wives. A wife with an Islamic appearance (veil) attracts attention.

Source: Stefan Aust et al., *Inside 9-11: What Really Happened* (New York: St. Martin's Press, 2001), pp. 289–292.

Document 7

Martyr's Blood

It is difficult for Westerners to understand the Muslim idea of martyrdom. Committing suicide for a political cause is a foreign concept in the West. But among Muslim extremists, martyrdom has a strong religious component. In the following excerpt from his essay, Morteza Motah-Hary explains the concept of martyrdom in words that the nineteen members of the September 11 plot understood well.

What does a martyr do? His function is not confined to resisting the enemy, and in the process, either giving him a blow or receiving a blow from him. Had that been the case we could say, that when his blood is shed, it goes to waste. But at no time is a martyr's blood wasted. It does not flow on the ground. Every drop of it is turned into hundreds and thousands of drops, nay into tons of blood, and is transfused into the body of his society. That is why the Holy Prophet has said: 'Allah does not like any drop, more than the drop of blood shed, in His way.' Martyrdom means transfusion of blood into a society, especially a society suffering from anemia. It is the martyr who infuses fresh blood into the veins of the society.

MARTYR'S COURAGE AND ZEAL

The distinctive characteristic of a martyr, is that he charges the atmosphere with courage and zeal. He revives the spirit of valor and fortitude, courage and zeal, especially divine zeal, among the people who have lost it. That is why Islam is always in need of martyrs. The revival of courage and zeal is essential for the revival of a nation.

MARTYR'S IMMORTALITY

A scholar serves the society through his knowledge. It is on account of his knowledge that his personality is amalgamated with the society, just as a drop of water is amalgamated with the sea. As the result of this amalgamation a part of personality, namely his thoughts and ideas become immortal. An inventor is amalgamated with the society through his inventions. He serves the society, but making himself immortal, by virtue of his skill and inventions. A poet makes himself immortal through his poetic art, and a moral teacher through his wise sayings.

Similarly, a martyr immortalizes himself in his own way. He gives invaluable fresh blood to the society. In other words, a scholar immortalizes his thoughts, an artist his art, an inventor his inventions, and a moral teacher his teachings. But a martyr, through his blood, immortalizes his entire being. His blood for ever flows in the veins of the society. Every other group of people can make only a part of its faculties immortal, but a martyr immortalizes all his faculties. That is why, the Holy Prophet said: 'Above every virtue, there is another virtue, but there is no virtue higher than being killed in the way of Allah.'

MARTYR'S INTERCESSION

There is a *hadith* which says, that there are three classes of people who will be allowed to intercede with Allah on the Day of Judgment. They are the prophets, *ulema* and martyrs. In this *hadith*, the *Imams* have not been mentioned expressly, but as the report comes down from our *Imams*, it is obvious that the term, '*Ulema*' stands for the true divines, who par excellence include the *Imams* themselves.

The intercession of the prophets is quite apparent. It is the intercession of the martyrs, which we have to comprehend. The martyrs secure this privilege of intercession because they lead the people onto the right path. Their intercession will be portrayal of the events which took place in this world.

The Commander of the Faithful, Imam Ali (P) says: 'Allah will bring forward the martyrs, on the Day of Judgment, with such pomp and splendor, that even the prophets if mounted, will dismount to show their respect for them.' With such grandeur, will a martyr appear on the Day of Judgment.

Source: Adam Parfrey (ed.), *Extreme Islam: Anti-American Propaganda of Muslim Fundamentalism* (Los Angeles: Feral House, 2001), pp. 9–10. Permission granted by Feral Press to reprint this statement. www.feralhouse.com.

Document 8

Memorandum from Richard A. Clarke for Condoleezza Rice Informing Her about the Al-Qaeda Network (January 25, 2001)

On January 25, 2001, Richard A. Clarke, a holdover from the Clinton administration and the head of counterterrorism efforts in that administration, sent a memorandum to Condoleezza Rice, then National Security Advisor to the Bush administration, about al-Qaeda. This memo was Clarke's first effort to have the Bush administration take into account the danger emanating from Osama bin Laden and al-Qaeda.

MEMORANDUM FOR CONDOLEEZZA RICE
FROM: Richard A. Clarke
SUBJECT: Presidential Policy Initiative/Review—The Al-Qaida Network

Condi asked today that we propose major Presidential policy reviews or initiatives. We urgently need such a Principal level review on the al Qida network.

Just some Terrorist Group?

As we noted in our briefings for you, al Qida is not some narrow, little terrorist issue that needs to be included in broader regional policy. Rather, several of our regional policies need to address centrally the transnational challenge to the US and our interests posed by the al Qida network. By proceeding with separate policy reviews on Central Asia, the GCC, North Africa, etc. we would deal inadequately with the need for a comprehensive multi-regional policy on al Qida. Al Qida is the active, organized, major force that is using a distorted version of Islam as its vehicle to achieve two goals:

- to drive the US out of the Muslim world, forcing the withdrawal of our military and economic presence in countries from Morocco to Indonesia;
- to replace moderate, modern, Western regime in Muslim counties with theocracies modeled along the lines of the Taliban.

Al Qida affects centrally our policies on Pakistan, Afghanistan, Central Asia, North Africa and the GCC. Leaders in Jordan and Saudi Arabia see al Qida as a direct threat to them. The strength of the network of organizations limits the scope of support friendly Arab regimes can give to a range of US policies, including Iraq policy and the Peace Process. We would make a major error if we underestimated the challenge al Qida poses, or over estimated the stability of the moderate, friendly regimes al Qida threatens.

Pending Time Sensitive Decisions

At the close of the Clinton Administration, two decisions about al Qaida were deferred to the Bush Administration.

- First, should we provide the Afghan Northern Alliance enough assistance to maintain it as a viable opposition force to the Taliban/al Qida? If we do not, I believe that the Northern Alliance may be effectively taken out of action this Spring when fighting resumes after the winter thaw. The al Qida 55th Brigade, which has been a key fighting force for the Taliban, would then be freed to send its personnel elsewhere, where they would likely threaten US interests. For any assistance to get there in time to effect the Spring fighting, a decision is needed now.
- Second, should we increase assistance to Uzbekistan to allow them to deal with the al Qida/IMU threat? [remainder of content of this section removed at the request of the CIA as operational detail]

Three other issues awaiting addressal now are:

- First, what the new Administration says to the Taliban and Pakistan about the importance we attach to ending the al Qida sanctuary in Afghanistan. We are separately proposing early, strong messages to both.
- Second, do we propose significant program growth in the FY02 budget for anti-al Qida operations by CIA and counter-terrorism training and assistance by State and CIA?
- Third, when and how does the Administration choose to respond to the attack on the USS Cole. That decision is obviously complex. We can make some decisions, such as those above, now without yet coming to grips with the harder decision about the Cole. On the Cole, we should take advantage of the policy that we "will respond at a time, place, and manner of our own choosing/and not be forced into knee jerk responses."

Attached is the year-end 2000 strategy on al Qaida developed by the last Administration to give to you. Also attached is the 1998 strategy. Neither was a "covert action only" approach. Both incorporated diplomatic, economic, military, public diplomacy and intelligence tools. Using the 2000 paper as background, we could prepare a decision paper/guide for a PC review.

1. Threat Magnitude: Do the Principles agree that the al Qida network poses a first order threat to US interests in a number of regions, or is this analysis a "chicken little" over reaching and can we proceed without major new initiatives and by handling this issue in a more routine manner?
2. Strategy: If it is a first order issue, how should the existing strategy be modified or strengthened? Two elements of the existing strategy that have not been made to work effectively are a) going after al Qida's money and b) public information to counter al Qida propaganda.
3. FY02 Budget: Should we continue the funding increases into the FY02 for State and CIA programs designed to implement the al Qida strategy?
4. Immediate [blacked out] Decisions: Should we initiate [blacked out] funding to the Northern Alliance and to the Uzbek's?

Please let us know if you would like such a decision/discussion paper or any modifications to the background paper.

Concurrences by: Mary McCarthy, Dan Fried, Bruce Reidel, Don Camp

Source: Barbara Elias, *National Security Archive Electronic Briefing Book,* no. 147. (http://www.gwu.edu/~nsarchiv/NSAEBB/NSAEBB147/clarke%20memo.pdf).

Document 9

Letter from Brian F. Sullivan, Retired FAA Special Agent to U.S. Senator John Kerry (May 7, 2001)

This letter, from a retired FAA Special Agent to U.S. Senator John Kerry, is important because it shows recognition of the problems with aviation security by a person in the field. The letter expressed Sullivan's concern about lax screening at checkpoints. He was also concerned about the culture in the FAA that promotes people up the chain of command even as they blocked needed reforms.

May 7, 2001
The Honorable John F. Kerry
304 Russell Senate Office Building
Washington, DC 20510

Dear Senator Kerry:

There was a very disturbing investigative report last night (Sunday evening May 6) on Channel 25 FOX News at 10PM regarding airport security. Although the report focused on Logan Airport and TF Green in Rhode Island, as a recently retired FAA Special Agent, I know this is a national problem, not one simply unique to New England Region. I've asked my friend Steve Elson, another former FAA Special Agent, to forward a video copy of the report to you. Both of us are willing to testify before Congress should the need arise and we are both committed to doing whatever is necessary to improving our aviation security system. We are hopeful that you would show the video to your peers, Senator McCain and members of any House committee dealing with aviation security.

The FAA does everything it can to prevent news reports of this nature under the guise of being a public safety issue, which should not be given a public form. Unfortunately, the report once again demonstrated what every FAA line agent already knows: the airport passenger screening system simply doesn't work as intended. The FAA would prefer to continue to promulgate a façade of security, than to honestly assess the system. Management knows how ineffective the current system is, but continues to tell Congress that our airport screening is an effective deterrent.

FAA official point of a 95+% success rate of FAA screening checkpoint tests, particularly when reassuring the flying public and Congress. They do this even though they know that every time a Red Team, or news reporter in this instance, tests the system, the exact opposite occurs with a failure rate of 95+%. The difference is realistic testing versus tests designed to avoid enforcement litigation problems with the airlines. It is a clear example of self fulfilling prophecy, whereby the tests are designed to produce a desired outcome, rather than to truly reflect the status of aviation security.

FAA management will point to a decline in incidents of hijacking since the system was put into effect in the '70s. My question is, "Have they kept up with the times?" Do you see a horde of Cuban exiles just waiting to commit air piracy to return to Havana? Or, has the threat become more refined over the years? I've stood along the Potomac and watched our big air ships fly in low and slow along the river. What protection is there against a rogue terrorist with a Stinger missile? While the FAA has focused on screening for handguns, new threats have emerged, such as chemical and biological weapons. Do you really think a screener could detect a bottle of liquid explosives, small battery and detonator in your carry on baggage? And with the concept of Jihad, do you think it would be difficult for a determined terrorist to get on a plane and destroy himself and all other passengers? The answers to these questions are obvious.

The FAA was dubbed "The Tombstone Agency" by Mary Schiavo, the former DOT OID. The reason is that the agency never seems to act until there has been an air tragedy. Think for a moment how vital the air transportation industry is to our overall economic well being as a nation. Think what the result would be of a coordinated attack which took down several domestic flights on the same day. The problem is that with our current screening system, this is more than possible. Given time, considering current threats, it is almost likely. We don't have to wait for a tragedy to occur to act. There are simple, cost effective means to improve the system now.

The DOT OIG has become an ineffective overseer of the FAA, particularly since Mary Schiavo's departure. Scathing reports have been developed on airport/airline security and FAA facility security. Still, the culture continues to perpetuate itself and managers have been promoted up the chain despite the fact that they've supported this façade of security and abused line agents who dare to speak the truth. The answer here is not to fire a few hapless low paid screeners or continue to issue meaningless fines against the airlines. The answer is to change the prevailing culture within Civil Aviation Security at the FAA from one concerned with continuing to support the façade, to one committed to protecting the traveling public. Let our agents do their job. Don't stifle initiative and independent thought and observations. Don't continue to silence those who refuse to buy the party line and actually attempt to reveal the façade.

It is time for the truth to be known, before an incident occurs. It is not in the best interests of public safety to continue this façade of security. Hopefully, FOX 25 will distribute this report to all its national affiliates and encourage similar testing. National TV news magazines could also help bring focus. Perhaps we can force a public forum where line agents, could testify before Congress and finally secure an honest assessment of aviation security, as well as some positive change.

Thank you,
Brian F. Sullivan
FAA Spec Agent (Ret.)

Source: Andrew R. Thomas, *Aviation Insecurity: The New Challenges of Air Travel* (Amherst, NY: Prometheus Books, 2003), pp. 225–226. Permission obtained from Brian F. Sullivan to reprint this letter.

Document 10

Letter from Michael Canavan, Associate Administrator for Civil Aviation Security to FAA Federal Security Managers (May 30, 2001)

Over the years the Federal Aviation Administration (FAA) had developed an overly strong relationship with the aviation industry. This letter reveals how close this relationship was. The FAA was willing to compromise on aviation security because the aviation industry wanted only the basics. It was not so much that the aviation industry was uninterested in safety, but that it was more concerned about cost and profitability. This letter to FAA federal security managers from Michael Canavan, FAA Associate Administrator for Civil Aviation Security, calls for flexibility in dealing with the aviation industry. Rather than acting as a regulatory agency, the FAA was to be a partner with the aviation industry in solving problems.

Action: Compliance and enforcement philosophy
From: Associate Administrator for Civil Aviation Security, ACS-1
To: Managers, Civil Aviation Security Division 700's, Federal Security Managers

As we work with the aviation industry, it is important to remember that our primary goal as a regulatory agency is to gain compliance. While I know there are circumstances that present difficult choices, it would be helpful to explain our approach to compliance and enforcement issues.

As I outlined in the ACS strategic plan, the safety and security of the flying public will depend upon the FAA and industry maintaining a candid, respectful, and mutually responsive business relationship. To be effective in this relationship, we need to be flexible. While I expect regulated parties to comply with regulatory requirements, there will be times when we find areas of noncompliance. When we do, I want to fully consider the actions the party has taken to fix the problem. I want to work with industry to develop action plans to permanently correct problems that have resulted in violations. To encourage industry to join us in this effort I do not expect us to impose a civil penalty against a regulated party for certain unaggravated violations, if we believe the party has successfully implemented a permanent fix that will resolve violations. To answer questions you may have about this new philosophy and how it will work, detailed guidance will be provided to you shortly.

I want to continue to give our partners a realistic opportunity to comply with the regulations and to work with us.

Source: Andrew R. Thomas, *Aviation Insecurity: The New Challenges of Air Travel* (Amherst, NY: Prometheus Books, 2003), p. 227. Letter from Canavan in the possession of Brian F. Sullivan, who has given permission to reprint this government document.

Document 11

Presidential Daily Briefing (August 6, 2001)

Presidents receive daily briefings from various agencies. This particular Presidential Daily Brief (PDB) has become controversial because it included a warning from the CIA that Osama bin Laden wanted to strike at targets in the United States. A representative of the CIA presented the PDB at Crawford, Texas on August 6, 2001. This document was declassified and approved for release on April 10, 2004.

Bin Laden Determined to Strike in US

Clandestine, foreign government, and media reports indicate Bin Ladin since 1997 has wanted to conduct terrorist attacks in the US. Bin Ladin implied in US television interviews in 1997 and 1998 that his followers would follow the example of the World Trade Center bomber Ramzi Yousef and "bring the fighting to America."

After US missile strikes on his base in Afghanistan in 1998, Bin Ladin told followers he wanted to retaliate in Washington, according a [blacked out] service.

An Egyptian Islamic Jihad (EIJ) operative told an [blacked out] service at the same time that Bin Ladin was planning to exploit the operative's access to the US to mount a terrorist strike.

The millennium plotting in Canada in 1999 may have been part of Bin Ladin's first serious attempt to implement a terrorist strike in the US. Convicted plotter Ahmed Ressam has told the FBI that he conceived the idea to attack Los Angeles International Airport himself, but that Bin Ladin lieutenant Abu Zubaydah encouraged him and helped facilitate the operation. Ressam also said that in 1998 Abu Zubaydah was planning his own US attack.

Ressam says Bin Ladin was aware of the Los Angeles operation.

Although Bin Ladin has not succeeded, his attacks against the US Embassies in Kenya and Tanzania in 1998 demonstrate that he prepares operations years in advance and is not deterred by setbacks. Bin Ladin associates surveilled our Embassies in Nairobi and Dar es Salaam as early as 1993, and some members of the Nairobi cell planning the bombings were arrested and deported in 1997.

Al-Qaida members—including some who are US citizens—have resided in or traveled to the US for years, and the group apparently maintains a support structure that could aid attacks. Two al-Qaida members found guilty in the conspiracy to bomb our Embassies in East Africa were US citizens, and a senior EIJ member lived in California in the mid-1990s.

A clandestine source said in 1998 that a Bin Ladin cell in New York was recruiting Muslim-American youth for attacks.

We have not been able to corroborate some of the more sensational threat reporting, such as that from a (blacked out) service in 1998 saying that Bin Ladin wanted to hijack a US aircraft to gain the release of "Blind Shykh" 'Umar' Abdel-Rahman and other US-held extremists.

Nevertheless, FBI information since that time indicates patterns of suspicious activity in this country consistent with preparations for hijackings or other types of attacks, including recent surveillance of federal buildings in New York.

The FBI is conducting approximately 70 full field investigations throughout the US that it considers Bin Ladin-related. CIA and the FBI are investigating a call to our Embassy in the UAE in May saying that a group of Bin Ladin supporters was in the US planning attacks with explosives.

Source: Steven Strasser (ed.), *The 9/11 Investigations* (New York: PublicAffairs, 2004), pp. 546–547.

Document 12

Brian Sullivan's E-mail to Michael Canavan, FAA Associate Administrator for Civil Aviation Security about Aviation Security (August 16, 2001)

Michael Canavan's May 30, 2001, letter, in which he defined his preferred approach for dealing with aviation security compliance issues, caused uncertainty among the FAA's rank and file. This uncertainty led to this e-mail from Brian Sullivan, an FAA agent. He made the case that what was actually going on differed from the philosophy announced by Canavan. Problems of aviation security were pointed out by FAA agents but were not being acted upon. Sullivan wanted senior FAA personnel to check on the progress of a problem to make sure something was done.

Subject: Compliance and Enforcement Philosophy
From: Brian Sullivan
To: Michael Canavan

Your C&E makes sense and is "well intentioned" but is being abused by field management to close cases without findings, and as the basis for not opening cases, despite the fact that violations persist.

Your intent was to work with the regulated parties and develop action plans to permanently correct problems. Here's what's really happening: A problem is identified. Instead of opening a case, we work with industry to develop the required plan. The agents go out and find that the problem persists, but field management won't allow them to open a case, incorrectly citing your May 30th memorandum as the basis for their decision. As a result we have a paper fix. Nice looking plans, but no real fix. The façade of security continues. Our line agents continue to experience the frustration of not being allowed to do their jobs.

The only way to confirm what I am saying is to check on the ground. What's the old military saying, "What goes right is what a commander checks," or something like that? When the FOX25 report was done at Logan in May, the reporter went back a few weeks later, after the dust had settled, and re-checked the same screening checkpoints with the same negative result, despite assurances from the BOS CASFO and airport/airlines. I know FOX could easily determine if these current action plans work as intended. Let me suggest that it would be better if you looked at some of the action plans and test them with a red team see if they actually work. I know our field agents have re-checked violations after the action plans have been developed only to find that the same violation persists. Plans aren't worth the paper they are written on unless they work. The only way to determine if they really work is to test them with an "honest broker" and that can't be done by our line agents if their management won't open up cases when problems persist.

If you doubt what I'm saying, this is very easy to check. I know you get more with honey than you can with vinegar, but compliance requires both the carrot and the stick, if it is to be truly effective. The industry is primarily concerned with the bottom line ($) and will give security the attention it merits, only if we are perceived as both willing to work with them, while at the same time committed to both compliance and enforcement. If they think we are soft and they can get away with paper plans, that is exactly what they'll do. The key is to insure that the action plans do, in fact, permanently correct the problems which have resulted in violations. That is not happening. When the plans don't correct the problem, we have to have field management willing to open up cases and support our line agents who find that violations persist.

I hope this is helpful information. I'm not looking for a response. I just want to help you make your philosophy work as intended

Best wishes. We are hearing some good things since your arrival.

Source: Andrew R. Thomas, *Aviation Insecurity: The New Challenges of Air Travel* (Amherst, NY: Prometheus Books, 2003), p. 229. Permission to reprint this e-mail has been given by Brian F. Sullivan.

Document 13

Mohamed Atta's Letter of Advice for Hijackers
(September 2001)

Mohamed Atta allegedly wrote a five-page handwritten document in Arabic to prepare the members of his al-Qaeda team for their mission on September 11, 2001. This letter was found in Atta's suitcase, which was left behind at Logan Airport in a suitcase with other papers because Atta was late in boarding American Airlines Flight 11. There is some question whether Atta wrote this document, but it is certainly written in language that he believed in. The document served as both a spiritual exhortation for the mission and a checklist for the teams.

The Last Night

1. Make an oath to die and renew your intentions. Shave excess hair from the body and wear cologne. Shower.
2. Make sure you know all aspects of the plan well, and expect the response, or a reaction from the enemy.
3. Read al-Tawba and Anfal [traditional war chapters from the Koran] and reflect on their meanings and remember all of the things that God has promised for the martyrs.
4. Remind your soul to listen and obey [all divine order] and remember that you will face decisive situations that might prevent you from 100 percent obedience, so tame your soul, purify it, convince it, make it understand and incite it. God said: "Obey God and his messenger, and do not fight amongst yourselves or else you will fail. And be patient, for God is with the patient."
5. Pray during the night and be persistent in asking God to give you victory, control and conquest, and that he may make your task easier and not expose us.

6. Remember God frequently, and the best way to do it is to read the Holy Koran, according to all scholars, as far as I know. It is enough for us that it [the Koran] are [*sic*] the words of the Creator of the Earth and the planets, the One that you will meet [on the Day of Judgment].

7. Purify your soul from all unclean things. Completely forget something called "this world" [or "this life"]. The time for play is over and the serious time is upon us. How much time have we wasted in our lives? Shouldn't we take advantage of these last hours to offer good deeds and obedience?

8. You should feel complete tranquility, because the time between you and your marriage [in heaven] is very short. Afterward begins the happy life, where God is satisfied with you, and eternal bliss "in the company of the prophets, the companions, the martyrs and the good people, who are all good company." Ask God for his mercy and be optimistic, because [the prophet], peace be upon him, used to prefer optimism in all his affairs.

9. Keep in mind that, if you fall into hardship, how will you act, and how will you remain steadfast and remember that you will return to God and remember that anything that happens to you could never be avoided, and what did not happen to you could never have happened to you. This test from Almighty God is to raise your level [a reference to the levels of heaven] and erase your sins. And be sure that it is a matter of moments, which will then pass, God willing, so blessed are those who win the great reward of God. Almighty God said: "Did you think you could go to heaven before God knows whom [*sic*] amongst you have fought for Him and are patient?"

10. Remember the words of Almighty God: "You were looking to the battle before you engaged in it, and now you see it with your own two eyes." Remember: "How many small groups beat big groups by the will of God." And his words: "If God gives you victory, no one can beat you. And if he betrays you, who can give you victory without Him? So the faithful put their trust in God."

11. Remind yourself of the supplications and of your brethren and ponder their meanings. [The morning and evening supplications, and the supplications of entering a town, and . . . the supplications said before meeting the enemy.]

12. Bless your body with some verses of the Koran [done by reading verses in one's hands and then rubbing the hands over whatever is to be blessed], the luggage, clothes, the knife, your personal effects, your ID, your passport, and all of your papers.

13. Check your weapons before you leave and long before you leave. (You must make your knife sharp and you must not discomfort your animal during the slaughter.)

14. Tighten your clothes [a reference to one making sure his clothes will cover his private parts at all times], since this is the way of the pious generations after the prophet. They would tighten their clothes before battle. Tighten your shoes well, wear socks so that your feet will be solidly in your shoes. All of these are worldly things [that humans can do to control their fate, although God decrees what will work and what will not] and the rest is left to God, the best One to depend on.

15. Pray the morning prayer in a group and ponder the great rewards of that prayer. Make supplications afterward, and do not leave your apartment unless you have performed ablution before leaving, because (The angels will ask for your forgiveness as long as you are in a state of ablution, and will pray for you). This saying of the prophet was mentioned by [Yaba ibn Shair] al-Nawawi in his book, *The Best of Supplications*. Read the words of God: "Did you think that We created you for no reason. . . ." from the al-Mu'minum chapter.

The Second Stage

When the taxi takes you to (M) [this initial could stand for matar, airport in Arabic] remember God constantly while in the car. (Remember the supplication for entering a car, for entering a town, the supplication of place and other supplications.) . . .

When you have reached (M) and have left the taxi, say a supplication of place ["O Lord, I ask you for the best of this place, and ask you to protect me from its evils"], and everywhere you go say that prayer and smile and be calm, for God is with the believers. And the angels protect you without you feeling anything. Say this supplication: "God is more dear than all of his creation." and Say: "O Lord, protect me from them as you wish.". . . [More supplications follow]:

1. They will come back [from battle] with God's blessings.
2. They were not harmed.
3. And God was satisfied with them.
[Many Koranic verses and statements of the Prophet follow.]

Fear is a great worship. The allies of God do not offer such worship except for the one God, who controls everything . . . with total certainty that God will weaken the schemes of the non-believers. God said: "God will weaken the schemes of the non-believers."

You must remember your brothers with all respect. No one should notice that you are making the supplication, "There is no God but God," because if you say it 1,000 times no one will be able to tell whether you are quiet or remember God. [More Koran verses]

Also, do not seem confused or show signs of nervous tension. Be happy, optimistic, calm because you are heading for a deed that God loves and will accept [as a good deed]. It will be the day, God willing, you spend with the women of paradise.

Smile in the face of hardship young man/For you are heading toward eternal paradise..

You must remember to make supplications wherever you go, and anytime you do anything, and God is with his faithful servants, he will protect them and make their tasks easier, and give them success and control, and victory and everything. . . .

Third Stage—When You Ride the Plane

When you ride the (T) [probably for tayyara, airplane in Arabic], before your foot steps in it, and before you enter it, you make a prayer and supplications. Remember that this is a battle for the sake of God. As the prophet, peace upon him, said: An action for the sake of God is better than all of what is in this world, or as he said. When you step inside the (T), and sit in your seat begin with the known supplications that we have mentioned before. Be busy with the constant remembrance of God. God said: "Oh ye faithful, when you find the enemy be steadfast, and remember God constantly so that you may be successful." When the (T) moves, even slightly, toward (Q) [unknown reference], say the supplication of travel. Because you are traveling to Almighty God, so be attentive on this trip. . . .

And then it takes off. This is the moment that both groups come together. So remember God, as he said in his Book: "Oh Lord, pour your patience upon us and make our feet steadfast and give us victory over the infidels." And his works: "And the only thing they said Lord, forgive our sins and excesses and make our feet steadfast and give us victory over the infidels." And his prophet said: "O Lord, you have revealed the book, you move the clouds, you gave us victory over the enemy, conquer them and give us victory over them." Give us victory and make the ground shake under their feet. Pray for yourself and all of your brothers that they may be victorious and hit their targets and [unclear] and ask God to grant you martyrdom facing the enemy, not running away from it, and for him to grant you patience and the feeling that anything that happens to you is for him.

Then every one of you should prepare to carry out his role in a way that would satisfy God. You should clench your teeth, as the pious early generations did.

When the confrontation begins, strike like champions who do not want to go back to this world. Shout, "Allahu Akbar," because this strikes fear in the hearts of nonbelievers. God said: "Strike above the neck, and strike at all of their extremities." Know that the gardens of paradise are waiting for you in all their beauty, and the women of paradise are waiting, calling out, "Come hither, friend of God." They have dressed in their most beautiful clothing.

If God decrees that any of you are to slaughter, you should dedicate the slaughter to your fathers . . . because you have obligations toward them. Do not disagree, and obey. If you slaughter, do not cause the discomfort of those you are killing, because this is one of the practices of the prophet, peace be upon him. On one condition: that you do not become distracted . . . and neglect what is greater, paying attention to the enemy. That would be reason, and would do more damage than good. If this happens, the deed at hand is more important than doing that, because the deed is an obligation, and [the other thing] is optional. And an obligation has priority over an option.

Do not seek revenge for yourself. Strike for God's sake. One time Ali bin Abi Talib [a companion and close relative of the Prophet Muhammad], may God bless him, fought with a nonbeliever. The nonbeliever spit on Ali, may God bless him. Ali . . . did not strike him. When the battle was over, the companions of the prophet asked him why he had not smitten the nonbeliever. He said, "After he spat at me, I was afraid that I would be striking at him in revenge for myself, so I lifted my sword." After he renewed his intentions, he went back and killed the man. This means that before you do anything, make sure that your soul is prepared to do everything for God only.

Then implement the way of the prophet in taking prisoners. Take prisoners and kill them. As Almighty God said, "No prophet should have prisoners until he has soaked the land with blood. You want the bounties of this world [in exchange for prisoners] and God wants the other world [for you], and God is all-powerful, all-wise."

If everything goes well, every one of you should pat the other on the shoulder in confidence. . . . Remind your brothers that this act is for Almighty God. Do not confuse your brothers or distract them. He should give them glad tidings and make them calm, and remind them [of God] and encourage them. How beautiful it is for one to read God's words, such as: "And those who prefer the afterlife over this world should fight for the sake of God." And his words: "Do not suppose that those who are killed for the sake of God are dead, they are alive. . . ." And others. Or they should sing songs to boost their morale, as the pious first generations did in the throes of battle, to bring calm, tranquility, and joy to the hearts of his brothers.

Do not forget to take a bounty, even if it is a glass of water to quench your thirst or that of your brothers, if possible. When the hour of reality approaches, the zero hour . . . wholeheartedly welcome death for the sake of God. Always be remembering God. Either end you life while praying, seconds before the target, or make your last words: "There is no God but God, Muhammad is his messenger."

Afterward, we will all meet in the highest heaven, God willing.

If you see the enemy as strong, remember the groups [that had formed a coalition to fight the Prophet Muhammad]. They were 10,000. Remember how God gave victory to his faithful servants. God said: "When the faithful saw the [size of the enemy army], they said, this is what God and the prophet promised, they said the truth. it only increased their faith."

And may the peace of God be upon the prophet.

Source: Barry Rubin and Judith Colp Rubin (eds.), *Anti-American Terrorism and the Middle East: A Documentary Reader* (Oxford: Oxford University Press, 2002), pp. 233–238.

Document 14

Oral Testimony from Survivors of the World Trade Center

The events of September 11 are almost impossible to comprehend, but the best testimony to the horrors of that day comes from the survivors. These survivors witnessed acts of heroism and unselfishness along with panic and desperation. They all commented on the number of people jumping to their deaths from the upper floors, and the terror of the collapse of first the South Tower and then the North Tower. Eyewitness testimony may be suspect in court trials, but as a way to personalize a tragedy it is indispensable.

Testimony of Joseph Pfeifer, Chief, Battalion 1, New York City Fire Department

I worked the night before in the firehouse, which is at 100 Duane Street, in lower Manhattan. Then that morning, somewhere around eight-thirty, we had a call to a possible gas leak in the street. So we went to the gas leak and there was a slight odor of gas in the street. No big deal. I had Engine 7 and Ladder 1 check some of the exposures. There was nothing inside the buildings. So we called Con Ed, and we were wrapping up with the operation there and standing around in the street. And then we hear this very loud plane coming overhead.

In Manhattan, you rarely hear planes because of the high buildings. So we all looked up. In almost disbelief, we see the plane pass, and it's flying so low. Our eyes followed it as it passed behind the buildings, and then it reappeared, and it appeared to me that it aimed right into the building. It smashed into the building. There was a large fireball. And then a couple of seconds later you heard the sound of the explosion. I told everybody to get in the rigs because we're going down there, to the Trade Center.

I got into a battalion car with Jules Naudet, the French film guy who made the 9/11 documentary tape. If you saw the tape, you saw our faces blank with disbelief that a plane was heading toward the Trade Center, followed by the actual impact. I picked up the department radio and I told them that a plane just hit the World Trade Center, and to transmit a second alarm. That was done immediately. That was the first official report of this happening.

We're heading down West Broadway, and I'm thinking to myself, What's the next step? What's the next thing I need to do? I picked up the radio again, and I told the dispatcher that this was a direct attack. I said I want a third alarm transmitted. "Have the second-alarm units report to the Trade Center, and the third-alarm units stage at Vesey and West Street."

We proceeded to the trade Center. We pull up to the front, underneath the canopy. I get out of the car. The firefighters get their gear. I throw my gear on, and we proceed into the building. As we go in, we see a couple of people badly burned right in the lobby. I proceeded to the fire command center of the Trade Center. I was met by a deputy fire safety director. I asked him if he knew what the floor the plane hit because it's very hard to tell from the outside exactly what floor. And he wasn't able to give me an exact floor. He said between the 78 and 80, but he wasn't sure.

My first thought was to organize, to find out information and then try to organize the firefighters that I had asked for. I needed to find out if we had any elevators. In the Trade Center, each of the towers had ninety-nine elevators. So it wasn't a simple job. It was not just walking over and checking one elevator bank. I had to send a number of people, from a number of companies, to see if any of the elevators were available to us. And what we found out, after a couple of minutes, was that we had no elevators. So we had to send people upstairs to find out what was going on and to attempt a rescue. I knew that we had somewhere around twenty floors of people above the fire, and I knew they were trapped. I knew the fire itself was too big to put out.

Deputy Peter Hayden came in and he took charge of the operation. My role was to support him, supply him with information, and continue communicating with the guys going up. Groups of firefighters were coming in. And we would brief them and then tell them the plan, and send them up. One of the engine companies that came in was Engine 33, which was my brother Kevin's. He was a lieutenant in 33, which is out of Great Jones Street, off the Bowery.

I was standing behind the fire command station, which is a high desk-type thing. And I remember seeing him walking over to me. And I said to myself, "What's he doing here?" He told me he was going to go on a special vacation and he was taking a number of mutuals off so he could study for the captain's test. So I thought his last tour had been the day before. I was very surprised to see him. But he came over to me, and I told him where we thought the lowest level of the fire possibly was, at 78. And I told him we didn't have any elevators available. And then we just spent a couple of seconds just looking at each other, with a real feeling of concern for each other. It was just a couple of seconds of staring at each other. And then he knew what he had to do and he slowly walked away to his men, who were standing maybe twenty feet away. I watched him walk away, and that was the last time I saw him.

This was maybe five minutes before the second plane hit. A lot of the high-ranking citywide tour commanders of the fire department stated coming in. We're trying to evaluate what's going on, what we have and who's coming in. We're trying to explain our rescue plan to people when the second plane hits the South Tower. We heard that. We saw debris coming down. A number of the chiefs got together. Deputy chief Peter Hayden and myself, citywide tour commander Donald Burns and Battalion Chief Orio Palmer. It was decided that we'd just split the group in half. One group would go into the South Tower. The other would stay in the North Tower.

Peter Hayden said, "I need Joe Pfeifer to stay with me. We'll take North Tower."

And Donald Burns said, "I'll take Orio, and we'll set up a command in tower 2."

What we tried to do at that point was to check out the repeater, the building repeater, because we were going to command channels. Orio and I tested it out together, and it failed. It did not work at all. So we had a communication difficulty right from the beginning.

So they went into the South Tower and we stayed with the North, knowing there was no communication between the two towers.

We tried a number of other communications solutions. We tried the repeater in the car. We also went to a different command channel. But our best system was knocked out with the first plane. Everything else from there would not be as good. High-rise communications are difficult at best because of the technology problems with radios.

I new that the B stairs had a special standpipe phone, which meant they had a jack where you could plug in a phone and talk down to the fire command board. So I physically gave people red phones. I said, "Hey, listen, right next to the standpipe you'll see a box. Plug this in and we'll have direct hard-wire communication."

We tried every possible means of communication that day. But even cell phones weren't working. But what goes through my head is that with each of the systems we tried, the redundancy of the systems still failed. I felt very frustrated. You can almost see it in the 9/11 film, the frustration on my face. I'm trying to call different chiefs, trying to access what's going on upstairs, and not being able to get through. Some of the messages did get through. We found we were able to talk at different levels at different times and at different spots in the building. We had a lot of people trapped in elevators, and we had a number of firefighters having chest pains. And we got those messages down, and we started to get people up to assist. But it was spotty at best.

It was almost like the closer you were, the less you knew. That's what happened. We weren't getting full intelligence reports of what was going on. If you watched the 9/11 tape, I don't think you saw any ranking law enforcement in the lobby. The helicopters were up, but we had no means to communicate with them. We tried a number of times to do that, but it wasn't happening and no one was coming in to volunteer any of that information to us. As we look back, we were the least informed. Resources were up there. Helicopters were able to assess the damage. My question is 'Who did they tell?' They didn't tell us. Or if they told anybody, whoever they told had a responsibility to tell us. But I think instead of blaming people, as we move forward I think we should just acknowledge that this is one of the areas that both departments need to work on, police and fire.

We heard this loud rumbling sound, which was the South Tower collapsing, but we didn't know that at the time. I thought that the elevators were coming down, or part of the building or the plane or something was crashing through the lobby, because it started to fill quickly with debris.

We ran around a little corner toward 6 World Trade. We pushed everybody around the corner. We actually huddled down at the base of the escalator, the escalator that leads up to 6 World Trade and then to the North Bridge over West Street. But now this whole area, which was brightly lit, became totally black. We stayed there until the rumbling stopped, and we knew we were alive.

But I thought it was a localized collapse. I never even suspected that the second tower collapsed. I figured whatever happened we're in the middle of it and we're okay.

I said, "Tower 1 command to all units. Evacuate the building. Evacuate the building." And that was heard, I got acknowledgement. Then I heard it go up farther, meaning that somebody, one of the chiefs, picked up the transmission. Then I heard it repeated again on the handy talkies, so I knew my call to get everybody out of the building was heard. And later on talking to firefighters, they said they heard me.

But I never knew the second tower collapsed. Nor did I hear any message of that. But I had to get the other guys out of the building because something was wrong and we were no longer able to assess what was going on. Now were in a mode where we have to figure out how to escape. We didn't know what occurred, so the concern was to get everybody out and regroup.

We went across the West Bridge with Jules and an EMS lieutenant. I went back and forth a few times and still didn't know that the South Tower had collapsed. You couldn't see it. What you saw was smoke. Many times when you get a big fire, smoke covers the building and you don't see the building. But you know the building is still there. So when we looked, we were at a bad angle. It was just dust that covered where the building would be. A minute later Chief Hayden came and was standing in the street, and still I did not know that the South Tower collapsed.

We were only out there a few minutes when we heard a loud rumbling sound, almost like a train if you're standing underneath an overpass. And somebody yelled, "The building's coming down. Run." I ran toward the river, and I guess Jules was with me. I had all my gear, the bunker gear, but I didn't have a mask. and I guess Jules ran faster than I, and as we get about twenty yards up the block, I see him huddled between a couple of cars in just a T-shirt. I figured, I have the helmet and the gear. I'll be able to protect him. So I actually jumped on top of him. He didn't know it was me at that time. And then I heard all the crashing and the steel and now the street goes totally black. As a firefighter you kind of expect blackness inside of a burning building. But outside in broad daylight, you don't.

At that point, I thought we were going to die. I could only think of my wife and kids and how much I would like to see them again. I thought of Kevin right after. I thought, he's going to be okay. We told him to get out, he'll be okay. There are a lot of firemen around. It's hard for me to find him. He'll come and find me. You know, I'm there with a white helmet. I'm a lot more visible than all the other guys. All the other guys look the same. So I thought, he'll see the white helmet and he'll find me.

I tried to call him on the radio. It didn't work. And I said, "Okay, the radio's not doing well today anyway." And then a number of hours passed by and still no Kevin. So I decided to take a walk around the site. Let me see if there's anybody from 33. And I saw 33's rig, and for some reason I checked the riding list, even though I knew he was in the building.

I remember walking north on West Street, walking through the blackness of downtown because there were no lights. It was at that point I realized my brother was gone, and hundreds of firefighters were gone, and all I could think of was how much we really used to love working downtown, and all the times we used to talk on the phone, or at the house, or at parties about the job, and I realized that all that was gone.

We had the memorial for my brother. And then in February, I got a phone call to come to the Trade Center right away. And I knew they had found him. I went down to the Trade Center and they were in the process of digging him out. For me, that was the toughest part. I was pretty cool and calm in that command mode, but I think at that point I left it all behind and I just knelt there next to his body in the midst of all the steel and the rubble. And then we carried him through the field of twisted steel and it was almost overwhelming because everything became a reality of what took place there and how horrible it was.

We actually brought him up a dirt hill and we had about a hundred firefighters salute as we passed by with a flag over his body. We put in an ambulance, and I jumped in. They closed the doors and I sat there. And there were a lot of tears. But after sitting there alone with him for a while, I started to remember all the good times we had. He only lived six blocks away from me in Middle Village, so I always saw him. So in the middle of tears, there was some sort of peace or tranquility. I remember sitting in the ambulance saying how horrible this was. This was the worst I could imagine. And then after a few minutes I felt a calmness. It's very strange, but it was my time with him, which I'm really glad I had. Not only did I see him going into the towers, but I brought him out.

A couple of days after September 11, I met Dennis Tardio, who was the captain of Engine 7. He stopped me on the stairs to the firehouse, and he said to me, "I owe my life to your brother."

I asked him what he meant. He said when he was coming down the stairs, he was coming down the C stairs, and for some strange reason he made eye contact with my brother. And my brother called him over and said, "Dennis, you can't get down these stairs. It leads you out into all the debris" He said, "You need to switch to the B stairs."

Dennis got out of the building and within thirty seconds the building came down. He said if it weren't for Kevin, he wouldn't be here. And I know for a fact, if they had gone down the other stairs, it would have led out onto the mezzanine level and there would never have been enough time to get out of the building.

Testimony of Robert Leder, Executive, SMW Trading Company
Our office is on the eighty-fifth floor of 1 World Trade Center. I was looking outside the window, facing the Empire State Building, when I saw the plane coming into the building. There was such a dramatic change of atmospheric pressure from the plane hitting. The building swayed from the impact, and it nearly knocked me off of my chair. Our ceiling imploded. Some of our walls began to implode. I saw people coming past the window. I don't think these were people who jumped. I think people must have sucked out of the windows because of the pressure.

The first thing that came to my mind was to call my wife. I told her that the World Trade Center had just been hit by a plane. She didn't believe me, and she just went about her business. Right after I spoke with her, I opened a door to see what was going on and this black billowing smoke came straight at us. I shut the door right away. I wasn't sure what was going on in the hallway. The whole office reeked of jet fuel, or kerosene. I started to get really nervous because I wasn't sure if we were going to be able to get out. People wanted to say in my office. They said, "Relax, everything's going to be fine."

And my exact words were, "I'm getting the fuck out of here, and I don't care what anybody else does."

I had no idea where the stairwell was. I just never thought of looking for one. We saturated our jackets with water, and people across the hall directed us to the stairwell. We started to go down and it was packed. But there was a quick pace and the stairwell wasn't smoky. Maybe there was a little bit of smoke, and there was a little bit of stench of burning, but it wasn't that bad.

By the time we got down to the seventy-something floor, fires were coming out of where a wall used to be. It was almost like a scene out of a horror movie. But it was not as chaotic as I thought it was going to be. Everybody was orderly and well mannered. Everybody was staying on the right-hand side of the stairs and letting people that were severely hurt go down on the other side. And this was before we saw any firefighters or police officers coming up. As we got farther and farther down, people started to calm down more, thinking that we're getting out and everything was going to be okay.

At around the 50th floor, I got a cell phone call through to my wife. I told her everything was okay and I'd call her when I got out. This must have been a minute before the second plane hit. I never heard it. We had no idea that 2 World Trade was struck by a plane. Thank God we didn't know. If we had, there would have been panic.

It was around the thirtieth floor when firefighters started to come up. They were all running up on the left side and we were going down on the right side. One after another, just running up with all their gear. You saw each one of these young firefighters running up with all their gear, and they knew what was going on with the other World Trade Center building. But they never said a word. You couldn't even see it in their faces.

The smoke actually started to get thicker as we got farther and farther down. At the twenty-second floor, I stopped my friend Billy and we helped an elderly woman. She had this huge bag with her that was filled with things from her desk, and she looked like she was having trouble. I grabbed her bag and I walked in front of her. Billy walked behind her, and we walked slowly. People were now passing us. It must have taken us an extra ten to fifteen minutes to get outside.

Once there, I was almost fixated on the debris, the body parts and blood. My friend Billy had to snap me out of it and wake me up. We were walking between the Gap and the PATH train when people started to scream, "Run, Run, Run. Oh, my God." We had no clue what was happening. And then we felt this wave and started to hear a rumbling. And the next thing you knew it was darkness. I thought it was over, I thought we were dying. I didn't know what was happening, but we threw the elderly lady to the ground and all three of us got into a ball against a little wall and we prayed. I'm not a religious person, but I prayed to God, hoping that we would be okay.

I still did not know if I was alive or dead. My eyes were wide open and I couldn't see anything. It was blacker than black. I couldn't even cough or breathe because

I had so much soot in my throat and in my mouth. And then it started to settle, and I realized I was alive.

I started to scream for some sort of a light. "Does anybody have a lighter?" Nobody answered me. My friend Billy finally said something. The lady was also okay. Finally, a huge floodlight went on, and then another, and I began to see all the EMS workers who were there with us. And they kept leading us out. I've never really noticed EMS workers, or police officers or firefighters. But I was there and now I know. These people are the most amazing people I've ever come across. They were not out for themselves. They stayed in there, making a light path fro everybody else to find a way out.

When I finally got out it looked like a nuclear winter. I was walking, but I was in shock. I still had no clue what was going on. I was walking down the street and looking down and seeing all the e-mails and pictures, and then seeing this white manila folder with the letter J on it from a law office or a doctor's office. This is after 2 World Trade Center collapsed, and it didn't even occur to me that it collapsed. I was still thinking, How did this happen from a small plane hitting out building?

My life dramatically changed on that day. I'm not the same person. I don't feel safe anymore. I don't conduct myself in the same manner that I used to because I'm always on alert. I'm a quieter person now. I fear death now. I'm waiting for it to happen. I haven't had a restful sleep since this whole thing happened. I've been taking medication to help me sleep, but it doesn't work. I mean, there are days that I sleep because I'm so tired that my body has no other choice. But more often than not, I get maybe three hours of sleep a night. I'm a restless person, that's my nature. But I'm worse than I ever was, and it's not good. I feel myself just breaking down, my whole body. I've been getting help, but it doesn't seem to be doing much.

Obviously, time heals everything as you get further and further away. But the memory stays. I have nightmares. The visions I saw aren't going away. Seeing all that carnage sticks in my mind. Seeing the plane and feeling the plane hit was terrible. It was just a frightening experience. Now I carry a flashlight in my bag and an air filter mask that was given out at my exchange a week after the attacks. I'm waiting for something else to happen. And if something else is going to happen, I feel it will happen in New York. I didn't go to the World Series game because of the stress. My wife was frightened for me to go. My choice was letting her be frightened for the whole night, or just going home, which is what I ended up doing. I gave the tickets away. And these are things that I love, going to ball games, going to football games. Now I avoid crowds. I won't do it. And that's very sad, but I don't see there ever being a remedy to it.

Testimony of Bernard B. Kerik, Former Police Commissioner, New York Police Department

I was in my office that morning. I had just finished exercising. I had a workout room in the back of my office, and I went in the back to take a shower. I'd locked the outside door to my inner office, and all of a sudden I heard this banging on the door. You know, kicking, banging, people yelling. So I ran out and opened the door. I had a towel wrapped around me. Hector Santiago and John Picciano, my chief of staff, were there and they were yelling at me that a plane had just hit tower 1.

I said, "All right. Shut up. Calm down." They were screaming, and I said, "Relax. It's okay." In my mind, I was thinking that it was a small plane flying up the Hudson. You know, we deal with tragedy every day in this city—and accidents, major accidents and the like.

But they kept saying, "No you don't understand. It's the whole top of the building. It's enormous."

I said, "All right, get out of the way." So I walked out into my office with a towel draped around me. I walked through my personnel office and into my conference room. When I got in front of the TV, I was stunned by what I saw. I turned around and replied, "Who the hell said this was a plane?"

They said, "Well, that's what they're yelling over the radio." So I ran back to my desk and I called the mayor. He was uptown at a breakfast. I spoke to him and said, "Look, something has just happened at the towers. I'm heading down there. I'll meet you at the command center," which was the Office of Emergency Management in 7 World Trade.

I was dressed within minutes. I got in my car with Hector and Craig Taylor. We got to West Broadway between Barclay and, Vesey and I said, "Stop the car." I got out and I looked up at the tower. I could see the smoke and the debris, and then I saw these things coming from the top of the building. It was so high up. I thought it was debris. But as it got closer to the ground I realized that people were jumping from the building. I've been in this business for twenty-six years and I've done everything under the sun. I've been involved in gun battles. I had partners that were killed. Hector and I were in a shooting. He got shot. But I've never felt as helpless as I did on that morning. You couldn't yell to these people and ask them to stop, or make them stop. I guess that had a choice: stay within a two-thousand-degree inferno, or jump. And they were jumping.

I told the guys to back the car away from he building. We were only about a half-block from the towers. They backed the car up Barclay Street. I was talking on the radio, telling the guys to bring in resources, activating rapid mobilizations from around the city, calling in cops from every precinct.

I turned around to say something to Hector when there was this enormous explosion. I looked up and the other building, building 2, was sort of exploding and igniting above. And I thought, Now what's happened? How did that building ignite this other building. I don't know what was going through my head, but all of a sudden somebody yelled, "Run." And Hector grabbed me by the shirt, and we started running up West Broadway. Debris and body parts and the plane and the building, it was all coming down right on top of us. Hector got his in the back of the leg with a piston or some piece of the plane. We ducked behind the post office behind 7 World Trade and waited for the entire thing to stop.

I looked back out. I saw the damage. At that point, I could hear aviation and the pilots yelling on the radio that it was a commercial airliner. I realized at that minute that we were under attack. I yelled to John to get on the telephone to call headquarters, but there was no phone service. The cell phones were down, so we're calling on the radio. I'm yelling for them to get aviation to close down the airspace. We needed air support, and I'm screaming at these guys to get me air support.

They're looking at me, like "Is there a fucking number to call for an F-16?" Like "Who do we call? How do we do that?"

But aviation had taken care of that and closed down the airspace. They had called in the military. I ordered the entire city to be shut down at that point. All bridges and tunnels closed. No entry. No exit. My main concern at that point was that there could be other secondary attacks set up on the ground. They're hitting us from above, did they do anything on the ground? Are they on the ground? My other concern was who the hell they were. Who are they? You know, as all of these events were unfolding, you're trying to put it all together. You're trying to think of so many things at once.

Then I thought about other targets—police headquarters, City Hall, the U.N., the Empire State Building. That's what was running through my mind. And as I thought of each target, I would tell my staff to start evacuating these buildings.

Within three or four minutes after the second plane hit, the mayor pulled up. I ran up the block and I stopped his car just north of Barclay. He got out of the car. He stood there with me. We were looking at the building and I was telling him what had just happened.

He made a comment to me, some kind of comment, like "We're in uncharted territory. The city has never experienced anything like this." I forget exactly how he said it, but it was something to that effect. And then he asked where the command posts were going to be, and I told him they were going to have to set one up on West Street or on the west side of the towers.

He said, "All right, let's go around to West Street. We'll go down west and we'll look at the damage from the other side of the building and see what they are doing there."

So we walked west on Barclay and then south on West Street. We stopped and met with First Deputy Commissioner Bill Feehan from the fire department; Chief Peter Ganci; ESU Sergeant John Coglin; Mychal Judge, the chaplain; and Ray Downey. They were setting up their staging area right across from tower 1. My guys kept pushing me to get into a command center, and I was telling the mayor, "Look, we have to go back north on West Street. We've got to get out of here."

The mayor wanted to talk to the White House. I said, "We've got to get you out of here and into a command center. You can call the White House from there." So we said goodbye to everybody and started walking. Mychal Judge grabbed the mayor and said, "Be careful and God bless you."

So we all went into 75 Barclay with the mayor; his chief of staff, Tony Carbonetti; Joe Lhota, the deputy mayor of operations; Steve Fishner, the criminal justice coordinator; and Sunny Mindel, the mayor's press secretary. The mayor got on the phone. They got through to the White House. As he was talking on the phone, somebody's pager said that the Pentagon had been hit. I've known the mayor for about eleven or twelve years, and I've never seen him look as worried or concerned about anything as much as he did when he was on the phone with the White House. He put the phone down and he said, "Well, that's not good at all. They've hit the Pentagon and they're evacuating the White House." It was a clear signal that this was no longer just about New York City. It was about the United States.

Then all of a sudden somebody slammed the door open in this office where we were standing and yelled to hit the deck. and just as they said it, the whole damned building started to shake. I started walking to the door to look outside and all the windows outside in that outer hallway of 75 Barclay started to shatter. Then there was this gush of smoke and soot, like this black dust. Hector grabbed me by the middle of my back and started pushing me to the back of the building. And everybody sort of followed. We didn't know what was going on. I didn't know if 75 Barclay was coming down, if another building was hit.

We went out through a back door and wound up in this maze of hallways. And every exit door was locked. We couldn't get out of this building, and it was filling up with smoke and debris. I remember thinking. All the shit I've been through in my entire life and I'm going to suffocate in this damn building.

Then in one of the basement areas we saw two maintenance guys. I don't know where they were coming from. I don't know what they were doing, but they were definitely as surprised to see us as we were to see them. We said, "We need to get out of here. We need to get as far away from the towers as possible. Can you open these doors?"

One of them said, "Yeah, absolutely." So he opened the doors, and we were in the lobby, I think, of 100 Church Street. The front of the lobby had these huge glass windows, and outside was solid pure white. You couldn't see anything. As we were standing there, in walked a guy covered in this white stuff from head to toe. His eyes were totally red and bloodshot. And it was my deputy commissioner of administration, Tibor Kerekes. We were in Korea together. We were in Saudi Arabia two different times together. He worked for me in New Jersey. He's my best friend. He walked in the door and his eyes were solid bloodred. He had been outside when the building fell and he ducked into one of those little three-foot openings in the side of the post office building. He stood there as all this debris came down around him. And now he was running into us. The mayor and I took him to the side. We were pouring water on his face and cleaning out his eyes.

We regrouped and started walking north on Church. We walked into the Tribeca Grand Hotel thinking we'd take the place over and set up the government in there. The advance people were up there, and they were running all over the building, getting phones, doing all this stuff. The mayor and I walked into the lobby. We looked around, and when we looked up, we saw that the entire ceiling was glass. There was an instantaneous feeling of being uncomfortable, I looked at the mayor, he looked at me, and we just walked right out the door. We didn't say anything. We just kept walking and everybody followed us right out of the building. We got back on Church Street and kept walking north.

We got to a firehouse. Everybody was gone. The firehouse was locked up. We had to break in. We broke in the door and then started making some phone calls and started putting together some mobilization plans. We needed to create a command center for city government. I said, "Let's go to the police academy. We can run the city from there." And that's what we did. We set up an enormous conference room in the police academy where the mayor and the fire commissioner and myself were able to call in all the other agencies and started working on a response to the attack.

I don't remember where we were when tower 1 came down. But I can remember the look on Tommy Von Essen's face. He knew that a lot of his guys were in those buildings. I can just remember seeing him at the academy. He was in a daze. We all were in a daze.

As for the mayor, I guess you'd have to know him to understand this. If there was a major tragedy on December 31, if something had happened on the afternoon of the 31st, his last day in office, he would have reacted no differently than he did in September. I made a comment to him, I guess it was around December 20, a week or so away from the end of his term. He used to have daily staff meetings at eight o'clock every day. And Tommy and I used to joke about it, because before September 11 we didn't go to the dailies. We went once a week. Now we were going to dailies and it was a week away from the end of his term, and I said, "Why do we have to have a daily? Next week we're outta here." I was joking.

And the mayor said, "Why? Because you're the police commissioner and I'm the mayor until December 31, that's why."

It was just another lesson in dealing with the mayor and working with him, and witnessing his work ethic and his integrity and what he did and how he did it. He set the tone on September 11. We didn't do anything that we hadn't done before. It was just far more enormous and far bigger than anything we had ever one, imagined, and two, experienced. I mean, I was a really active cop. I'm probably the highest decorated police commissioner that's ever served this city. I was awarded the medal of Valor. I'd been involved in gun battles. I knew. I'd been around. And yet to witness this, and to be there, was like nothing that I would have ever imagined.

Martin Glynn's Tribute to Police Officer Moira Smith

I was one of the last people to see Police Officer Moira Smith before she perished in the collapse of the World Trade Center. I remember her very vividly because my experience was personal, intense, and unique. This is to document what she was doing in those final minutes.

I have to background this story by saying that my wife has been a flight attendant for a major US Airline for over twenty years. During that time, she has received extensive training in emergency evacuation procedures. I have seen her practice the drill for evacuating passengers from a fiery aircraft on many occasions. I always felt that she was very sincere about executing her responsibility in such a situation. Her rehearsals included details that would never occur to the average person. For example, she was trained to touch a door with the back of her hand before opening it. If the door was so hot that it burned her hand, she would still be able to use the front of her hand to hold a rope should that be necessary. The dedication and intensity with which she executed these exercises left me no doubt about her intention to perform in an emergency situation.

On 9/11, I entered 2 WTC moments before the first tower was struck. I took the express elevator to the 78th floor sky lobby and everything appeared normal. I entered the local elevator and pressed 84. The elevator stopped on the 82nd floor and a young man leapt into the car just as the door was closing. He was screaming, "Terrorists, go down." I asked him what he had seen, but he was in such a state of shock he couldn't communicate. He was crouched in the corner and kept saying, "Fire! Fire!"

The elevator continued up to my floor but I didn't get out. I kept trying to find out what the young man had seen. When we got back down to the sky lobby, the scene has changed completely. The floor was packed, and people were lined up ten deep in front of the express elevators to go back down. We weren't sure if the elevators were going to be running, so many of us started down the stairs.

At first, it was a slow march. There were people streaming into the descending crowd on every floor. However, when we had gone down about ten floors, the flow of people joining us stopped. I thought that perhaps the situation had clarified, and I decided to view the scene for myself.

The first reentry door was on the sixtieth floor. I asked a fellow who was walking around locking up offices where I could go to see the North Tower. He pointed down a hallway and said, "It's that way, but don't look. It's too horrible!"

I went anyway. When I got to the window, I looked up and saw the flames shooting out of the top floors. I looked down and saw three distinct large pools of blood. I reckon the largest was thirty yards across. The bodies were mixed in with the wreckage and I could make out several legs sticking out of the debris. I looked back up just to see a man in a white shirt jumping from a top floor. I saw his face clearly. My eyes followed him down till the ground came into focus, then I looked away.

My reaction was very physical and intense. My stomach turned, my knees became wobbly, and my eyes saw black. I almost passed out.

I thought that by exiting the building under these circumstances I would add to the confusion and impede the rescue workers. I decided to sit down and wait for the emergency to get under control. I had been sitting for about 15 minutes, when the second plane hit our building. We knew something enormous had happened because the building shook and the temperature rose by ten degrees in an instant.

There were about ten of us who had been sitting around in the reception area on that floor. We all got up quickly and hurried down the steps. The staircase was open now and we were moving quite fast.

After we had gone down several floors, we came to a cripple woman lying on a landing between floors. Her walking cane was by her side and she was looking at the people hurrying by. She was yelling, 'I'm going to die. I'm going to die.' I felt a pang of guilt as I continued past her with the rest of the crowd. My mind flashed images of my wife alone in the bed and my sons without a father. Nothing else mattered, I had to get out.

When we got down to about the fifth floor, we caught up with the tail end of the main crowd. The trek down the steps became a slow march again. I looked back to see who was behind us. There I saw an Oriental fellow carrying the crippled woman on his back.

I didn't fault myself for being a coward. Rather, I admired him for being calm and composed in this emergency situation. I thought, 'I could have done that too—or at least I could have helped out—but I'm not thinking—I'm panicked.' As we stood there in the dimly light staircase, I was thinking about the carnage I would witness when we came out into the plaza lobby. I was trying to brace myself. To be prepared for the worst.

We exited the stairwell to a ramp which led toward the main plaza. A slow moving line progressed along the ramp to a down escalator which connected to the underground passageway being used to exit the compound. Moira stood at the end of the ramp directing the traffic down the escalator. She had her flashlight in her right hand and she was waving it like a baton. She was repeating over and over—"Don't look! Keep Moving."

I immediately had the sensation that I knew what had happened there before. I thought: groups of people had come through here and stopped to look at the horror of the situation. There was mass hysteria and the exit paths were blocked. She broke it up and got things moving again. Now she's making sure it doesn't happen again.

It was a very intense personal experience for me. It was like I was in a scene that I had witnessed before only this time—instead of my wife rescuing strangers—it was me being rescued by Moira.

I came to the end of the ramp and I was standing squarely in front of Moira, I leaned to the left to try to look past her to see the plaza. She quickly matched my motion and blocked my vision saying "don't look." Our eyes made direct contact. My eyes said to her, "I know how bad it is and I understand what you're doing." Her face was full of pain and her eyes said to me, "In this horrific situation, this is the best and only thing I can do."

The mass of people exiting the building felt the calm assurance that they were being directed by someone in authority who was in control of the situation. Her actions seemed ordinary, even commonplace. She insulated the evacuees from the awareness of the dangerous situation they were in, with the result that everything preceded smoothly.

In my company—sixty one people perished—one hundred eighty survived. Afterwards, I asked several of my fellow employees if they had noticed the woman police officer at the escalator landing. They said, "Yeah—she was directing traffic."

A statue of Moira—holding her flashlight while evacuating the building—would be an excellent way to pay tribute to the heroism of the NYPD on 9/11. As a work of art, it would work on many levels.

- It commemorates the Supreme Sacrifice in an understated way that will encourage viewers to look twice.
- It will have special meaning for women. Moira's job on 9/11 was without heraldry, yet she may have been responsible for saving more lives than anyone else.

Greg Trevor, Official in the Public Affairs Department of the Port Authority of New York and New Jersey

A Race to Safety: What Was It Like Inside One World Trade Center?
My life was spared by 11 minutes.

On Sept. 11, my coworkers and I escaped One World Trade Center at 10:18 a.m. The building collapsed seconds before 10:29 a.m.

I owe my life to three things: a knit tie, a quick-thinking Port Authority Police officer; and the foresight of the architects and engineers who designed the World Trade Center strong enough to withstand direct hits from jets—and enable an estimated 25,000 people to escape.

When the first of two 767s hit the Twin Towers at 8:46 a.m., I was standing behind my desk on the south side of the 68th floor of One World Trade Center, in the Public Affairs Department of the Port Authority of New York and New Jersey.

I had been working or nearly two hours, and had just finished a phone call to a colleague at Newark International Airport. I stood to stretch my legs and looked out the window at the Statue of Liberty, which sparkled from the sunlight of that unusually bright morning.

I was nearly knocked to the floor by the impact of the first plane, which slammed into the north side of Tower One more than 20 floors above me. I heard a loud thud, followed by an explosion. The building felt like it swayed about 10 feet to the south. It shuddered back to the north, then shimmied back and forth.

Out the window I saw a parabola of flame fall toward the street, followed by a blizzard of paper and glass. Then I heard two sounds: emergency sirens on the street, and phones ringing across the 68th floor—calls from reporters wondering what had happened.

Dazed but anxious to get out, I ran to the office of my department Director, Kayla Bergeron. She was already on the phone to the Port Authority's Chief Operating Officer Ernesto Butcher. I got on Kayla's other line and contacted the Port Authority Police Department's headquarters in Jersey City.

Within a few minutes, we gathered the staff, threw files and notepads into our bags, and prepared to evacuate the floor. It began to fill with grainy smoke.

We forwarded the office phones to the Port Authority's Central Police Desk in Jersey City, so the media could leave messages while we escaped. Ana Abelians, a member of our staff, said two media calls were holding. I replied, "You get one, I'll get the other one, we'll get rid of them and get the hell out of here."

I picked up the pone. "Greg Trevor here."

"Hi, I'm with NBC national news. If you could hold on for about 5 minutes, we're going to put you on for a live phone interview."

"I'm sorry, I can't. We're evacuating the building."

"But this will only take a minute."

"I'm sorry, you don't understand. We're leaving the building right now."

He seemed stunned. "But but, this is NBC NATIONAL news." (Apparently, I don't have to risk by life for the local NBC affiliate, but no sacrifice is too great for the NATIONAL news.)

I said "I'm sorry" once more, then hung up.

For more than an hour, we joined thousands of fellow World Trade Center workers who patiently descended the emergency stairwells.

I wasn't scared at first. My initial feelings were disorientation and disbelief. When we entered the stairwell, all we knew was that a plane had struck the building. It didn't make sense. (How could a plane hit a 110-story building on such a clear day?) Because we were in the stairwell, we didn't feel the impact of the second plane hitting Two World Trade Center.

I tried to call my wife, Allison, several times by cell phone, but couldn't get through. Fortunately, I reached my colleague, Pasquale DiFulco, through my interactive pager.

Pasquale, who began the day on vacation and was watching CNN, called Allison to let her know I was safe. He also used his pager to tell us what was really going on.

9:32 a.m. page from Pasquale: AA 676 from Boston crashed into 1wtc. FBI reporting plane was hijacked moments before crash saw second plane crash live on CNN into 2 wtc. Bush just made announcement possible terrorist attack.

9:36 a.m.: At least 1,000 injuries—CNN

9:41 a.m.: Fire at the Pentagon

9:43 a.m. page to Pasquale: Oh Christ

9:43 a.m. page from Pasquale: Pentagon and White House being evacuated

9:46 a.m.: Fire on mall in Washington

9:49 a.m.: FAA closes all flights nationwide

9:52 a.m.: Plane hit Pentagon

9:54 a.m.: Capitol treasury also evacuated

Despite this news, our long walk in search of safety remained calm and orderly. We had conducted regular fire drills, so we knew what to do. Every few floors, we would stop, move to the right of the stairwell and make room for injured people walking down—and firefighters and Port Authority officers running up.

Then we reached the fifth floor just before 10 a.m.

We heard a loud rumble. The building shook violently. I was thrown from one side of the stairwell to the other.

We didn't know it at the time, but Tower Two had just collapsed.

Our stairwell filled with smoke and concrete dust. Breathing became difficult. The lights died. A steady stream of water, about 4 inches deep, began running down the stairs. It felt like we were wading through a dark, dirty, rapid river—at night in the middle of a forest fire.

The smartest decision I made that day was to wear a knit tie to work. I put the blue tie over my nose and mouth to block the smoke and dust. To keep from hyperventilating, I remembered the breathing exercises my wife and I learned in our Lamaze classes.

Someone yelled that we should put our right hand on the shoulder of the person in front of us and keep walking down. We descended one more flight, to the fourth floor, when I heard someone say: "Oh shit, the door's blocked."

The force from the collapse of Tower Two had apparently jammed the emergency exit. We were ordered to turn around and head back up the stairs, to see if we could transfer to another stairwell.

Now we were wading against the current of that dark, dirty river. Others were still trying to walk down. People were starting to panic.

For the first time, I was afraid we wouldn't make it. I whispered a quick prayer: "Lord, please let me see my family again."

Then I closed my eyes, and made mental pictures of my family's faces: Allison's beautiful brown eyes; our 5-year-old son Gabriel's deep blue eyes and dimples; our 2-year-old son Lucas' blond ringlets.

I remember thinking: Their faces will keep me calm. And if I die, they will be the last thing on my mind.

During this ordeal, Pasquale sent me a series of frantic pages that didn't go through.

10 a.m. page from Pasquale: Please tell my I r OK Please respond. Another explosion at wtc

10:02 a.m.: Part of 2 wtc has collapsed. Is everyone ok?

10:06 a.m.: Please respond

10:12 a.m.: Where are you? 2 wtc just collapsed?

I don't know how many minutes it took for emergency workers to clear the exit. But when they did, thank God that Port Authority Police Officer David Lim was there.

David is a K-9 officer whose partner, Sirius, was killed in the attacks. He was later trapped in the rubble for nearly five hours. David had the presence of mind to figure out a way to get us all turned around and headed back downstairs. Over and over, he shouted: "Down is good! Down is good!"

When I heard that, I shouted "Down is good!" up the stairwell. Like an echo, I heard others shout "Down is good!" up the line.

Now we darted down the stairs as quickly as possible.

The emergency exit led to the mezzanine level of Tower One. We walked several hundred feet to a glass door that led outside.

The mezzanine was filled with dull-beige concrete dust—on the floor, in the air, caked against the floor-to-ceiling windows. It felt like we were walking through a huge, dirty snow globe that had just been shaken.

It was even worse when we walked outside, near Six World Trade Center. The plaza was a minefield of twisted metal, covered by a layer of concrete dust several inches thick. I am grateful for that dust, because it means I didn't see any bodies.

As we were leaving the building, my pager buzzed with a message from Al Frank, a reporter with the Newark Star-Ledger who has covered the Port Authority for years.

10:17 a.m. page from Al Frank: Are you okay?

I replied a minute later, as we were walking along the outside of Six World Trade: We're out of the building. Everyone is fine.

Relieved but fatigued, we sprinted down the stairs between Six and Five World Trade, then turned up Church Street and headed north.

I looked back at the Trade Center. The upper third of Tower One was on fire. There was so much smoke and dust, I couldn't tell that Tower Two had collapsed.

At 10:24 a.m., I received a page from Kayla, my boss, who was walking about half a block behind me: Where shall we go?

I walked back to her and said we should go to the entrance of the Holland Tunnel, because I knew Port Authority Police officers would be there.

We continued walking north toward the Holland. A few minutes later, we heard an NYPD officer shout: "Run for your lives!"

We ran north for several blocks. We felt a deafening rumble, followed by a thick cloud of black smoke and brown dust.

When we finally outraced the cloud, we had almost reached the Holland Tunnel. I was standing next to coworker, John Toth, who was limping with a bloody knee.

"John, are you all right?"

"They're gone, Greg."

"Who's gone, Jon?"

"Not who. Both towers, they're gone."

I didn't believe him. Then I looked back to where the Twin Towers should have been.

All I saw was smoke and sky. One World Trade Center had stayed up for more than 1 hour and 40 minutes after the first attack, enabling thousands of us to escape.

We walked the remaining blocks to the mouth of the Holland Tunnel. Military jets flew overhead.

Our clothes, hair and faces still covered with dust, we crammed into Port Authority Police cars, which took us to our temporary offices in Jersey City.

About an hour later, I wrote the first draft of our first statement after the attacks on the only form of communication I had left—my interactive pager.

Our hearts and our prayers go out to the families of the countless people—including many members of the Port Authority family—who were killed today in this brutal and cowardly attack. All PA facilities are closed until further notice. We at the PA are going everything within out power to assist the families of the victims, and to co-operate with federal, state and local authorities to capture the perpetrators of this attack and bring them to justice.

My personal recovery has been steady in the months that have followed the attacks on the World Trade Center.

Our department worked out of Jersey City for more than two months—at first, in rotating 12-hour shifts. As we mourn the loss of 75 friends and colleagues, we have answered the deluge of questions from media around the world—about security, the recovery and our own experiences.

I returned to Ground Zero for days after the attacks. The experience was unnerving and humbling—not because of what's there, but what used to be there. I looked up at the hole in the sky where our offices used to be, and thought about how easily we could have been trapped up there.

I often feel waves of sadness, thinking about the loss and the suffering.

I think about the 37 Port Authority Police officers and commanders who died helping others escape—particularly Captain Kathy Mazza, the first woman Commandant of the Port Authority Police Academy.

She led a group of Police Academy instructors into Tower One a few minutes after the first attack. Most of them didn't make it out. Kathy, a former operating room nurse and one of the finest people I've ever known, was the first female Port Authority Police officer in the department's 73-year history to be killed in the line of duty.

Sometimes when I'm walking down a street, I stop, lean back my head, take a deep breath of clean air—and remember those frightful minutes when we were denied this pleasure.

Cigarette smoke bothers me a lot, but food tastes much better.

My thighs ached for four days from the stairwell evacuation. My wife says my skin was dull gray for the first two days.

In mid-December, I was in bed for a week with pneumonia—a condition caused in part by the stress and exhaustion from September 11 and its aftermath.

Although my children don't fully understand what happened, they want to cuddle more.

Therapy has been very helpful. It has shown me that I am at the beginning of a very long journey. Some days I make a lot of progress; other days I stand still.

My goal is to get as far down the road as possible. But no matter how far I go, I know that there's no way I'll get back to Sept. 10.

I've saved my tie—still caked in smoke and dust—in a sealed bag. I've also saved my dust-covered shoes.

Source: Mitchell Fink and Lois Mathias (eds.), *Never Forget: An Oral History of September 11, 2001* (New York: ReganBooks, 2002): Joseph Pfeifer, pp. 17–22; Robert Leder, pp. 51–53; Bernard B. Kerik, pp. 109–113. Source for Martin Glynn testimony is http://www.moirasmith.com/. Source for Greg Trevor testimony is http://www.coping.org/911/survivor/race.htm/. Oral testimonies and tribute by Martin Glynn used by permission. Greg Trevor and his wife Allison Salerno Trevor can be reached at allisonsalerno@verizon.net.

Document 15

Pentagon Attack

The attack on the Pentagon has received much less attention than that on the World Trade Center, or than United Airlines Flight 93, but it was still a major attack. Casualties were high, with many of the survivors suffering bad burns. Lieutenant Colonel Ted Anderson's account gives an idea of what happened on September 11 at the Pentagon.

Ted Anderson, Lieutenant Colonel, U.S. Army, Legislative Liaison Officer to the U.S. Congress in the Pentagon

My portfolio deals with current operations for the army worldwide. So I go in extremely early, between 4 and 5 A.M., in order to read overnight cable traffic from Europe and destinations beyond. From there, I try to get in a little physical training and then begin the normal duty day with everybody else.

We had a morning meeting scheduled at 7:45, which I attended. I picked up a cup of coffee on the way back, chitchatted with a few folks, and made it back into the office. Then I noticed that all of my colleagues were huddled near an overhead television. Probably four or five lieutenant colonels and three civilian secretaries and everybody seemed extremely quiet. We're usually a pretty rambunctious group of folks. Some of the ladies were crying. I had no idea what had happened. And then I stared at the TV, and it showed the towers, both burning. Then the clip came on showing the replay of the second airplane striking tower 2. Two of the aviators in our office said, "Well, that's it. There's all the proof you need right there. That's no accident." And I knew he was right. And immediately I knew that this was some kind of state-sponsored terrorism. Renegade terrorists cannot conduct a coordinated attack that successfully.

I walked back to my cubicle and sat down. I pulled up my e-mail and then all of a sudden I just got this real eerie feeling. I don't know, call it nineteen years in the army, combat experience, deployments worldwide, constant level of preparedness. So I immediately got up from my cubicle and walked out the mall entrance to the guard location, where the defense protective services folks are at. I knew the guys on duty. I asked them if they were aware of what had occurred in New York. They were just getting some of the details. And I stated, "Hey, look, guys, we need to upgrade security here. Has anybody given any thought of upgrading the threat level."

And he said, "Sir, I'm sure that they're talking about that now. Let me radio in." So he called in and found out that sergeants and the officers at the headquarters location were in a meeting talking about what upgraded security precautions they should take. So I felt a little bit better. I mean, we had talked about what a tremendous target the Pentagon was and how vulnerable we were, previously.

I walked back to my office, sat down, and pulled up some more of the e-mail and started corresponding with the daily activity across the Potomac on the Hill, and my phone rang. It was my wife, who lives in Fayetteville, North Carolina. My wife is a sixth-grade schoolteacher at Stedman Middle School, and she was in class with her students and they had the TV on and were watching the activity live and discussing what was going on. And my wife said, "Hey, I know somebody in Washington. Let's call him and we'll get an instant update as to what's going on and what they think in Washington."

So we talked briefly, and she was relaying information to her students as I was describing it to her. I told her that we could only assume at this point that it was some sort of coordinated attack. But I also told her to make sure that her students understood that we should not jump to conclusions and point fingers at anyone, because we had done that in the Oklahoma tragedy and we were extremely embarrassed that we had alienated the entire Arab community. I could hear her explaining that to her students, all about the Oklahoma bombing, when the plane hit the Pentagon. It was a loud roar, and I mean the building literally shook. And there was a sucking sound, which I believe was the oxygen escaping as the jet fuel poured into the corridors right down the hall from us and ignited, taking all the oxygen out of the air.

Our ceiling caved in. The lights went out, but the phone was still working, I was still on with my wife. I was a little stunned, just for an initial second, and then I said, "Listen, we have been bombed. I have to go." And I hung up the phone. I didn't even wait for a response.

I didn't know at first that it was a plane. I initially assumed for about the first two minutes that a bomb had been left somewhere in the building, and the bomb went off.

I screamed for everybody in the office to get out. I got up and moved, and that was the last time I was ever in that cubicle. We lost everything: twenty years of medical records, everything on my hard drive, personal files, my Class A uniform, everything.

I moved out into the hallway out the back door and went into the main corridor between corridors 4 and 5. The plane actually hit between corridors 2 and 3. I positioned myself in the main corridor and was looking up and down the corridor to see if I could see smoke or fire or anything. And I noticed people just meandering out of their offices, looking around, having basic discussions, and I just started barking orders to get out of the building. Now here I am, dressed for legislative business with Congress. I've got on a nice suit with a striped shirt, tie, and suspenders And I am screaming at full-bird colonels and general officers to move out of the building, just barking orders, screaming. And they listened to me. They all started moving and they tried to get out of the mall entrance but the guards had mistakenly thought that they were under attack from the outside of the building. So they secured that entrance. They had taken out most of their small arms, machine guns, etc., and brought them all out. It looked like they were preparing to defend the doors there. So I started moving people toward the center of the Pentagon. This all took place within two minutes.

The Pentagon is structured by a series of rings. The center of the Pentagon is the A-ring, and then it goes out in rings B, C, D, and E. The E-ring is the last ring around the building. It is basically the wall, the last corridor before you exit the building. So I'm at the E-ring and I kick open a fire exit and scream for people to follow me out that way. I motion for them to move off to the northeast, toward north parking. We have two parking lots, north parking and south parking. I think you've got enough for about fifty thousand parking spaces on each side. I turned to my left and I saw a field of scattered debris. It was all gray and metallic. Everybody was moving to my right, and I turned to my left and ran toward the debris. There's nobody with me except Chris Braman, a noncommissioned office, an NCO, and he is in civilian clothes. He's a cook for the chief of staff of the army, and he was wearing black pants and a polo shirt with his emblem on it.

As we get to the debris field, I know that it's an airplane because of the chunks of charred steel. I'm running at full speed and I'm seeing the billowing smoke and the flames from around the helipad area of the Pentagon. I'm not paying attention to what I'm doing and I fell right into huge pieces of the aircraft and trip over it. I picked myself up and ran directly toward the fire, and at this point I notice that there are two fire trucks on that side which are maintained at the helipad area. It's basically the fire department at the Pentagon. One truck is parked outside and a truck is parked inside the garage. The outside truck was completely engulfed in flames from taking part of the impact of the airplane. The other truck was protected. It was inside the garage and there were three firefighters on duty, two of which I knew, and they pulled the truck out of the garage and were beginning to turn the water cannon on top of the truck. They were the only people out there. I didn't see anybody else.

I got as close to the building as I could, trying to find a door that we could get into. We found two women out on the ground next to the building. Initially, I thought that they had been blown out of their offices, or they had just jumped, but I found out later that they had been thrown out by people who were rescuing folks inside the building.

One woman was conscious. The other was unconscious. I picked up the conscious lady. She had a broken hip and was in horrible, horrible pain. She had flash burns as well. Both ladies had been terribly flash-burned. We were pretty close to the fire now. The fire was bearing down on us. The heat was horrendous. I made sure she understood that I was there, and that we were going to pull her out of there and move her away from the building. I told her it was going to hurt, and I picked her up and threw her on my back. She screamed in pain. I ran her about four hundred yards to the other side of the helipad and laid her down.

The NCO carried the other lady and followed me. We laid them there and other people came up to render aid to them.

Chris and I ran back to the building. We found a window that was pretty well blasted out and we tore the remaining shards of glass along the bottom out and gained entry. Inside we just screamed for people to come toward our voices. We couldn't see anything. The smoke was billowing and it was hard to breathe.

I got on the floor and I felt my way down the wall and I felt a body right in front of the door. It was a woman, extremely heavyset. She was conscious. She was bleeding from the ears and the mouth and she was definitely in shock. She was pinned against a wall by a huge safe. It was a six-drawer safe that had fallen and it was wedged up against her. We were either going to leave her there and let her burn, or we were going to waste some serious time getting her out of there. We had no choice. We had to go ahead and try to get her out. It seemed like forever, but we were finally able to pull her free. We weren't able to lift her. We had to drag her from the building.

Chris and I went back into the building and this time we were trying to figure out what we were going to do. We wanted to crawl from the outside door to the E-ring corridor. As we were trying to get out bearings, some type of fuel outside next to the fire department area blew up. A propane storage tank, I think. And when this thing blew up, it knocked us both down inside that office that we were in. When I pulled myself up, the whole time trying to shield my face with my elbow, I noticed this bright flash that went by me. I thought it was the ceiling caving in. And I heard Chris scream, "Help me." It was a person on fire, trying to get out of the building. Chris knocked him down and I jumped on top of him. We smothered the fire on this guy. He wasn't totally engulfed in flames, just the front part of this guy, from his head down to his lower torso including his legs. We rolled him on the ground and he was screaming, fully conscious, and we picked him up immediately and just carried him out. We got him as far away from the building as we could and gently laid him down. He was burned, horribly, horribly burned from the top of his head all the way to the bottom of his feet. He had no color in his eyes. It was all white.

There are three things that I remember from that day more than anything else. That is one of them. I could see it was a civilian because he had a suit on. You could see that he had a white shirt on, but the whole front of everything had been burnt away. The back of his collar was still affixed, the belt to his pants was still affixed and melted into the side of his body. Everything else was just charred black down the front.

Now this guy is screaming and we were finally able to figure out that he was saying something. He was yelling, "There are people behind me, in the corridor. You have to get the people in the corridor out." He was just screaming this over and over again.

Chris and I looked around and we noticed that more firemen were showing up. Arlington County Fire Department was there, along with Fairfax County Fire Department and Washington, D.C., Fire Department. We ran back toward the same door and all we needed to do now was negotiate this twenty-five feet to that E-ring corridor, and we'll get to the people in that corridor. If we could just get to them, we can lead them back out.

We were getting ready to make entry again, and the firemen stopped us. We had a little confrontation there, I must tell you. I've been instructed by the army to not explain what really happened there, but it was a very lively conversation. I grabbed one of the firefighters and basically told him, "Look, I know you're doing your job, and I know you have our best interests at heart, but here's the bottom line. You have two choices, you can either stay out here, or you can go in with us, and that's basically all I want to talk about. We're wasting time."

Other firemen showed up and they physically restrained us and pulled us away from the building. I am completely and totally out of my mind at this point, reverting to full combat mode. So did Chris. He had been in the Ranger regiment. He fought in Mogadishu. And as far as I was concerned, this was a combat situation. You've got all the horrors of combat. You've got the smells, the sounds of agony and despair. You've got everything there, all of the elements of combat except for the actual lead that's flying through the air. Nobody's shooting at you.

Still, it's an unwritten code that we live by. If you saw *Black Hawk Down*, you know we don't leave anyone behind. I knew there were people inside the building, as did Chris, and it didn't matter that they were civilians. It didn't matter that they were contractors or vendors. We were all one team, one fight. I consider the civilians for the Department of Defense just as important, if not more important then the military folks. The DOD civilians basically run the army and the Pentagon. I knew there were wounded in there and we needed to go in and get them. You can't leave your wounded behind, period. But I was restrained and pulled back.

A three-star general showed up, along with a couple other generals, and I explained to them what was going on. This three-star general basically felt the same way I did, and he went to the on-site fire commander and said, "Look, I will take full responsibility. We're going to mount a rescue effort. We've got two guys here that have already been inside. They will lead our rescue effort, but we need to make an attempt to go in and get our people out." He was overruled by the fire captain.

I have since come to know that the fire captain was correct. I am now certain that they saved my life, and I'm certain they saved Chris's life, as well. My whole outlook on the American firefighter changed that day. I've become Mr. Fan of the Fire Department. Those guys were the real heroes of the day for me. I have talked to firemen who later went into that area and there was no way out. That last burned guy we brought out was the last person of the building alive on the exterior side of the Pentagon. He is alive. The two ladies we brought out both lived. The heavyset woman, unfortunately, died.

Later that afternoon I was able to call and relay a message to my wife that I was okay. The firemen were fully involved in fighting the fire now. They were inside the structure and they were totally involved. I just sat and watched. I was in awe of them the whole afternoon. As darkness fell, the 3rd Infantry Regiment across the river, the old-guard soldiers, showed up in mass, about 250 soldiers, and they relieved us. Basically we were told to go home. "Thanks, you guys did a great job, but the infantry's here to take over."

I remember laying down outside along with a buddy of mine from the same office and we were trying to figure out how we were going to get home. Of course, we didn't bring anything out of the building with us. Everything was inside, including my car keys. Our cars were in the north parking lot and that part of the lot was now a crime scene because part of the aircraft had fallen there, so it was roped off. So we're trying to figure out where the closest metro is. The Pentagon metro site was closed down, so we needed to walk over to Crystal City, which was probably a ten-minute walk at most. So we started strolling off, two well-dressed guys who looked like they had fallen off the turnip truck and dragged through an onion field. We were caked in soot and blood, and it was just nasty looking. I mean, we looked like hell. So we walked over to Crystal City and walked down the metro station, which was running free. The gates were open. We got on a train headed toward Springfield, Virginia, and people looked at us in disbelief. But nobody said anything to us. We looked like bomb victims. And one of the other things that I remember—the first was about that guy's eyes—the second thing is that nobody spoke on the train. It was total silence. Everybody was in shock. Even couples that were together, nobody was talking. They just stared out of the train, stared at each other in just total disbelief.

I got off at my stop and had to walk about four blocks to my house. I didn't have my keys with me, so I had to ask the manager of the building to let me in. He tried to let me in, but his key didn't work so he had to pull the lock off. I was exhausted, I went out and laid down in the grass and went to sleep. The maintenance guy had to come and find me. When I got in, I took a forty-minute shower, cried for thirty minutes, and then spent the rest of the night trying to answer about fifty voice mails. The phone just kept ringing all night. People called from Bulgaria, from Puerto Rico, from Colombia, all over the United States. Finally, you can only tell the story so many times. It physically wears you out. At about eleven o'clock, I had had it and I went to sleep. I slept for a couple of hours and then woke up, you know, and thought it was all a bad dream. I popped on the news, and, of course, I couldn't get away from the story. This was about two in the morning and I just decided to get up and go to work. I put on my battle dress uniform, my fatigues and my boots. I grabbed gear figuring that I'm going to be at work for a while. I got in a car and drove up the 595. And as soon as I turned onto 595, I could see the glow, the orange glow in the distance. As I got closer to it, the glow got brighter. Coming over the break in the horizon you could see that the building was on fire. The ceiling portion of the Pentagon was burning, and it was out of control. I remember very distinctly at about three-ten in the morning, parking my car and seeing this building on fire and people going into work. And that's the last of the three things I'll always remember about that day: Ten thousand people showed up to work at the Pentagon that morning and the building was still on fire. It just made me extremely proud of what I was doing and where I was working to know that a building can be burning out of control and still ten thousand people came to work because they knew number one, we were probably going to be at war, and number two, that there were still dead people in the building who needed to be brought out and identified.

Source: Mitchell Fink and Louis Mathias (eds.), *Never Forget: An Oral History of September 11, 2001* (New York: ReganBooks, 2002): Ted Anderson, pp. 145–151. Oral testimony used by permission.

Document 16

United Airlines Flight 93

Of all the events on September 11, the hijacking of United Airlines Flight 93 was the most dramatic because of the heroic reaction of its passengers. Realizing that the hijackers were on a suicide mission, the passengers attempted to regain control of the aircraft. The fact that they failed to save their own lives does not diminish their effort. Here is the account of Tom Burnett's role in the effort to regain control of the airliner.

Deena Burnett, Wife of Tom Burnett, Passenger on United Airline Flight 93

Tom was in New York for a business meeting. I did not talk to him on the tenth. Normally, he called at least once a day unless he was terribly busy, and he did call on the tenth, but I was out. He left a message on the answering machine and for whatever reason he did not call my cell phone. I took it to mean that he was very busy. It was very unusual not to talk to him.

On the morning of September 11, I was awakened by the three children running into my room, as normal for most mornings. They came in a little before six [Pacific time] and I immediately got up and out of bed. It was Anna Clare's first day of preschool, so we were very excited about getting downstairs and getting breakfast over and being on time. Anna Clare and our two five-year-old twins, Halley and Madison, told me what they wanted for breakfast. I turned on the television. Our kitchen and family room are connected and you can easily see the television. I normally turn it on to check the weather so I can see how to dress the children.

I noticed that on every station there was a news report about the World Trade Center, and as I turned it back to channel 7, ABC News, they showed an airplane flying through one of the towers. I thought, my goodness, air traffic control must be terribly messed up. They're sending airplanes into the towers by accident.

The phone rang, and it was my mom, who said, "Deena, have you seen the television? They're saying this is an American Airlines flight that's gone into the towers, Tom's in New York, isn't he?"

I said, "Yes, he is, but don't worry, Mom, that's not his plane. He wouldn't be on American. He'd be flying United or Delta."

She said, "Well, do you know what time he was leaving?"

And I said, "No, but it should have been fairly early in the morning. He said he'd be home by noon." I could tell by her voice that she was concerned, and I reassured her: "Mom, don't worry. Planes crash all the time and Tom's never on them. Of all the thousands of planes in the sky, the likelihood of that being Tom's is just very slim. It can't possibly be his." She said, "Okay, I'll stop worrying," and she hung up.

I turned the news up again. The more I watched and listened, the more concerned I became. I kept trying to do the math in my mind: if he's coming in at noon and there's a three-hour time difference and it's a five-hour flight, what time would he have taken off and which airport would he have taken off from?

And then I thought, okay, I can call his cell phone. I tried to remember if he had an itinerary. Normally he would have left one with me, but it was such a short trip that he did not leave one. I thought about called his secretary, Kim, and realized it was too early to call, that she wouldn't be in at the office. I couldn't find her home phone number and didn't want to wake her anyway. And then I thought about calling his mom. Maybe she would know what time he was leaving and what flight he was on. And while I was trying to decide whether or not I should worry her, the phone rang again and it was Tom's mother. I made breakfast for the children while I was on the phone with her. And her first question was "Do you know where Tom is?"

I said, "No, I don't. I was hoping you would know." And while we were trying to provide each other with information and figure out the situation, the phone rang in on call-waiting, and I said, "Oh, let me go. That may be him."

And so I clicked over, and I looked at the phone and I saw on the caller ID that it was Tom's cell phone. I was relieved, thinking that if he was on his cell phone, he was in the airport somewhere and was fine. I brought the phone back to my mouth and ear and said, "Tom, are you okay?"

And he said, "No, I'm not. I'm on an airplane that's been hijacked. It's United Flight 93." And he told me what was going on. "They're already knifed a guy. I think one of them has a gun." I started asking questions, and he said, "Deena, just listen." He went over the information again and said, "Please call the authorities," and he hung up.

I just felt a jolt of terror run through my whole body. It was as if I'd been struck by lightning. I couldn't believe how I felt. I started reaching for the phone book, and for papers, going back and forth in the kitchen, pacing up and down the counter, trying to figure out who to call. I didn't know what I was looking for. Then I thought, 911. I have to call 911. Maybe they can tell me who I need to call for a hijacking. I dialed their number, and while the phone was ringing I thought, they're going to think I am nuts. What can I say to them to make them believe me?

A woman answered 911. She asked, "Is this an emergency?"

And I said, "Well, yes. I don't know. Yes. My husband is on a pane that's been hijacked. He called me from the airplane and told me that they have guns on board the plane."

And she started repeating me. "Your husband's on a plane that's been hijacked?" I said yes, and she said, "Okay, let me transfer you." She transferred me to another lady, I believe a supervisor, who eventually transferred me to a man at the FBI. And he transferred me to a special agent. As I was explaining the situation and Tom's phone call, the phone rang in again on call-waiting, and I said, "I have to go."

He said, "Call me back if it's him," and I wrote his number down quickly.

And I clicked over and it was Tom again, and the first thing he said was, "They're in the cockpit." And I told him about the World Trade Center. He hadn't known about it yet. As soon as I told him, he relayed that information to the people sitting around him.

And he said, "Oh, my God, it's a suicide mission." And he started asking questions: "Who's involved? Was it a commercial airplane? What airline was it? Do you know how many airplanes are involved?" He was really pumping me for information about what was going on, anything that I knew. And he was relaying my answers to people sitting around him. Then he told me he had to go and he hung up.

I started calling United to find out what kind of plane he was on and they told me it was a 757. And of course, they didn't know anything about the hijacking.

I was sitting in a chair. I had fed the girls their breakfast. They were sitting on the sofa watching an airplane fly into the World Trade Center and saying, "Mom is that Dad's plane?" And I said no. Because when he first called, they had gathered around me and they wanted to talk to him, and I said that he would talk them later. They seemed to be fine with that. I just reassured them that Dad was fine and they shouldn't worry about him.

And then a news reporter came on saying that the Pentagon had been hit, and I started wailing. I mean, really wailing, making a noise that I did not know I could make, thinking that it was Tom's plane that had hit the Pentagon. I began to tremble. The girls were watching me and they started laughing. I had made a strange noise, not a crying noise but a sound of sorrow and grief and pain.

And when they saw the tears fall down my face and that I wasn't laughing, that I wasn't playing with them, they began to get concerned, and they ran over to me, and they started crying. I realized at that point that I needed to get control of myself, that I was alarming the children. And so I tried to contain myself.

The phone rang again and it was Tom and he said, "Deena."

I said, "Tom, you're okay," thinking that he had survived the plane crash. He said no. And I said, "They just hit the Pentagon." And I knew that he was assessing the situation and trying to figure out how to solve the problem that they were in.

He repeated the same questions: "Who's involved? How many planes are involved? Which airlines?" And he told the people around him that a plane had just hit the Pentagon, and I could hear people talking and spreading the news in the background and I could hear their concern and I could hear people gasping as if they were surprised and shocked. Tom came back on the phone and said, "I'm putting a plan together. We're going to take back the airplane."

I asked, "Who's helping you?"

He said, "Different people, several people. There's a group of us. Don't worry. We're going to do something." Then he said, "I'm going to call you back," and he hung up. And then he called back about five minutes till seven. I didn't even say hello. I just said, "Tom."

He asked, "Is there anything new?" I said no. He was very quiet this time, very calm. He had been very calm and collected through the other conversations, but he was very solemn in this conversation, and I couldn't hear anything in the background. I could hear the roar of the engines and I could tell that he was sitting in a seat and very still and not walking around like he had been. He asked, "Where are the kids?"

I said, "They're fine. They're sitting at the table. They're asking to talk to you."

He said, "Tell them I'll talk to them later."

"I called your parents. They know about your plane being hijacked," I told him. He scolded me: "You shouldn't have worried them. How are they doing?"

"They're okay. They're with Mary and Martha."

"Good." It was just silent, and I could feel my heart racing. Tom said, "We're waiting until we're over a rural area. We're going to take back the airplane."

I became very frightened and I begged, "No, no, Tom. Just sit down, be still, be quiet, and don't draw attention to yourself."

He said, "No, Deena. If they're going to crash this plane into the ground, we're going to have to do something."

I asked, "What about the authorities?"

He said, "We can't wait for the authorities. I don't know what they can do anyway. It's up to us." He said, "I think we can do it." And neither of us said anything for a few seconds.

Then I said, "What do you want me to do? What can I do?"

"Pray, Deena, just pray."

"I am praying. I love you."

Tom said, "Don't worry. We're going to do something," then he hung up. And he never called back.

I kept waiting. I held onto the telephone for almost three hours waiting for him to call back to tell me that he had landed the plane and that everything was fine and that he would be home later. I started thinking about what I could cook for dinner. I was thinking about sending the kids to school, and who could come pick them up, because I didn't want to miss his phone call when he called. I thought about calling his parents to tell them that everything was fine, that Tom was in control, but I was afraid I would miss his call if I called anyone. So I just sat there.

A policeman showed up around the third or fourth phone call to sit with me. A neighbor who had seen the police car came over to see if the children were okay. Tom's sister, Mary, called from her cell phone, and I told her about the hijacking. Their other sister Martha and she went over to their parents' house, and called me to let me know that they were there. So there were actually many telephone calls coming in that morning, between his phone calls. Police officers and FBI agents called on the phone to ask if I had talked to Tom again. I updated them briefly, so I wouldn't tie up my telephone.

By the time his fourth phone call came, firemen had shown up on the front lawn. The children went in and out of the house, looking at all the police cars and fire trucks. I dressed them for school while still holding onto the telephone.

At about ten o'clock I realized that I had been running around the house all morning in my pajamas. I had Tom's old blue robe on. I had not showered or anything. I had not heard from Tom for about three hours, and I just thought I really needed to get dressed. So I went upstairs. I had the telephone with me. And it was really the first time I had released it. I put it. I put it on the ledge by the shower so that in the event I didn't hear it, I could see it ring. I never took my eyes off the telephone while I was showering. It was a very fast shower. I got dressed, and I went downstairs. The policeman was standing at the bottom, and I could tell by the look on his face that something was wrong. I asked him what was wrong, and he said, "I think I have bad news for you."

I remember turning toward the television and seeing that there had been another plane crash. And I ran over to the TV and I asked, "Is that Tom's plane?"

And he said, "Yes, it's Flight 93." I just felt my knees buckle and he pretty much carried me over to the sofa. I was so weak I couldn't even feel the ground beneath me. And I just started crying. It felt as though the tears were coming from the depths of my heart. I was just incredibly, incredibly sad. And I felt so alone. I've never felt such emptiness as I experienced those few moments.

I handed the policeman the telephone. But I kept thinking, people can survive a plane crash. And if he survived, he's going to call. But I looked down and I noticed that the phone battery was dead. The policeman hung it back up on the charger.

It was very difficult. All I wanted to do was go to church. I knew that my children were fine. They had gone off to school, and the principal had called to let me know that the kids were okay and that they did not know about the airplane yet. Several parents were picking up their children from school that day, but I decided to let mine stay in school. I thought that being there was better than being at home and seeing me fall apart. I felt like I needed some to decide how to handle the emotions. And so I went to church. The policeman took me to church, and by the time I left, I knew that the media was looking for me. I went out the back door. The media was already there, questioning the priest who had been brought in earlier that day. I went home. The policeman who had been staying with me all day told me that I needed to brace myself because they were going to find out who I was and where I lived, and I needed to be ready for the onslaught of the media.

I remember being incredibly frightened about speaking to the press. I didn't know what to say. I didn't know what to do. But by six that evening, they had found our house and began knocking on the door and asking to come in or have me come out. And I spent the evening just crying and being with friends and having neighbors come in and out and having family call me on my cell phone to offer their condolences.

And so the next day, I decided that I would face the media, hoping that if I did interviews for one day, they'd leave us alone and we could go on with our lives. They came in droves, packs and packs of news reporters, and many as could fit in my living room. And I remember them saying that my husband was being touted as a hero. It made me laugh to think about Tom's reaction to being called a hero.

They asked me why I was laughing, and I said, "If you knew my husband, you would know that he would laugh at being called a hero. He would tell you that all he was trying to do was get home to his family." He realized the danger of the situation he was in, and he assessed the situation and tried to solve the problem based on the fact that he was a good man and knew right from wrong. He knew it was the right thing to do, not because he was trying to be a hero.

I found that having people call him a hero was a very difficult balance, maybe even an impossible balance. There was incredible pride on my part for his actions on Flight 93. And yet, there was the incredible pain of this loss that we suffered and the fact that my children no longer had a father, and that their father had been cut so short of being able to accomplish what he had planned to in life. I think we will struggle with the balance of the loss versus the pride.

Source: Mitchell Fink and Louis Mathias (eds.), *Never Forget: An Oral History of September 11, 2001* (New York: ReganBooks, 2002): Deena Burnett, pp. 190–196. Oral testimony used by permission.

Document 17

Dog Handlers at Ground Zero

Finding survivors in the wreckage of the World Trade Center was a daunting task. Dog teams were indispensable to that effort. As days passed, the searchers could only hope to find bodies and body parts so that the victims could be identified and their families could have closure. The dog teams were even more critical to these later efforts. It was hard on the dogs, but they performed admirably.

Mark Dawson, Canine Handler for FEMA at Ground Zero

I'm a paid firefighter and a canine handler for Massachusetts Task Force 1, which is part of the Federal Emergency Management Agency program, FEMA. We are one of twenty-eight teams in the country.

We arrived in New York City at 10 P.M. on 9/11. We went down to the site on Church Street for a review of the area we were going to search. We gathered information and split up into two groups, a day shift and a night shift. I worked the night shift for the next eight days.

There were still some large fires burning in the crater area on the night of the attacks. First I went to the edge of the rubble at building 2 with my dog, Elvis, who is a six-year-old black Lab, an advanced, certified dog in the FEMA program. I was taken aback by the devastation and I wondered whether we could work effectively in the pile. Elvis worked extremely well through a lot of hazardous areas. There were large void spaces under the surface of the rubble. We were able to climb down into them on ladders. We also lowered the dogs with rope harnesses down into void spaces that we weren't able to climb to, or that ladders couldn't reach. We got to one elevator shaft area the first night. We heard a pass alarm, which is the device firefighters use in an emergency situation, so they can be located. But in this case, there was no one in the area. It was just the device.

After that, we went to another area, about five stories down. There were streams of water and an out-of-control fire. Sometimes we were pulled out of areas because of the possible collapse of several buildings. We did a search of the first and basement floors of 4 World Trade Center and came up with no victims and no alerts in the area. Then we were asked to go down to an area where they thought they heard some pinging. We went a full story down into a large void area a store area. We did a search and came across a number of mannequins. Apparently, it was a Halloween shop and they were used to display things. Elvis was searching through that area and he showed some unusual behavior when he approached the mannequins. They looked like deceased bodies.

We then worked the rest of the mall area into the subway. We went into a Hallmark store, and it was pretty weird because the cards and everything were still on the shelves. There's all this destruction around you, and then there's this card shop where all the cards are perfectly placed in a row. It was pretty eerie. There were no indications of any survivors. In a lot of the shops it appeared like people had dropped everything and run out. Things were still in place. Back in the clerk's room, the money trays were still sitting on the desks.

We did a number of void searches on the second night, and again we came up with no live victims. Elvis is not a cadaver dog. Elvis is an air-scent dog. He has been exposed to cadaver work, but when he does hit a cadaver, his tail will go between his legs. He's usually very cautious, as if he's nervous of the area. We did have two indications of cadavers the third night, on the back side of the building 6. One was confirmed. We work with two dogs in the area. If a dog has an indication or an alert, we bring a second dog in to verify it. Then we bring the technical search people in with cameras and listening devices to pick up sight or sound of any trapped victims. Then the rescue guys follow to extricate the subject.

On the fourth night, or maybe the tail end of the third night, thunderstorms rolled through, and they did not allow us to go back on the pile because the metal was slippery. They were concerned with risk and safety issues. So we ended up doing building searches of the surrounding buildings. Elvis and I went to the Federal Building with a team out of Sacramento and searched the eighteen stories. We found some plane parts on the roof and systematically worked each floor after that. Again the scene was eerie. Usually when you do buildings searches, things aren't in place. But here we were finding offices with briefcases on the desks, Dunkin' Donuts coffee cups with only one or two sips gone, jackets and sport coats on the backs of doors and chairs.

We learned in Oklahoma that a dog's drive decreases over a period of several days when there is a lack of live finds. The cleanliness of the dogs is also important. Some of the dogs were depressed, and a bath would start to spark them up and drive them back to work again. Knowing these things, we positively rewarded our dogs for every act that they did. Whenever we came out of an area without finding anyone, we hid a rescuer, which would serve as a live victim for Elvis. That kept his drive and his spirits up.

What we did down there proved to be beneficial to the animals. As a FEMA team we're made up of a little bit of everybody: doctors, regular citizens, engineers, firefighters, police officers. And although we don't see the magnitude of what the firefighter see, we do deal with death on a daily basis.

Elvis's drive has not changed one bit. He still loves his job. If I tell him he's going to go search somewhere, he runs to the front door. There are so many things that we do with our animals to get them ready for days like September 11, and since then I think we're even a little more alert too. As we go by buildings today, we think of possible search scenarios. It's part of the world right now. But you know, we can do the job if called upon again.

Source: Mitchell Fink and Louis Mathias (eds.), *Never Forget: An Oral History of September 11, 2001* (New York: ReganBooks, 2002): Mark Dawson, pp. 235–237. Oral testimony used by permission.

Document 18

President George W. Bush's Address to the Nation (September 11, 2001)

Americans were in a state of shock on September 11, 2001. The unthinkable had happened: a terrorist attack on the United States had killed over 3,000 Americans without any way to fight back. President Bush had been as startled as anybody else in the United States. In this speech, which he gave during the evening of September 11, 2001, he tried to reassure Americans that its government was going help in the recovery and deal with the terrorists.

Today, our fellow citizens, our way of life, our very freedom came under attack in a series of deliberate and deadly terrorist acts. The victims were in airplanes or in their offices: secretaries, businessmen and –women, military and federal workers, moms and dads, friends and neighbors.

Thousands of lives were suddenly ended by evil, despicable acts of terror. The pictures of airplanes flying into buildings, fires burning, huge structures collapsing have filled us with disbelief, terrible sadness and a quiet, unyielding anger.

These acts of mass murder were intended to frighten our nation into chaos and retreat. But they have failed. Our country is strong. A great people has been moved to defend a great nation.

Terrorist attacks can shake the foundations of our biggest buildings, but they cannot touch the foundation of America. These acts shatter steel, but they cannot dent the steel of American resolve.

America was targeted for attack because we're the brightest beacon for freedom and opportunity in the world. And no one will keep that light from shining.

Today, our nation saw evil, the very worst of human nature, and we responded with the best of America, with the daring of our rescue workers, with the caring for strangers and neighbors who came to give blood and help in any way they could.

Immediately following the first attack, I implemented our government's emergency response plans. Our military is powerful, and it's prepared. Our emergency teams are working in New York City and Washington, D.C., to help with local rescue efforts.

Our first priority is to get help to those who have been injured and to take every precaution to protect our citizens at home and around the world from further attacks.

The functions of our government continue without interruption. Federal agencies in Washington which had to be evacuated today are reopening for essential personnel tonight and will be open for business tomorrow.

Our financial institutions remain strong, and the American economy will be open for business as well.

The search is under way for those who are behind these evil acts. I've directed the full resources for our intelligence and law enforcement communities to find those responsible and bring them to justice. We will make no distinction between the terrorists who committed these acts and those who harbor them.

I appreciate so very much the members of Congress who have joined me in strongly condemning these attacks. And on behalf of the American people, I thank the many world leaders who have called to offer their condolences and assistance.

America and our friends and allies join with all those who want peace and security in the world, and we stand together to win the war against terrorism.

Tonight I ask for your prayers for all those who grieve, for the children whose worlds have been shattered, for all whose sense of safety and security has been threatened. And I pray they will be comforted by a power greater than any of us spoken through the ages in Psalm 23: "Even though I walk through the valley of the shadow of death, I fear no evil for you are with me."

This is a day when all Americans from every walk of life unite in our resolve for justice and peace. America has stood down enemies before, and we will do so this time.

None of us will ever forget this day, yet we go forward to defend freedom and all that is good and just in our world.

Thank you. Good night and God bless America.

Source: Barry Rubin and Judith Colp Rubin (eds.), *Anti-American Terrorism and the Middle East: A Documentary Reader* (Oxford: Oxford University Press, 2002), pp. 319–320.

Document 19

Interview with Mullah Omar Muhammad (September 21, 2001)

Mullah Omar (Umar) Muhammad was the head of the Taliban government of Afghanistan until the fall of 2001. He had gained power by winning battles with his Taliban soldiers. His government imposed a harsh brand of Islamic law. Muhammad had received Osama bin Laden with open arms even though bin Laden had already initiated attacks against the United States. Though he rarely met or talked to representatives of the world outside of Afghanistan, he gave an interview, which was broadcast on September 21, 2001 on Voice of America, in which he gave his reasons why he did not expel bin Laden after the September 11, 2001, attacks in the United States.

Question: Why don't you expel Usama bin Ladin?

Umar: This is not an issue of Usama bin Ladin. It is an issue of Islam. Islam's prestige is at stake. So is Afghanistan's tradition.

Question: Do you know that the United States has announced a war on terrorism?

Umar: I am considering two promises. One is the promise of God, the other is that of Bush. The promise of God is that my land is vast. If you start a journey on God's path, you can reside anywhere on this earth and will be protected. . . . The promise of Bush is that there is no place on earth where you can hide that I cannot find you. We will see which one of these two promises fulfilled.

Question: But aren't you afraid for the people, yourself, the Taliban, your country?

Umar: Almighty God . . . is helping the believers and the Muslims. God says he will never be satisfied with the infidels. In terms of worldly affairs, America is very strong. Even if it were twice as strong or twice that, it could not be strong enough to defeat us. We are confident that no one can harm us if God is with us.

Question: You are telling me you are not concerned, but Afghans all over the world are concerned.

Umar: We are also concerned. Great issues lie ahead. But we depend on God's mercy. Consider our point of view: if we give Usama away today, Muslims are not pleading to give him up would then be reviling us for giving him up. . . . Everyone is afraid of America and wants to please it. But Americans will not be able to prevent such acts like the one that has just occurred because America has taken Islam hostage. If you look at Islamic countries, the people are in despair. They are complaining that Islam is gone. But people remain firm in their Islamic beliefs. In their pain and frustration, some of them commit suicide acts. They feel they have nothing to lose.

Question: What do you mean by saying America has taken the Islamic world hostage?

Umar: America controls the government of the Islamic countries. The people ask to follow Islam, but the governments do not listen because they are in the grip of the United States. If someone follows the path of Islam, the government arrests him, tortures him or kills him. This is the doing of America. If it stops supporting those governments and lets the people deal with them, then such things won't happen. America has created the evil that is attacking it. The evil will not disappear even if I die and Usama dies and others die. The United States should step back and review its policy. It should stop trying to impose its empire on the rest of the world, especially on Islamic countries.

Question: So you won't give Usama bin Ladin up?

Umar: No. We cannot do that. If we did, it means we are not Muslims . . . that Islam is finished. If we were afraid of attack, we could have surrendered him the last time we were threatened and attacked. So America can hit us again, and this time we don't even have a friend.

Question: If you fight America with all your might—can the Taliban do that? Won't America beat you and won't your people suffer even more?

Umar: I'm very confident that it won't turn out this way. Please note this: there is nothing more we can do except depend on Almighty God. If a person does, then he is assured that the Almighty will help him, have mercy on him and he will succeed.

Source: Barry Rubin and Judith Colp Rubin, *Anti-American Terrorism and the Middle East: A Documentary Reader* (Oxford: Oxford University Press, 2002), pp. 247–249. Permission to reproduce this interview granted by Oxford University Press.

Document 20

Environmental Protection Agency's Press Release (September 13, 2001)

One of the ongoing controversies stemming from September 11 has been the health problems experienced by workers who hunted for survivors, located bodies, and cleaned up the debris at the World Trade Center. There was a tremendous cloud of dust and debris in the air for weeks after the collapse of the twin towers and other buildings. One of the first actions of the U.S. government was to send Environmental Protection Agency (EPA) agents to test the air quality. In a series of press releases beginning on September 13, Christie Whitman, head of the EPA, reassured the rescue crews and the public that the level of air contaminants was low. This information was later to be questioned after a significant number of workers at the site began to have respiratory illnesses that led to long-term disabilities or death. The document presented here is the first of the EPA press released that came out on September 13.

EPA Initiates Emergency Response Activities, Reassures Public about Environment Hazards

U.S. Environmental Protection Agency Administrator Christie Whitman today announced that the EPA is taking steps to ensure the safety of rescue workers and the public at the World Trade Center and the Pentagon disaster sites, and to protect the environment. EPA is working with state, federal, and local agencies to monitor and respond to potential environmental hazards and minimize any environmental effects of the disasters and their aftermath.

At the request of the New York City Department of Health, EPA and the U.S. Department of Labor's Occupational Safety and Health Administration (OSHA) have been on the scene at the World Trade Center monitoring exposure to potentially contaminated dust and debris. Monitoring and sampling conducted on Tuesday and Wednesday have been very reassuring and potential exposure of rescue crews and the public to environmental contaminants [*sic*].

EPA's primary concern is to ensure that rescue workers and the public are not exposed to elevated levels of asbestos, acidic gases or other contaminants from the debris. Sampling of ambient air quality found either no asbestos or very low levels of asbestos. Sampling of bulk materials and dust found generally low levels of asbestos.

The levels of lead, asbestos and volatile organic compounds in air samples taken on Tuesday in Brooklyn downwind from the World Trade Center site, were not detectable or not of concern.

Additional sampling of both ambient air quality and dust particles was conducted Wednesday night in lower Manhattan and Brooklyn, and results were uniformly acceptable.

"EPA is greatly relived to have learned that there appears to be no significant levels of asbestos dust in the air in New York City," said Administrator Whitman. "We are working closely with rescue crews to ensure that all appropriate precautions are taken. We will continue to monitor closely."

Public health concerns about asbestos contamination are primarily related to long-term exposure. Short-term, low-level exposure of the type that might have been produced by the collapse of the World Trade Center buildings is unlikely to cause significant health effects. EPA and OSHA will work closely with rescue and cleanup crews to minimize their potential exposure, but the general public should be very reassured by initial sampling.

EPA and OSHA will continue to monitor and sample for asbestos, and will work with the appropriate officials to ensure that rescue workers, cleanup crews and the general public are properly informed about appropriate steps that should be taken to ensure proper handling, transportation and disposal of potentially contaminated debris or materials.

EPA is taking steps to ensure that response units implement appropriate engineering controls to minimize environmental hazards, such as water sprays and rinsing to prevent or minimize potential exposure and limit releases of potential contaminants beyond the debris site.

EPA is also conducting downwind sampling for potential chemical and asbestos releases from the World Trade Center debris site. In addition, EPA has deployed federal On-Scene Coordinators to the Washington, D.C. Emergency Operations Center, Fort Meade, and FEMA's alternative Regional Operations Center in Pennsylvania and has deployed an On-Scene Coordinator to the Virginia Emergency Operations Center.

Under its response authority, EPA will use all available resources and staff experts to facilitate a safe emergency response and cleanup.

EPA will work with other involved agencies as needed to:

- procure and distribute respiratory and eye protection equipment in cooperation with the Dept. of Health and Human Services;
- provide health and safety training upon request;
- design and implement a site monitoring plan;
- provide technical assistance for site control and decontamination; and
- provide some 3,000 asbestos respirators, 60 self-contained breathing apparatuses and 10,000 protective clothing suits to the two disaster sites.

New York Governor George E. Pataki has promised to provide emergency electric generators to New York City in efforts to restore lost power caused by Tuesday's tragedy, and EPA will work with State authorities to expedite any necessary permits for those generators.

OSHA is also working with Consolidated Edison regarding safety standards for employees who are digging trenches because of leaking gas lines underground. OSHA has advised Con Edison to provide its employees with appropriate respirators so they can proceed with emergency work, shutting off gas leaks in the city.

Source: Office of Inspector General U.S. Environmental Protection Agency Report No. 2003-P-00012 (http://www.epa.gov/wtc/stories/headline_091301.htm).

Document 21

Statements by Federal Emergency Management Agency on Its Response to the Terrorist Attacks on the World Trade Center in New York City and the Pentagon before the United States Senate's Committee on Environment and Public Works (October 16, 2001)

In 2001, the Federal Emergency Management Agency (FEMA) operated twenty-eight teams from around the United States. It was FEMA's responsibility to react to the events of September 11, and following those events, FEMA mobilized twenty-six of those teams to travel to New York City and Washington, D.C. Of these teams twenty-one went to New York and five to Washington. Despite some deficiencies caused by the lack of equipment at times, these FEMA teams operated effectively under harsh conditions. These three statements, given on October 16, 2001 before the Senate's Committee on Environment and Public Works, show how they performed and the difficulties that they had to deal with in a scene of destruction.

STATEMENT OF JOE M. ALLBAUGH, DIRECTOR, FEDERAL EMERGENCY MANAGEMENT AGENCY

Actually, I'll be brief in my remarks because I know you have several questions. I'd just like to begin by telling that these folks sitting on the front row are the true heroes of everyday American life. They represent heroes, many men and women who put their lives on the line, whom we often take for granted, as Senator Voinovich said. They're always first in line for budget cuts and last in line for recognition. I think, as a result of September 11, that maybe these brave men and women will be due the admiration that they so richly deserve, putting their lives on the line every minute of every day all across this country.

Five weeks ago this morning, our world was transformed. At that time, President Bush told me to make sure that the Federal Government would provide whatever assistance was needed in New York, Pennsylvania and at the Pentagon. That mission is still a work in progress, but I can assure you and the American public that FEMA's response was swift and comprehensive and our commitment of continued support is unwavering.

Since September 11, I've spent many days at Ground Zero in New York City. I visited the site in Pennsylvania, was inside the Pentagon the Saturday after the event. Those places are where the true heroes are—those who were in their offices at work, grabbing a cup of coffee, on an airplane; and those who were first to respond to the tragic events—the firefighters, the police officers, the emergency medical technicians.

All are gone now, but I can assure you they're not forgotten. Our prayers are still with those folks and their families. Working hand-in-hand with Governor Pataki, Mayor Giuliani, Fire Commissioner Tommy Von Essen and Police Commissioner Bernard Kerik and many others, we've begun the painful process of recovery.

Beginning on September 11, FEMA deployed 26 of our 28 national urban search and rescue teams. Twenty-one went to New York, ultimately, the last one checking out of New York a week ago this last Sunday. Five went to northern Virginia at the Pentagon site. The New York City Office of Emergency Management's Task Force was among the first responders at the World Trade Center. Its leader, Chief Ray Downey, a person I was lucky to know, a great partner of FEMA, was on the scene. Tragically, he and his team never made it out.

I watched our rescue teams join New York City's finest and Virginia's finest, working shoulder to shoulder around the clock to find their brothers and sisters and fellow citizens. These sites are truly hallowed ground. Now our rescue teams have gone home and we are fully engaged in the recovery process. We have millions of tons of debris still to be moved out of New York City. It will take months. As of this morning, we've only moved out 300 million tons. It doesn't sound like very much compared to what we have to move.

Before and since the President signed the disaster declarations for Pennsylvania, for New Jersey, for Virginia and New York, FEMA activated the Federal response plan. To your point, Senator Voinovich, I think what we planned to do in this event worked just like it was supposed to, according to the Federal response plan.

We activated our emergency operations center here and in our 10 regions. We established disaster field offices in Virginia, New York and New Jersey and declared these disasters with public assistance at 100 percent for eligible cost. Our biggest concern currently is to make sure that the right assistance is getting to the right people. Many people need counseling; they will need counseling for a long time to come. Many qualify for individual assistance. I want to make sure that those people are helped.

In addition, we are there to help States and local governments with their public assistance needs, such as their public buildings, roads, streets, and emergency protective measures, making sure that these men and women are reimbursed for their time, material, their equipment in proper fashion.

In the past month, thousands of Federal employees have been working day and night at our disaster field offices at these three sites. Today we still have 1,300 employees deployed to New York City. Our job is not finished, but we will see it through to the end.

In the meantime, we're currently looking at all aspects of our disaster response in those three States to determine the lessons learned to be better prepared for the future. We're also working with President Bush and his Administration on any new legislative needs. As we continue to move forward with the recovery, I will let you know promptly if there is any new need for authorities.

Let me conclude on a personal note, if you don't mind. I attended about 10 days ago and spoke at the funeral of Captain Terry Haddon in New York City. Two weeks prior to that, on August 29, I had the fortune to sit down with his coworkers at Rescue One on 43rd Street in New York City to have a lunch with those individuals. Chief Ray Downey was there, with 13 or 14 of us around the table. We had a great time.

I try to stop in our country's firehouses every opportunity that I'm out on the road. It is amazing what I'm able to learn, what their needs are, what their wishes, wants, hopes. They are a true family in those firehouses all across the country. In that short 1½–2 hours, I became, I thought, a small part of their family.

The night before Terry's funeral, I attended a wake in New York City, and his wife Beth, who subsequently found out that she was pregnant with their first child after September 11—Terry never knew—handed me a small card. On one side it was a short life history of Terry. On the back part of the card was the Fireman's Prayer. I'd like to close just with the last sentence of that prayer, because I think it says so much about men and women who wear the uniform of our country's military. It says so much about the firemen and firewomen and the police officers and the emergency responders and all those individuals who lost their lives on September 11.

It goes like this: "If, according to my fate, I am to lose my life, please bless with Your protecting hand my family, friends and wife." For Terry Haddon, Ray Downey, Joey Angelini, Dennis Mohica and thousands of other souls that were lost on that fateful day, I hope that those of us still living and thriving can help provide that protecting hand to all the families and loved ones.

STATEMENT OF EDWARD P. PLAUGHER, CHIEF, ARLINGTON COUNTY, VIRGINIA, FIRE DEPARTMENT

Thank you very much. It is indeed a pleasure to be here this morning. It's also a great deal of pleasure and an honor to represent the men and women, not only of the Arlington County Fire Department, but also of the Nation. Hopefully my remarks will assist the cause of improving our capability to respond to any type of incident.

Again, I want to thank you are allowing me to be here today. I understand that you as a committee are deeply concerned, as are all of us, with the tragic events of September 11. These events have a profound impact on the men and women of my fire department and on the Nation's fire service as a whole.

I have prepared remarks which I hope will be entered into the record, and I'll just highlight a couple of the key points in order to be brief here this morning, to allow my colleagues ample time to testify.

It is an opportunity for me, however, to talk about the incident at the Pentagon. First of all, you need to know, I think, is that our response to the Pentagon began when one of our engine companies who was responding to another routine call noticed the plane and its route to the Pentagon and was actually a witness to the incident. Immediately, the northern Virginia automatic mutual aid program was activated. Units from Fort Myer, Alexandria, Fairfax County and the National Airport Fire Department responded from the initial alarm.

The second alarm units included units from the District of Columbia as well as from Montgomery County and Prince George's County, MD. These first responding fire units fought a fire that was triggered by 6,000 gallons of jet fuel in the world's largest office building.

The Federal Emergency Management Agency, in their response to the attack on the Pentagon and its aftermath, was superb. FEMA and their front line urban search and rescue teams, which were mobilized from Fairfax County, Virginia Beach, Montgomery County, MD; Memphis, TN, and then later on, we received assistance from New Mexico to provide relief for the exhausted rescue personnel.

I must tell you, Mr. Chairman and members of the committee, that the FEMA urban search and rescue teams made an outstanding contribution to our effort. These teams are comprised of dedicated professionals whose hard work and unyielding efforts should not be overlooked.

Two resources that were brought to bear to the incident scene by FEMA come to mind and stand out in my mind. First was the search dog capability. It's a unique and absolutely critical, necessary component of a structural collapse search that allows for swift and thorough search for victims that could not otherwise have been possible. Second, the urban search and rescue team brings in specially trained urban search and rescue structural engineers that allow us to then proceed into the building with safety being paramount to all the personnel on the scene.

However, there's a couple of areas that I think we can do to improve our business, and that is the business of response to our community, particularly in these types of incidents. That is what the director was just talking about, the ability to have a clear understanding of the local first responders, of what does the urban search and rescue team bring to an incident, and particularly the capability of this being taught at the National Fire Academy.

I also think that we need to have a clear understanding of the capability that is being developed for these urban search and rescue teams. In other words, what I mean is there needs to be a standardized list of equipment that is well understood and that we can count on when deployed. It also occurs to me that this complement of equipment and response capability should be developed with a panel of experts that seeks out local advice so that the folks of us who have been there will allow them to be able to adjust their response capability based upon our now new experiences.

We just heard again about the need for additional equipment. Most urban each and rescue teams—which in my earlier career in Fairfax County, I was fortunate enough to be one of the founding members of the team, and participated in its early structure—we realize that they are multiple deep in personnel, but not multiple deep in equipment. We think that now is the time that we could fix that.

We are, in fact, very lucky and very privileged in the Washington Metropolitan area to have two urban search and rescue teams in our midst, both Montgomery County, MD and Fairfax County, VA. This is a unique situation in our community.

However, one of the things that we also focused on, and we realized early on in this particular incident at the Pentagon, is that there was a need for some command overhead teams. These command overhead teams would be chief officers who would be experienced in dealing with these incidents and bring to bear that extra chief level officer capability. We think that maybe there's an opportunity for this to come out in the future.

The level of cooperation and mutual assistance between FEMA and the Arlington County Fire Department was excellent. There are many moving parts to an effective response to a terrorist incident. Each of us must have a good expectation of our own responsibilities of the different agencies.

In the final analysis, what transpired at the Pentagon, under the circumstances, was dealt with professionally and to the best of each of our abilities. We at the Arlington County Fire Department learned valuable lessons with regard to our own abilities and our limits. It is our hope that we can use those lessons to further a more effective preparedness approach.

I personally testified last spring before the House Transportation Committee on a piece of legislation designed to address this issue. A Senate companion bill, Senate bill 1453, the Preparedness Against Terrorism Act of 2001, was recently introduced by Senator Bob Smith and referred to this committee. This bill codifies the Office of National Preparedness at FEMA that President Bush created earlier this year. It creates a President's Council that will be charged with the development of a single national strategy on terrorism preparedness, that will include measurable preparedness goals.

We applaud Present Bush's designation of Governor Tom Ridge of Pennsylvania as our new Homeland Security coordinator. However, it seems to us that Senate bill 1453 could and would bring focus and legal authority to this new effort. It is my understanding that the Bush Administration has significant input into this bill, and I urge you to make whatever modifications are necessary to address Governor Ridge's role and to act favorably on the bill in sending it to the full Senate for consideration as quickly as possible.

STATEMENT OF JEFFREY L. METZINGER, FIRE CAPTAIN, SACRAMENTO, CA METROPOLITAN FIRE DISTRICT; MEMBER, FEMA URBAN SEARCH AND RESCUE TEAM

Good morning Mr. Chairman and members of the committee. I'm Captain Jeff Metzinger. I'm with the Sacramento Metropolitan Fire District in northern California. I'm also a member of California's Urban Search and Rescue Team, California Task Force 7.

Like the others here, I am also honored and very humbled to be talking to you this morning, representing the thousands of firefighters across this country who put their lives on the line every day.

We were dispatched to the World Trade Center on the morning of September 11, as so many other teams were. I keep a journal with me wherever I go, and I brought it with me today and I'm going to read some excerpts for you. It's a habit I've had for a long time, and I think there's some value in there.

I'll start out on Wednesday, September 12.

We're finally leaving for New York City and everyone is anxious to get to work. As we approach the Hudson River from New Jersey, you can see a large column of smoke coming up from the site where the World Trade Center used to stand.

This is my first trip to New York City, and I feel sad about what I see. The traffic is incredible, even with a full police escort. The corners are filled with people, and we're just now a few blocks away from the large smoke column I had seen earlier. We arrive at the Javits Convention Center by 7 p.m. and set up our base of operations. There's other teams coming in as well, including teams from Los Angeles, Missouri, Indianapolis, Riverside, California, Pennsylvania, Massachusetts and Ohio.

Our 62 person team is divided into two teams, where we alternate 12-hour shifts, working 24 hours around the clock. It's assigned to the Blue team, working the night shift. The first night, on September 13, we loaded into the bus and headed into our sector to go to work. We met up with the Gray team and did a pass-on Street.

The scene was surreal. There were people everywhere. Smoke continued to drift from the massive piles of rubble. The expanse of the disaster is difficult to comprehend. Several searches were conducted by our search dogs in the vicinity of Tower Seven. The technical search cameras were also used, but we had no luck finding any victims.

The following night, our team was working again, looking for an assignment. The dogs alerted an area, but at a very dangerous location. It was too unstable to enter. That night there was thunder, lightning, wind and heavy rains pounding upon us. Frequently, debris—large pieces of metal were blowing off the roofs of adjacent buildings. Our task force leader determined it wasn't safe for us to go any farther, we didn't want to lose any further lives.

The next afternoon we had a briefing from our task force leader at our base and were told that President Bush would be visiting our facility that day. I was privileged to meet and shake hands with President Bush, with Senator Hillary Rodham Clinton, and the governor and the mayor were also present. It was quite an experience, and their visit was very much appreciated by all.

That night on the bus we were headed back to work, still hundreds of people lining the streets of New York City, cheering us as we go by. Traffic was so congested that we finally stopped the bus, got off and walked the last few blocks to the Church and Dey command post. Tonight our search team is finally getting to do some work, putting up a rope system to lower one of our members down into the debris crater near Church Street. The objective here is to place a cellular phone antenna down lower that might assist with victim locations.

The following night we were headed back to work and again people were lining the streets, cheering, waving flags, holding signs, lighting candles. It was a sight that warmed us even as we went in. This particular night, our search and rescue teams were assigned to search the buildings around the outer perimeter of the plaza area. There are several 30-plus story buildings around the World Trade Center plaza. We conducted searches from basement to roof, every door was opened, every space was checked. We climbed the stairwells, taking on one building at a time.

We didn't find any victims. Every floor of every building we searched was marked and completed. The assignment took a lot of toll on our legs that night.

On Sunday, during our briefing, we were told that three top New York fire chiefs were laid to rest that day. Firefighter Chaplain Ward Cockerton said a prayer for the victims and for the safety of the team members that are still working here.

Tonight we're going to work between buildings five and six, possible going underground. We hear that there's up to six levels below the street grade. So we reported to the Church and Dey command post that night and I personally got assigned my first job as head rigger, which is my assignment with the team. Steve of Massachusetts Task Force One was there, and he and I worked with four New York City iron workers through the night, using a 90-10 crane, moving tons of debris all night long.

The following day we were back at work on the same crane, and a new group of iron workers. We made a connection with some guys by the name of Mike, Rich and Kevin. They're all great people. I found that the New York iron workers and construction workers are just incredibly great folks.

We cut and moved tons of steel again tonight. In the middle of the night I found a child's doll in the rubble, and I realized suddenly how much I missed my family. I heard our response team found a victim this morning, a police officer. Our hopes for a live rescue are starting to dim.

The next day we were back on the bus to the work site again. I'm already tired. We've averaged about 3 hours of sleep per night. Even when we get time to rest, you can't sleep.

Heading back to the crane, we worked all night again, moving steel, looking for bodies. I've noticed for several nights that there's very little debris that's recognizable. There's no desks, there's no chairs, carpet or sheet rock or anything else you'd associate with an office building, just the steel structure. There are still no victims in the area we're working in.

On September 18, we're back in the pile again, moving steel and searching for victims. Today the smell of death is more evident. I found a business card of a man with an office on the 83rd floor of one of the towers, and I wondered what his fate was at that moment. I said a prayer for him and hoped he is alive and well. I'm still not sure what his fate is.

Around midnight that night, the crane operation was halted while they were moving in a larger crane. When the crane shut down, I joined forces with some of the New York firefighters. Two of the battalion chiefs were out there with their sleeves rolled up, working right alongside of us. We were moving debris by hand, and that was a very solemn night. Went home tired that day.

The following day, Thursday, September 20, we started heading home, packing our equipment. It's been a long 10 days and everyone is exhausted. The team physician just diagnosed me with bronchitis. The dust we've been breathing all week finally caught up to us. Many others in the team had the same complaint of headache, sore throat, sinus congestion and sometimes fever. But most of all, everybody's troubled that we didn't find any victims.

Finally, on Friday, we land back in northern California, Travis Air Force Base, and we get a full police escort all the way back to Sacramento. Every freeway overpass for 40 miles was covered with fire engines, police cars and citizens cheering us home. It was a warm reception.

We arrived in Sacramento to a similar greeting of family, friends, co-workers and media. I realized then for the people of Sacramento that we were their connection to this tragedy on the East Coast. It felt good to be home, but I felt like a part of me was still in New York. When I go to sleep, I still dream that I'm there. It doesn't leave us.

I just want to close and say that firefighters and law enforcement and EMS people are going to continue to be the first responders arriving at these incidents, and the toll is tremendous. The toll is tremendous on what I saw on the New York City firefighters, and for those of us who just came there and left, it took a toll as well, physically and mentally. We owe it to ourselves to be prepared for future incidents, to take care of our responders and make sure that we are afforded everything that we can possibly to do to be ready for the next one.

Source: U.S. Senate Committee on Environment and Public Works, United States Senate, *FEMA's Response to the Sept. 11th Attacks* (Washington, D.C.: U.S. Government Printing Office, 2003), pp. 44–55.

Document 22

Dawn Interview with Osama bin Laden
(November 10, 2001)

The Pakistani newspaper Dawn conducted a wide-ranging interview with Osama bin Laden concerning his views on the September 11 attacks. Bin Laden gave this interview on November 10, 2001, in the middle of the American campaign to overthrow the Taliban and capture or kill him. In this interview bin Laden states his reasons for war against the United States and the use of terrorism against civilians. At this time bin Laden was still reluctant to take responsibility for the September 11 attacks, but he acknowledged that al-Qaeda had access to chemical and nuclear weapons.

Question: After [the] American bombing of Afghanistan on October 7, you told al-Jazira television that the September 11 attacks had been carried out by some Muslims. How did you know they were Muslims?

Bin Ladin: The Americans themselves released a list of suspects of the September 11 attacks saying that the persons named were involved in the attacks. They were all Muslims, of whom fifteen belonged to Saudi Arabia, two were from the United Arab Emirates, and one from Egypt. . . . [A] *fateha* [funeral] was held for them in their homes. But America said they were hijackers.

Question: In your statement of October 7, you expressed satisfaction over the September 11 attacks, although a large number of innocent people perished in them. Hundreds among them were Muslims. Can you justify the killing of innocent men in the light of Islamic teachings?

Bin Ladin: This is a major point in jurisprudence. In my view, if an enemy occupies a Muslim territory and uses common people as a human shield, then it is permitted to attack that enemy. For instance if bandits barge into a home and hold a child hostage, then the child's father can attack the bandits, and in that attack even the child may get hurt. America and its allies are massacring us in Palestine, Chechnya, Kashmir and Iraq. The Muslims have the right to attack America in reprisal. The Islamic *Sharia* says Muslims should not live in the land of the infidel for long. The September 11 attacks were not targeted at women and children. The real targets were America's icons of military and economic power. The holy prophet (peace be upon him) was against killing women and children. When he saw a dead woman during a war he asked, Why was she killed? If a child is above thirteen and wields a weapon against Muslims, then it is permitted to kill him. The American people should remember that they pay taxes to their government, they elect their president, their government manufactures arms and gives them to Israel, and Israel uses them to massacre Palestinians. The Congress endorses all government measures, and this proves that . . . [all of] America is responsible for the atrocities perpetrated against Muslims. [All of] America because they elect Congress. I ask the American people to force their government to give up anti-Muslim policies. The American people had risen against their government's war in Vietnam. They must do the same today. The American people should stop the massacre of Muslims by their government.

Question: Can it be said that you are against the American government, not the American people?

Bin Ladin: Yes! We are carrying on the mission of our Prophet Muhammad (peace be upon him). The mission is to spread the word of God, not to indulge in massacring people. We ourselves are the target of killings, destruction, and atrocities. We are only defending ourselves. This is defensive *jihad*. We want to defend our people and our land. That is why I say that if we don't get security, the Americans, too, would not get security. This is a simple formula that even an American child can understand. This is the formula of live and let live.

Question: The head of Egypt's al-Azhar [Islamic university] has issued a *fatwa* against you saying that the views and beliefs of Usama bin Ladin have nothing to do with Islam. What do you have to say about that?

Bin Ladin: The *fatwa* of any official *alim* [religious figure] has no value for me. History if full of such *ulama* [clerics] who justify *riba* [economic interest], who justify the occupation of Palestine by the Jews, who justify the presence of American troops around Harmain Sharifain [the Islamic holy places in Saudi Arabia]. These people support the infidels for their personal gain. The true *ulama* support the *jihad* against America. Tell me, if Indian forces invaded Pakistan what would you do? The Israeli forces occupy our land and the American troops are on our territory. We have no other option but to launch *jihad*.

Question: Some Western media claim that you are trying to acquire chemical and nuclear weapons. How much truth is there in these reports?

Bin Ladin: I heard the speech of [the] American president Bush [on November 7]. He was scaring the European countries that Usama wanted to attach with weapons of mass destruction. I wish to declare that if America used chemical or nuclear weapons against us then we may retort with chemical and nuclear weapons. We have the weapons as a deterrent.

Question: Where did you get these weapons from?

Bin Ladin: Go to the next question.

Question: Demonstrations are being held in many European countries against American attacks on Afghanistan. Thousands of protesters were non-Muslims. What is your opinion about these non-Muslim protesters?

Bin Ladin: There are many innocent and good-hearted people in the West. American media instigates them against Muslims. However, some good-hearted people are protesting against American attacks because human nature abhors injustice. The Muslims were massacred under the UN patronage in Bosnia. I am aware that some officers of the state department had resigned in protest. Many years ago the U.S. ambassador in Egypt had resigned in protest against the policies of President Jimmy Carter. Nice and civilized people are everywhere. The Jewish lobby has taken America and the West hostage.

Question: Some people say that war is no solution to any issue. Do you think that some political formula could be found to stop the present war?

Bin Ladin: You should put this question to those who have started this war. We are only defending ourselves.

Question: If America got out of Saudi Arabia and the al-Aqsa mosque was liberated, would you then present yourself for trial is some Muslim country?

Bin Ladin: Only Afghanistan is an Islamic country. Pakistan follows the English law. I don't consider Saudi Arabia an Islamic country. If the Americans have charges against me, we too have a charge sheet against them.

Question: Pakistan's government decided to cooperate with America after September 11, which you don't consider right. What do you think Pakistan should have done but to cooperate with America?

Bin Ladin: The government of Pakistan should have the wishes of the people in view. It should not have surrendered to the unjustified demands of America. America does not have solid proof against us. It just has some surmises. It is unjust to start bombing on the basis of those surmises.

Question: Had America decided to attack Pakistan with the help of India and Israel, what would we have done?

Bin Ladin: What has America achieved by attacking Afghanistan? We will not leave the Pakistani people and the Pakistani territory at anybody's mercy. We will defend Pakistan. But we have been disappointed by [Pakistan's leader] General Pervez Musharraf. He says that the majority is with him. I say the majority is against him.

Bush has used the word "crusade." This is a crusade declared by Bush. It is no wisdom to barter off blood of Afghan brethren to improve Pakistan's economy. He will be punished by the Pakistani people and Allah.

Right now a great war of Islamic history is being fought in Afghanistan. All the big powers are united against Muslims. It is *sawad* [a good religious deed] to participate in this war. . . .

Question: Is it correct that a daughter of Mullah Umar is your wife or your daughter is Mullah Umar's wife?

Bin Ladin: [laughs] All my wives are Arabs and all my daughters are married to Arab *mujahidin*. I have a spiritual relationship with Mullah Umar. He is a great and brave Muslim of this age. He does not fear anyone but Allah. He is not under any personal relationship or obligation to me. He is only discharging his religious duty. I, too, have not chosen this life out of any personal consideration.

Source: Barry Rubin and Judith Colp Rubin (eds.), *Anti-American Terrorism and the Middle East: A Documentary Reader* (Oxford: Oxford University Press, 2002), pp. 261–264. Used by permission of Dawn Group of Newspapers, Karachi, Pakistan.

Document 23

Bin Laden's Homage to the Nineteen Students
(December 26, 2001)

On December 26, 2001, the Arab news network al-Jazeera broadcast a statement by Osama bin Laden in which he issued an homage to the nineteen students that had carried out the attacks on September 11, 2001. Prior to this statement, bin Laden had made no publication statement owning up to his role in the events of September 11, and he had made allusions that it was the responsibility of another group. By December 2001, the Taliban had lost control of the military situation in Afghanistan to the Northern Alliance and its American allies, and bin Laden was on the run. With little to lose, bin Laden took the opportunity to honor the nineteen martyrs of September 11. An important point to note in this statement is bin Laden's emphasis on strikes against the American economy. It seems that attacking against the economy of the United States is at least as important as the military campaign. The following is most of that statement, with some opening prayers omitted.

Three months after the blessed strikes against global unbelief and its leader America, and approximately two months after the beginning of this vicious Crusader campaign against Islam, we should discuss the meaning of these events, which have revealed things of the greatest importance to Muslims. It has become all too clear that the West in general, with America at its head, carries an unspeakable Crusader hatred for Islam. Those who have endured the continuous bombing from American aeroplanes these last months know this only too well.

How many innocent villages have been destroyed, how many millions forced out into the freezing cold, these poor innocent men, women, children who are now taking shelter in refugee camps in Pakistan while America launches a vicious campaign based on mere suspicion?

If America had evidence that could prove with degree of certainty who did this deed [9/11], then it would attribute it to Europe, to the IRA, for example. There were many ways in which it could have dealt with the problem, but even though it was merely a matter of suspicion, the real, ugly face of Crusader hatred for the Islamic world immediately manifested itself in all is clarity.

At this point I would like to emphasize the fact that the struggle between us and America is of the utmost gravity and importance, not only to Muslims but to the entire world. On the basis does America accuse this group of emigrants who wage *jihad* for God's sake, against whom there is no evidence other than that of injustice, oppression, and hostility?

The history of the Arab *mujahidin* who waged *jihad* for the grace of God Almighty is as clear as can be. In the face of the Soviet Union's despicable terrorism against children and innocents in Afghanistan twenty years ago, these Arab *mujahidin* rose up and left their jobs, universities, families, and tribes to earn the pleasure of God, to help God's religion and to help these poor Muslims.

It is inconceivable that those who came to help the poor people today came to kill innocents, as is being alleged. History recounts that America supported everyone who waged *jihad* and fought against Russia, but when God blessed these Arab *mujahidin* with going to help those poor innocent women and children in Palestine, America became angry and turned its back, betraying all those who had fought in Afghanistan.

What is happening in Palestine today is extremely clear, and something about which all of humanity since Adam can agree. Some may get corrupted, and people differ on many issues, but there are some whom God Almighty keeps from corruption, in contrast to those whose souls have become deviant and have reached an excessive degree of oppression and hostility. But one issue on which people are agreed, even if they themselves have been the victims of oppression and hostility, is that you cannot kill innocent children.

The deliberate killing of innocent children in Palestine today is the ugliest, most oppressive, and hostile act, and something that threatens all of humanity.

History knows that one who kills children, even if rarely, is a follower of Pharaoh. God Almighty favoured the sons of Israel when He helped them escape from Pharaoh. "Remember when We saved you from Pharaoh's people, who subjected you to terrible torment, slaughtering your sons and sparing only your women." Slaughtering children was something for which the head of oppression, unbelief, and hostility, Pharaoh, was famous, yet the sons of Israel have done the same thing to our sons in Palestine. The whole world has witnessed Israeli soldiers killing Muhammad al-Durreh and many others like him.

People across the entire world, both in East and West, are contravening their faiths by denying these deeds, but America goes on supporting those oppressors and enemies of our sons in Palestine. God Almighty has decreed that if someone reaches such an excessive degree of hostility that he kills another unlawfully, this is the most abhorrent deed, but it is yet more abhorrent to kill innocent children. God Almighty says: "On account of (his deed), We decreed to the Children of Israel that if anyone kills a person—unless in retribution for murder or spreading corruption in the land—it is as if he kills all mankind, while if any saves a life it is as if he saves the lives of all mankind."

So in fact it is as if Israel—and those backing it in America—have killed all the children in the world. What will stop Israel killing our sons tomorrow in Tabuk, al-Jauf and other areas? What would the rulers do if Israel broadened its territory according to what they allege is written in their false, oppressive unjust books, which said that "Our borders extend as far as Medina?" What will rulers do except submit to this American Zionist lobby?

Rational people must wake up, or what befell Muhammad al-Durreh and his brothers will happen tomorrow to their sons and women. There is no strength or power save in God.

The matter is extremely serious. This disgraceful terrorism is practiced by America in its most abhorrent form in Palestine and in Iraq. This terrible man Bush Sr., was the reason for the murder of over a million children in Iraq, besides all the other men and women [who have been killed].

The events of 22nd Jumada al-Hani, or Aylul (September 11) are merely a response to the continuous injustice inflicted upon our sons in Palestine, Iraq, Somalia, southern Sudan, and other places, like Kashmir. The matter concerns the entire *umma*. People need to wake up from their sleep and try to find a solution to this catastrophe that is threatening all of humanity.

Those who condemn these operations [9/11] have viewed the event in isolation and have failed to connect it to previous events or to the reasons behind it. Their view is blinkered and lacks either a legitimate or a rational basis. They merely saw others in America and the media decrying these operations, so they did the same themselves.

These people remind me of the wolf who, seeing a lamb, said to it: "You were the one who polluted my water last year." The lamb replied: "It wasn't me," but the wolf insisted: "Yes it was." The lamb said: "I was only born this year." The wolf replied: "Then it was your mother who polluted my water," and he ate the lamb. When the poor ewe saw her son being torn by the wolf's teeth, her maternal feelings drove her to give the wolf a hard butt. The wolf cried out: "Look at this terrorism!" And all the parrots repeated what he said saying "Yes, we condemn the ewe's butting of the wolf." What do you think about the wolf eating the ewe's lamb?

These blessed, successful strikes are merely a reaction to events in our land in Palestine, in Iraq, and in other places. America has continued this policy with the coming of George Bush Jr., who began his term with violent air strikes on Iraq to emphasize the policy of oppression and hostility, and to show that the blood of Muslims has no value.

This blessed reaction came by the grace of God Almighty showing very clearly that this haughty, domineering power, America, the Hubal of the age, is based on great economic power, but it is soft. How quickly it fell from the sky, by the grace of God Almighty.

It was not nineteen Arab states that did this deed [9/11]. It was not Arab armies or ministries who humbled the oppressor who harms us in Palestine and elsewhere. It was nineteen post-secondary students—I beg God Almighty to accept them—who shook America's throne, struck its economy right in the heart, and dealt the biggest military power a mighty blow, by the grace of God Almighty.

Here we have clear proof that this destructive, usurious global economy that America uses, together with its military force, to impose unbelief and humiliation on poor peoples, can easily collapse. Those blessed strikes in New York and the other places forced it to acknowledge the loss of more than a trillion dollars, by the grace of God Almighty. And they used simple means—the enemy's airplanes and schools—without even the need for training camps. God gave them the chance to teach a harsh lesson to these arrogant people who think that freedom only has meaning for the white race, and that other peoples should be humiliated and subservient, not even rising up when they strike us, as they did previously in Iraq.

I say that American military power, as demonstrated recently in Afghanistan, where it poured down all its anger on these poor people, has taught us great and important lessons in how to resist this arrogant force, by the grace of God Almighty.

By way of example, if the front line with the enemy is 100km long, this line should also be deep. In other words, it is not enough for us to have a defense line 100, 200, 300 metres deep. It should be a few kilometres deep, with trenches dug all the way along and through it, so that the intensity of the American bombing is exhausted before it destroys these lines, and so that light, quick forces can move from one line to another and from one defense position to another.

We made use of this tactic after the intense American bombardment on the northern and Kabul lines, and in this way the years pass and, with the will of God Almighty, American will not break the *mujahidin* lines.

Furthermore, it is well known that there are two elements to fighting; there is the fighting itself and then there is the financial element, such as buying weapons. This is emphasized in many verses of the Qur'an, such as the following: "God has purchased the persons and possessions of the believers in return for the Garden."

So the struggle is both financial and physical. Even if he distance between us and the American military base is very great, and our weapons do not match up to their planes, we are able to soak up the pressure of these strikes with our broad defense lines. And in another way it is possible to strike the economic base that is the foundation of the military base, so when their economy is depleted they will be too busy with each other to be able to enslave poor peoples.

So I say that it is very important to focus on attacking the American economy by any means available. Here we have seen the real crime of those who claim to call for humanity and freedom. Just a tiny quantity [of explosives]—7 grams' worth—is more than enough to account for anyone. But America, in her hatred for the Taliban and for Muslims, drops bombs weighing 7 tons on our brothers in the front lines. That is equivalent to seven thousand kilograms, or seven million grams, even though 7 grams is more than enough for one person.

When the young men—we beg God to accept them—exploded less than two tons [of explosive] in Nairobi, America said that this was a terrorist strike, and that this is a weapon of mass destruction. But they have no qualms about using two bombs weighing seven million grams each.

After the Americans bombed entire villages for no reason other than to terrify people and make them afraid of hosting Arabs or going near them, their minister of defense got up and said that that was their right, meaning effectively that they had their right to annihilate people so long as they were Muslim and not American. This is the clearest and most blatant crime. Everyone who hears them saying that they did such things "by mistake" knows that this is the clearest and most brazen lie.

Some days ago, the Americans announced that they hit al-Qaeda positions in Khost and had dropped a bomb on a mosque, which they said was a mistake. After investigations it became clear that scientists in Khost were saying their Ramadan evening prayers and had a meeting afterwards with the hero *mujahid* sheikh Jalal al-Din Haqqani, one of the foremost leaders of the *jihad* against the Soviets, who has resisted this American occupation of Afghan land. So they bombed the mosque and Muslims while they wee at prayers, killing 105 of them. God save Sheikh Jalal, we hope that He blesses his life.

This is Crusader hatred. So those who speak out and say that they condemn terrorism, but do not pay attention to the consequences, should take note. Our terrorism against America is a praiseworthy terrorism in defense against the oppressor, in order that America will stop supporting Israel, who kills our sons. Can you not understand this? It is very clear.

America and the western leaders always say that Hamas and Islamic Jihad in Palestine, and other such militias, are terrorist organizations. If self-defense is terrorism, what is legitimate? Our defense and our fight is no different to that of our brothers in Palestine like Hamas. We fight for "There is no God but God." The world of God is the highest and that of God's enemies is the lowest. So let us relieve the oppression of the poor people in Palestine and elsewhere.

Every possible analysis clearly shows all sensible Muslims should stand in the trenches, because this is the most dangerous, aggressive, violent, and fierce Crusader war against Islam. With God's will, America's end will not be far off. This will be nothing to do with the poor slave bin Laden, whether dead or alive. With God's grace, the awakening has begun, which is one of the benefits of these operations. I hope that God Almighty will take those young men to martyrdom and bring them together with the Prophet, the martyrs, and the righteous.

Those young men did a very great deed, a glorious deed. God rewarded them and we pray that their parents will be proud of them, because they raised Muslims' heads high and taught America a lesson it won't forget, with God's will.

As I warned previously in an interview on the ABC channel, by involving itself in a struggle with the sons of Saudi Arabia, America will forget the Vietnam crisis, with the grace of God Almighty. What is yet to come will be even greater.

From Saudi Arabia fifteen young men set out—we pray to God to accept them as martyrs. They set out from the land of faith, where lies the Muslims' greatest treasure, where faith returns, as our Prophet rightly said, to Medina, just as the snake returns to its hole. Another two came from the Eastern Peninsula, from the Emirates, another from the Levant, Ziad al-Jarrah, and another from the land of Egypt, Mohammed Atta, may God accept all of them as martyrs.

With their actions they provided a very great sign, showing that it was this faith in their hearts that urged them to do these things, to give their soul to "There is no god but God". By these deeds they opened a great door for good and truth. Those we hear in the media saying that martyrdom operations should not be carried out are merely repeating the desires of the tyrants, America and its collaborators.

Every day, from east to west, our *umma* of 1200 million Muslims is being slaughtered, in Palestine, in Iraq, Somalia, Western Sudan, Kashmir, the Philippines, Bosnia, Chechnya, and Assam. We do not hear their voices, yet as soon as the victim rises up and offers himself on behalf of his religion, people are outraged. 1200 million Muslims are being slaughtered without anyone even knowing, but if anyone comes to their defense, those people just repeat whatever the tyrants want them to say. They have neither common sense nor authority.

There is a clear moral in the story of the boy, the king, the magician, and the monk, of people offering themselves for "There is no god but God". There is also another meaning, which is that victory is not only a question of winning, which is how most people see it, but of sticking to your principles.

God mentioned the people of the trench and immortalized their memory by praising them for being resolute in their faith. They were given a choice between faith and being thrown into the fire. They refused not to believe in God, and so they were thrown into hell. At the end of the story of the boy, when the tyrant king ordered that the believers should be thrown in the pit, a poor mother came carrying her son. When she saw the fire she was afraid that harm would befall her son, so she went back. But the Prophet relates, her son told her: "be patient, mother, for you are in right."

No Muslim would ever possibly ask: what did they benefit? The fact is that they were killed—but this is total ignorance. They were victorious, with the blessings of God Almighty, and with the immortal heavens that God promised them. Victory is not material gain; it is about sticking to your principles.

And in the sayings of our Prophet, there is the story about the uneducated boy, the magician and the monk. One day an animal was blocking the road, and the boy said, "Today, I'll find out who is better, the monk or the magician." Because he was lacking in knowledge, he did not as yet understand which one was better, so he asked God to show him. If the monk was more beloved to God Almighty, then he would be able to kill the animal. So the boy picked up the rock and threw it at the animal, and it dropped dead. The monk turned to him and said: "My son, today you are better than me," even though he was far more knowledgeable than this ignorant young boy. Nevertheless, God Almighty lit up this boy's heart with the light of faith, and he began to make sacrifices for the sake of "There is no god but God."

This is a unique and valuable story which he youth of Islam are waiting for their scholars to tell them, which would show the youth that these (the 9/11 attackers) are the people who have given up everything for the sake of "There is no god but God," and would tell them what the scholar told the boy: "Today, you are better than us."

This is the truth. The measure of virtue in this religion is, as the saying of our Prophet goes, the measure of faith—not only collecting knowledge but using it. According to this yardstick, whoever fights them [unbelievers] physically is a believer, whoever fights them verbally is a believer, and whoever fights them with his heart is a believer. Nothing can be more essentially faithful than this. These people fought the great unbelief with their hands and their souls, and we pray to God to accept them as martyrs.

The lord of martyrs Hamza bin Abd al-Muttalib, said that God illuminated a unknown man's heart with faith, and he stood up against an unjust imam, who rebuked him and killed him, as is written in the *al-Jami al-Sahih*.

He won a great victory that not one of the noble followers or companions could achieve. God Almighty raised him up to the status of lord of the martyrs. This is something that our Prophet emphasized. so how could any sane Muslim say, "What did he benefit from it?" This is clear error and we ask God for good health.

God opened the way for these young men to tell America, the head of global unbelief, and its allies, that they are living in falsehood. They sacrificed themselves for "There is no god but God."

We have spoken much about these great events, but I will sum things up by emphasizing the importance of continuing *jihadi* action against American, both militarily and economically. America has been set back with the help of God Almighty, and the economic bleeding still goes on today. Yet still we need more strikes. The youth should strive to find the weak points of the American economy and strike the enemy there.

Before I finish, I should mention those heroes, these true men, these great giants who erased the shame from the forehead of our *umma*. I should like to recite poetry in praise of them and all those who follow the same path as Muhammad.

But before that, I would like to stress one point, which is that these battles going on around the clock today in Afghanistan against the Arab *mujahidin* and particularly the Taliban, have clearly shown just how powerless the American government and it soldiers really are. Despite the great developments in military technology, they can't do anything without relying on apostates and hypocrites. So what is the difference today between Babrak Karmal, who brought in the Russians to occupy his country, and the deposed president Burhan al-Din (and *din* has nothing to do with him)? What difference is there between the two? One brought Russians to occupy the land of Islam and the other brought Americans. As I said, this clearly shows the weakness of the American soldier, by the grace of God Almighty. So you should seize this chance, and the youth should continue the *jihad* and work against the Americans. I'll finish with some lines of poetry in memory of those heroes from the land of Hijaz, the land of faith, from Ghamid and Zahran, from Bani Shah, from Harb, from Najd, and we pray to God to accept them all, and in memory of those who came from Holy Mecca, Salem and Nawaf al-Hazmi, Khaled al-Mihdhar, or those who came from Medina, the radiant, who left life and its comforts for the sake of "There is no god but God."

I testify that these men, as sharp as a sword,
Have persevered through all trials,
How special they are who sold their souls to God,
Who willingly bared their chests as shields.
Though the clothes of darkness enveloped us and the poisoned tooth bit us,
Though our homes overflowed with blood and the assailant desecrated
    our land,
Though from the squares the shining of swords and horses vanished,
And the sound of drums was growing
The fighters' winds blew, striking their towers and telling them:
We will not cease our raids until you leave our fields.

                                           [poem by Yusuf Abu Hilala]

Source: Bruce Lawrence (ed.), *Messages to the World: The Statements of Osama bin Laden* (London: Verso, 2005), pp. 145–157. Reprinted with permission.

Document 24

White House Declaration on the Human Treatment of al Qaeda and Taliban Detainees (February 7, 2002)

The decision to classify al-Qaeda and Taliban detainees as unlawful detainees has become controversial. After some deliberation about the status of al-Qaeda and Taliban prisoners, White House and Justice Department lawyers finally came up with the classification of "unlawful detainees," a classification that meant that these detainees were not prisoners of war and thus had no rights under the Geneva Convention. This ruling, which President George W. Bush accepted, has meant that the detainees basically have no rights except those determined by the U.S. government. This ruling has been attacked by both the international community and elements within the United States. This document explains the justification for the unlawful detainees ruling.

THE WHITE HOUSE
WASHINGTON
February 7, 2002

MEMORANDUM FOR:
    THE VICE PRESIDENT
    THE SECRETARY OF STATE
    THE SECRETARY OF DEFENSE
    THE ATTORNEY GENERAL
    CHIEF OF STAFF TO THE PRESIDENT
    DIRECTOR OF CENTRAL INTELLIGENCE
    ASSISTANT TO THE PRESIDENT FOR NATIONAL SECURITY
      AFFAIRS
    CHAIRMAN OF THE JOINT CHIEFS OF STAFF
SUBJECT: Human Treatment of al Qaeda and Taliban Detainees

1. Our recent extensive discussions regarding the status of al-Qaida and Taliban detainees confirm that the application of Geneva Convention

Relative to the Treatment of Prisoners of War of August 12, 1949, (Geneva) to the conflict with al-Qaida and the Taliban involves complex legal questions. By its terms, Geneva applies to conflicts involving "High Contracting Parties," which can only be states. Moreover, it assumes the existence of "regular" armed forces fighting on behalf of states. However, the war against terrorism ushers in a new paradigm, one in which groups with broad, international reach commit horrific acts against innocent civilians, sometimes with the direct support of states. Our nation recognizes that this new paradigm—ushered in not by us, but by terrorists—requires new thinking in the law of war, but thinking that should nevertheless be consistent with the principles of Geneva.

2. Pursuant to my authority as commander in chief and chief executive of the United States, and relying on the opinion of the Department of Justice dated January 22, 2002, and on the legal opinion rendered by the attorney general in his letter of February 1, 2002, I hereby determine as follows:

   a. I accept the legal conclusion of the Department of Justice and determine that none of the provisions of Geneva apply to our conflict with al-Qaida in Afghanistan or elsewhere throughout the world because, among other reasons, al-Qaida is not a High Contracting Party to Geneva.

   b. I accept the legal conclusion of the attorney general and the Department of Justice that I have the authority under the Constitution to suspend Geneva as between the United and Afghanistan, but I decline to exercise that authority at this time. Accordingly, I determine that the provisions of Geneva will apply to our present conflict with the Taliban. I reserve the right to exercise the authority in this or future conflicts.

   c. I also accept the legal conclusion of the Department of Justice and determine that common Article 3 of Geneva does not apply to either al-Qaida or Taliban detainees, because, among other reasons, the relevant conflicts are international in scope and common Article 3 applies only to "armed conflict not of an international character."

   d. Based on the facts supplied by the Department of Defense and the recommendation of the Department of Justice, I determine that the Taliban detainees are unlawful combatants and, therefore, do not qualify as prisoners of war under Article 4 of Geneva. I note that, because Geneva does not apply to our conflict with al-Qaida, al-Qaida detainees also do not qualify as prisoners of war.

3. Of course, our values as a nation, values that we share with many nations in the world, call for us to treat detainees humanely, including those who are not legally entitled to such treatment. Our nation has been and will continue to be a strong supporter of Geneva and its principles. As a matter of policy, the United States Armed Forces shall continue to treat detainees humanely and, to the extent appropriate and consistent with military necessity, in a manner consistent with the principles of Geneva.

4. The United States will hold states, organizations, and individuals who gain control of United States personnel responsible for treating such personnel humanely and consistent with applicable law.

5. I hereby reaffirm the order previously issued by the secretary of defense to the United States Armed Forces requiring that the detainees be treated humanely

and, to the extent appropriate and consistent with military necessity, in a manner consistent with the principles of Geneva.

6. I hereby direct the secretary of state to communicate my determinations in an appropriate manner to our allies, and other countries and international organizations cooperating in the war against terrorism of global reach.

Source: Erik Saar and Viveca Novak, *Inside the Wire: A Military Intelligence Soldier's Eyewitness Account of Life at Guantanamo* (New York: Penguin Press, 2005), pp. 275–277.

Document 25

Testimony of Dr. W. Gene Corley on Behalf of the American Society of Civil Engineers before the Subcommittee on Environment, Technology and Standards and Subcommittee on Research of the U.S. House of Representatives Committee on Science (May 1, 2002)

Dr. W. Gene Corley testified before the U.S. House of Representatives' Committee on Science's Subcommittee on Environment, Technology and Standards and Subcommittee on Research on the scientific reasons for the collapse of the twin towers on September 11, 2001. A team of civil engineers had studied the problem and posited probable reasons for the collapse, but its members also called for more research on the issue. This eighteen-page report, written in response to this call, is too large to be reproduced verbatim, but there was considerable redundancy. Consequently, the first six pages of the report have been reproduced.

Following the September 11, 2001, attacks on New York City's World Trade Center, the Federal Emergency Management Agency (FEMA) and the Structural Engineering Institute of the American Society of Civil Engineers (SEI/ASCE), in association with New York City and several other federal agencies and professional organizations, deployed a team of civil, structural, and fire protection engineers to study the performance of buildings at the World Trade Center (WTC) site.

Founded in 1852, ASCE represents more than 125,000 civil engineers worldwide and is the country's oldest national engineering society. ASCE members represent the profession most responsible for the nation's built environment. Our members work in consulting, contracting, industry, government and academia. In addition to developing guideline documents, state-of-the-art reports, and a multitude of different journals, ASCE, an American National Standards Institute (ANSI) approved standards developer, establishes standards of practice such as the document known as ASCE 7 which provides minimum design loads for buildings and other structures. ASCE 7 is used internationally and is referenced in all of our nation's major model building codes.

The events of following the attacks in New York City were among the worst building disasters and resulted in the largest loss of life from any single building event in the United States. Of the 58,000 people estimated to be at the WTC Complex, over 3,000 lives were lost that day, including 343 emergency responders. Two commercial airliners were hijacked, and each was flown into one of the two 110-story towers. The structural damage sustained by each tower from the impact, combined with the ensuing fires, resulted in the total collapse of each building. As the towers collapsed, massive debris clouds, consisting of crushed and broken building components, fell onto and blew into surrounding structures, causing extensive collateral damage and, in some cases, igniting additional fires and causing additional collapses. In total, 10 major buildings experienced partial or total collapse and 30 million square feet of commercial office space was removed from service, of which 12 million belonged to the WTC complex.

Scope of the Study

The purpose of the FEMA/ASCE study was to see what could be learned to make buildings safer in the future. Building performance studies are often done when there is major structural damage due to events such as earthquakes or blasts. A better understanding of how buildings respond to extreme forces can help us design safer structures in the future.

Specifically, the scope of the FEMA/ASCE study was to:

• Review damage caused by the attack;
• Assess how each building performed under the attack;
• Determine how each building collapsed'
• Collect and preserve data that may aid in future studies; and
• Offer guidelines for additional study.

The team examined:

• The immediate effects of the aircraft impact on each tower;
• The spread of the fire following the crashes;
• The reduction in structural strength caused by the fires;
• The chain of events that led to the collapse of the towers; and
• How falling debris and the effects of the fires impacted the other buildings at the World Trade Center complex.

The team recommendations are present for more detailed engineering studies, to complete the assessments and produce improved guidance and tools for building design and performance evaluation.

World Trade Center 1 and World Trade Center 2

As each tower was struck, extensive structural damage, including localized collapse, occurred at the several floor levels directly impacted by the aircraft. Despite this massive localized damage, each structure remained standing. However, as each aircraft impacted a building, jet fuel on board ignited. Part of this fuel immediately burned off in the large fireballs that erupted at the impact floors. Remaining fuel flowed across the floors and down elevator and utility shafts, igniting intense fires throughout upper portions of the buildings. As these fires spread, they further weakened the steel-framed structures, eventually triggering total collapse.

The collapse of the twin towers astonished most observers, including knowledgeable structural engineers, and, in the immediate aftermath, a wide range of explanations were offered in an attempt to help the public understand these tragic and unthinkable events. However, the collapse of these symbolic buildings entailed a complex series of events that were not identical for each tower. To determine the sequence of events, likely root causes, and methods of technologies that may improve or mitigate the building performance observed, FEMA and ASCE formed a Building Performance Study (BPS) Team consisting of specialists in tall building design, steel and connection technology, fire and blast engineering, and structural investigation and analysis.

The SEI/ASCE team conducted field observations at the WTC site and steel salvage yards, removed and tested samples of the collapsed structures, viewed hundreds of images of video and still photography, conducted interviews with witnesses and persons involved in the design, construction, and maintenance of each of the affected buildings, reviewed available construction documents, and conducted preliminary analyses of the damage to the WTC towers.

With the information and time available, the sequence of events leading to the collapse of each tower could not be definitively determined. However, the following observations and findings were made:

- The structural damage sustained by each of the two buildings as a result of the terrorist attacks was massive. The fact that the structures were able to sustain this level of damage and remain standing for an extended period of time is remarkable and is the reason that most building occupants were able to evacuate safely. Events of this type, resulting in such substantial damage, are generally not considered in building design, and the fact that these structures were able to successfully withstand such damage is noteworthy.

- Preliminary analyses of the damaged structures, together with the fact the structures remained standing for an extended period of time, suggest that, absent other severe loading events, such as a windstorm or earthquake, the buildings could have remained standing in their damaged states until subjected to some significant additional load. However, the structures were subjected to a second, simultaneous severe loading event in the form of the fires caused by the aircraft impacts.

- The large quantity of jet fuel carried by each aircraft ignited upon impact into each building. A significant portion of this fuel was consumed immediately in the ensuing fireballs. The remaining fuel is believed either to have flowed down through the buildings or to have burned off within a few minutes of the aircraft impact. The heat produced by this burning jet fuel does not by itself appear to have been sufficient to initiate the structural collapses. However, as the burning jet fuel spread across several floors of the buildings, it ignited much of the buildings' contents, permitting fires to evolve across several floors of the buildings simultaneously. The heat output from these fires is estimated to have been comparable to the power produced by a large commercial generating station. Over a period of many minutes, this heat induced additional stresses into the damaged structural frames while simultaneously softening and weakening these frames. This additional loading and damage were sufficient to induce the collapse of both structures.

- The ability of the two towers to withstand aircraft impact without immediate collapse was a direct function of their design and construction characteristics, as was the vulnerability of the two towers to collapse as a result of the combined effects of the impacts and ensuing fires. Many buildings with other design and construction characteristics would have been more vulnerable to collapse in these events than the two towers, and few may have been less vulnerable. It was not the purpose of this study to assess the code-conformance of the building design and construction, or to judge the adequacy of these features. However, during the course of this study the structural and fire protection features of the building were examined. The study did not reveal any specific structural features that would be regarded as substandard, and, in fact, many structural and fire protection features of the design and construction were found to be superior to the minimum code requirements.

What Caused the Collapse of the Towers?

Our analysis showed that the impact alone did not cause the collapse of the towers, but instead, left the towers vulnerable to collapse from any significant additional force, such as from high winds, an earthquake, or in the case of the Twin Towers, the fires that engulfed both buildings. Without that second event, the team believes the towers could have remained standing indefinitely.

Although steel is very strong, it loses some of its strength when heated. To prevent that loss of strength, structural steel is protected with fireproofing and sprinkler systems. In the towers, fires raged through several floors simultaneously, ignited by the jet fuel and fed by a mixture of paper and furniture. The impact dislodged some fireproofing on the structural beams and columns, which made them vulnerable to fire damage. With the sprinkler system disabled, the fires raged uncontrollably, weakening the steel and leading to the collapse of the buildings.

Several building design features have been identified as key to the buildings' ability to remain standing as long as they did and to allow the evacuation of most building occupants. These included the following:

- Robustness and redundancy of the steel framing system;
- Presence of adequate egress stairways that were well marked and lighted; and
- The conscientious implementation of emergency exiting training programs for building tenants.

Similarly, several design features have been identified that may have played a role in allowing the buildings to collapse in the manner that they did and in the inability of victims at and above the impact floors to safely exit. These features should not be regarded either as design deficiencies or as features that should be prohibited in future building codes. Rather, these are features that should be subjected to more detailed evaluation, in order to understand their contribution to the performance of these buildings and how they may perform in other buildings. These include the following:

- The type of steel floor truss system present in these buildings and their structural robustness and redundancy when compared to other structural systems;
- Use of impact-resistant enclosures around egress paths;
- Resistance of passive fire protection to blasts and impacts in buildings designed to provide resistance to such hazards; and
- Grouping emergency egress stairways in the central building core as opposed to dispersing them throughout the structure.

Building Codes

During the course of this study, the question of whether building codes should be changed in some way to make future buildings more resistant to such attacks was frequently explored. Depending on the size of the aircraft, it may not be technically feasible to develop design provisions that would enable structures to be designed and constructed to resist the effects of impacts by rapidly moving aircraft, and the ensuing fires, without collapse. In addition, the cost of constructing such structures might be so large as to make this type of design intent practically infeasible.

Although the attacks on the World Trade Center are a reason to question design philosophies. The BPS Team believes there are insufficient data to determine whether there is a reasonable threat of attacks on specific buildings to recommend inclusion of such requirement in building codes. Some believe the likelihood of such attacks on any specific building is deemed sufficiently low to not be considered at all. However, individual building developers may wish to consider design provisions for improving redundancy and robustness for such unforeseen events, particularly for structures that, by nature of their design or occupancy, may be especially susceptible to such incidents. Although some conceptual changes to the building codes that could make buildings more resistant to fire or impact damage or more conducive to occupant egress were identified in the course of this study, the BPS Team felt that extensive technical, policy, and economic study of these concepts should be performed before any specific code change recommendations are developed. This report specifically recommends such additional studies. Future building codes revisions may be considered after the technical details of the collapses and other building responses to damage are better understood.

Surrounding Buildings

Several other buildings including the Marriott Hotel (WTC 3), the South Plaza building (WTC 4), the U.S. Customs building (WTC 6), and the Winter Garden experienced nearly total collapse as a result of the massive quantities of debris that fell on them when the two towers collapsed. The St. Nicholas Greek Orthodox Church just south of WTC 2 was completely destroyed by the debris that fell on it.

WTC 5, WTC 7, 90 West Street, 130 Cedar Street, Bankers Trust, the Verizon building, and World Financial Center 3 were impacted by large debris from the collapsing twin towers and suffered structural damage, but arrested collapse to localized areas. The performance of these buildings demonstrates the inherent ability of redundant steel-framed structures to withstand extensive damage from earthquakes, blasts, and other extreme events without progressive collapse.

The debris from the collapses of the WTC towers also initiated fires in surrounding buildings, including WTC 4, 5, 6, 7; 90 West Street; and 130 Cedar Street. Many of the buildings suffered severe fire damage but remained standing. However, two steel-framed structures experienced fire-induced collapse. WTC 7 collapsed completely after burning unchecked for approximately 7 hours, and a partial collapse occurred in an interior section of WTC 5. Studies of WTC 7 indicate that the collapse began in the lower stories, either through failure of major load transfer members located above and electrical substation structure or in columns in the stories above the transfer structure. The collapse of WTC 7 caused damage to the Verizon building and 30 West Broadway. The partial collapse of WTC 5 was not initiated by debris and is possibly a result of fire-induced connection failures. The collapse of these structures is particularly significant in that, prior to these events, no protected steel-frame structure, the most common form of large commercial construction in the United States, had ever experienced a fire-induced collapse. Thus, these events may highlight new building vulnerabilities, not previously believed to exist.

In the study of the WTC towers and the surrounding buildings that were subsequently damaged by falling debris and fire, several issues were found to be critical to the observed building performance in one or more buildings.

General Observations, Findings and Recommendations

These issues above fall into several broad topics that should be considered for buildings that are being evaluated or designed for extreme events. It may be that some of these issues should be considered for all buildings; however, additional studies are required before general recommendations, if any, can be made for all buildings. The issues identified from this study of damaged buildings in or near the WTC site have been summarized into the following points.

a. Structural framing systems need redundancy and/or robustness, so that alternative paths or additional capacity is available for transmitting loads when building damage occurs.

b. Fireproofing needs to adhere under impact and fire conditions that deform steel members, so that the coatings remain on the steel and prove the intended protection.

c. Connection performance under impact loads and during fire loads needs to be analytically understood and quantified for improved design capabilities and performance as critical components in structural frames.

d. Fire protection ratings that include the use of sprinklers in buildings require a reliable and redundant water supply. If the water supply is interrupted, the assumed fire protection is greatly reduced.

e. Egress systems currently in use should be evaluated for redundancy and robustness in providing egress when building damage occurs, including the issues of transfer floors, stair spacing and locations, and stairwell enclosure impact resistance.

f. Fire protection ratings and safety factors for structural transfer systems should be evaluated for their adequacy relative to the role of transfer systems in building stability.

What Significant Recommendations Does the Team Make in Its Report?

What may be most important is that the BPS Team does not recommend any immediate changes in building codes. The Team believes that there are a number of areas that need further study, and that there are some things that building designers could do to improve safety for occupants in building that might be possible terrorist targets.

In general terms, the FEMA/ASCE report suggests that critical building components such as the structural frame, the sprinkler system or the exit stairwells be designed to be more redundant, more robust, or both. Redundancy means, for example, that if some structural columns were shattered, the building would be designed to transfer the weight to other columns. Robustness means making the building stronger and better able to resist impact without collapse.

The team is also strongly urging additional study of the collapse of the buildings.

What Key Findings Impact All Existing Buildings?

The team found that some connections between the structural steel beams failed in the fire. This was most apparent in the collapse of World Trade Center Building 5, where the fireproofing did not protect the connections, causing the structure to fail.

The team is calling for more research and analysis of the how the connections weakened and how best to strengthen their resistance to future fires. Typically, fire resistance tests are limited to steel members, not to the steel connections. Furthermore, fireproofing is sprayed on the connections the same way it is applied to the trusses, though the steel in the trusses and joints may be made of different alloys.

Source: U.S. House of Representatives. Committee on Science, *9/11-Understanding the Collapse of the World Trade Center* (Washington, DC: U.S. Government Printing Office, 2003), pp. 29–43.

Document 26

Report by Eleanor Hill from the Joint Inquiry Staff Statement on the Intelligence on the Possible Terrorist Use of Airplanes (September 18, 2002)

The use by terrorists of commercial aircraft as a weapon in a suicide mission came as a surprise to the American public and terrorist experts alike. Yet the American intelligence community was aware of hints that terrorists had an interest in hijacking commercial aircraft. Just how much knowledge the American intelligence community had about this tactic was revealed in a report from the Joint Inquiry of the Senate's Select Committee on Intelligence and the House's Permanent Select Committee on Intelligence held between September 18 and 26, 2002. Eleanor Hill made this statement on the subject on September 18, 2002.

Central to the September 11 attacks was the terrorists' use of airplanes as weapons. In the aftermath of the terrorist attacks, there was much discussion about the extent to which our Government was, or could have been, aware of the threat of terrorist attacks of this type and the extent to which adequate precautions were taken to address that threat. We therefore asked the question: Did the Intelligence Community have any information in its possession prior to September 11, 2001 indicating that terrorists were contemplating using airplanes as weapons?

Based on our review to date of the requested information, we believe that the Intelligence Community was aware of the potential for this type of terrorist attack, but did not produce any specific assessments of the likelihood that terrorists would use airplanes as weapons.

Our review has uncovered several examples of intelligence reporting on the possible use of airplanes as weapons in terrorist operations. As with the intelligence reports indicating Bin Ladin's intentions to strike inside the United States, the credibility of the sources is sometimes questionable, and the information is often sketchy. Nevertheless, we did find reporting on this kind of potential threat, including the following:

- In December 1994, Algerian Armed Islamic Group terrorists hijacked an air France flight in Algiers and threatened to crash it into the Eiffel Tower. French authorities deceived the terrorists into thinking the plane did not have enough fuel to reach Paris and diverted it to Marseilles. A French anti-terrorist force stormed the plane and killed all four terrorists;
- In January 1995, a Philippine National Police raid turned up materials in a Manila apartment indicating that three individuals—Ramzi Yousef, Abdul Murad and Khalid Shaykh Mohammad—planned, among other things, to crash an airplane into CIA headquarters. The Philippine National Police said that the same group was responsible for the bombing of a Philippine airliner on December 12, 1994. Information on the threat was passed to the FAA, which briefed U.S. and major foreign carriers;
- In January 1996, the Intelligence Community obtained information concerning a planned suicide attack by individuals associated with Shaykh Omar Adb al-Rahman and a key al-Qa'ida operative. The plan was to fly to the United States from Afghanistan and attack the White House;
- In October 1996, the Intelligence Community obtained information regarding an Iranian plot to hijack a Japanese plane over Israel and crash it into Tel Aviv. An individual would board the plane in the Far East. During the flight, he would commandeer the aircraft, order it to fly over Tel Aviv, and then crash the plane into the city;
- In 1997, one of the units at FBI headquarters became concerned about the possibility of a terrorist group using an unmanned aerial vehicle (UAV) for terrorist attacks. The FBI and CIA became aware of reporting that this group had purchased a UAV. At the time, the agencies' view was that the only reason that this group would need a UAV would be for either reconnaissance or attack. There was more concern about the possibility of an attack outside the Untied States, for example, by flying a UAV into a U.S. Embassy or a visiting U.S. delegation;
- In August 1998, the Intelligence Community obtained information that a group of unidentified Arabs planned to fly an explosive-laden plane from a foreign country into the World Trade Center. The information was passed to the FBI and the FAA. The FAA found the plot highly unlikely given the state of that foreign country's aviation program. Moreover, they believed that a flight originating outside the United States would be detected before it reached its intended target inside the United States. The FBI's New York office took no action on the information, filing the communication in the office's bombing repository file. The Intelligence Community has acquired additional information since then indicating there may be links between this group and other terrorist groups, including al-Qa'ida;
- In September 1998, the Intelligence Community obtained information that Usama Bin Ladin's next operation could possibly involve flying an aircraft loaded with explosives into a U.S. airport and detonating it; this information was provided to senior U.S. officials in late 1998;

- In November 1998, the Intelligence Community obtained information that the Turkish Kaplancilar, and Islamic extremist group, had planned a suicide attack to coincide with celebrations marking the death of Ataturk. The conspirators, who were arrested, planned to crash an airplane packed with explosives into Ataturk's tomb during a government ceremony. The Turkish press said the group had cooperated with Usama Bin Ladin. The FBI's New York office included this incident in one of its Usama Bin Ladin databases;
- In February 1999, the Intelligence Community obtained information that Iraq had formed a suicide pilot unit that it planned to use against British and U.S. forces in the Persian Gulf. The CIA commented that this was highly unlikely and probably disinformation;
- In March 1999, the Intelligence Community obtained information regarding plans by al-Qa'ida member, who was a U.S. citizen, to fly a hang glider into the Egyptian Presidential Palace and then detonate the explosives he was carrying. The individual, who received hang glider training in the United States, brought a hang glider back to Afghanistan. However, various problems arose during the testing of the glider. He was subsequently arrested and is in custody abroad;
- In April 2000, the Intelligence Community obtained information regarding an alleged Bin Ladin plot to hijack a 747. The source, who was a "walk-in" to the FBI's Newark office, claimed that he had been to a training camp in Pakistan where he learned hijacking techniques and received arms training. He also stated that he was supposed to meet five to six other individuals in the United States who would also participate in the plot. They were instructed to use all necessary force to take over the plane because there would be pilots among the hijacking team. The plan was to fly the plane to Afghanistan, and if they would not make it there, that they were to blow up the plane. Although the individual passed an FBI polygraph, the FBI was never able to verify any aspect of his story or identify his contacts in the United States; and
- In August 2001, the Intelligence Community obtained information regarding a plot to either bomb the U.S. Embassy in Nairobi from an airplane or crash an airplane into it. The Intelligence Community learned that two people, who were reportedly acting on instructions from Usama Bin Ladin, met in October 2000 to discuss this plot.

The CIA disseminated several of these reports to the FBI and to agencies that would be responsible for taking preventive actions, including the FAA. The FAA has staff assigned to the DCI's CTC, the FBI's Counterterrorism Division, and to the State Department's Diplomatic Security Service go gather relevant intelligence for domestic use. The FAA is responsible for issuing information circulars, security directives and emergency amendments to the directives alerting domestic and international airports and airlines of threats identified by the Intelligence Community.

Despite these reports, the Intelligence Community did not produce any specific assessments of the likelihood that terrorists would use airplanes as weapons. Again, this may have been driven in part by resource issues in the area of intelligence analysis. Prior to September 11, 2001, the CTC had forty analysts to analyze terrorism issues worldwide, with only one of the five branches focused on terrorist tactics. As a result, prior to September 11, 2001, the only terrorist tactic, on which the CTC performed strategic analysis was the possible use of chemical, biological, radiological and nuclear weapons (CBRN) because there was more obvious potential for mass casualties.

At the FBI, our review found that, prior to September 11, 2001, support for ongoing investigations and operations was favored, in terms of allocating resources, over long-term, strategic analysis. We were told, during the course of our FBI interviews, that prevention occurs in the operational units, not through strategic analysis, and that, prior to September 11, the FBI had insufficient resources to do both. We were also told that the FBI's al-Qa'ida-related analytic expertise had been "gutted" by transfers to operational units and that, as a result, the FBI's analytic unit had only one individual working on al-Qa'ida at the time of the September 11 attacks.

While focused strategic analysis was lacking, the subject of aviation-related terrorism was included in some broader terrorist threat assessments, such as the National Intelligence Estimates (NIE) on terrorism. For example the 1995 NIE on terrorism mentioned the plot to down 12 U.S.-owned airliners. The NIE also cited the consideration the Bojinka conspirators gave to attacking CIA headquarters using an aircraft loaded with explosives. The FAA worked with the Intelligence Community on this analysis and actually drafted the section of the NIE addressing the threat to civil aviation. The section contained the following language:

> Our review of the evidence . . . suggests the conspirators were guided in their selection of the method and venue of attack by carefully studying security procedures in place in the region. If terrorists operating in this country [the United States] are similarly methodical, they will identify serious vulnerabilities in the security for domestic flights.

The 1997 update to the 1995 NIE on terrorism included the following language:

> Civil aviation remains a particularly attractive target in light of the fear and publicity the downing of an airliner would evoke and the revelations last summer of the US air transport sectors' vulnerabilities.

As a result of the increasing threats to aviation, Congress passed Section 310 of the Federal Aviation Reauthorization Act of 1996, requiring the FAA and the FBI to conduct joint threat and vulnerability assessments of security at select "high risk" U.S. airports and to provide Congress with an annual report. In the December 2000 report, the FBI and FAA published a classified assessment that suggested less concern about the threat to domestic aviation:

> FBI investigations confirm domestic and international terrorist groups operating within the U.S. but do not suggest evidence of plans to target domestic civil aviation. Terrorist activity within the U.S. has focused primarily on fundraising, recruiting new members, and disseminating propaganda. While international terrorists have conducted attacks on U.S. soil, these acts represent anomalies in their traditional targeting which focuses on U.S. interests overseas.

In short, less than a year prior to the September 11 attacks and notwithstanding historical intelligence information to the contrary, the FBI and FAA have assessed the prospects of a terrorist incident targeting domestic civil aviation in the United States as relatively low.

After September 11, 2001, the CIA belatedly acknowledged some of the information that was available regarding the use of airplanes as weapons. A draft analysis dated November 19, 2001, "The 11 September Attacks: A Preliminary Assessment," states:

> We do not know the process by which Bin Ladin and his lieutenants decided to hijack planes with the idea of flying them into buildings in the United States, but the idea of hijacking planes for suicide attacks had long been current in jihadist circles. For example, GIA terrorists from Algeria had planned to crash an Air France jet into the Eiffel Tower in December 1994, and Ramzi Yousef—a participant in the 1993 World Trade Center bombing—planned to explode 12 US jetliners in mid-air over the Pacific in the mid-1990s. Likewise the World Trade Center had long been a target of terrorist bombers.

Despite the intelligence available in recent years, our review to date had found no indications that, prior to September 11, analysts in the Intelligence Community were:

- Cataloguing information regarding the use of airplanes as weapons as a terrorist tactic;
- Sending requirements to collectors to look for additional information on this threat; or
- Considering the likelihood that Usama Bin Ladin, al-Qa'ida, or any other terrorist group, would attack the Untied States or U.S. interests in this way.

Source: Select Committee on Intelligence U.S. Senate and the Permanent Select Committee of Intelligence House of Representatives, *Joint Inquiry into Intelligence Community Activities before and after the Terrorist Attacks of Sept. 11, 2001* (Washington, DC: U.S. Government Printing Office, 2004), vol. 1, pp. 26–31.

Document 27

Report by Eleanor Hill from the Joint Inquiry Staff on the Intelligence Community's Knowledge of the September 11 Hijackers Prior to September 11, 2001 (September 20, 2002)

In another report from the Joint Inquiry Staff of the Senate's Selection Committee on Intelligence and the House's Permanent Select Committee on Intelligence, Eleanor Hill outlined the investigation of U.S. government agencies on the three known terrorist suspects before September 11. These three later participated in the suicide attacks on the World Trade Center and the Pentagon.

Three September 11 Hijackers Who Came to the Attention of the Intelligence Community Prior to September 11, 2001

What follows is a description of how the Intelligence Community developed information on three of the hijackers, and when the Intelligence Community had, but missed, opportunities both to deny them entry into the United States and, subsequently, to generate investigative and surveillance action regarding their activities within the United States. At this stage, we must also reiterate that this is only an unclassified summary of these events. While the Joint Inquiry Staff has studied this intelligence trail in great detail, some aspects involving intelligence sources and methods remain classified. A separate and more detailed classified report is also being submitted to the two Committees.

As mentioned earlier, the Joint Inquiry Staff has also requested that the written statements of the CDI and Director of the FBI be declassified. When they become available, they will further describe what the Intelligence Community now knows about the September 11 plot.

As background, we mention here that watchlists are important to U.S. Government efforts aimed at preventing criminals and terrorists from entering the

United States from overseas. The State Department, the Immigration and Naturalization Service (INS) and the U.S. Customs Service all maintain watchlists of named individuals. Names are added to the watchlists based on information provided by the Intelligence Community and various law enforcement agencies. When individuals apply for visas to enter the United States or present themselves to immigration officers at U.S. ports of entry—airports, seaports, and land border crossings—U.S. consular officers, INS officers, and Customs agents check their names against watchlists maintained by their respective agencies. If an individual's name is on a U.S. Government watchlist, he or she may be denied visas or denied entry into the United States.

The story begins in December 1999 with the Intelligence Community on heightened alert for possible terrorist activity as the world prepared to celebrate the new Millennium. A meeting of individuals believed at the time to be associated with Usama Bin Ladin's terrorist network took place in Kuala Lumpur, Malaysia from January 5 to 8, 2000. Khalid al-Mihdhar and Nawaf al-Hazmi were among those attending the meeting in Malaysia, along with an individual later identified as Khallad bin-Atash, a key operative in Usama Bin Ladin's terrorist network. The meeting took place at a condominium owned by an individual named Yazid Sufaat. Sufaat is the same individual who would later, in October 2000, sign letters identifying Zacarias Moussaoui as a representative of his company. U.S. authorities found these letters in the possession of Moussaoui after the September 11 attacks. Although it was not known what was discussed at the Malaysia meeting, the CIA believed it to be a gathering of al-Qa'ida associates. Several of the individuals attending the meeting, including al-Mihdhar and al-Hazmi, then proceeded to another Southeast Asian country.

By the time these individual entered Malaysia, the CIA determined Khalid al-Mihdhar's full name, his passport number, and birth information. Significantly, it also knew that he held a U.S. B-1/B-2 multiple-entry visa that had been issued to him in Jeddah, Saudi Arabia on April 7, 1999 and would not expire until April 6, 2000. Soon after these individuals departed Malaysia for another country on January 8, 2001, the CIA also received indications that Nawaf's last name might be al-Hazmi. Unbeknownst to the CIA, another arm of the Intelligence Community, the NSA, had information associating Nawaf al-Hazmi with the Bin Ladin network. NSA did not immediately disseminate that information, although it was in NSA's database. At this stage, Salim was known to the rest of the Intelligence Community as an associate of Khalid's and Nawaf's and that he was possibly Nawaf's brother. Al-Mihdhar's and Nawaf al-Hazmi's names could have been, but were not, added at this time to the State Department, INS, and U.S. Customs Service watchlists denying individuals entry into the United States.

A CIA communication in early January 2000 states that al-Mihdhar's travel documents, including his multiple entry visa for the United States, were shared with the FBI for further investigation. No one at the FBI recalls having received such documents at the time. No confirmatory record of the transmittal of the travel documents has yet been located at either the CIA or the FBI. In addition, while the Malaysian meeting was in progress, a CIA employee sent an e-mail to a CIA colleague, advising that he had briefed two FBI agents about what the CIA had learned about al-Mihdhar's activities. The CIA employee told us that he had, at the time, been assigned to work at the FBI Strategic Information

Operations Center to fix problems "in communicating between the CIA and the FBI." His e-mail, however, makes no mention of the CIA's determination that al-Mihdhar held a U.S. multiple-entry visa. The CIA employee notes in his e-mail that he had told the second FBI agent that:

> . . . this continues to be an [intelligence] operation. Thus far, a lot of suspicious activity has been observed but nothing that would indicate evidence of an impending attack or criminal enterprise. Told [the first FBI agent] that as soon as something concrete is developed leading us to the criminal arena or to known FBI cases, we will immediately bring FBI into the loop. Like [the first FBI agent] yesterday, [second FBI] stated that this was a fine approach and thanked me for keeping him in the loop.

The CIA employee told the Joint Inquiry Staff that he does not recall telling the FBI about Mihdhar's visa information and potential travel to the United States.

When interviewed by the Joint Inquiry Staff, neither FBI agent initially recalled discussions with the CIA employee about al-Mihdhar. The first agent did locate his own handwritten notes that indicated that he did speak with the employee about the Malaysia activities, probably in early January 2000. The second agent knows the CIA employee but does not recall learning about al-Mihdhar or the Malaysia meeting until after September 11, 2001. An e-mail from the second FBI agent to a superior at FBI headquarters has been located that relates the basic facts of the conversation with the CIA employee. The e-mail makes no mention of al-Mihdhar's visa information or possible travel to the United States. It concludes with "CIA is reporting relevant information as it becomes available."

The CIA maintained its interest in al-Mihdhar and al-Hazmi after their departure from Malaysia, with assistance from foreign authorities. A February 2000 CIA cable in response to a request by foreign authorities to become involved reiterated CIA's primacy in the case and intent "to determine what the subject is up to."

In early March 2000, CIA headquarters, including both the CTC and the special Bin Ladin unit, received information from an overseas CIA station involved in the matter that Nawaf al-Hazmi had entered the United States via Los Angeles International Airport on January 15, 2000. No further destination for Khalid al-Mihdhar was noted in the CIA cable. The cable carrying the information was marked "Action Required: None, FYI." The following day, another overseas CIA station noted, in a cable to the Bin Ladin unit at CIA headquarters, that it had "read with interest" the March cable, "particularly the information that a member of this group traveled to the U.S. . . . ." The CIA did not act on this information. Nor did it consider the possibility that, because Nawaf al-Hazmi and Khalid al-Mihdhar had been together in Malaysia and continued on together to another Southeast Asian country, there was a substantial probability that they would travel further together. In fact, al-Mihdhar, who had traveled with al-Hazmi, continued on with him to the United States on January 15, 2000.

Again, at this point, these two individuals, who later participated in the September 11 attacks, could have been added to the State Department's watchlist for denying individuals entry into the United States. Although the individuals had already entered the United States, the sharing of this information with the FBI and appropriate law enforcement authorities could have prompted investigative efforts to locate these individuals and surveil their activities within the United States. Unfortunately, none of these things happened. The Joint Inquiry Staff has interviewed the individual at CIA headquarters who had direct responsibility for tracking the movement of individuals at this meeting in Malaysia. That person does not recall seeing the March message. In his testimony before the Joint Inquiry on June 18, 2001, the DCI acknowledged that the CIA should have acted to add these individuals to the State Department's watchlist in March 2000 and characterized this omission as a mistake.

During the course of our interviews, we attempted to identify the reasons why that mistake occurred. We were told that there was, at the time, no formal system in place at the CTC for watchlisting suspected terrorists with indications of travel to the United States. CIA personnel also told us that they received no formal training on watchlisting. One CIA employee said they learned about the watchlisting process through "on-the-job training." Another CIA employee who had been aware of al-Mihdhar's participation in the Malaysia meeting told us that, prior to September 11, 2001, it was "not incumbent on CTC's special Bin Ladin unit to watchlist such individuals." Finally, a CTC employee who in 2000 handled the cable traffic on the Malaysia meeting told us that the meeting was not considered "important" (relative to other counterterrorist activities occurring at that time) and that there was "not enough people" to handle CTC's workload at the time. As a result, informational cables—such as the March 2000 message—received less attention than "action" items. Several other employees told us that they typically did not have time to even read information cables.

The failure to watchlist al-Mihdhar and al-Hazmi or, at a minimum, to advise the FBI of their travel to the United States, is perhaps even more puzzling because it occurred shortly after the peak of Intelligence Community alertness to possible Millennium-related terrorist attacks. In the fall of 1999, there was debate within the Intelligence Community about whether intelligence information that had been collected earlier that year meant that Usama Bin Ladin's network intended to carry out terrorist attacks in the midst of the celebrations ushering in the new Millennium. Intelligence information, along with the arrest of Ahmed Ressam at the U.S.-Canadian border, prompted the U.S. Government and various foreign governments to arrest, detain, and otherwise disrupt numerous individuals associated with Bin Ladin's network in various locations around the world. These disruption operations occurred between December 1999 and February 2000. Thus, the Malaysia meeting of January 5-8, 2000 and the March 2000 information that al-Hazmi had entered the United States developed at a time when the Intelligence Community had only recently confronted the real possibility of a Bin Ladin attack. However, it apparently was still focused on the organization and aftermath of the previous operations.

In interviews with the Joint Inquiry Staff, a number of working level CIA personnel who were following the Malaysia meeting and other terrorist activities in the Millennium timeframe have characterized the Malaysia meeting as just one of many counterterrorist efforts occurring at that time. In contrast, documents reviewed by the Joint Inquiry Staff show that the Malaysia meeting was deemed sufficiently important at the time that it was included—along with several other counterterrorist activities—in several briefings to the DCI in January 2000. We were told, however, that the matter was "dropped" when the CIA employee handling the matter moved on to other issues and, as a result, no CIA officer was following the al-Mihdhar group by the summer of 2000.

By March 2000, al-Mihdhar and Nawaf al-Hazmi had settled into a residence in San Diego. In the course of their time in San Diego, they used their true names on a rental agreement, as al-Mihdhar also did in obtaining a California motor vehicle photo identification card. In May 2000, they took flight lessons in San Diego but abandoned the effort. On June 10, 2000, al-Mihdhar left the Untied States on a Lufthansa flight from Los Angeles to Frankfurt.

Nawaf al-Hazmi remained in the United States. On July 7, 2000, a week shy of the expiration of the six-month visa to stay in the United States that he had been granted on January, 2000, al-Hazmi applied to the INS for an extension to his visa. He used on his INS application the Lemon Grove, California address for the residence that the shared with al-Mihdhar before the latter's departure in early June 2000. The INS recorded receipt of the extension request on July 27, 2000. The INS has advised the Joint Inquiry Staff that it assumes a receipt was generated and sent to al-Hazmi at the address he listed. Lemon Grove is the community al-Hazmi lived in until December 2000. At that time, he moved to Mesa, Arizona with Hani Hanjour, who in December had just returned to the United States and would later be the most likely hijacker to have piloted American Flight 77. The INS does not have a record of a further extension request by al-Hazmi, who remained in the United States illegally after his initial extension expired in January 2001.

On October 12, 2000, two individuals with ties to Usama Bin Ladin's terrorist network carried out an attack on *USS Cole* as the Navy destroyer was refueling in Aden, Yemen. In the course of its investigation of the attack, the FBI developed information indicating that an individual named Tawfiq Mahomed Saleh Atash, also known as Khallad, had been a principal planner in the *Cole* bombing and that two other participants in the *Cole* conspiracy had delivered money to Khallad at the time of the January 2000 Malaysia meeting. The FBI shared this information with the CIA, and it prompted analysts at CIA to take another look at the January 2000 meeting in Malaysia.

In that process, the CIA acquired information in January 2001 indicating that Khallad had attended the meeting in Malaysia. This information was significant because it meant that the other attendees, including al-Mihdhar and Nawaf al-Hazmi, had been in direct contact with the key planner in Usama Bin Ladin's terrorist network behind the *Cole* attack. However, CIA again apparently did not act and did not add Khalid al-Mihdhar and Nawaf al-Hazmi to the State Department's watchlist for denying individuals entry into the United States. At this time, Khalid al-Mihdhar was abroad, while Nawaf al-Hazmi was still in the United States.

In May 2001, personnel at the CIA provided an Intelligence Operations Specialist (IOS) at FBI headquarters with photographs taken in Malaysia, including one of al-Mihdhar. The CIA wanted the FBI to review the photographs to determine whether an individual in custody in connection with the FBI's *Cole* investigation (who had carried the money to a Southeast Asian country for Khallad in January 2000) could be identified in the photographs. When interviewed, the FBI IOS who received the photographs told the Joint Inquiry Staff that the CIA told her about Mihdhar's meeting in Malaysia and travel to another Southeast country, but said nothing about his potential travel to the United States. Nor did the CIA advise the FBI that the photographs were from a meeting that it believed Khallad had attended. Again, no action was taken to watchlist al-Mihdhar or al-Hazmi.

On June 11, 2001, FBI headquarters representatives and CIA representatives met with the New York FBI agents handling the *Cole* investigation. The New York agents were shown, but not given copies of, the photographs and told they were taken in Malaysia. When interviewed, one of the New York agents recalled al-Mihdhar's name being mentioned. He also recalled asking for more information on why the people in the photographs were being followed and for access to that information. The New York agents were advised they could not be told why al-Mihdhar and the others were being followed. An FBI headquarters representative told us in her interview that the FBI was never given specific information until it was provided after September 11, 2001. The CIA analyst who attended the New York meeting acknowledged to the Joint Inquiry Staff that he had seen the information regarding al-Mihdhar's U.S. visa and al-Hazmi's travel to the United States. But, he stated that he would not share information outside of the CIA unless he had authority to do so and unless that was the purpose of the meeting.

On June 13, 2001, Khalid al-Mihdhar obtained a new U.S. visa in Jeddah, using a different passport than the one he had used to enter the United States on January 15, 2001. On his visa application, he checked "no" in response to the question of whether he had ever been in the United States. On July 4, 2001, al-Mihdhar re-entered the United States.

On or about July 13, 2001, a CIA officer assigned to the FBI accessed CIA's electronic database and located a CIA cable, for which he had been searching, that contained information the CIA had acquired in January 2001 indicating that Khallad had attended the meeting in Malaysia. The presence of Khallad in Malaysia deeply troubled the CIA officer, who immediately sent an email from FBI headquarters to the DCI's CTC saying of Khallad: "This is a major league killer, who orchestrated the *Cole* attack and possibly the Africa bombings."

A review at the CIA of all prior cables concerning the Malaysia meeting was launched, a task that fell to an FBI analyst assigned to the CTC. On August 21, 2001, the FBI analyst put together two key pieces of information. These were the intelligence that the CIA had received in January 2000 that al-Mihdhar had a multiple entry visa to the United States and the Information it had received in March 2000 that Nawaf al-Hazmi had enter the United States on January 15, 2000. Working with an INS representative assigned to the CTC, the analyst obtained information that al-Mihdhar had entered the United States on January 15, 2000 and had departed on June 10, 2000. Additional investigation revealed that al-Mihdhar had re-entered the United States on July 4, 2001, with a visa that allowed him to stay in the United States through August 22. CIA suspicions were further aroused by the timing of al-Mihdhar's and al-Hazmi's arrival in Los Angeles in January 2000, the same general timeframe in which Algerian terrorist and Bin Ladin associate Ahmed Ressam was to have arrived in Los Angeles to conduct terrorist operations.

On August 23, 2001, the CIA sent a cable to the State Department, INS, Customs Service, and FBI requesting that "Bin Ladin related individuals"—al-Mihdhar, Nawaf al-Hazmi, and two other individuals at the Malaysia meeting—be watchlisted immediately and denied entry into the United States "due to their confirmed links to Egyptian Islamic Jihad operatives and suspicious activities while traveling in East Asia." Although the CIA believed al-Mihdhar was in the United States, placing him on the watchlist would enable authorities to detain him if he attempted to leave.

Meanwhile, the FBI headquarters' Usama Bin Ladin Unit sent to the FBI's New York field office a draft document recommending the opening of an intelligence investigation on al-Mihdhar ". . . to determine if al-Mihdhar is still in the United States." It also stated that al-Mihdhar's confirmed association with various elements of Bin Ladin's terrorist network, including potential association with two individuals involved in the attack on *USS Cole*, "make him a risk to the national security of the United States." This document was sent to New York in final form on August 28. New York FBI agents told us that they tried to convince FBI headquarters to open a criminal investigation on al-Mihdhar, given the importance of the search and the limited resources that were available to intelligence investigations. FBI headquarters declined to do so because there was, in its view, no way to connect al-Mihdhar to the ongoing *Cole* investigation without using some intelligence information.

At the State Department, a visa revocation process was begun immediately. Al-Mihdhar, Nawaf al-Hazmi, Khallad, and the other individual who had been at the Malaysia meeting were added to the watchlists maintained by INS and Customs Service, on the chance that they had not yet entered the United States.

The FBI contacted the Bureau of Diplomatic Security at the State Department on August 27, 2001 to obtain al-Mihdhar's and Nawaf al-Hazmi's visa information. The visa information was provided to the FBI on August 29, 2001. It revealed that, on entering the United States on July 4, 2001, al-Mihdhar had indicated on his application that he would be staying at a Marriott hotel in New York City. An FBI agent working with a Naval Criminal Investigative Service agent determined on September 5, 2001 that al-Mihdhar had not registered at any New York area Marriott hotel, including the Marriott World Trade Center Hotel. On September 10, 2001, the New York FBI field office prepared a request that the FBI office in Los Angeles check registration records for all Sheraton Hotels located in the Los Angeles metropolitan area. The request also asked the Los Angeles field office to check with Untied Airlines and Lufthansa for travel and alias information since al-Mihdhar and al-Hazmi had used those airlines when they entered and when al-Mihdhar departed the United States. The Los Angeles FBI office conducted the search after September 11, 2001, with negative results.

In short, the CIA had obtained information identifying two of the 19 hijackers, al-Mihdhar and al-Hazmi, as suspected terrorists carrying visas for travel to the United States al long as eighteen months prior to the time they were eventually watch-listed on August 24, 2001. There were numerous opportunities during the tracking of these two suspected terrorists when the CIA could have alerted the FBI and other U.S. law enforcement authorities to the probability that these individual either were or would soon be in the United States. That was not done, nor were they placed on watchlists denying them entry into the United States. In his closed-door testimony of June 18, 2000, before the Joint Inquiry, as mentioned earlier, the DCI acknowledged that the CIA had made a mistake in not watch-listing these two individuals prior to August 2001.

It is worth noting that the watchlists mentioned above are aimed at denying named individuals from entering the United States. Prior to September 11, 2001, these watchlists were not used to screen individuals boarding domestic flights within the United States. Thus, even though al-Mihdhar and al-Hazmi had been placed on U.S. watchlists two weeks prior to September 11, 2001, this did not prevent them from boarding American Flight 77 on September 11.

Beyond the watchlist issue, the story of al-Mihdhar and al-Hazmi also graphically illustrates the gulf that apparently existed, at least prior to September 11, 2001, between intelligence and law enforcement counterterrorist efforts. An effective defense against terrorist groups such as al-Qa'ida requires close collaboration between both law enforcement and foreign intelligence agencies as well as within the FBI between the unit responsible for criminal investigations and the unit responsible for counterintelligence and counterterrorism investigations. There are a number of factors that make effective integration of law enforcement and intelligence investigations against terrorism difficult. These include differences in experience, tactics, objectives, legal authorities, and concern for protecting intelligence sources and methods. A brief explanation of certain legal distinctions between law enforcement and foreign intelligence investigations is important to understand aspects of how CIA and FBI dealt with information about the hijackers as well as the FBI's handling of the Moussaoui investigation.

The May 17, 2002 opinion of the United States Foreign Intelligence Surveillance Court (FISC) concerning "minimization procedures" that control the dissemination of information collected by the FBI pursuant to the Foreign Intelligence Surveillance Act (FISA) addresses the legal issue of the appropriate relationship between the law enforcement and foreign intelligence aspects of counterterrorism investigation. Historically, the U.S. Government has recognized two distinct, albeit occasionally overlapping, spheres of investigative activity; domestic criminal investigations and foreign intelligence collection. The former is the exclusive province of federal, state and local law enforcement agencies; the National Security Act of 1947 forbids the CIA from having any internal security or law enforcement powers. Domestic law enforcement activity is carefully circumscribed by constitutional protections in the 4th, 5th, and 6th amendments and various statutory controls on electronic surveillance and physical searches. In general, the government is required to establish probable cause to believe a search will obtain evidence of criminal activity in order to obtain a search warrant in a criminal investigation.

Foreign intelligence collection, on the other hand, is the responsibility of the Intelligence Community under the guidance of the DCI. Collection of such information is carefully regulated when U.S. persons are the targets or when electronic surveillance or physical searches are conducted in the United States against foreign powers or their agents pursuant to FISA. The rules governing foreign intelligence collection are different than those pertaining to the collection and dissemination of information for law enforcement purposes. In general, this differentiation is explained by the national security purpose of foreign intelligence collection, i.e, to enable the conduct of foreign policy and military operations and to counter hostile intelligence services and international terrorists. While it is possible that evidence of criminal conduct may be obtained in the course of such a surveillance, the FISC's May 17 opinion holds that the acquisition of such evidence may not be the primary purpose of such a surveillance. Surveillance for domestic law enforcement purposes, by contrast, obviously may be conducted for the purpose of subsequent criminal prosecution.

The existence of two categories of surveillance rules and the perceived need to keep them discrete raises practical problems in managing an investigation that straddles the divide as counterintelligence and counterterrorism investigations often do. The first question is whether to apply criminal or foreign intelligence rules in a particular case. The second is how to regulate coordination and interaction between intelligence and law enforcement personnel.

One way to ensure against violation of rules limiting such coordination and interaction is the imposition of a "wall" that requires someone not involved in either the foreign intelligence surveillance or the criminal investigation to decide what information should be passed from intelligence personnel to criminal investigators. That is one issue the FISC addresses in the May 2002 opinion mentioned above.

There is, however, a second type of wall that can also limit the flow of information to criminal investigators from intelligence agencies; that wall exists to protect foreign intelligence sources and methods from disclosure in a criminal prosecution. Intelligence agencies often provide information to the FBI, for example, with a limitation that it may only be used for lead purposes as distinct from evidentiary purposes. In the case of al-Mihdhar and al-Hazmi, evidently, assisting the important *USS Cole* criminal investigation was deemed insufficient to justify breaching the "wall" that prevented the full sharing of relevant intelligence information with the agents handling that criminal investigation.

An August 29, 2001 e-mail exchange between FBI headquarters and a FBI agent in New York is illustrative. The agent, who had been involved in the *Cole* criminal investigation since the day of that attack, asked FBI headquarters to allow New York to use the full criminal investigative resources available to the FBI to find al-Mihdhar. Headquarters responded that its National Security Law Unit advised that this could not be done. This was the exchange:

- From FBI Headquarters: "A criminal agent CAN NOT be present at the interview. This case, in its entirety, is based on [intelligence]. If at such time as information is developed indicating the existence of a substantial federal crime, that information will be passed over the wall according to the proper procedures and turned over for follow-up criminal investigation." [Emphasis in original.]
- From FBI agent, New York: "Whatever has happened to this—someday someone will die—and wall or not—the public will not understand why we were not more effective and throwing every resource we had at certain 'problems.' Let's hope the [FBI's] National Security Law Unit will stand behind their decisions then, especially since the biggest threat to us now. UBL is getting the most "protection.'"

Within two weeks after the September 11 attacks, the FBI prepared an analysis of Bin Ladin's responsibility as part of the State Department's development of a "White Paper" that could be shared with foreign governments. That analysis relied, at least in part, on the connection between the attack on the *USS Cole* investigation and al-Mihdhar and al-Hazmi:

> Even at this early state of the investigations, the FBI has developed compelling evidence which points to Usama Bin Ladin an al-Qa'ida as the perpetrators of this attack. By way of illustration, at least two of the hijackers met with a senior al-Qa'ida terrorist, the same al-Qa'ida terrorist which reliable information demonstrates orchestrated the attack on the *USS Cole* and who was involved in the planning of the East Africa Embassy Bombings.

The two hijackers referred to were al-Mihdhar and al-Hazmi. The senior al-Qa'ida terrorist was Khallad. The place that they met was Malaysia. Thus, the facts linking these two individuals to Khallad and therefore to Usama Bin Ladin formed the crux of the case made by the State Department to governments around the world that Usama Bin Ladin should be held accountable for the September 11 attacks.

Source: Select Committee on Intelligence U.S. Senate and the Permanent Select Committee of Intelligence House of Representatives, *Joint Inquiry into Intelligence Community Activities before and after the Terrorist Attacks of Sept. 11, 2001* (Washington, DC: U.S. Government Printing Office, 2004), vol.1, pp. 310–330.

Document 28

Statement of a Special Agent of the Federal Bureau of Investigation (September 20, 2002)

In a statement before the Joint Committee on Intelligence, an unnamed FBI special agent expressed his unhappiness with "the wall" that separated intelligence gathering from criminal investigations. This barrier meant that once a criminal investigation had been launched, information could no longer be shared with the intelligence-gathering agents in the FBI or with any other agency of the U.S. government. Legal opinion at FBI headquarters was that this distinction was sacrosanct. Even if the information concerned national security there could be no exceptions. This reasoning was part of the FBI's risk-avoidance strategy before September 11.

Mr. Chairmen, Vice Chairman Shelby, Ranking Member Pelosi, and members of the Committees, I am a Special Agent of the Federal Bureau of Investigation assigned to the New York field office. I appreciate your invitation to appear before your committees today in connection with you Joint Inquiry into the tragic events of September 11, 2001. I fully understand the responsibility with which you have been charged. I intend to cooperated with you and answer your questions to the best of my ability.

I am speaking to you today as an individual agent. The views I express, therefore, are my own, not necessarily those of the FBI, although I believe that my concerns are shared by many fellow agents. I hope by appearing here today I might help in a small way to assure that the men and women of the FBI and others in the Intelligence Community, have access to the information necessary to carry out their sworn duty to protect the people of the United States.

I have no wish in the remarks that follow to be critical of any person. Whether they are at (FBI) Headquarters or in the field, FBI personnel work their hearts out to perform our mission. I am before you today to address practices that frustrate us all. Much has been written about how the FBI does not share information with local law enforcement agencies, but the American people must realize that the FBI does not always have access to the information itself, nor is all information the FBI possesses available to all of its agents. It is my belief that the former problem is due to the fear that the Bureau may "run ahead" or "mess up" a current or future operation of one of our sister agencies—and the latter is primarily due to decisions that have snowballed our of the Foreign Intelligence Surveillance Act (FISA) Court. A concept known as "The Wall" has been created within the Law Enforcement and Intelligence Communities. From my perspective, and in its broadest sense—"The Wall" is an information barrier placed between elements of an intelligence investigation and those of a criminal investigation. In theory— again same perspective—it is there to ensure that we, the FBI, play by the rules in our attempts to gather evidence in a criminal case and Federal prosecution.

I have tried to write this statement knowing full well that its contents and my testimony will be studied by the enemy. Along those lines—much detail has been left out and if I may humbly remind everyone that questions regarding sources, other possible operations, and investigative methods in this forum should be approached with extreme caution.

As an aside, may I say I firmly believe prevention is best served by allowing the Law Enforcement Community—Federal and local—to conduct sound, sometimes exigent investigations, with access to all information that the US Government and Liaison Governments possesses. These investigations build sources, evidence, connections and information—and are not simply reactive. I would like to assure the American people that in my almost seven (7) years in the Bureau, the FBI has always been in the Prevention—if I may—"Game."

Before going further, I would like to offer a few words of introduction so that you [are] aware of the background that I bring to the questions before the Committees. Between 1985 and 1993, I served in the military. After a brief stint in the private sector, I joined the FBI in December 1995, and was assigned to the New York Field Office's Joint Terrorism Task Force in July 1996. From July 1996 through October 1997, I worked on the TWA Flight 800 investigation. In October 1997, I was assigned to the squad that had responsibilities for Taliban and Pakistan matters. Following the East Africa Embassy bombings in August 1998, I was part of the first team on the ground, spending a cumulative total of over 30 weeks abroad investigating the bombings.

In early 1999, I joined the New York Field Office's Usama Bin Laden (UBL) case squad, which is responsible for the overall investigation of UBL and Al-Qaeda. Immediately after the attack on the USS Cole in Aden, Yemen on October 12, 2000, I was assigned as one of the case agents and worked on that case—Adenbom—until the attacks of September 11, 2001. Since then I have also worked on general UBL matters and have been deployed 12 weeks overseas, working along side other Intelligence Community components. I mention this fact because, although there are issues about the sharing of information with FBI investigators by the CIA—my experience is the FBI and the Intelligence Community have worked successfully together. The people of the United States should take great pride in the service and sacrifice of the men and women of all the US Agencies and DOD deployed overseas—many of whom I have had the privilege of working with overseas.

Briefly, "The Wall" and implied, interpreted, created or assumed restrictions regarding it, prevented myself and other FBI Agents working a criminal case of the

New York Field Office from obtaining information from the Intelligence Community, regarding Khalid Al-Mihdhar and Nawaf Al-Hazmi in a meeting on June 11, 2001. At the time, there was reason to believe that Al-Mihdhar and Al-Hazmi had met with a suspect connected to the attack against the USS Cole. The situation came to a head during the fourth week of August 2001, when, after it was learned that Al-Mihdhar was in the country, FBI HQ representatives said that FBI New York was compelled to open an "intelligence case" and that I nor any of the other "criminal case" investigators assigned to track Al-Qaeda could attempt to locate him. This resulted in a series of e-mails between myself and the FBI HQ analyst working the matter.

In my e-mails, I asked where this "The New Wall" was defined. I wrote on August 29, 2001: "Whatever has happened to this—someday someone will die—and wall or not—the public will not understand why we were not more effective and throwing every resource we had at certain 'problems'. Let's hope the National Security Law Unit will stand behind their decisions then, especially since the biggest threat to us now, UBL, is getting the most protection." I was told in response that "we [at Headquarters] are all frustrated with this issue," but "These are the rules. NSLU does not make them up." I hope, Messrs. Chairmen, these proceedings are the time to break down the barriers and change the system which makes it difficult for all of us, whether we work at FBI, HQ or in the field, at the FBI or elsewhere, to have and be able to act on the information that we need to do our jobs.

Personally, I do not hold any US Government affiliated individual or group of individuals responsible for the attacks on September 11, 2001. I truly believe that if given a chance, anyone of them would given or sacrificed anything to have prevented what occurred. Then, and now, I hold the system responsible. Information is power in this system of Intelligence and Law Enforcement. This will never change—nor could or should it. In addition to "The Wall", the system as it currently exists, however, seduces some managers, agents, analysts, and officers into protecting turf and being the first to know and brief those above. Often these sadly mistaken individuals, use "The Wall" described herein, and others—real and imagined—to control that information.

I, myself, still have two key questions today that I believe are important for this committee to answer. The detailed answers to them will deserve, and be afforded, the scrutiny of a nation, and must stand the test of time and exhaustive investigation. First, if the CIA passed information regarding Al-Mihdhar and Al-Hazmi to the FBI prior to the June 11, 2001 meeting—in either January 2000 or January 2001—then why was that information not passed, either by CIA or FBI Headquarters personnel immediately to the New York case agents, criminal or "Intel", investigating the murder of 17 sailors in Yemen when more information was requested? A simple answer of "The Wall" is unacceptable. Second, how and when did we, the CIA and the FBI, learn that Al-Mihdhar came into the country on either or both occasions, in January 2000 and or July 2001 and what did we do with the information?

On September 11, 2001, I spent the morning on the streets with other agents and Joint Terrorism Task Force (JFFT) personnel around the World Trade Center, providing whatever help we could. I and several of my co-workers were within blocks when both towers came down. Within minutes of the second strike on the

Southern Tower, we asked a senior fireman heading towards the South Tower what we could do. At the time, he was getting out of his fire truck and looking at the towers. By the Grace of God he turned to us and replied that he did not know what we could do—but that we were not going anywhere close to the buildings without a respirator. I do not know who he was but I truly believed he saved our lives. I also believe that based on the direction that he was looking, towards the Southern Tower, that moments later he entered that tower and perished in the attack. It's taken a while for his response, but I believe that the task before this committee, and in some small way—me being here today—is what that brave fireman is telling us, all of us, "what we can do."

If we do not change the system—if I may say again—"someday someone will die—and wall or not—the public will not understand why we were not more effective and throwing every resource we had at certain 'problems'."

Thank you for this opportunity and privilege of appearing before you today. I would, of course, welcome your questions.

Source: Select Committee on Intelligence U.S. Senate and the Permanent Select Committee of Intelligence House of Representatives, *Joint Inquiry into Intelligence Community Activities before and after the Terrorist Attacks of Sept. 11, 2001* (Washington, DC: U.S. Government Printing Office, 2004), vol.1, pp. 368–370.

Document 29

Report of the Joint Inquiry Staff by Eleanor Hill on the FBI's Handling of the Phoenix Electronic Communication (September 24, 2002)

One of the controversies of the September 11 investigations was the failure of the FBI headquarters to react to the report of an FBI's Phoenix field agent about the number of Middle Eastern men taking pilot lessons and the potential danger to U.S. security. The Joint Inquiry Staff investigated this failure and presented its report on September 24, 2002, before the Joint Senate and House Committees on Intelligence.

The Phoenix Electronic Communication

The Joint Inquiry Staff's interim statement to the Committees on September 18, 2002 discussed the indications of an impending terrorist attack detected by the Intelligence Community in the summer of 2001 and the warnings that intelligence resulted in. In that same timeframe, an FBI special agent in the FBI's Phoenix field office generated a document that has been subsequently described in media reports as the "Phoenix memo." It is known within the FBI as the Phoenix Electronic Communication, or "Phoenix EC." "EC" is an FBI term of art. ECs are the primary type of document used by the FBI for internal communications. In this statement, we use the terms "Phoenix memo" and "Phoenix EC" interchangeably.

The Joint Inquiry Staff reviewed the Phoenix EC and its handling by FBI headquarters with the following questions in mind:

- What did the EC say?
- Why did the special agent write it?
- Who handled it within FBI headquarters and what reaction did it elicit?
- Does FBI headquarters' handling of the document illuminate any broader, systemic problems within the FBI?

Introduction

On July 10, 2001, a Special Agent (SA) in the FBI's Phoenix Division sent an EC to individuals in the Usama Bin Ladin Unit (UBLU) and the Radical Fundamentalist Unit (RFU) within the Counterterrorism Division at FBI headquarters and to several SAs on an International Terrorism squad in the New York Field Office. In the EC, the SA outlined his concerns that there was a coordinated effort underway by Usama Bin Ladin to send students to the United States for civil aviation-related training. He noted that there were an "inordinate number of individuals of investigative interest" attending this type of training in Arizona and speculated that this was part of an effort to establish a cadre of individuals in civil aviation, who would be in position to conduct terrorist activity in the future.

The EC contained a number of recommendations that the agent asked FBI headquarters to consider implementing. Apparently, the communication did not raise any alarms at FBI headquarters or in the New York office. In fact, New York personnel who reviewed the EC found it to be speculative and not particularly significant. New York already knew that many Middle Eastern flight students, including several associated with Bin Ladin, trained in the United States. They believed that Bin Ladin needed pilots to transport goods and personnel in Afghanistan, and, at the time, viewed pilots connected to Bin Ladin in that light. About a week after its receipt, headquarters personnel determined that no follow-up action was warranted in the Phoenix EC recommendations. No managers at FBI headquarters took part in that decision or even saw the communication before September 11, 2001. No one apparently considered the significance of the Phoenix EC in light of what else confronted the FBI counterterrorist team during the summer of 2001: the unprecedented increase in terrorist threat reporting, the investigation and arrest of Zacarias Moussaoui in August 2001, and the possible presence of Bin Ladin associates al-Mihdhar and al-Hazmi in the United States.

Our review of the circumstances surrounding the Phoenix memo reveals a number of weaknesses at the FBI that, if left uncorrected, will continue to undercut counterterrorist efforts. The FBI handling of the Phoenix EC is symptomatic of a focus on short-term operational priorities, often at the expense of long-term, strategic analysis. Throughout this review, we have found that the FBI's ability to handle strategic analytic products, such as the Phoenix EC, was, at best, limited prior to September 11, 2001. Inadequate information sharing within the FBI, particularly between the operational and analytic units, is also highlighted by our review of the Phoenix EC. Several of the addresses on the EC, especially at the supervisory level, did not receive it prior to September 11 due to limitations in the electronic dissemination system. Those limitations are consistent with the complaints we have repeatedly heard throughout this inquiry about the FBI's technology problems. Finally, the case-driven, law enforcement approach, while important and extremely productive in terms of the FBI's traditional mission, does not generally "incentivize" attention to big-picture, preventive analysis and strategy. This is particularly true where there is no direct and immediate impact on an ongoing criminal prosecution.

In that context, the Joint Inquiry Staff found that the Phoenix memo was not the first time the FBI had confronted concerns about Middle Eastern individuals studying aviation topics in the United States. In 1998, the FBI's chief pilot in Oklahoma City drafted a memo expressing concern about the number of Middle

Eastern flight students there and his belief that they could be planning a terrorist attack. Also in 1998, the FBI had received reporting that a terrorist organization planned to bring students to the United States to study aviation and that a member of that organization had frequently expressed an intention to target civil aviation in the United States. Yet another terrorist organization, in 1999, allegedly wanted to do the same thing, triggering a request from FBI headquarters to 24 field officers to investigate and determine the level of the threat. To date, our review has found that the field officers conducted little to no investigation in response to that request.

Our inquiry found that, given the lack of information sharing across units in FBI headquarters, personnel who saw the Phoenix memo had no knowledge of any of these prior instances involving other terrorist groups. Since the prior reporting did not directly relate to al-Qa'ida, they were unable to evaluate the Phoenix EC in the context of what was known about likely terrorist strategies favored by other, similar groups. As terrorist groups increasingly associate with and support each other, information sharing and overarching strategic analysis is critical to success in counterterrorist efforts. This is particularly important to the FBI's efforts here in the United States, where the members of the various groups tend to associate with each other.

Finally, while the Phoenix EC does not include by name any of the hijackers involved in the September 11, 2001 attacks, our review confirmed that the FBI now believes that one of the individuals named in the EC was connected to Hani Hanjour, who is now believed to have piloted American Flight 77. The individual named in the EC has been connected both through witness statements and flight school records to Hanjour. This individual first came to the attention of the FBI in 1999, but when the FBI went to investigate him, they determined that he had left the United States, and an investigation was not opened. The FBI was apparently unaware that he had returned to the United States in the summer of 2001 and may have been associating with Hanjour and several other Islamic extremists. These issues will be discussed at greater length in subsequent sections.

Summary of the Phoenix EC

In an interview with the Joint Inquiry Staff, the special agent in Phoenix who wrote the EC said that he first became concerned about aviation-related terrorism in the early 1990s. He was working on two cases in which Libyans with suspected terrorist ties were working for U.S. aviation companies. One of these individuals had a Masters degree in a technical field, yet was working in menial jobs at the airport as a skycap and then a baggage handler. The other individual was working as a technical avionics officer for a domestic airline and was charged with overseeing the complete overhaul of aircraft and with checking for structural integrity. In addition, several Bin Ladin operatives had lived and traveled to the Phoenix area in the past, one of whom was Wadih El-Hage, a Bin Ladin lieutenant convicted for his role in the 1998 embassy bombings. He had lived in the Tucson area for several years in the 1980s. The Phoenix SA believes that El-Hage established a Usama Bin Ladin support network in Arizona while he was living there and that this network is still in place.

The agent stated that the idea of possible terrorists having easy access to aircraft conjured up visions of Pan Am 103. The Phoenix agent told the Joint Inquiry

Staff that, in authoring the EC, he never imagined terrorists using airplanes as was done on September 11. His primary concern was that Islamic extremists, studying everything from aviation security to flying, could be learning how to hijack or destroy aircraft and to evade airport security.

In April 2000, the agent interviewed the individual who was the subject of the Phoenix EC. When he interviews foreign nationals they usually tend to be at least somewhat intimidated in their first contact with the FBI. By contrast, this individual told the agent directly that he considered the U.S. government and military legitimate targets of Islam. In looking around the individual's apartment, the agent noticed a poster of Bin Ladin and another poster of wounded Chechnyan mujaheddin fighters. He was also concerned by the fact that this individual was from a poor Middle Eastern country and had been studying a non-aviation related subject prior to his arrival in the United States.

The agent also described for us another incident that increased his suspicion about the Middle Eastern flight students in the Phoenix area. During a physical surveillance of the subject of the Phoenix EC, the agent determined that he was using a vehicle registered to another individual. In 1999, the owner of the car and an associate of his were detained for trying to gain access to the cockpit of a commercial airliner on a domestic flight. They told the FBI that they thought the cockpit was the bathroom and they accused the FBI of racism. They were released after an investigation, the FBI closed the case, and the two were not prosecuted. A year later, the individual's name was added to the State Department's watchlist after intelligence information was received indicating that he may have gotten explosive and car bomb training in Afghanistan. In August 2001, the same individual applied for a visa to re-enter the United States and, as a result of the watchlisting, was denied entry.

In May 2001, after a brief time investigating a series of arsons, the Phoenix special agent was reassigned to work international terrorism matters. To get back up to speed, he reviewed case files of terrorism cases on his squad. In the course of the review, he became increasingly concerned by the number of individuals of potential investigative interest enrolled in aviation training. At that point, he began to draft the EC, which he completed by July 10, 2001.

The Phoenix EC focuses on 10 individuals who were the subjects of FBI investigations. These individuals were Sunni Muslim, and were from Kenya, Pakistan, Algeria, the United Arab Emirates, India, and Saudi Arabia. Not all were in flight training; several were aeronautical engineering students, and one was studying international aviation security. One of the individuals under investigation was the primary focus of the Phoenix EC.

This individual had come to the Phoenix agent's attention when it was learned that he was a member of the al-Muhajiroun, whose spiritual leader was a strong supporter of Bin Ladin and who had issued a number of *fatwas* against the United States, one mentioning airports as a possible target. The subject of the Phoenix investigation was enrolled at Embry Riddle University and was taking aviation-related security courses. As a member of the al-Muhajiroun, he was organizing anti-U.S. and anti-Israeli rallies and calling for jihad. The investigation of this individual led to the opening of investigations on six of his associates, also involved in aviation training. The remaining three subjects in the Phoenix EC, although involved in aviation subjects, were not known to associate with the others.

We asked the Phoenix agent whether he had received any intelligence from FBI headquarters or from other Intelligence Community agencies that contributed to the suspicions he raised in the EC. According to him, the Phoenix office did not receive FBI, Intelligence Community, or foreign intelligence service products on a regular basis. He told us that he believes that prior to September 11, 2001 the FBI was not running counterterrorism as a national level program; he often has felt that he's "out on an island" in Phoenix. He said that, prior to headquarters downsizing, the FBI used to do a better job of disseminating intelligence products to the field. He does not believe that sufficient resources are devoted to counterterrorism even though it is officially a Tier I program. In his words, counterterrorism and counterintelligence have always been considered the "bastard stepchild" of the FBI because these programs do not generate the statistics that other programs do, such as Violent Crimes/Major Offenders or drugs.

The Phoenix EC makes four recommendations and requests that FBI headquarters consider implementing them:

- Headquarters should accumulate a list of civil aviation university/colleges around the country;
- FBI offices should establish liaison with the schools;
- Headquarters should discuss the Phoenix theories with the intelligence community;
- Headquarters should consider seeking authority to obtain visa information on individuals seeking to attend flight schools.

Phoenix Office's Actions Prior to Sending the EC

While he was developing the EC, the Phoenix agent attended a meeting in May-June 2000 of a local intelligence working group. At the meeting the agent told the attendees about the individual under investigation who was attending Embry Riddle University. He asked if anyone had information on Islamic extremists showing up at aviation schools. No one offered any information. The agent told the Joint Inquiry Staff that he had also discussed his theories with other members of the Phoenix Joint Terrorism Task Force. The Joint Inquiry Staff's examination of records had determined that he also requested the routine intelligence community checks be run on the subjects of the EC. In March 2001, the agent's supervisor in Phoenix attended a meeting in Long Beach where he mentioned the Phoenix theories about civil aviation. The CIA was made aware of the FBI information, but had no relevant information to offer.

As he was drafting the EC, the Phoenix agent contacted an Intelligence Operations Specialist (IOS) at FBI headquarters whom he had known for a number of years to use as a sounding board. The IOS provided him with several names to include on the addressee list. Around the same time, another agent at the same Phoenix squad called the FAA's counterterrorism representative at FBI headquarters to inquire about the legality of the Middle Eastern students attending aviation schools. The FAA representative said that, as long as the students were in legal immigration status, their attendance was legal.

Headquarters' Response to the EC

When he sent the EC to the Counterterrorism Division at FBI headquarters the Phoenix agent requested in a "lead" that both the RFU and UBLU consider implementing the suggested actions that he had set out.[1] On July 30, 2001, an Intelligence Assistant (IA) in the RFU at FBI headquarters assigned the lead to an IOS. The IOS appears to have been picked, not because the assignment was within her programmatic area of responsibility, but because her name was the first non-supervisory name on the addressee list. At the time, this was typical of the way in which leads were assigned in the unit. The IOS recalls the lead arriving in her electronic folder on the system but did not receive a hard copy of the document from the IA. After reviewing the EC, the IOS determined that the project should be handled by someone in the UBLU.

The RFU IOS contacted a UBLU IOS to effect a transfer. The UBLU IOS did not want the lead transferred but agreed to take responsibility for her unit's response. The UBLU IOS also received a hard copy of the document. The UBLU IOS then consulted two other IOSs in her unit, mentioning specifically the paragraph in the EC about obtaining visa information. Their discussion centered on the legality of the proposal and whether it raised profiling issues. The IOS also decided to forward the EC to the Portland office because an individual named in the EC, with ties to suspected terrorists arrested in the Middle East in early 2001, was an employee of an airline and had previously lived and studied in the northwestern United States.

On August 7, 2001, after receiving no objection from the Phoenix office, the EC was forwarded to an intelligence analyst in Portland via e-mail, stating that the document "basically puts forth a theory on individuals being directed to come here to study aviation and their ties to extremists. Nothing concrete or whatever, but some very interesting coincidences. I thought it would be interesting to you considering some of the stuff you were coming up with in PD [Portland]. Let me know if anything strikes you." The Portland analyst has told the Joint Inquiry Staff that she had spoken to the UBLU IOS on several occasions about the aviation-related ties of terrorist subjects in the Portland and Seattle areas. She did not take action on the communication or disseminate it any further, as it was only sent to her for informational purposes.

The UBLU IOS informed the Joint Inquiry Staff that she affixed a note to her copy of the EC, on which she jotted down several items to follow up on. She recalls that her first item was to review the intelligence investigations of another individual who was the only Usama Bin Ladin pilot she knew about.[2] She assumes she would have also written that she should call agents in two FBI field offices who

---

[1] This is an FBI system through which the office sending a communication can request that the receiving office(s) take some follow-up action or conduct additional investigation. In the "lead" section of the communication, the sending office can outline exactly what action or investigation that it is requesting that the receiving office conduct. Once the lead has been completed (or "covered" in FBI vernacular), the receiving office will inform the sending office as to the results of the investigation or as to the action taken.

[2] According to documents reviewed by the Joint Inquiry, this individual was not the only pilot with ties to Usama Bin Ladin known to the FBI at that time.

were familiar with this individual. The note was on her copy of the EC that she provided to the Department of Justice Inspector General (IG). The IG has informed the Joint Inquiry Staff that they recall seeing the note during their interview of the IOS but cannot locate it.

On August 7, 2001, both IOSs decided that the lead should be closed. In the electronic system, the RFU IOS noted that the lead was "covered-consulted with UBLU, no action at this time, will reconvine [sic] on this issue." The UBLU IOS maintains that she fully intended to return to the project once she had time to do additional research, but that September 11 occurred, and she had not yet had an opportunity to return to the project.

Both IOSs also said they considered assigning the Phoenix project to a headquarters analytic unit but decided against it. In an interview with a supervisory agent in the UBLU, the Joint Inquiry Staff was told that the EC should have been assigned to an analytic unit because it was a long-term, labor-intensive suggestion, and the analytic units would have more time to devote to it then the operational units. There appear to be a number of factors bearing on why the project was not assigned to the analysts that will be discussed later in this statement.

Did FBI Headquarters Management Review the Phoenix EC Prior to September 11?

The chiefs of both the RFU and UBLU informed the Joint Inquiry Staff that they did not see the Phoenix communication prior to September 11. Moreover, neither remembers even hearing about the flight school issue until after September 11. At the Joint Inquiry Staff's request the FBI audited their central records system; the audit supports their statements.

Both the IOSs are unsure, but think they might have mentioned the EC to their unit chiefs prior to September 11. The UBLU IOS said in an interview with the Joint Inquiry Staff that she told her supervisor that Phoenix had sent in a communication about Usama Bin Ladin sending pilots for training and that she planned to do some research before determining what to do about the recommendations in the EC. However, in her interview with the Department of Justice IG in November 2001, she stated that she had not discussed the EC with any supervisory personnel until after the EC was closed. The RFU IOS said she could not recall but might have mentioned the EC to her supervisor in passing.

FBI Headquarters Weaknesses Demonstrated by Handling of Phoenix EC

The manner in which FBI headquarters handled the Phoenix EC provides a valuable window into the FBI's operational environment prior to September 11 and illustrates several procedural weaknesses that have been recognized and are currently being corrected.

The manner in which the Phoenix EC was handled demonstrated how strategic analysis took a back seat to operational priorities prior to September 11. That many in the U.S. Government believed an attack of some type was imminent in the summer of 2001 apparently only served to further de-emphasize strategic analysis. For example, the IOS handling the Phoenix EC was primarily concerned with an individual in the EC who was connected to individuals arrested overseas; the IOS paid less attention to the flight school theories. For his part, the RFU Chief said he was seeing about 1000 pieces of mail daily and could not keep up. His solution was to assign the review of intelligence reports to his IOS. Even the analytic unit responsible for strategic analysis was largely producing tactical products to satisfy the operational section. In fact there was no requirement to handle projects with nationwide impact, such as the Phoenix EC, any different than any other project. This has now been changed. Any lead of the type such as Phoenix represented now can be raised to the section chief level.

The handling of the Phoenix EC also exposed information sharing problems between FBI headquarters elements. A number of analysts commented that the UBLU and RFU frequently do not share information with the International Terrorism Analytic Unit. The supervisor of the UBLU said that the Investigative Services Division, of which the analytic unit is a part, was not a major player and that often information was not shared with it.

Had the project been transferred to the analytic unit, the capability to conduct strategic analysis on al-Qa'ida was limited because five of the unit's analysts had transferred into operational units. The Joint Inquiry Staff has been told that every time a competent new analyst arrived, the UBLU or RFU would either try to recruit them as IOSs or would refuse to share information. This allowed the UBLU and RFU to control the information flow. The end result, unfortunately, is that there is no one left whose role is to perform strategic analysis.

Even if the project had been assigned to the al-Qa'ida analyst in the analytic unit, there can be no guarantee that the various reports about using airplanes as weapons and terrorists sending students to flight school in the United States would have been pieced together. However, there was only one analytic unit at FBI headquarters responsible for counterterrorism, and there were five operational units. It is easier to share information within one unit than it is among five units.

The handling of the Phoenix EC also illustrates the extent to which technological limitations affect information flow at the FBI. A number of individuals who were addressees on the EC have stated that they did not see it prior to September 11. Audits of the system support their statements. The FBI's electronic system is not designed to ensure that all addressees on a communication actually receive it. Instead the electronic version of the document is sent to the unit and then forwarded electronically only to the individual to whom the lead is assigned. Furthermore, the system is capable of recognizing units only if they are precisely designated in the leads section; otherwise, a unit would not receive the communication. In the case of an inaccurate address the communication would be sent into either the Counterterrorism Division's main electronic folder or to the International Terrorism Operations Section's folder where it would sit until the secretaries checked their folders and forwarded it on to the appropriate unit for handling. In fact, the electronic system was considered so unreliable that many FBI personnel, both at the field offices and FBI headquarters, use e-mail instead. In the case of important communications, they double-check to ensure it is not being neglected. Several FBI personnel interviewed conceded that it was possible that "routine" leads, on which there was no direct communication, were falling through the cracks. RFU and UBLU policies in effect at the time the Phoenix EC was sent gave the person to whom the lead was assigned the discretion to make the determination as to which people in the unit needed to see the report. One person said that he was not certain why the Phoenix agent put all the addresses on the EC but believes the IOS probably made the decision that this was more of an issue for the UBLU and did not need to be routed around to all of the people on the addressee list in the RFU.

The Joint Inquiry Staff has been informed that the FBI recently determined that there are 68,000 outstanding and unassigned leads assigned to the counterterrorism division dating back to 1995. Since many FBI personnel have not been using the electronic system for these purposes, it is difficult to know how many of these leads have actually been completed. The counterterrorism division's management is currently looking into this situation.[3]

Links from the Phoenix EC to September 11, 2001

FBI officials have noted, both in public statements and Congressional testimony that the September 11 hijackers did not associate with anyone of investigative interest. However, there is evidence that hijacker Hani Hanjour, who was unknown to the Intelligence Community and law enforcement agencies prior to September 11, 2001, was an associate of an individual mentioned in the Phoenix EC. This individual had been engaged in flight training in the United States, and the FBI believed that he was possibly a radical fundamentalist. The evidence connecting this individual to Hanjour is described below. There are several possible reasons, which will also be discussed below, why this individual's association with Hanjour did not bring Hanjour to the FBI's attention prior to September 11, 2001.

The FBI believes that, beginning in 1997, Hanjour and the individual named in the Phoenix EC trained together at a flight school in Arizona. Several instructors at the flight school say they were associates and one thinks they may have carpooled together. Through various record checks, the FBI has confirmed five occasions when the Phoenix subject and Hanjour were at the flight school on the same day. On one occasion in 1999, the flight school logs indicate that Hanjour and this individual used the same plane. According to the flight instructor, the individual mentioned in the Phoenix EC was there as an observer. The rules of the flight school were such that for this individual to observe, Hanjour would have had to approve of his presence in the aircraft. Another individual informed the FBI after September 11, 2001 that this individual and Hanjour knew each other, both from flight training and through a religious center in Arizona.

The FBI's evidence linking the two in the summer of 2001 is not as strong. The FBI has located records from a flight school in Phoenix indicating that on one day in June 2001, Hanjour and several other individuals signed up to use the Cessna simulator. The next day, the two individuals who signed up with Hanjour the previous day, came to the facility with the individual mentioned in the Phoenix EC. An employee of the flight school has informed the FBI that he recalls a fourth individual being there with him but cannot remember who. Another employee of the flight school has placed Hanjour and this individual together during that time frame, although she was not completely confident in her identification.

---

[3]The Joint Inquiry Staff has asked the FBI for further details and explanation on the status of these outstanding leads, and what actions are being taken to address this situation.

The FBI attempted to investigate this individual in May 2001, but discovered that he was out of the country. The FBI was apparently unaware that he returned to the United States soon after, and may have been associating with Hanjour and several other Islamic extremists.[4] A Phoenix agent told the JIS that had the individual been in the country in May 2001, they would have opened an investigation. However, the Phoenix office generally did not open investigations on individuals whom they believed had permanently left the United States. Although there were no legal bars to opening an investigation. FBI HQ discouraged this practice. The Phoenix office also did not notify the INS, State Department, or the CIA of their interest in this individual.

No one can say whether the FBI would have developed an investigative interest in Hanjour had they opened an investigation on the individual mentioned in the Phoenix EC prior to September 11, 2001. The Joint Inquiry Staff is also not suggesting that if they had, it would have necessarily led to the discovery of the September 11 plot. However, this example provides additional evidence that at least some of the hijackers may have been less isolated and more integrated into their communities than was previously thought. If the hijackers were, in fact, associating with individuals of investigative interest, and were not keeping to themselves as has been portrayed, there are more significant questions as to whether or not they should have come to the FBI's attention prior to the attacks. These associations continue to raise questions about the FBI's knowledge and understanding of the radical fundamentalist network in the United States prior to September 11, 2001.

This case also raises question about the FBI's policy and practice prior to September 11, 2001 regarding the initiation of investigations on individuals outside of the United States. The Phoenix FBI agent noted that this policy and practice have since been changed. It also provides a valuable illustration of how crucial it is for the FBI to coordinate its investigations internally and with other U.S. Government agencies, particularly when individuals are traveling into and out of the United States.

For this system to work effectively, and for the FBI to be aware when individuals of previous investigative interest return to the United States, they have to have close contact with INS and CIA. Unfortunately, it appears that prior to September 11, 2001, there was no system in place to ensure coordination. In this case, the FBI did not notify the INS, State Department, or the CIA of their interest in the Phoenix subject. Therefore, this individual was able to get into the United States without any notification to the FBI that he had returned. Supposedly coordination with INS and CIA is much better now, and the FBI does a better job of notification to those agencies.

Finally, the Phoenix subject's name was not provided to the TIPOFF watchlist at the State Department nor the NAILS watchlist at INS. The individual's name and information regarding his terrorist associations and background were provided to the TIPOFF program by the FBI and the CIA after the September 11

---

[4]The Joint Inquiry Staff is still attempting to determine whether the FBI's Phoenix office was aware of this individual's presence in the United States in the summer of 2001. The JIS has interviewed three agents in Phoenix about this issue, and received slightly contradictory answers. The JIS has asked the FBI for clarification on this issue.

attacks. It is only by identifying this individual to the TIPOFF and NAILS watch-list that the FBI could have been assured that he would be kept out of the United States.

Previous FBI Focus at U.S. Flight Schools

The Phoenix EC was not the first occasion that the FBI had been concerned about terrorist groups sending individuals to the United States for aviation study. The EC should be understood in this broader context. It is also important to note that neither individuals involved in drafting the Phoenix EC nor the FBI personnel who worked on it at FBI headquarters were aware of this broader context.

In 1981, the U.S. military was involved in hostilities with the Libyan Air Force in the Gulf of Sidra. President Reagan made the decision to deport all Libyan students in the Untied Stated involved in either aviation or nuclear studies. In May 1983, the INS published a rule in the Federal Register, terminating the nonimmigrant status of Libyan nationals or individuals acting on behalf of Libyan entities engaged in aviation-or nuclear-related education. The INS turned to the FBI for assistance in locating any such individuals. On May 6, 1983, FBI headquarters sent a "priority" communication to all field offices, asking the field offices for assistance in complying with the INS request. The Joint Inquiry Staff has not been able to locate all of the relevant records, so it is not clear how many students the FBI located and deported.

In 1998, the Chief Pilot of the FBI's Oklahoma City Field Office contacted an agent on the office's counterterrorism squad to inform him that he had observed a large number of Middle Eastern males at Oklahoma flight schools. An intra-office communication to the counterterrorism squad supervisor was drafted noting the Chief Pilot's concern that the aviation education might be related to planned terrorist activity, and his speculation that light planes would be an ideal means of spreading chemical or biological agents. The communication was sent to the office's "Weapons of Mass Destruction" control file. It appears to have been for informational purposes only. There is no indication that any follow-up action was either requested or conducted.

The FBI received reporting in 1998 that a terrorist organization might be planning to bring students to the United States for training at a flight school. The FBI was aware that individuals connected to the organization had performed surveillance and security tests at airports in the United States and made comments suggesting an intention to target civil aviation. There is no indication that this organization actually followed through on their plans.

In 1999, reporting was received that yet another terrorist organization was planning to send students to the United States for aviation training. The purpose of this training was unknown, but the terrorist organization leaders viewed the requirement as being "particularly important" and were reported to have approved an open-ended amount of funding to ensure its success. In response, an operational unit in the Counterterrorism Section at FBI headquarters sent a communication to 24 field offices, asking them to pay close attention to Islamic students in their area from the target country who were engaged in aviation training. This communication was sent to the Phoenix Office's International Terrorism squad, but the Phoenix SA does not recall this reporting. The Phoenix SSA was not assigned to the Phoenix Office at the time.

The communication requested that field offices "task sources, coordinate with the INS, and conduct other logical inquiries, in an effort to develop and intelligence baseline" regarding this terrorist group's use of students. To this point, there is no indication that the FBI field offices conducted any investigation after receiving the communication. The analyst who drafted the communication indicated that he did receive several calls from field offices, but that the calls were either to seek additional guidance or to raise concerns about the Buckley Amendment implications of investigating at schools. (The Buckley Amendment is part of the 1974 Family Educational Rights and Privacy Act, which bars post secondary educational institutions which receive federal funding from releasing student's personal information without their written consent.)

In November 1999, to address these concerns, the FBI sent a letter to INS explaining the intelligence and requesting a database search for individuals studying in the United States from the target country. Any information provided by the INS would be sent to the field offices, which would conduct appropriate investigations in coordination with local INS agents. According to interviews, the INS never provided any information in response to the request.

The project was subsequently assigned to the International Terrorism Analytic Unit at FBI headquarters. The analyst assigned to the project determined that there were 75 academic institutions offering flight education in the United States. He also located via the Internet an additional 1000 flight schools. In November 2000, the analyst sent a communication to the FBI field offices, informing them that no information was uncovered concerning this terrorist group's recruitment of students studying aviation and stated that "further investigation by FBI field offices is deemed imprudent" by FBI headquarters.

The former unit chief of the operational unit involved in this project told the Joint Inquiry Staff that he was not surprised by the apparent lack of vigorous investigative action by the field offices. He believes that the field offices' calls requesting additional guidance or raising Buckley Amendment issues were just "excuses" and that the field offices should have known full well how to go about this effort. In his view, this type project was like "drilling for oil," in that you drill in many different spots, almost all of which are unsuccessful but the reward from one successful "drilling" is worth the effort. In his opinion, the field offices did not like to undertake difficult labor-intensive projects like this with a high risk of failure. The FBI's culture often prevented headquarters from forcing field offices to take investigative action that they were unwilling to take. He told us that the FBI was so decentralized, and the Special Agents in Charge wielded such power, that when field agents complained to a supervisor about a request from headquarters, FBI headquarters management would generally back down.

Missed Opportunity to Connect Phoenix to Similar Investigations?

The personnel working on the Phoenix EC at FBI headquarters were not aware of the prior reporting on terrorist groups sending aviation students to the United States and did not know that FBI headquarters had undertaken a systematic effort in 1999 to identify Middle Eastern flight students in the United States. This is not surprising considering the lack of information sharing in the FBI. According to interviewees, this is a problem not only at FBI headquarters but at the field offices as well. Agents often will only be familiar with cases on their own squad and will not know about investigations on other squads.

Had the headquarters personnel working on the Phoenix EC known about the 1999 efforts by FBI headquarters to locate foreign nationals at flight schools, it might have affected how they handled the EC. The IOSs handling the EC were concerned about the legal implications of following through on the recommendations but were unaware of similar efforts in the past whereby the INS and FBI had established an arrangement to provide the FBI with foreign nationals' student visas for investigative purposes. Unfortunately, instead of approaching FBI lawyers to determine whether there were legal obstacles to implementation, the IOSs decided among themselves that the EC raised profiling issues.

This lack of information sharing among personnel working different targets poses increasing problems for the FBI faced with a national security environment and the growth of the "International Jihad" movement, making it difficult to link individuals to specific foreign powers or terrorist groups. Some FBI personnel expressed concern that the FBI's labeling of individuals as associated with particular terrorist organizations is not always accurate. For example, an individual affiliated with al-Qa'ida may associate with Hamas members in the United States and be labeled Hamas based on these associations. If such an individual is being worked out of another unit, the traditional lack of information sharing makes it unlikely the al-Qa'ida unit will learn about the investigation. This affects the unit's ability to develop a comprehensive understanding of al-Qa'ida presence and operations in the United States. There may also be al-Qa'ida information directly relevant to the investigation about which personnel working Hamas are unaware.

New York FBI Office Actions in Connection with the Phoenix EC

The Phoenix EC was sent to two investigators in the FBI's New York field office who specialize in Usama Bin Ladin cases. They were asked to "read and clear" but were not asked to take any follow-up action. A Joint Inquiry Staff audit of electronic records shows that at least three people in New York saw the EC prior to September 11. It does not appear to have received much attention or elicited concern. Two of the three do not recall the communication prior to September 11, 2000. The third remembered reading it but said it did not resonate with him because he found it speculative.

The New York agents interviewed stated that they were well aware that Middle Eastern men frequently came to the United States for flight training. This was not surprising as it was considered the best and most reasonably priced place to train. According to them, many foreign nationals got their commercial flight training here.

A communication noting that Middle Eastern men with ties to Usama Bin Ladin were receiving flight training in the United States would not necessarily be considered particularly alarming because New York personnel knew that individuals connected to al-Qa'ida had previously received flight training in the United States. In fact, one of these individuals trained at the Airman Flight School in Norman, Oklahoma, the same place where Zacarias Moussaoui trained prior to his arrival Minnesota. Mohammed Atta and another of the hijackers visited this same flight school but decided not to enroll there. The commonly held view at the FBI prior to September 11 was that Bin Ladin needed pilots to operate aircraft he had purchased in the United States to move men and material. Also, several pilots with al-Qa'ida ties testified for the U.S. Government during the course of the Embassy bombing trial.

However, the FBI had also received reporting that was not entirely consistent with this view of Usama Bin Ladin's pilots. Two of the pilots had been through al Qa'ida training camps in Afghanistan where they were trained to conduct terrorist domestic U.S. aircraft.

Source: Select Committee on Intelligence U.S. Senate and the Permanent Select Committee of Intelligence House of Representatives, *Joint Inquiry into Intelligence Community Activities before and after the Terrorist Attacks of Sept. 11, 2001* (Washington, DC: U.S. Government Printing Office, 2004), vol.1, pp. 436–450.

Document 30

Report of the Joint Inquiry Staff by Eleanor Hill on the FBI Investigation of Zacarias Moussaoui (September 24, 2002)

The Joint Inquiry Staff investigated the FBI's mishandling of the Zacarias Moussaoui case and issued a report for the Senate and House's intelligence committees on September 24, 2002. This report was critical in the steps taken to arrest Moussaoui and the failure to capitalize on his arrest.

Zacarias Moussaoui came to the attention of the FBI during a period of time when the Intelligence Community was detecting numerous indicators of an impending terrorist attack against U.S. interests somewhere in the world. Moussaoui was in the custody of the INS on September 11, 2001. Our review has, in part, focused on whether information resulting from the FBI's investigation of Moussaoui could have alerted the U.S. Government to the scope and nature of the attacks that occurred on September 11, 2001.

Moussaoui has been indicted and faces a criminal trial this fall. Among other things, Moussaoui has been charged with conspiracy to commit aircraft piracy "with the result that thousands of people died on September 11, 2001." In order to avoid affecting the course of that proceeding, the Joint Inquiry Staff has limited the amount of detail in this presentation while attempting to provide a general understanding of the facts of the investigation.

Our review of the FBI's investigation to date has identified three issues in particular, to which I would draw Members' attention:

- Differences in the way the FBI's field offices and headquarters components analyzed and perceived the danger posed by the facts uncovered during the FBI's investigation of Moussaoui prior to September 11, 2001.
- The tools available to the FBI under the Constitution and laws of the United States to investigate that danger, notably the Foreign Intelligence Surveillance

Act (FISA), and whether FBI personnel were well organized and informed about the availability of those tools; and

* Whether the substance, clarity, and urgency of the threat warning provided by the FBI to other parts of the Intelligence Community corresponded to the danger that had been identified.

For purposes of this interim report, the American public should understand that under FISA, the FBI can obtain a court order authorizing a physical search or electronic surveillance, such as a wiretap, if it can demonstrate that the subject: (1) is an agent of a foreign power, which can be a foreign country or an international terrorist group, and (2) is, among other things, engaged in international terrorism, or activities in preparation therefore, on behalf of that foreign power. Court orders issued under FISA are classified and are issued by the Foreign Intelligence Surveillance Court (FISC).

The FBI's focus at the time Moussaoui was taken into custody appeared to the Joint Inquiry Staff to have been almost entirely on investigating specific crimes and not on identifying linkages between separate investigations or on sharing information with other U.S. Government agencies with counterterrorist responsibilities. No one at FBI headquarters apparently connected Moussaoui, the Phoenix memo, the possible presence of Khalid al-Mihdhar and Nawaf al-Hazmi in the United States, or the flood of warnings about possible terrorist attacks during the summers of 2001.

The Joint Inquiry Staff has determined that Moussaoui contacted the Airman Flight School in Norman, Oklahoma by e-mail on September 29, 2000 and expressed interest in taking lessons to fly a small Cessna aircraft. On February 23, 2001, he entered the United States at Chicago's O'Hare Airport. He was traveling on a French passport and this allowed him to stay in the United States without a visa for 90 days, until May 22, 2001. On February 26, 2001, he began flight lessons at Airman Flight School.

On August 11, 2001, Moussaoui and his roommate, Hussein al-Attas, arrived in Egan, Minnesota and checked into a hotel. Moussaoui began classes at Pam Am Flight School there on August 13, 2001.

While Airman Flight School provided flight lessons in piloting Cessnas and similar small aircraft, Pan Am Flight School provided ground training and access to a Boeing 747 flight simulator used by professional pilots. Most of Pan AM's students are either newly hired airline pilots who use the flight simulator for initial training or are active airline pilots who use the equipment for an update or refresher training. Although anyone can sign up for lessons at Pan Am, the typical student has a pilot's license, is employed by an airline, and has several thousand flight hours. Moussaoui had none of these qualifications.

Based on concerns expressed by a private citizen, the FBI's Minneapolis Field Office opened an international terrorism investigation of Moussaoui on August 15, 2001.

The FBI's Minneapolis Field Office hosts and is part of a Joint Terrorism Task Force, of JTTF. Agents of the INS share space and work closely with the FBI in Minneapolis and were able to immediately determine that Moussaoui had been authorized to stay in the United States only until May 22, 2001. Thus, Moussaoui was 'out of status' at the time—August—that the FBI began investigating him.

On the same day the Minneapolis field office learned about Moussaoui, it asked both the CIA and the FBI's legal attaché in Paris for any information they had or could get on Moussaoui. At the same time, they also informed FBI headquarters of the investigation. The supervisory agent in Minneapolis told the Joint Inquiry Staff that FBI headquarters had suggested that Moussaoui be put under surveillance, but that Minneapolis did not have enough agents to do that. Furthermore, the Minneapolis agents believed that it was more important to prevent Moussaoui from getting any additional flight training.

After conducting several interviews, the FBI agents, along with two INS agents, went to Moussaoui's hotel. The INS agents temporarily detained Moussaoui and his roommate, Hussein al-Attas, while checking to determine if they were legally in the United States. Al-Attas showed the INS that he had a valid student visa and agreed to allow the agents to search his property in the hotel room. The INS agents determined that Moussaoui had not received an extension to allow him to stay in the United States beyond May 22, 2001, so they took him into custody. The agents packed Moussaoui's belongings, noticing that he had a laptop computer among his possessions.

After Moussaoui's detention, the Minneapolis supervisory agent called the office's legal counsel and asked if there was any way to search Moussaoui's possessions without his consent. He was told he had to obtain a search warrant.

Over the ensuing days, the Minneapolis agents considered several alternatives, including trying to obtain a criminal search warrant, seeking a search warrant under the FISA, and deporting Moussaoui to France after arranging for the French authorities to search Moussaoui's possessions and share their findings with the FBI. Adding to the sense of urgency, a supervisor in the INS's Minneapolis office told the FBI that INS typically does not hold visa waiver violators like Moussaoui for more than 24 hours before returning them to their home countries. Under the circumstances, however, the INS said it would hold Moussaoui for seven to ten days.

On Saturday, August 18, Minneapolis sent a detailed memorandum to FBI headquarters. That memorandum described the Moussaoui investigation and stated that it believed that Moussaoui posed a threat.

The Joint Inquiry Staff has been told in interviews with the Minneapolis agents that FBI headquarters advised against trying to obtain a criminal search warrant as that might prejudice any subsequent efforts to get a search warrant under FISA. Under FISA, a search warrant could be obtained if they could show there was probable cause to believe Moussaoui was an agent of a foreign power and either engaged in terrorism or was preparing to engage in terrorism. FBI headquarters was concerned that if a criminal warrant was denied and then the agents tried to get a warrant under FISA, the court would think the agents were trying to use authority for an intelligence investigation to pursue a criminal case.

During this time frame an attorney in the National Security Law Unit of FBI headquarters asked the counsel in the Minneapolis field office if she had considered trying to obtain a criminal warrant and she replied that a FISA warrant would be the safer course. Minneapolis also wanted to notify the Criminal Division about Moussaoui through the local U.S. Attorney's Office, believing it was obligated to do so under Attorney General guidelines that required notification when there is a "reasonable indication" of a felony. FBI headquarters advised that Minneapolis did not have enough evidence to warrant notifying the Criminal Division.

The FBI case agent in Minneapolis had become increasingly frustrated with what he perceived as a lack of assistance from the Radical Fundamentalist Union (RFU) at FBI headquarters. He had had previous conflicts with the RFU agent over FISA issues and believed headquarters was not being responsive to the threat Minneapolis had identified. At the suggestion of a Minneapolis supervisor, the Minneapolis case agent contacted an FBI official who was detailed to the CTC. The Minneapolis agent shared the details of the Moussaoui investigation with him and provided the names of associates that had been connected to Moussaoui. The Minneapolis case agent has told the Joint Inquiry Staff that he was looking for any information that CTC could provide that would strengthen the case linking Moussaoui to international terrorism.

On August 21, 2001, the Minneapolis case agent sent an e-mail to the supervisory special agent in the RFU who was handling this matter urging that the U.S. Secret Service in Washington, D.C. be apprised of the threat potential there indicated by the evidence. In an interview with the Joint Inquiry Staff, the RFU agent to whom the e-mail was addressed said that he told the Minneapolis agent that he was working on a notification to the entire Intelligence Community, including the Secret Service, about the threat presented by Moussaoui.

The RFU supervisory special agent sent a teletype on September 4, 2001, recounting the FBI's interviews of Moussaoui and al-Attas, and other information it had obtained in the meantime. The teletype, however, merely recounted the steps in the investigation. It did not place Moussaoui's actions in the context of the increased level of terrorist threats during the summer of 2001, nor did it provide its recipients with any analysis of Moussaoui's actions or plans, or information about what type of threat he may have presented.

A CIA officer detailed to FBI headquarters learned of the Moussaoui investigation from CTC in the third week of August 2001. The officer was alarmed about Moussaoui for several reasons. CIA stations were advised of the known facts regarding Moussaoui and al-Attas and were asked to provide any relevant information they might have.

On Wednesday, August 22, the FBI legal attaché's office in Paris provided its report. That report began a series of discussion between Minneapolis and the RFU at FBI headquarters focusing on whether a specific group of Chechen rebels were a "recognized" foreign power, one that was on the State Department's list of terrorist groups and for which the Foreign Intelligence Surveillance Court had previously granted orders. The RFU agent believed that the Chechen rebels were not a "recognized" foreign power and that, even if Moussaoui were to be linked to them, the FBI could not obtain a search warrant under FISA. Thus, the RFU agent told the Minneapolis agents that they needed to somehow connect Moussaoui to al-Qa'ida, which he believed was a "recognized" foreign power. This led the Minneapolis agents to attempt to gather information showing that the Chechen rebels were connected to al-Qa'ida.

Unfortunately this dialogue was based on a misunderstanding of FISA. The FBI's Deputy General Counsel told the Joint Inquiry Staff that the term "recognized foreign power" has no meaning under FISA and that the FBI can obtain a search warrant under FISA for an agent of any international terrorist group, including the Chechen rebels. But because of the misunderstanding Minneapolis spent the better part of three weeks trying to connect the Chechen group to al-Qa'ida.

The Minneapolis case agent contacted CTC, asking for additional information concerning connections between the group and al-Qa'ida; he also suggested that the RFU agent contact CTC for assistance on the issues. The RFU agent responded that he had all the information he needed and requested that Minneapolis work through FBI headquarters when contacting CTC. Ultimately, the RFU agent agreed to submit Minneapolis' FISA request to the attorneys in the FBI's National Security Law Unit (NSLU) for review.

The Joint Inquiry staff interviewed several FBI attorneys with whom the RFU agent consulted about Moussaoui. All have confirmed that they advised the RFU agent that the evidence was insufficient to link Moussaoui to a foreign power. One of the attorneys also told the RFU agent that the Chechen and his rebels were not a "recognized foreign power". The attorneys also told the Staff that, if they had been aware of the Phoenix memo, they would have forwarded the FISA request to the Justice Department's Office of Intelligence Policy Review (OIPR). They reasoned that the particulars of the Phoenix memo changed the context of the Moussaoui investigation and made a stronger case for the FISA warrant. None of them saw the Phoenix memo before September 11.

Two FBI agents assigned to the Oklahoma City Field Office's international terrorism squad visited Airman Flight School in Norman, Oklahoma on August 23. In September of 1999, one of the agents had been assigned a lead from the Orlando Field Office to visit the flight school concerning another individual who had been identified as Usama Bin Ladin's personal pilot and who had received flight training at Airman. The agent had not been given any background information about this individual. Although he told us that he thought that this lead had been the most significant information he had seen in Oklahoma City, the agent did not remember the lead when he returned to the flight school two years later to ask questions about Moussaoui. He told the Joint Inquiry Staff that he should have connected the two visits but that he did not have the time to do so.

During a conversation on August 27, 2001, the RFU agent told the Minneapolis supervisor that the supervisor was getting people "spun up" over Moussaoui. According to his notes and his statement to the Joint Inquiry Staff, the supervisor replied that he was trying to get people at FBI headquarters "spun up" because he was trying to make sure that Moussaoui "did not take control of a plane and fly it into the World Trade Center." The Minneapolis agent said that the headquarters agent told him, "[T]hat's not going to happen; we don't know he's a terrorist. You don't have enough to show he is a terrorist. You have a guy interested in this type of aircraft—that is it." The headquarters agent does not remember this exchange. The Minneapolis supervisor told the Joint Inquiry Staff that he had no reason to believe that Moussaoui was planning an attack on the World Trade Center; he was merely trying to get headquarters' attention.

In a subsequent conference call with FBI headquarters, the chief of the RFU Unit told Minneapolis that a specific recognized foreign power, such as HAMAS, was necessary to get a FISA search warrant.

On August 28, 2001, after reviewing the request for a search warrant, the RFU agent edited it and returned the request to Minneapolis for comment. The RFU agent says that it was not unusual for headquarters agents to make changes to field submissions in addition to changes made by the NSLU and OIPR. The major substantive change that was made was the removal of information about connections between the Chechen rebels and al-Qa'ida. The RFU agent said he removed it because he believed this information was insufficient and that, if he received approval from the NSLU to use the Chechen rebels as a foreign power, he would have added it back to an expanded section about Chechnya.

After the edit was complete, the RFU agent briefed the FBI Deputy General Counsel. The Deputy General Counsel told the Joint Inquiry Staff that he agreed with the RFU agent that there was insufficient information to show that Moussaoui was an agent of a foreign power, but that the issue of a 'recognized' foreign power did not come up. After that briefing, the RFU agent sent an e-mail to Minneapolis saying that the information was even less sufficient than he had previously thought because Moussaoui would actually have to be shown to be a part of a movement or organization.

After concluding that there was insufficient information to show that Moussaoui was an agent of any foreign power, the FBI's focus shifted to arranging for Moussaoui's planned deportation to France on September 17. French officials would search his possessions and provide the results to the FBI. Although the FBI was no longer considering a search warrant under FISA, no one revisited the idea of attempting to obtain a criminal search warrant, even though the only reasons for not attempting to obtain a criminal search warrant—the concern that it would prejudice a request under FISA—no longer existed.

On Thursday, September 4, 2001, FBI headquarters sent a teletype to the Intelligence Community and other U.S. Government agencies, including the Federal Aviation Administration (FAA), providing information about the Moussaoui investigation. The teletype noted that Moussaoui was being held in custody but did not describe any particular threat that the FBI thought he posed, for example, whether he might be connected to a larger plot. The teletype also did not recommend that the addressees take any action or look for any additional indicators of a terrorist attack, nor did it provide any analysis of a possible hijacking threat or provide any specific warnings. The following day the Minneapolis case agent hand-carried the teletype to two employees of the FAA's Bloomington, Minnesota office and orally briefed them on the status of the investigation. The two FAA employees told the Joint Inquiry Staff that the FBI agent did not convey any sense of urgency about the teletype and did not ask them to take any specific action regarding Moussaoui. He just wanted to be sure the FAA had received the cable.

Prior to September 11, 2001, no one at the FBI canvassed other individuals in the custody of and cooperating with the U.S. Government in connection with past terrorism cases to see if any of those individuals knew Moussaoui.

The final preparations for Moussaoui's deportation were underway when the September 11 attacks occurred.

Source: Select Committee on Intelligence U.S. Senate and the Permanent Select Committee of Intelligence House of Representatives, *Joint Inquiry into Intelligence Community Activities before and after the Terrorist Attacks of Sept. 11, 2001* (Washington, DC: U.S. Government Printing Office, 2004), vol.1, pp. 450–456.

Document 31

Testimony of Richard A. Clarke before the National Commission on Terrorist Attacks upon the United States (March 24, 2004)

Richard A. Clarke was the leading counterterrorism expert for both the Clinton and Bush administrations. After he left office in 2003, Clarke became the leading critic of the Bush administration's handling of terrorism before September 11. Clarke is also famous for being the only U.S. government official who apologized to the families of the victims for the failures of government to prevent September 11. In this testimony before the 9/11 Commission, Clarke outlines the basics of the policies toward terrorism held by both the Clinton and Bush administrations. The following is an excerpt from that testimony.

I am appreciative of the opportunity the Commission is offering for me to provide my observations about what went wrong in the struggle against al Qida, both before and after 9-11. I want the families of the victims to know that we tried to stop those attacks, that some people tried very hard. I want them to know why we failed and what I think we need to do to insure that nothing like that ever happens again.

I have testified for twenty hours before the House-Senate Joint Inquiry Committee and before this Commission in closed hearings. Therefore, I will limit my prepared testimony to a chronological review of key facts and then provide some conclusions and summary observations, which may form the basis for further questions. My observations and answers to any questions are limited by my memory, because I do not have access to government files or classified information for purposes of preparing for this hearing.

I was assigned to the National Security Council staff in 1992 and had terrorism as part of my portfolio until late 2001. Terrorism became the predominant part of my duties during the mid-1990s and I was appointed National Coordinator for Counter-terrorism in 1998.

1. *Terrorism without US Retaliation in the 1980s:* In the 1980s, Hezbollah killed 278 United States Marines in Lebanon and twice destroyed the US embassy. They kidnapped and killed other Americans, including the CIA Station chief. There was no direct US military retaliation. In 1989, 259 people were killed on Pan Am 103. There was no direct US military retaliation. The George H.W. Bush administration did not have a formal counter-terrorism policy articulated in an NSC Presidential decision document.

2. *Terrorism Early in the Clinton Administration:* Within the first few weeks of the Clinton administration, there was terrorism in the US: the attack on the CIA gatehouse and the attack on the World Trade Center. CIA and FBI concluded at the time that there was no organization behind those attacks. Similarly, they did not report at the time that al Qida was involved in the planned attack on Americans in Yemen in 1992 or the Somali attacks on US and other peacekeepers in 1993. Indeed, CIA and FBI did not report the existence of an organization named al Qida until the mid-1990s, seven years after it was apparently created. Nonetheless, the 1993 attacks and then the terrorism in the Tokyo subway and the Oklahoma City bombing caused the Clinton Administration to increase its focus on terrorism and to expand funding for counter-terrorism programs.

   As a result of intelligence and law enforcement operations, most of those involved in the World Trade Center attack of 1993, the planned attacks on the UN and New York tunnels, the CIA gatehouse shootings, the Oklahoma City bombing, and the attempted assassination of former President Bush were successfully apprehended.

   The Clinton Administration responded to Iraqi terrorism against the US in 1993 with a military retaliation and against Iranian terrorism against the US in 1996 at Khobar Towers with a covert action. Both US responses were accompanied by warning that further anti-US terrorism would result in greater retaliation. Neither Iraq nor Iran engaged in anti-US terrorism subsequently. (Iraqis did, of course, later engage in anti-US terrorism in 2003–4.)

3. *Identifying the al Qida Threat:* The White House urged CIA in 1994 to place greater focus on what the Agency called "the terrorist financier, Usama bin Ladin." After the creation of a "virtual station" [Alec Station] to examine bin Ladin, CIA identified a multi-national network of cells and of affiliated terrorist organizations. That network was attempting to wage "jihad" in Bosnia and planned to have a significant role in a new Bosnian government. US and Allied actions halted the war in Bosnia and caused most of the al Qida related jihadists to leave. The White House asked CIA and DOD to develop plans for operating against al Qida in Sudan, the country of its headquarters. Neither department was able successfully to develop a plan to do so. Immediately following Usama bin Ladin's move to Afghanistan, the White House requested that plans be developed to operate against al Qida there. CIA developed ties to a group which reported on al Qida activity, but which was unable to mount successful operations against al Qida in Afghanistan. CIA opposed using its own personnel to do so.

4. *Sudan:* While bin Ladin was in Sudan, he was hosted by its leader Hasan Turabi. Under Turabi, Sudan had become a safe haven for many terrorist groups, but bin Ladin had special status. He funded many development programs such as roads and dined often with Turabi and his family. Turabi and bin Ladin were ideological brethren. Following the assassination attempt on Egyptian President Mubarek, the US and Egypt successfully proposed UN sanctions on Sudan because of its support of terrorism. Because of the growing economic damage to Sudan due to its support of terrorism, bin Ladin offered to move to Afghanistan. Sudan at no time detained him, nor was there ever a credible offer by Sudan to arrest and render him. This is in contrast to Sudan's arrest of the terrorist known as Carlos the Jackal, who the Sudanese then handed over in chains to French authorities.

5. *1998 Turning Point:* In 1996, CIA had been directed to develop its capability to operate against al Qida in Afghanistan and elsewhere. CIA operations identified and disrupted al Qida cells in several countries. In 1997, a federal grand jury began reviewing evidence against al Qida and in 1998 indicted Usama bin Ladin. Several terrorists, including bin Ladin, issued a fatwa against the United States.

    In August, al Qida attacked two US embassies in East Africa. Following the attacks, the United States responded militarily with cruise missile attacks on al Qida facilities. President Clinton was widely criticized for doing so. A US Marine deployment combined with CIA activity, disrupted a third attack planned in Tirana, Albania.

    President Clinton requested the Chairman of the Joint Chiefs to develop follow-on military strike plans, including the use of US Special Forces. The Chairman recommended against using US forces on the ground in Afghanistan, but placed submarines with cruise missile off shore awaiting timely intelligence of the location of Usama bin Ladin.

    The President also requested CIA to develop follow-on covert action plans. He authorized lethal activity in a series of directives which progressively expanded the authority of CIA to act against al Qida in Afghanistan.

    Diplomatic activity also increased, including UN sanctions against the Taliban regime in Afghanistan and pressure on Pakistan to cooperate further in attempts to end the Taliban support for al Qida.

6. *National Coordinator:* In 1998, I was appointed by the President to a newly created position of National Coordinator for Security, Infrastructure Protection and Counter-terrorism. Although the Coordinator was appointed to the Cabinet level NSC Principals Committee, the position was limited at the request of the departments and agencies. The Coordinator had no budget, only a dozen staff, and no ability to direct actions by the departments or agencies. The President authorized ten security and counter-terrorism programs and assigned leadership on each program (e.g. Transportation Security) to an agency lead.

7. *1999:* The Clinton Administration continued to pursue intelligence, including covert action, military, law enforcement, and diplomatic activity to disrupt al Qida.

    CIA was unable to develop timely intelligence to support the planned follow-on military strikes. On three occasions, CIA reported it knew where Usama bin Ladin was, but all three times the Director of Central Intelligence recommended against military action because of the poor quality of the intelligence. Eventually, the US submarines on station for the military operation returned to normal duties. CIA's assets in Afghanistan were unable to utilize the lethal covert action authorities and CIA recommended against placing its own personnel in Afghanistan to carry out the operations. Captures of al Qida personnel outside of Afghanistan continued.

In December 1999 intelligence and law enforcement information indicated that al Qida was planning attacks against the US. The President ordered the Principals Committee to meet regularly to prevent the attacks. That Cabinet level committee met throughout December, 1999 to review intelligence and develop counter-measures. The planned al Qida attacks were averted.

Despite our inability to locate Usama bin Ladin in one place long enough to launch an attack, I urged that we engage in a bombing campaign of al Qida facilities in Afghanistan. That option was deferred by the Principals Committee.

8. *Terrorists in the US:* FBI had the responsibility for finding al Qida related activities or terrorists in the US. In the 1996–1999 timeframe, they regularly responded to me and to the National Security Advisor that there were no known al Qida operatives or activities in the US. On my trips to FBI offices, I found that al Qida was not a priority (except in the New York office). Following the Millennium Alert, FBI Executive Assistant Director Dale Watson attempted to have the field offices act more aggressively to find al Qida related activities. The Bureau was, however, less than proactive in identifying al Qida related fund raising, recruitment, or other activities in the United States. Several programs to increase our ability to respond to terrorism in the US were initiated both in the FBI and in other departments, including programs to train and equip first responders.

9. *2000:* The President, displeased with the inability of CIA to eliminate the al Qida leadership, asked for additional options. The NSC staff proposed that the Predator, unmanned aerial vehicle, be used to find the leadership. CIA objected. The National Security Advisor, however, eventually obtained Agency agreement to fly the Predator on a "proof of concept" mission without any link to military or CIA forces standing by. CIA wanted to experiment with the concept before developing a command and control system that incorporated Predator information with attack capabilities. The flights ended when the high winds of winter precluded the operation of the aircraft. The experiment had proved successful in locating the al Qida leadership.

In October 2000, the USS Cole was attacked in Yemen. Following the attack, the Principals considered military retaliation. CIA and FBI were, however, unwilling to state that those who had conducted the attack were al Qida or related to the facilities and personnel in Afghanistan. The Principals directed that the Politico-Military Plan against al Qida be updated with additional options. Among those options were aiding Afghan factions to fight the Taliban and al Qida and creating an armed version of the Predator unmanned aircraft to use against the al Qida leadership.

Military strike options, including cruise missiles, bombing, and use of US Special Forces were also included.

As the Clinton Administration came to an end, three attacks on the US had been definitively tied to al Qida (the World Trade Center 1993, the Embassies in 1998 and the Cole in 2000), in which a total of 35 Americans had been killed over eight years.

To counter al Qida's growing threat, a global effort had been initiated involving intelligence activities, covert action, diplomacy, law enforcement, financial action, and military capability. Nonetheless, the organization continued to enjoy a safe haven in Afghanistan.

10. *2001:* On January 24, 2001 I requested in writing an urgent meeting of the NSC Principals committee to address the al Qida threat. That meeting took place on September 4, 2001. It was preceded by a number of Deputies Committee meetings, beginning in April. Those meetings considered proposals to step up activity against al Qida, including military assistance to anti-Taliban Afghan factions.

In June and July, intelligence indicated an increased likelihood of a major al Qida attack against US targets, probably in Saudi Arabia or Israel. In response, the interagency Counter-terrorism Security Group agreed upon a series of steps including a series of warning notices that an attack could take place in the US. Notices were sent to federal agencies (Immigration, Customs, Coast Guard, FAA, FBI, DOD, and State), state and local police, airlines, and airports.

In retrospect, we know that there was information available to some in the FBI and CIA that al Qida operatives had entered the United States. That information was not shared with the senior FBI counter-terrorism official (Dale Watson) or with me, despite the heightened state of concern in the Counter-terrorism Security Group.

Observations and Conclusions

Although there were people in the FBI, CIA, Defense Department, State Department, and White House who worked very hard to destroy al Qida before it did catastrophic damage to the US, there were many others who found the prospect of significant al Qida attacks remote. In both CIA and the military there was reluctance at senior career levels to fully utilize all of the capabilities available. There was risk aversion. FBI was, throughout much of this period, organized, staffed, and equipped in such a way that it was ineffective in dealing with the domestic terrorist threat from al Qida.

At the senior policy levels in the Clinton Administration, there was an acute understanding of the terrorist threat, particularly al Qida. That understanding resulted in a vigorous program to counter al Qida including lethal covert action, but it did not include a willingness to resume bombing of Afghanistan. Events in the Balkans, Iraq, the Peace Process, and domestic politics occurring at the same time as the anti-terrorism effort played a role.

The Bush Administration saw terrorism policy as important but not urgent, prior to 9-11. The difficulty in obtaining the first Cabinet level (Principals) policy meeting on terrorism and the limited Principals' involvement sent unfortunate signals to the bureaucracy about the Administration's attitude toward the al Qida threat.

The US response to al Qida following 9-11 has been partially effective. Unfortunately, the US did not act sufficiently quickly to insert US forces to capture or kill the al Qida leadership in Afghanistan. Nor did we employ sufficient US and Allied forces to stabilize that country. In the ensuing 30 months, al Qida has morphed into a decentralized network, with its national and regional affiliates operating effectively and independently. There have been more major al Qida related attacks globally in the 30 months since 9-11 than there were in the 30 months preceding it. Hostility toward the US in the Islamic world has increased since 9-11, largely as a result of the invasion and occupation of Iraq. Thus, new terrorist cells are likely being created, unknown to US intelligence.

To address the continuing threat from radical Islamic terrorism, the US and its allies must become increasingly focused and effective in countering the ideology that motivates that terrorism.

Source: Richard A. Clarke, *Against All Enemies: Inside America's War on Terror* (New York: Free Press, 2004), pp. 293–297.

Document 32

Testimony of Mary Fetchet, Founding Director, Voices of September 11th, on the Need for Reform in a Hearing of the Senate's Committee on Government Affairs (August 17, 2004)

Members of the families of victims of September 11 testified before various Senate and House committees. Perhaps the most poignant was the testimony of Mary Fetchet, who lost a son on September 11. She was the founding director of the Voices of September 11th and appeared before the Senate's Committee on Government Affairs on August 17, 2004. This is a transcript of her statement before the Committee, in which she demanded reform.

Honorable Chairman Collins. Senator Lieberman and other distinguished members of the Governmental Affairs Committee, I am honored to be here today to testify on behalf of the 9/11 families. My name is Mary Fetchet. I am a member of the 9/11 Families Steering Committee and founding director and president of Voices of September 11th, a 9/11 family advocacy group. More importantly, I am the mother of Brad Fetchet, who tragically lost his life at the age of 24 in the terrorist attacks on the World Trade Center on September 11th.

We appreciate your urgency in holding this hearing to address the critical task of implementing the recommendations made by the 9/11 Commission. We are equally indebted to the 9/11 commissioners and their staff who worked tirelessly in a bipartisan manner over the last year to examine those events that led to the attacks and to develop recommendations to prevent future tragedies. The commission may not have answered all our questions but its report does offer a much needed overall strategy to develop a comprehensive foundation for creating a safer America.

The challenge now before all of us is whether we have the national will to combat our political bureaucracy, general inertia and the influence of special interest groups in order to enact the comprehensive set of recommendations to improve our national security. The work will not be easy. It is, however, essential, if we are to protect our families and our country.

The last three years have been a painful education for me. It began on September 11th, 2001 when my husband contacted me at work to let me know Brad had called him shortly after the first plane hit Tower One. Brad was on the 89th floor of Tower Two and he wanted to reassure us that he was okay. He was shaken because he had seen someone fall from the 91st floor, quote, "all the way down." But Brad told my husband he expected to remain at work for the remainder of the day. The Port Authority, after all, had used the PA system to ensure everyone in Tower Two that they were safe and directed them to remain in the building. Brad remained with his co-workers in their office as they were told. Other individuals who attempted to evacuate Tower Two at that time were ordered back up to their offices. Shortly after my husband's call, I witnessed the plane hit Tower Two on television. The image is forever etched in my mind as it was at that movement that I knew our country was under attack and that my son Brad was trapped in a high-rise building that he wouldn't be able to escape.

I never had the opportunity to speak with Brad. We later learned from a message he left his girlfriend at 9:20 a.m. that he was attempting to evacuate after his building was hit by the second plane.

Obviously, Brad and his co-workers never made it out. He and nearly 600 other individuals in Tower Two who should have survived if they had been directed to evacuate died senselessly because of unsound directions. As a mother, it didn't make sense to me that they were directed to remain in a 110-story building after the high rise building next door had been hit by a plane, had a gaping hole in its side and was engulfed in flames.

Since that day, I have come to recognize the inadequacies in our overall preparedness as well as the grave responsibilities and the inexcusable inertia of our political system. As with many who worked on the 9/11 Commission's Family Steering Committee, I came to Washington as a political novice, unfamiliar with politics of the political system, without a party affiliation. Every election day, I voted for individuals irrespective of political party who I thought would best represent our country.

However, my political involvement ended as I cast my ballot assuming, like most, that my elected officials would act in my best interest, ensure my family's safety and counter any terrorist attacks. I believed that my government was a comprehensive organization whose officials and agencies, in the best interest of national security would share intelligence, collaborate and coordinate their counterterrorism efforts. Sadly, I was wrong.

I, like others, have also tried to make sense of my son's death and those of the nearly 3,000 other innocent victims by collecting and scrutinizing newspaper reports on 9/11 issues. Two important themes quickly became apparent. One system didn't fail our country. Virtually all systems failed. They failed to follow existing procedures and failed to have protocols or effective lines of communication in place, leading to widespread breakdowns in our preparedness, defense and emergency response. The other painful realization is that our government is often paralyzed by partisanship and complacent to a fault.

Our sad and frightening pre-9/11 history includes pervasive failures and shortcomings within and amongst government agencies due to breakdowns in communication on all levels, lack of direction and overall strategic plan and a disconnect between policy, priorities and allocation of funds. More specifically, failures occurred due to intelligence agencies not sharing information within and amongst their organizations despite their common responsibility to protect our country. Not leveraging or updating technology already in place, which would have helped identify and stop these terrorists from entering out country or passing through domestic airport security point checks, ultimately preventing them from turning passenger planes into weapons

Inadequate or failed procedures in communications systems that prevented emergency response teams from effectively working with each other, connecting to workers in the World Trade Center and communicating with outside agencies such as airports and buildings that had already been identified as targets. The failure of the North American Air Defense Command and the FAA to have a protocol in place to rapidly identify and respond to hijacked planes. Failure of the FBI to process and act on Colleen Rowley's report in the Phoenix memo which would have identified terrorists and the potential for planes to be used as weapons.

Failure of the legislators to act on earlier recommendations to address the threat of terrorism such as those proposed by the Hart-Rudman Commission and those related to airline security by the Gore Commission. Allowing special interest groups to undermine and block preventative safety measures that could have prevented 9/11 attacks in an effort to save money. Failure of our government and its intelligence agencies to have an overall strategy to establish and coordinate policies, priorities and procedures based on the escalating threat of terrorism.

Colonel Randall Larsen and Ruth A. Davis of the ANSER Institute for Homeland Security summed up the situation facing pre-9/11 America in an article published in *Strategic Review* in the spring of 2001, obviously before 9/11. Quote, "What is needed now is leadership from the administration," they wrote. "There is widespread concern that threats to our homeland are both real and growing. However, one of the most troubling questions yet to be answered is whether substantial changes, such as those recommended by Hart-Rudman or Collins-Horowitz, can be made unless America experiences a tragic wakeup call." Ultimately, Larsen and David asked, "Will the administration and Congress have the vision and courage to act before we experience another Pearl Harbor or something far worse that could change the course of history?"

We all recognize that we have experienced another Pearl Harbor, now known as September 11th. The administration and Congress did not have the vision or the courage to act on previous information. Now, three years after this tragic event and the death of nearly 3,000 innocent victims, it is apparent that the status quo is unacceptable and reform is necessary. The questions we now face are two-fold: Are we prepared and if not, are we ready to move decisively to embrace a comprehensive overhaul such as the ones presented by the 9/11 Commission?

As a nation, we remain amazingly ill-prepared to prevent an attack or at least minimize its impact. This is specially frightening since we are under a greater threat than ever.

Consider for a moment, we live under a heightened national terrorist alert. And yet, three years later, systems have not been put in place to educate our families, our schools, our communities on how to prepare for another attack. Several initiatives have been put in place since 9/11. Yet many of the core problems within and amongst government agencies have not been addressed.

Communication systems are still inadequate. Community- and citywide preparedness plans have not been effectively established or communicated; government agencies and legislative groups do not effectively share or leverage intelligence and general information or even readily accept it from the public as I know firsthand. An effective government-wide control center for all intelligence has yet to be established. Crucial congressional oversight and budgetary control of this effort is not in place. No one is in charge.

Some in Washington have warned that it may take three to five years to enact all the measures needed. That is not acceptable to the 9/11 families or the American people. Our enemies are preparing to strike us now and the longer we wait to move decisively, the greater advantages and opportunities they have to harm us.

Former Defense Secretary William Cohen put the impact of unchecked aggression into perspective six years ago in speaking to New York's Council on Foreign Relations. Quote, "No government can permit others to attack its citizens with impunity if it hopes to retain the loyalty and confidence of those it's charged to protect." End quote. Americans have lost faith in our government and its ability to protect us. You have to act now to restore it.

I recognize the challenge with moving a federal bureaucracy, however well meaning, in a new direction. Like any system, change and restructuring are difficult. Special interest groups, turf battles and simple fear of an unknown can all work against reform. Yet, when American lives are at stake, indifference or inertia is unacceptable. I am confident you will recognize what is at stake and are up to the challenge. We must embrace a complete and interlinking set of recommendations proposed by the 9/11 Commission.

This plan should include the creation of a National Counterterrorism Center and the appointment of a National Intelligence Director who reports directly to the White House. The NID should oversee all national intelligence and counterterrorism activities, develop an overall strategy to promote national and regional preparedness, coordinate policies, priorities and protocols among the 15 intelligence agencies, authorize and allocate the budget and resources to execute the strategy, ensure qualified individuals are appointed to key posts and have the ability to hire, fire and more importantly promote individuals who are proactive in the fight against the war on terrorism.

The aim is simple. A coordinated and comprehensive approach to gathering information and operating our intelligence agencies. I recognize that this committee is charged with solely examining intelligence issues. But we must not allow ourselves to become shortsighted or piecemeal in our approach to America's safety. We must examine and embrace all the commission's 41 recommendations for they are interconnected.

As Governor Kean has mentioned, the success of the reorganization is also dependent upon changes made in foreign policy, public diplomacy, border and transportation security and national preparedness. Effective implementation is reliant on legislation, executive order and a willingness to maintain a consistent strategy in each of these areas. Is there a risk in transition? Absolutely.

Governor Kean, chairman of the 9/11 Commission, acknowledged as much in his report. He warned, however, that there is even more risk in doing nothing. We cannot afford to continue with the status quo. We must act now.

Ultimately, I want to do what I wasn't able to do on September 11th. I want to protect my children and keep them safe. I can't bring my son Brad back but I can, in his memory, push for a safer America. When critical reforms are implemented to make our country safer, I'll know that neither Brad's life nor the lives of nearly 3,000 others who perished on September 11th were lost in vain.

As a result of research into the horrific circumstances of my son's death, I came to realize that our country was unprepared for the threat of terrorism despite forewarning. I now recognize that I can't just be an observer but have an obligation and a responsibility as an American citizen to be educated and aware of the larger issues that impact the safety of my family and friends. I encourage all Americans to read the 9/11 Commission report and to contact their elected officials to urge them to act expeditiously in a nonpartisan fashion to enact reform.

Again, I want to thank you for this opportunity to express my views. My hope is that these hearings will lead to critical reforms. We now look to you, our elected officials, for leadership, courage and fortitude to embrace the recommendations. The safety of our families, our communities and our country rests in your hands.

Source: U.S. Senate Governmental Affairs Committee, *Voicing the Need for Reform: The Families of 9/11* (Washington, DC: U.S. Government Printing Office, 2004), pp. 5–9.

Document 33

Assessment of the FBI on Pre-9/11 Intelligence
(August 18, 2004)

In testimony before the Senate Judiciary Committee on August 18, 2004, Slade Gorton, a commissioner on the 9/11 Commission gave his interpretation of the FBI's record on dealing with domestic intelligence on terrorism leading up to the events of September 11. The list of deficiencies had led the members of the commission and its staff to consider the formation of an American version of the British MI5, but they decided against it in favor of reforming the FBI.

The FBI has, for several decades, performed two important but related functions. First, it serves as our premier federal law enforcement agency investigating possible violations of federal criminal statutes and working with federal prosecutors to develop and bring cases against violators of those laws. Second, it is an important member of the intelligence community, collecting information on foreign intelligence or terrorist activities within the United States. That information can be used either for additional counterintelligence or counter-terrorism investigation, or to bring criminal prosecutions.

We focused on the FBI's performances as an intelligence agency, combating the al Qaeda threat within the United States before 9/11. And like the joint inquiry of the Senate and House Intelligence Committees before us, we found that performance seriously deficient.

Finally, when FBI agents did develop important information about possible terrorist related activities, that information often did not get effectively communicated either within the FBI itself or in the intelligence community as a whole.

Within the FBI itself, communication of important information was hampered by the traditional case-oriented approach of the agency and the possessive case file mentality of FBI agents. As this committee is only too familiar with the information technology problems that have long hampered the FBI's ability to "know what it knows." Even when information was communicated to the field from headquarters, it didn't always come to the attention of the director or other top officials who should have seen it. This was the case in the now-famous incident of the summer of 2001 of the Phoenix electronic communication about Middle Eastern immigrants and flight schools, and the Minneapolis field office's report to headquarters about the arrest of Zacarias Moussaoui.

The other internal barrier to the communication information between the FBI intelligence officials and the FBI criminal agents and the federal prosecutors was the wall between intelligence and law enforcement that developed in the 1980s and reinforced in the 1990s. Through a combination of court decisions, pronouncements from the Department of Justice and its Office of Intelligence Policy and Review and risk-averse interpretations of those pronouncements by the FBI, the flow of information between the intelligence and criminal sides of the FBI and the Justice Department was significantly choked off, a phenomenon that continued until after 9/11, when the Congress enacted the PATRIOT Act and when the Justice Department successfully appealed a FISA court decision that effectively reinstated the wall.

These failures in internal communications were exacerbated by a reluctance of the FBI to share information with its sister agencies in the intelligence community, with the National Security Council at the White House, and with state and local law enforcement agencies. This culture of non-sharing was by no means unique to the FBI, but the FBI was surely one of the worst offenders.

The FBI, under the leadership of its current director, Robert Mueller, has undertaken significant reforms to try to deal with these deficiencies and build a strong capability in intelligence and counterterrorism. These include the establishment of an Office of Intelligence, headed by an Associate Director, Maureen Baginski, who is an experienced manager of intelligence systems. The FBI has embarked on an ambitious program to recruit qualified analysts, to train all agents in counterterrorism, and to develop career tracks for agents who want to specialize in counterterrorism or intelligence. The agency is also making progress, albeit slowly, in upgrading its internal information technology system. But, as Director Mueller himself has recognized, much more remains to be done before the FBI reaches its full potential as an intelligence agency.

Because of the history of serious deficiencies and because of lingering doubts about whether the FBI can overcome its deep-seated law enforcement culture, the commission gave serious consideration to proposals to move the FBI's intelligence operation to a new agency devoted exclusively to intelligence collection inside the United States, a variant of the British security service popularly known as MI5.

We decided not to make such a recommendation for several reasons, set forth in our Report. Chief among them were the disadvantages of separating domestic intelligence from law enforcement and losing the collection resources of FBI field offices around the country, supplemented by their relationships with state and local law enforcement agencies. Another major reason was civil liberties concerns that would arise from creating outside of the Justice Department an agency whose focus is on collecting information from and about American citizens, residents, and visitors. The rights and liberties of Americans will be better safeguarded, we believe, if this sensitive function remains in an agency trained and experienced in following the law and the Constitution, and subject to the supervision of the Attorney General.

We also believe that while the jury is still out on the ultimate success of the reforms initiated by Director Mueller, the process he has started is promising. And many of the benefits might be realized by creating a new agency will be achieved, we're convinced, if our important recommendations on restructuring the Intelligence Community—creation of a National Counterterrorism Center and a National Intelligence Director with real authority to coordinate and direct the activities of our intelligence agencies—are implemented. An FBI that is an integral part of the NCTC and is responsive to the leadership of the National Intelligence Director will work even more effectively with CIA and other intelligence agencies, while retaining the law enforcement tools that continue to be an essential weapon in combating terrorism.

What the commission recommends therefore is that further steps be taken by the president, the Justice Department and the FBI itself to build on the reforms that have been undertaken already and to institutionalize those reforms so that the FBI is permanently transformed into an effective intelligence and counterterrorism agency. The goal, as our report states, is to create within the FBI a specialized and integrated national security workforce of agents, analysts, linguists and surveillance specialists who create a new FBI culture of expertise in national security and intelligence. This Committee will have a vital oversight role in monitoring progress by the FBI and ensuring that this new capacity so critical to our nation is created and maintained.

Source: U.S. Judiciary Committee, *The 9/11 Commission and Recommendations for the Future of Federal Law Enforcement and Border Security* (Washington, DC: U.S. Government Printing Office, 2004), pp. 5–12.

Document 34

Testimony by Lee Hamilton, Vice Chairman of the 9/11 Commission, before the House of Representatives' Financial Services Committee (August 22, 2004)

One weapon against terrorist plots is to attack terrorist financing. This approach had only been tentatively used before September 11. In testimony before the House of Representatives' Financial Services Committee Lee Hamilton, the vice chairman of the 9/11 Commission, outlined the difficulty of and potential problems with cutting off the finances of terrorist groups. He also traced the history of al-Qaeda's support for the September 11th conspiracy.

While commissioners have not been asked to review or approve this staff report—indeed, I first saw it only a few hours ago—we believe the work of the staff on terrorist finance issues will be helpful to your own consideration of these issues.

After the September 11 attacks, the highest-level U.S. government officials publicly declared that the fight against al Qaeda financing was as critical as the fight against al Qaeda itself. It was presented as one of the keys to success in the fight against terrorism: If we choke off the terrorists' money, we limit their ability to conduct mass-casualty attacks.

In reality, stopping the flow of funds to al Qaeda and affiliated terrorist groups has proved to be essentially impossible. At the same time, tracking al Qaeda financing is an effective way to locate terrorist operatives and supporters, and to disrupt terrorist plots. Our government's strategy on terrorist financing thus has changed significantly from the early post-9/11 days. Choking off the money remains the most visible and important—it's an important aspect of our approach, but it is not our only, or even most important, goal. Making it harder for terrorists to get money is a necessary, but insufficient, component of the overall strategy.

Following the money to identify terrorist operatives and sympathizers provides a particularly powerful tool in the fight against terrorist groups. Use of this tool almost always remains invisible to the general public, but it is a critical part of the overall campaign against al Qaeda. Today, the United States government recognizes—appropriately, in our view—that terrorist-financing measures are simply one of many tools in the fight against al Qaeda.

The September 11 hijackers used U.S. and foreign financial institutions to hold, move and retrieve their money. The hijackers deposited money into U.S. accounts, primarily by wire transfers and deposits of cash or travelers checks brought from overseas. Additionally, several of them kept funds in foreign accounts, which they accessed in the United States through ATM and credit card transactions. The hijackers received funds from facilitators in Germany and the United Arab Emirates or directly from Khalid Sheikh Mohammed, KSM, as they transited Pakistan before coming to the United States. The plot cost al Qaeda somewhere in the range of $400,000 to $500,000, of which approximately $300,000 passed through the hijackers' bank accounts in the United States.

While in the United States, the hijackers spent money primarily for flight training, travel and living expenses; extensive investigation has revealed no substantial source of domestic financial support. Neither the hijackers nor their financial facilitators were experts in the use of the international financial system. They created a paper trail linking them to each other and their facilitators. Still, they were adept enough to blend into the vast international financial system easily without doing anything to reveal themselves as criminals, let alone terrorists bent on mass murder.

The money-laundering controls in place at the time were largely focused on drug trafficking and large-scale financial fraud. They could not have detected the hijackers' transactions. The controls were never intended to, and could not, detect or disrupt the routine transactions in which the hijackers engaged.

There is no evidence that any person with advance knowledge of the impending terrorist attacks used that information to profit by trading securities. Although there has been consistent speculation that massive al Qaeda-related "insider trading" preceded the attacks, exhaustive investigation by federal law enforcement and the securities industry has determined that unusual spikes in the trading of certain securities were based on factors unrelated to terrorism.

Al Qaeda and Osama bin Laden obtained money from a variety of sources. Contrary to common belief, Bin Laden did not have access to any significant amounts of personal wealth, particularly after his move from Sudan to Afghanistan. He did not personally fund al Qaeda, either through an inheritance or businesses he was said to have owned in Sudan.

Al Qaeda's funds, approximately $30 million per year, came from the diversion of money from Islamic charities. Al Qaeda relied on well-placed financial facilitators who gathered money from both witting and unwitting donors, primarily in the Gulf Region.

No persuasive evidence exists that al Qaeda relied on the drug trade as an important source of revenue, had any substantial involvement with conflict diamonds, or was financially sponsored by any foreign government. The United States is not, and has not been, a substantial source of al Qaeda funding, although some funds raised in the United States may have found their way to al Qaeda and its affiliate groups.

Before 9/11, terrorist financing was not a priority for either domestic or foreign intelligence collection. Intelligence reporting on this issue was episodic, insufficient, and often inaccurate.

Although the National Security Council considered terrorist financing important in its campaign to disrupt al Qaeda, other agencies failed to participate to the NSC's satisfaction. There was little interagency strategic planning or coordination. Without an effective interagency mechanism, responsibility for the program was dispersed among a myriad of agencies, each working independently.

The FBI gathered intelligence on a significant number of organizations in the United States suspected of raising funds for al Qaeda or other terrorist groups. The FBI, however, did not develop an endgame for its work. Agents continued to gather intelligence, with little hope that they would be able to make a criminal case or otherwise disrupt the operations of these organizations.

The FBI could not turn these investigations into criminal cases because of insufficient international cooperation, a perceived inability to mingle criminal and intelligence investigations due to the wall between intelligence and law enforcement matters, sensitivities to overt investigations of Islamic charities and organizations, and the sheer difficulty of prosecuting most terrorist-financing cases. Nonetheless, FBI street agents had gathered significant intelligence on specific groups.

On a national level, the FBI did not systematically gather and analyze the information its agents developed. It lacked a headquarters unit focusing on terrorist financing. Its overworked counterterrorism personnel lacked time and resources to focus specifically on financing. The FBI as an organization therefore failed to understand the nature and extent of the jihadist fund-raising problem within the United States or to develop a coherent strategy for confronting the problem. The FBI did not and could not fulfill its role to provide intelligence on domestic terrorist financing to government policymakers. The FBI did not contribute to national policy coordination.

The Department of Justice could not develop an effective program for prosecuting terrorist finance cases. Its prosecutors had no systematic way to learn what evidence of prosecutable crimes could be found in the FBI's intelligence files, to which it did not have access.

The U.S. intelligence community largely failed to comprehend al Qaeda's methods of raising, moving, and storing money. It devoted relatively few resources to collecting the financial intelligence that policymakers were requesting or that would have informed the larger counterterrorism strategy.

The CIA took far too long to grasp basic financial information that was readily available—such as the knowledge that al Qaeda relied on fundraising, not bin Laden's personal fortune. The CIA's inability to grasp the true source of bin Laden's funds frustrated policymakers. The U.S. government was unable to integrate potential covert action or overt economic disruption into the counterterrorism effort.

The lack of specific intelligence about al Qaeda financing, and intelligence deficiencies, persisted through 9/11. The Office of Foreign Assets Control, the Treasury organization charged by law with searching out, designating, and freezing bin Laden assets, did not have access to much actionable intelligence.

Before 9/11, a number of significant legislative and regulatory initiatives designed to close vulnerabilities in the U.S. financial system failed to gain traction. They did not gain the attention of policymakers. Some of these, such as a move to control foreign banks with accounts in the United States, died as a result of banking industry pressure. Others, such as a move to regulate money remitters, were mired in bureaucratic inertia and a general anti-regulatory environment.

It is common to say the world has changed since 9/11. This conclusion is especially apt in describing U.S. counterterrorist efforts regarding financing. The U.S. government focused for the first time on terrorist finance and devoted considerable energy and resources to the problem. As a result, we now have a far better understanding of the methods by which terrorists raise, move, and use money. We have employed this knowledge to our advantage.

With a new sense of urgency post 9/11, the intelligence community, including the FBI, created new entities to focus on and bring expertise to the question of terrorist fund-raising and the clandestine movement of money. The intelligence community uses money flows to identify and locate otherwise unknown associates of known terrorists, and has integrated terrorist-financing issues into the larger counterterrorism effort.

Equally important, many of the obstacles hampering investigations have been stripped away. The current intelligence community approach appropriately focuses on using financial transactions, in close coordination with other types of intelligence, to identify and track terrorist groups rather than to starve them of funding.

Still, understanding al Qaeda's money flows and providing actionable intelligence to policymakers present ongoing challenges because of the speed, diversity, and complexity of the means and methods for raising and moving money, the commingling of terrorist money with legitimate funds, the many layers and transfers between donors and the ultimate recipients of the money, the existence of unwitting participants, including donors who give to generalized jihadist struggles rather than specifically to al Qaeda, and the U.S. government's reliance on foreign government reporting for intelligence.

Bringing jihadist fund-raising prosecutions remains difficult in many cases. The inability to get records from other countries, the complexity of directly linking cash flows to terrorist operations or groups, and the difficulty of showing what domestic persons knew about illicit foreign acts or actors all combine to thwart investigations and prosecutions.

The domestic financial community and some international financial institutions have generally provided law enforcement and intelligence agencies with extraordinary cooperation. This cooperation includes providing information to support quickly developing investigations, such as the search for terrorist suspects at times of emergency. Much of this cooperation is voluntary and based on personal relationships.

It remains to be seen whether such cooperation will continue as the memory of 9/11 fades. Efforts to create financial profiles of terrorist cells and terrorist fundraisers have proved unsuccessful, and the ability of financial institutions to detect terrorist financing remains limited.

Since the September 11 attacks and the defeat of the Taliban, al Qaeda's budget has decreased significantly. Although the trend line is clear, the U.S. Government still has not determined with any precision how much al Qaeda raises or from whom or how it spends its money. It appears that the al Qaeda attacks within Saudi Arabia in May and November 2003 have reduced, some say drastically, al Qaeda's ability to raise funds from Saudi sources. There has been both an increase in Saudi enforcement and a more negative perception of al Qaeda by potential donors in the Gulf.

However, as al Qaeda's cash flows have decreased, so, too, have its expenses, generally owing to the defeat of the Taliban and the disbursement of al Qaeda.

Despite our efforts, it appears that al Qaeda can still find money to fund terrorist operations. Al Qaeda now relies to an even greater extent on the physical movement of money and other informal methods of value transfer, which can pose significant challenges for those attempting to detect and disrupt money flows.

Source: U.S. House of Representatives, Financial Services Committee, *9/11 Commission Report: Identifying and Preventing Terrorist Financing* (Washington, DC: U.S. Government Printing Office, 2004), pp. 5–13.

Document 35

The Aviation Security System and the 9/11 Attacks (2004)

The staff of the 9/11 Commission did an in-depth analysis of the aviation security system as it operated on September 11, 2001. Staff members built upon the investigative work completed by other federal agencies to trace the deficiencies that allowed the al-Qaeda operatives to seize four commercial aircraft and use them as weapons against the United States. Material in this document comes from Staff Statement No. 3.

THE ENEMY VIEW

We approach the question of how the aviation security system failed on September 11 by starting from the perspective of the enemy, asking, "What did al Qaeda have to do to complete its mission?"

Some time during the late 1990s, the al Qaeda leadership made the decision to hijack large, commercial, multi-engine aircraft and use them as a devastating weapon as opposed to hijacking a commercial aircraft for use as a bargaining tool. To carry out that decision would require unique skill sets:

- terrorists trained as pilots with the specialized skill and confidence to successfully fly large, multi-engine aircraft, already airborne, into selected targets;
- tactics, techniques, and procedures to successfully conduct in-flight hijackings; and
- operatives willing to die.

To our knowledge, 9/11 was the first time in history that terrorists actually piloted a commercial jetliner in a terrorist operation. This was new. This could not happen overnight and would require long term planning and sequenced operational training.

The terrorists had to determine the tactics and techniques needed to succeed in hijacking an aircraft within the United States. The vulnerabilities of the U.S. domestic commercial aviation security system were well advertised through numerous unclassified reports from agencies like the General Accounting Office and the Department of Transportation's Inspector General. The News media had publicized those findings.

The al Qaeda leadership recognized the need for more specific information. Its agents observed the system first-hand and conducted surveillance flights both internationally and with the United States. Over time, this information allowed them to revise and refine the operational plan. By the spring of 2001, the September 11 operation had combined intent with capabilities to present a real and present threat to the civil aviation system. As long as operational security was maintained, the plan had a high probability of success in conducting multiple, near simultaneous attacks on New York City and Washington, DC.

Let us turn now to a more specific look at the security system in place on September 11 related to anti-hijacking.

INTELLIGENCE

The first layer of defense was intelligence. While the FAA was not a member of the U.S. Intelligence Community, the agency maintained a civil aviation intelligence division that operated 24 hours per day. The intelligence watch was the collection point for a flow of threat related information from federal agencies, particularly the FBI, CIA, and State Department. FAA intelligence personnel were assigned as liaisons to work within these three agencies to facilitate the flow of aviation related information to the FAA and to promote inter-departmental cooperation. The FAA did not assign liaisons to either the National Security Agency or the Defense Intelligence Agency but maintained intelligence requirements with those agencies.

Intelligence data received by the FAA went into preparing Intelligence Case Files. These files tracked and assessed the significance of aviation security incidents, threats and emerging issues. The FAA's analysis of this data informed its security policies, including issuance of FAA Information Circulars, Security Directives, and Emergency Amendments. Such Security Directives and Emergency Amendments are how the FAA ordered air carriers and/or airports to undertake certain extraordinary security measures that were needed immediately above the established baseline.

While the staff has not completed its review and analysis as to what the FAA knew about the threat posed by al Qaeda to civil aviation, including the potential use of aircraft as weapons, we can say:

First, no documentary evidence reviewed by the Commission or testimony we have received to this point has revealed that any level of the FAA possessed any credible and specific intelligence indicating that Osama Bin Ladin, al Qaeda, al Qaeda affiliates or any other group were actually plotting to hijack commercial planes in the United States and use them as weapons of mass destruction.

Second, the threat posed by Osama Bin Ladin, al Qaeda, and al Qaeda affiliates, including their interest in civil aviation, was well known to key civil aviation security officials. The potential threat of Middle Eastern terrorist groups to civil aviation security was acknowledged in many different official FAA documents. The FAA possessed information claiming that associates with Osama Bin Ladin in the 1990s were interested in hijackings and the use of an aircraft as a weapon.

Third, the potential for terrorist suicide hijacking in the United States was officially considered by the FAA's Office of Civil Aviation Security dating back to at least March 1998. However in a presentation the agency made to air carriers and airports in 2000 and early 2001 the FAA discounted the threat because, "fortunately, we have no indication that any group is currently thinking in that direction."

It wasn't until well after the 9/11 attacks that the FAA learned of the "Phoenix EC"—an internal FBI memo written in July of 2001 by an FBI agent in the Phoenix field office suggesting steps that should be taken by the Bureau to look more closely at civil aviation education schools around the country and the use of such programs by individuals who may be affiliated with terrorist organizations.

Fourth, the FAA was aware prior to September 11, 2001, of the arrest of Zacarias Moussaoui in Minnesota, a man arrested by the INS in August of 2001 following reports of suspicious behavior in flight school and the determination that he had overstayed his visa waiver period. Several key issues remain regarding what the FAA knew about Moussaoui, when they knew it, and how they responded to the information supplied by the FBI, which we are continuing to pursue.

Fifth, the FAA did react to the heightened security threat identified by the Intelligence Community during the summer of 2001, including issuing alerts to air carriers about the potential for terrorist acts against civil aviation. In July 2001, the FAA alerted the aviation community to reports of possible near-term terrorist operations . . . particularly on the Arabian Peninsula and/or Israel. The FAA informed the airports and air carriers that it had no credible evidence of specific plans to attack U.S. civil aviation. The agency said that some of the currently active groups were known to plan and train for hijackings and had the capability to construct sophisticated improvised explosive devices concealed exercise prudence and demonstrate a high degree of alertness.

Although several civil aviation security officials testified that the FAA felt blind when it came to assessing the domestic threat because of the lack of intelligence on what was going on the American homeland as opposed to overseas, FAA security analysts did perceive an increasing terrorist threat to U.S. civil aviation at home. FAA documents, including agency accounts published in the Federal Register on July 17, 2001, expressed the FAA's understanding that terrorist groups were active in the United States and maintained an historic interest in targeting aviation, including hijacking. While the agency was engaged in an effort to pass important new regulations to improve checkpoint screener performance, implement anti-sabotage measures and conduct ongoing assessments of the system, no major increases in anti-hijacking security measures were implemented in response to the heightened threat levels in the spring and summer of 2001, other than general warnings to the industry to be more vigilant and cautious.

Sixth, the civil aviation security system in the Untied States during the summer of 2001 stood, as it had for quite some time, at an intermediate aviation security alert level—tantamount to a permanent Code Yellow. This level, and its corresponding security measures, was required when:

Information indicates that a terrorist group or other hostile entity with a known capability of attacking civil aviation is likely to carry out attacks against U.S. targets; or civil disturbances with a direct impact on civil aviation have begun or are imminent.

Without actionable intelligence information to uncover and interdict a terrorist plot in the planning stages or prior to the perpetrator gaining access to the aircraft in the lead-up to September 11, 2001, it was up to the other layers of aviation security to counter the threat.

We conclude this section with a final observation. The last major terrorist attack on a U.S. flagged airliner had been with smuggled explosives, in 1988, in the case of Pan Am 103. The famous Bojinka plot broken up in Manila in 1995 had principally been a plot to smuggle explosives on airliners. The Commission on Aviation Safety and Security created by President Clinton in 1996, named the Gore Commission for its chairman, the Vice President, had focused overwhelmingly on the danger of explosives on aircraft. Historically, explosives on aircraft had taken a heavy death toll, hijackings had not. So, despite continued foreign hijackings leading up to 9/11, the U.S. aviation security system worried most about explosives.

PRESCREENING

If intelligence fails to interdict the terrorist threat, passenger prescreening is the next layer of defense. Passenger prescreening encompasses measures applied prior to the passenger's arrival at the security checkpoint. Prescreening starts with the ticketing process, and generally concludes with passenger check-in at the airport ticket counter.

The hijackers purchased their tickets for the 9/11 flights in a short period of time at the end of August 2001, using credit cards, debit cards, or cash. The ticket record provides the FAA and the air carrier with passenger information for the prescreening process.

The first major prescreening element in place on 9/11 was the FAA listing of individuals known to pose a threat to commercial aviation. Based on information provided by the Intelligence Community, the FAA required air carriers to prohibit listed individuals from boarding aircraft or, in designated cases, to assure that the passenger received enhanced screening before boarding. None of the names of the 9/11 hijackers were identified by the FAA to the airlines in order to bar them from flying or subject them to extra security measures. In fact, the number of individuals subject to such special security instructions issued by the FAA was less than 20 compared to the tens of thousands of names identified in the State Department's TIPOFF watch list.

The second component of prescreening was a program to identify those passengers on each flight who may pose a threat to aviation. In 1998, the FAA required air carriers to implement a FAA-approved computer-assisted passenger prescreening program (CAPPS) designed to identify the pool of passengers most likely in need of additional security scrutiny. The program employed customized, FAA-approved criteria derived from a limited set of information about each ticketed passenger in order to identify "selectees."

FAA rules required that the air carrier only screen each selectee's checked baggage for explosives using various approved methods. However, under the system in place on 9/11, selectees—those who were regarded as a risk to the aircraft—were not required to undergo any additional screening of their person or carry-on baggage at the checkpoint.

The consequences of selection reflected FAA's view that non-suicide bombing was the most substantial risk to domestic aircraft. Since the system in place on

9/11 confined the consequences of selection to the screening of checked bags for explosives, the application of CAPPS did not provide any defense against the weapons and tactics employed by the 9/11 hijackers.

On American Airlines Flight 11, CAPPS chose three of the five hijackers as selectees. Since Waleed al Shehri checked no bags, his selection had no consequences. Wail al Shehri and Satam al Suqami had their checked bags scanned for explosives before they were loaded onto the plane.

None of the Flight 175 hijackers were selected by CAPPS.

All five of the American Airlines Flight 77 hijackers were selected for security scrutiny. Hani Hanjour, Khalid al Mihdhar, and Majed Moqed were chosen via the CAPPS criteria, while Nawaf al Hazmi and Salem al Hazmi were made selectees because they provided inadequate identification information. Their bags were held until it was confirmed that they had boarded the aircraft.

Thus, for the hijacker selectees Hani Hanjour, Nawaf al Hazmi, and Khalid al Mihdhar, who checked no bags on September 11, there were no consequences for their selection by the CAPPS system. For Salem al Hazmi, who checked two bags, and Majed Moqed, who checked one bag, the sole consequence was that their baggage was held until after their boarding on Flight 77 was confirmed.

Ahmad al Haznawi was the sole CAPPS selectee among the Flight 93 hijackers. His checked bag was screened for explosives and then loaded on the plane.

CHECKPOINT SCREENING

With respect to checkpoint screening, Federal rules required air carriers "to conduct screening . . . to prevent or deter the carriage aboard airplanes of any explosive, incendiary, or a deadly or dangerous weapon on or about each individual's person or accessible property, and the carriage of any explosive or incendiary in check baggage." Passenger checkpoint screening is the most obvious element of aviation security.

At the checkpoint, metal detectors were calibrated to detect guns and large knives. Government-certified x-ray machines capable of imaging the shapes of items possessing a particular level of acuity were used to screen carry-on items. In most instances, these screening operations were conducted by security companies under contract with the responsible air carrier.

As of 2001 any confidence that checkpoint screening was operating effectively was belied by numerous publicized studies by the General Accounting Office and the Department of Transportation's Office of Inspector General. Over the previous twenty years they had documented repeatedly serious, chronic weakness in the systems deployed to screen passenger and baggage for weapons or bombs. Shortcomings with the screening process had also been identified internally by the FAA's assessment process.

Despite the documented shortcomings of the screening system, the fact that neither a hijacking nor a bombing had occurred domestically in over a decade was perceived by many within the system as confirmation that it was working. This explains, in part, the view of one transportation security official who testified to the Commission that the agency thought it had won the battle against hijacking. In fact, the Commission received testimony that one of the primary reasons to restrict the consequences of CAPPS "selection" was because officials thought that checkpoint screening was working.

The evolution of checkpoint screening illustrates many of the systemic problems that faced the civil aviation security system in place on 9/11. The executive and legislative branches of government, and the civil aviation industry were highly reactive on aviation security matters. Most of the aviation security system's features had developed in response to specific incidents, rather than in anticipation. Civil aviation security was primarily accomplished through a slow and cumbersome rulemaking process—a reflection of the agency's conflicting missions of both regulating and promoting the industry. A number of FAA witnesses said this process was the "bane" of civil aviation security. For example, the FAA attempted to set a requirement that it would certify screening contractors. The FAA Aviation Reauthorization Act of 1996 directed the FAA to take such action, which the 1997 Gore Commission endorsed. But the process of implementing this action had still not been completed by September 11, 2001.

Those are systemic observations. But, to analyze the 9/11 attack, we had to focus on which items were prohibited and which were allowed to be carried into the cabin of an aircraft. FAA guidelines were used to determine what objects should not be allowed into the cabin of an aircraft. Included in the listing were knives with blades 4 inches long or longer and/or knives considered illegal by local law; and tear gas, mace, and similar chemicals.

These guidelines were to be used by screeners, to make a reasonable determination of what items in the possession of a person should be considered a deadly or dangerous weapon. The FAA told the air carriers that common sense should prevail.

Hence the standards of what constituted a deadly or dangerous weapon were somewhat vague. Other than for guns, large knives, explosives and incendiaries, determining what was prohibited and what was allowable was up to the common sense of the carriers and their screening contractors.

To write out what common sense meant to them, the air carriers developed, through their trade associations, a Checkpoint Operations Guide. This document was approved by the FAA. The edition of this guide in place on September 11, 2001, classified "box cutters," for example, as "Restricted" items that were not permitted in the passenger cabin of an aircraft. The checkpoint supervisor was required to be notified if an item in this category was encountered. Passengers would be given the option of having those items transported as checked baggage. "Mace," "pepper spray," as well as "tear gas" were categorized as hazardous materials and passengers could not take items in that category on an airplane without the express permission of the airline.

On the other hand, pocket utility knives (less than 4 inch blade) were allowed. The Checkpoint Operations Guide provided no further guidance on how to distinguish between "box cutters" and "pocket utility knives."

One of the checkpoint supervisors working at Logan International Airport on September 11, 2001, recalled that as of that day, while box cutters were not permitted to pass through the checkpoint without the removal of the blade, any knife with a blade of less than four inches was permitted to pass through security.

In practice, we believe the FAA's approach of admonishing air carriers to use common sense about what items should not be allowed on an aircraft, while also approving the air carrier's checkpoint operations guidelines that defined the industry's "common sense," in practice, created an environment where both parties could deny responsibility for making hard and most likely unpopular decisions.

What happened at the checkpoints? Of the checkpoints used to screen the passengers of Flights 11, 77, 93 and 175 on 9/11, only Washington Dulles International Airport had videotaping equipment in place. Therefore the most specific information that exists about the processing of the 9/11 hijackers is information about American Airlines Flight 77, which crashed into the Pentagon. The staff has also reviewed testing results for all the checkpoints in question, scores of interviews with checkpoint screeners and supervisors who might have processed the hijackers, and FAA and FBI evaluations of the available information. There is no reason to believe that the screening on 9/11 was fundamentally different at any of the relevant airports.

Return again to the perspective of the enemy. The plan required all of the hijackers to successfully board the assigned aircraft. If several of their number failed to board, the operational plan might fall apart or their operational security might be breached. To have this kind of confidence, they had to develop a plan they felt would work anywhere they were screened, regardless of the quality of the screener. We believe they developed such a plan and practiced it in the months before the attacks, including in text flights, to be sure their tactics would work. In other words, we believe they did not count on a sloppy screener. All 19 hijackers were able to pass successfully through checkpoint screening to board their flights. They were 19 for 19. They counted on beating a weak system.

Turning to the specifics of Flight 77 checkpoint screening, at 7:18 a.m. Eastern Daylight Time on the morning of September 11, 2001, Majed Moqed and Khalid al Mihdhar entered one of the security screening checkpoints at Dulles International Airport. They placed their carry-on bags on the x-ray machine belt and proceeded through the first magnetometer. Both set off the alarm and were subsequently directed to a second magnetometer. While al Mihdhar did not alarm the second magnetometer and was permitted through the checkpoint, Moqed failed once more and was then subjected to a personal screening with a metal detection hand wand. He passed this inspection and then was permitted to pass through the checkpoint.

At 7:35 a.m. Hani Hanjour placed two carry-on bags on the x-ray belt in the Main Terminal checkpoint, and proceeded, without alarm, through the magnetometer. He picked up his carry-on bags and passed through the checkpoint. Salem al Hazmi successfully cleared the magnetometer and was permitted through the checkpoint. Nawaf al Hazmi set off the alarms for both the first and second magnetometers and was then hand-wanded before being passed. In addition, his shoulder-strap carry-on bag was swiped by an explosive trace detector and then passed.

Our best working hypothesis is that a number of the hijackers were carrying permissible utility knives or pocket knives. One example of such a utility knife is the "Leatherman" item. We know that at least two knives like this were actually purchased by hijackers and have not been found in the belongings the hijackers left behind. The staff will pass this around. Please be careful. The blade is open. It locks into position. It is very sharp.

According to the guidelines on 9/11, if such a knife were discovered in the possession of an individual who alarmed either the walk-through metal detector or the hand wand, the item would be returned to the owner and permitted to be carried on the aircraft.

ONBOARD SECURITY

Once the hijackers were able to get through the checkpoints and board the plane, the last layer of defense was onboard security. That layer was comprised of two main components: the presence of law enforcement on the flights and the so-called "Common Strategy" for responding to in-flight security emergencies, including hijacking, devised by the Federal Aviation Administration in consultation with industry and law enforcement.

But on the day of September 11, 2001, after the hijackers boarded, they faced no significant security obstacles. The Federal Air Marshal Program was almost exclusively directed to international flights. Cockpit doors were not hardened. Gaining access to the cockpit was not a particularly difficult challenge.

Flight crews were trained not to attempt to thwart or fight the hijackers. The object was to get the plane to land safety. Crews were trained, in fact, to dissuade passengers from taking precipitous or "heroic" actions against hijackers.

CONCLUSION

From all of the evidence staff has reviewed to date, we have come to the conclusion that on September 11, 2001, would-be hijackers of domestic flights of U.S. civil aviation faced these challenges:

- avoiding prior notice by the U.S. intelligence and law enforcement communities;
- carrying items that could be used as weapons that were either permissible or not detectable by the screening systems in place; and
- understanding and taking advantage of the in-flight hijacking protocol of the Common Strategy.

A review of publicly available literature and/or the use of "test runs" would likely have improved the odds of achieving those tasks.

The "no-fly" lists offered an opportunity to stop the hijackers, but the FAA had not been provided any of their names, even though two of them were already watchlisted in TIPOFF. The prescreening process was effectively irrelevant to them. The on-board security efforts, like the Federal Air Marshal program, had eroded to the vanishing point. So the hijackers really had to beat just one layer of security—the security checkpoint process.

Plotters who were determined, highly motivated individuals, who escaped notice on no-fly lists, who studied publicly available vulnerabilities of the aviation security system, who used items with a metal content less than a handgun and most likely permissible, and who knew to exploit training received by aircraft personnel to be non-confrontational were likely to be successful in hijacking a domestic U.S. aircraft.

Source: Steven Strasser (ed.), *The 9/11 Investigations* (New York: Public Affairs, 2004). 9-11 Commission Staff Statement No. 3. pp. 34–46.

Document 36

Letter from Brian F. Sullivan to Thomas Kean, Chairman of the National Commission on Terrorist Attacks Upon the United States (2004)

Brian F. Sullivan, former FAA Special Agent, wrote this letter to Thomas Kean, the Chairman of the 9/11 Commission, toward the end of the commission's investigation of September 11. He was still concerned over the state of aviation security and the lack of accountability of those in charge at the time of the attacks. Not only were there reprimands for bad decisions, but many of those receiving such reprimands had been subsequently promoted to higher commands. Sullivan was worried about the culture of bureaucracy within the federal aviation security.

Thomas Kean, Chairman
National Commission on Terrorist Attacks Upon the United States
301 7th Street SW
Room 5125
Washington, DC 20407

Dear Chairman Kean:

I recently had an opportunity to review FBI Whistleblower Sibel Edmunds's open letter to you as chairman of the 9/11 Commission and felt compelled to write in support of her observations. She was spot on when she spoke to failed transparency, the lack of accountability and information provided yet inexplicably left out of your final report, I see the same omissions vis a vis aviation security, as she has cited regarding the FBI and intelligence.

First and foremost is the question of accountability. Not a single FAA manager, responsible for the insecurities of 9/11 has been held accountable for allowing our last line of defense to be so vulnerable on that fateful day, instead, some of the same people were transferred into and in some instances promoted into key positions within the Transportation Security Administration.

The end result is that the culture of bureaucracy within federal aviation security didn't change and we've ended up with expected result. Two examples would be failed leadership in the development of CAPPII and the GAO's recent report on how poorly federal screeners are performing. The *Seattle Times* recently completed a series on just how porous our aviation security remains today. The bottom line is that the American taxpayer is not getting what we paid for in terms of enhanced aviation security and the TSA is not all it can be.

Let's look for a moment at information, which was provided to the Commission, but left out of your report. Perhaps this information will be included in your updated/revised staff statements or in assessments of the individual airports exploited on 9/11 (Boston's Logan Airport, Dulles and Newark); but in order to insure some level of transparency and provide the media with some focus for national review. I'll list just a few here.

1. The Massachusetts Governor's Carter Commission report, with its findings relative to FAA, airline and Massport security.
2. The April '01 memorandum from Massport's Director of Security, Joe Lawless to his leadership, which cited terrorist ties to Logan Airport and the need to address known vulnerabilities there.
3. The Counter Technology Inc report on Logan's security, six pages of which were critical of Massport leadership vis a vis security, but were removed from the original report after a meeting with Massport's General Counsel.
4. The Logan Airline Managers Council (LAMCO), in conjunction with the FAA's Federal Security Manager at Logan rejecting Joe Lawless's proposal for the Mass State Police to begin undercover testing of screening checkpoints in July '01.
5. Jan Garvey, the head of the FAA, failing to react after an FAA Administrator's Hotline complaint in the summer of '01 regarding security concerns at Logan, which included a hand delivered tape of the local FOX affiliate's April '01 expose of security shortcomings, to include the very same screening checkpoints which would be exploited by the terrorists on 9/11.
6. Reported sighting of Mohammed Atta at Logan in May and early September involved in suspicious activity in the Operations Area and surveillance of checkpoints.

These are but a few issues reported to the Commission, but for some reason, left out of the final report. Probably the most significant of all was the Office of Special Counsel's Report and DOT OIG response, which stated how FAA's leadership failed to manage its own Red Team and take action on its findings.

The Commission made a couple of generic recommendations regarding aviation security, but in failing to address accountability left the action in the hands of the TSA. The problem here is that until the Commission recognizes and holds accountable those failed FAA Civil Aviation Security managers, who gave us the insecurities of 9/11 and then were transferred into and some cases promoted into key positions within the TSA, that organization will remain dysfunctional and unable to enact the Commission's aviation security recommendations.

Accountability must be established first if there is to be any reasonable expectation that those recommendations will be brought to fruition.

The Commissioners must address the TSA's shortcomings, in order to change the prevailing culture within aviation security. Layers of bureaucracy must be eliminated, incompetents replaced by competents and local autonomy granted, in as much as is possible, to the Federal Security Directors at our airports. The TSA as it now stands, is a bloated bureaucracy made dysfunctional by overcentralization.

Somehow the media euphoria and infatuation with the 9/11 Commission in the aftermath of its report must be replaced with some critical analysis regarding accountability and aviation security. Both were given short shift in the Commission's final report.

I am not willing to see the façade of aviation security, as promulgated by the TSA continue on unabated and I'm hopeful that we can enlist the support of the 9/11 Commissioners to help address the accountability issue, particularly if you are serious about your aviation security recommendations being effectively implemented.

A response, open or closed, would be appreciated.

Respectfully submitted:

Brian F. Sullivan
FAA Special Agent (Retired)
New England Region

Source: Brian F. Sullivan, "An Open Letter to Thomas Kean," *Scoop Independent News* [New Zealand] (August 13, 2004), p. 1. Letter reprinted with the permission of Brian F. Sullivan.

Document 37

Comments of Representative Maxine Waters (D-CA) on Saudi Financial Support for Al-Qaeda before the House of Representatives' Financial Services Committee (August 22, 2004)

One of the controversial aspects of financial support for al-Qaeda has been the role of the Saudis. Saudi financial support played a role in the success of the Taliban in Afghanistan, and later in other regimes that advanced Wahhadism. Representative Maxine Waters (D-CA) used the House Financial Services Committee to challenge the 9/11 Commission's conclusion that there was no money funneled by Saudis to al-Qaeda. Lee Hamilton then made a measured reply to the congresswoman's points.

REP. MAXINE WATERS (D-CA): I'd like to commend Chairman Kean, Vice Chairman Hamilton and other members of the 9/11 Commission and the Commission staff for the care and attention that obviously went into these documents. And I thank all of them for their work. They have certainly performed an exceptional public service.

Mr. Chairman and members, I'm going to take a line of questioning that may be a little bit uncomfortable, but I think it is absolutely necessary.

First of all, I'd like to note that as it is reported, the 9/11 commission confirmed last month that it had found no evidence that the government of Saudi Arabia funded al Qaeda terrorist network and the 9/11 hijackers received funding from Saudi citizen Omar al-Bayoumi or Princess Haifa Faisal, wife of Ambassador to the United States Prince Bandar Sultan. I'd like to ask what went into that investigation that would lead you to that conclusion.

And the reason I would like to ask that is there are so many reports. *Time* magazine, for example, reported that the Saudis still appear to be protecting charities associated with the royal family which funnel money to terrorists.

Also, as you know, there has been a lot written lately about the relationship of both President Bush and his father to the Saudis, not only their personal friendships but their money relationships—relationships that include the Harken Energy, Halliburton and the Carlyle Group. And of course a lot has been written about the $1 million that was funded to the Bush library by the Saudis.

Also, it is noted that in this cozy relationship that this administration has with the—have with the Saudis, it goes so far as to identify that Robert Jordan, the ambassador that was appointed to Saudi Arabia, had no diplomatic experience, does not speak Arabic and cannot be considered a serious diplomat as it relates to representing our interests in a country where many of us have very, very serious concerns.

So I would like to know how did the commission reach the conclusion or find no evidence that the government of Saudi Arabia funded—furnished al Qaeda or the network with any funds, or that they're not still funding these charities. Did you have CIA information that helped you to document that? As a matter of fact, it appears that before 9/11, according to *U.S. News*—a 1996 CIA report found that a third of the 50 Saudi-backed charities it studied were tied to terrorist groups.

Similarly, a 1998 report by the National Security Council had identified the Saudi government as the epicenter of terrorist funding, becoming the single greatest force in spreading Islamic fundamentalism and funneling hundreds of millions of dollars to jihad groups and al Qaeda cells around the world.

Now I must admit that this information that I'm reading to you now came from the Center for American Progress.

I won't go on any further, I think you get the picture. What I'm trying to say to you is, if you've come to this conclusion that the Saudi government had no— is not responsible for continuing to fund these charities, where dollars ended up with some of the 9/11 hijackers, how did you come to this conclusion? And what have you explored about this relationship of this administration to the Saudi government? Obviously it's very cozy. They helped to escort members of Osama bin Laden's family out of the country. The princess who was found to have been giving money to charities associated with 9/11 hijackers—all leads us to a conclusion that this cozy relationship has to be broken up, and there's something to this funding.

LEE HAMILTON: Thank you very much, Congressman Waters. The Saudi connection with al Qaeda is a very, very important matter to look at.

And you really do have to make a distinction between the activities of the Saudi government prior to the spring of 2003, when they were attacked themselves, and then again later I think in November in 2003; that time frame, pre-attacks in Saudi Arabia and post-attacks in Saudi Arabia. Saudi Arabia is a key part of any international effort to fight terrorist financing.

You asked us how we reached the conclusion. The conclusion was that we found no evidence, as you have stated correctly, that the Saudi government, as an institution or as individual senior officials of the Saudi government, supported al Qaeda. Now we sent investigators to Saudi Arabia. We reviewed all kind of information and documents with regard to—that are available in the intelligence community. We listened to many, many people who talked to us about these things. We followed every lead that we could. This is an ongoing investigation. I think it will continue; we're not going to have the final word on it.

We did find in this—the pre-attack period, pre-Saudi Arabia attack period, that there was a real failure to conduct oversight in the Saudi government. There was a lack of awareness of the problem, and a lot of financing activity we think flourished. We think that Saudi cooperation was ambivalent and selective, and we were not entirely pleased with it. Then along came those attacks, and in the spring of 2003 and after that period we believe the performance of the Saudi government improved quite a bit, and a number of deficiencies were corrected.

The Saudi government needs to continue its activities to strengthen their capabilities to stem the flow from Saudi sources to al Qaeda, and we have to work very, very closely with the Saudis in order to get that done. But we do not have any evidence that the government itself or senior officials of the government were involved in al Qaeda financing, and I think our diplomatic efforts there over a period of time have been helpful. But no one, I think, would say that we have resolved all of the problems with the Saudis. So we have to continue to send a message to the Saudi government that the Saudis must do everything within their power—everything within their power—to eliminate al Qaeda financing from Saudi sources.

Source: U.S. House of Representatives, Financial Services Committee, *9/11 Commission Report: Identifying and Preventing Terrorist Financing* (Washington, DC: U.S. Government Printing Office, 2004), pp. 12–13.

Document 38

Curt Weldon's Testimony about Able Danger
(September 20, 2005)

In 2005, shortly after the final report of the 9/11 Commission appeared, news about a secret military project with the name Able Danger surfaced, and a controversy ensued. This project had supposedly identified Mohamed Atta and others as al-Qaeda operatives well before the events of September 11, 2001. Representative Curt Weldon (R-PA), member of the House of Representatives Armed Services Committee, has led the campaign to disclose information about Able Danger. On September 20, 2005, Weldon gave testimony before the Senate Judiciary Committee on Able Danger and Intelligence Information Sharing. His remarks follow.

Mr. Chairman [Senator Arlen Spector], I am dismayed and frustrated, however, with the response of our government to information about the program Able Danger. The Defense Department has acknowledged that a program, Able Danger, existed and operated during the 1999–2000 time period, authorized by the Chairman of the Joint Chiefs of Staff, and carried out by SOCOM, with the help of the Army. DOD has stated publicly that five individuals, including an Army lieutenant colonel, recipient of the Bronze Star, who's in the room today, and a Navy Annapolis graduate ship commander, have emphatically claimed that they worked on or ran Able Danger and identified Mohammed Atta and three other 9/11 terrorists over 1 year prior to the Trade Center attack.

These five individuals have told me, your staff, and others, that Able Danger amassed significant amounts of data, primarily from open sources about al Qaeda operations worldwide, and that this data continued to be used through 2001 in briefings prepared for the Chairman of the Joint chiefs of Staff and others.

These two brave military officers have risked their careers to come forward to simply tell the truth and to help America fully understand all that happened prior to 9/11 that had or might have had an impact on the most significant attack ever against our country and our citizens. These individuals have openly expressed their willingness to testify here today without subpoenas, but have been silenced by the Pentagon. They have been prevented from testifying, according to the Pentagon, due to concerns regarding classified information, in spite, Mr. Chairman, of the Pentagon's claims to members of the House Armed Services Committee two weeks ago that the bulk of the data used by Able Danger was open-source, which was why the DOD lawyers claim that no certificates were needed to certify the destruction of massive amounts of data that had been collected. Mr. Chairman, you can't have it both ways. It's either classified or it's not. But what the Pentagon has done the last two weeks is they've contradicted themselves.

Another former DOD official (J. D. Smith) told me and your staff, and was prepared to testify today—and he's in the room—that he worked on the data collection and analysis used to support Able Danger. He was prepared to state, as he told us, that he had an Able Danger chart, with Mohamed Atta identified, on his office wall at Andrews Air Force Base until DOD Investigative Services removed it. At risk to his current employment, he has told us, and is prepared to testify under oath, in direct rebuttal to the claims of the 9/11 commissioners that he was aware of the purchase of Mohamed Atta's photograph from a California contractor, not from the U.S. legal identity documents. He was prepared to discuss the extensive amount of data collected and analyzed about al Qaeda. Underscoring the fact that Able Danger was never about one chart or one photograph but, rather, was and is about massive data collected and assembled against what Madeleine Albright declared to be, in 1999, an international terrorist organization. He, too, has been silenced. Another former DOD official will testify today that he was ordered to destroy up to 2.5 terabytes of data. Now, I don't know what a terabyte of data is, so we contacted the Library of Congress. It's equal to one-fourth of all the entire written collection that the Library of Congress maintains. This information was amassed through Able Danger that could still be useful today. He will name the individual who ordered him to destroy that data, and will state for the record that the customer for that data, General Lambert of SOCOM, was never consulted about that destruction and expressed his outrage upon learning that the destruction had taken place.

An FBI employee that I identified has met with your committee staff, and was prepared to testify today that she arranged three meetings with the FBI Washington Field office in September of 2000 for the specific purpose of transferring al Qaeda Brooklyn cell/Able Danger information to the FBI for their use. In each instance, she has stated that meetings were canceled at the last minute by DOD officials. She has not been allowed to testify publicly today.

The 9/11 commission was created by Congress with my full support. I have publicly championed many of their recommendations. On four separate occasions, I attempted to brief the commission on specifics related to intelligence problems, lack of intelligence collaboration, the NOA concept—the national operations analysis (hub) that I had pursued in '99 and 2000—and the work of the LIWA and Able Danger. Except for one five-minute telephone call with Tom Kean, I was unable to meet with 9/11 commissioners and/or staff. In fact, I had my chief of staff hand-deliver questions to be asked of George Tenet, and others, to the commission on March the 24th of 2004, which I will enter into the record. They were never used and the questions were never asked. It was, in fact, a member of the 9/11 commission who encouraged me to pursue the Able Danger story after I briefed him on June 29th of 2005.

He informed me that the 9/11 commission staff had never briefed the commission members on Able Danger. He said that the facts had to be brought out. When the 9/11 commission first responded to questions about Able Danger, they changed their story and spin three times in three days. This is not what Congress intended. All the people involved with Able Danger should have been interviewed by the 9/11 commission.

Because Able Danger ceased to formally exist before the administration came into office, I understand why there might have been a lack of knowledge about the program and its operations. In fact, when I first met with Steve Cambone—and I'm the one that introduced him to Tony Shaffer, who is here today—he told me that he was at a significant disadvantage, that I knew more about Able Danger than he did.

But that is not an excuse to not pursue the complete story of Able Danger. In fact, Mr. Chairman, DOD never conducted an actual investigation. And this came up in our Armed Services meeting two weeks ago. No oaths were given, no subpoenas were issued; rather, an informal inquiry was initiated.

A thorough review of Able Danger, its operations and data collected and analyzed, and recommendations for data transfer to other agencies, could have and should have been completed by more than one member of Congress using one staffer. Instead, over the past three months, I have witnessed denial, deception, threats to DOD employees, character assassination, and now silence. This is not what our constituents want. It is unacceptable to the families and friends of the victims of 9/11 and flies in the face of every ideal upon which this country was founded.

Over the past six weeks, some have used the Able Danger story to make unfair public allegations, to question the intentions or character of 9/11 commissioners or to advance conspiracy theories. I have done none of this. When I learned details of Able Danger in June, I talked to 9/11 commissioners personally and staff. I delivered a comprehensive floor speech on June 27th of 2005 and methodically briefed the House chairs of Armed Services, Intelligence, Homeland Security and Justice Appropriations.

This story only became public—even though significant portions were first reported in a Heritage Foundation speech that I gave, still available online, on January 28, 2003—when Government Security News ran a story on August the 1st of 2005, followed by a front-page story in the *New York Times* on August the 2nd of 2005.

My goal now, Mr. Chairman, is the same as it was then—the full and complete truth for the American people about the run-up to 9/11. Many Americans lost family and friends on 9/11. Michael Horrocks was a neighbor of mine in Pennsylvania, a former Navy pilot, graduate of Westchester, like myself. He was at the controls of one of the planes on 9/11.

He left behind a wife and two kids. We built a playground in his honor at his kids' school. Ray Downey was a personal friend. As a New York deputy fire officer, he took me through the garage of the Trade Center towers in 1993, the first time bin Laden hit us. We worked together. In fact, he gave me the idea for the creation of the Gilmore Commission, which I authorized—which I authored and added to the Defense Authorization Bill in 1997.

On September 11th, 2001, he was a New York City Fire Department chief of all rescue. The 343 firefighters, including Ray, who were all killed were under

Ray's command as he led the largest and most successful rescue effort in the history of mankind.

I promised Michael's wife and kids and Ray's wife and kids and grandkids that we would not stop until the day that we had learned all the facts about 9/11. Unfortunately, Mr. Chairman, that day has not yet arrived. We must do better.

Source: *Congressional Record* (Oct. 20, 2005) Page H8979, Page H8981, Page H8982, and Page H8983.

Document 39

Essay by Ward Churchill (September 11, 2001)

The essay "'Some People Push Back': On the Justice of Roosting Chickens," by University of Colorado professor Ward Churchill, was written shortly after September 11, 2001, but there was little reaction to it until 2004, when it became notorious. Many people became outraged, and politicians began threatening both Churchill and the university. Besides defending the motives of the hijackers, Churchill made charges about the guilt of the victims, calling them "little Eichmanns." Churchill's provocative prose led to demands that he be fired from his tenured position. The university administration first defended his academic freedom rights and then instituted a panel to investigate his research. This panel concluded that Churchill should be fired or suspended for academic misconduct with regard to his research. Churchill has since lost his job, and legal proceedings are about to commence that should take several years. The complete text of Churchill's essay is included, and he sometimes uses unconventional spelling.

When queried by reporters concerning his views on the assassination of John F. Kennedy in November 1963, Malcolm X famously—and quite charitably, all things considered—replied that it was merely a case of 'chickens coming home to roost.'

On the morning of September 11, 2001, a few more chickens—along with some half-million dead Iraqi children—came home to roost in a very big way at the twin towers of New York's World Trade Center. Well, actually, a few of them seem to have nestled in at the Pentagon as well.

The Iraqi youngsters, all of them under 12, died as a predictable—in fact, widely predicted—result of the 1991 US 'surgical' bombing of their country's water purification and sewage facilities, as well as other 'infrastructural' targets upon which Iraq's civilian population depends for its very survival.

If the nature of the bombing were not already bad enough—and it should be noted that this sort of 'aerial war' constitutes a Class 1 Crime Against Humanity, entailing myriad gross violations of international law, as well as every conceivable standard of 'civilized' behavior—the death toll has been steadily ratcheted up by US-imposed sanctions for a full decade now. Enforced all the while by a massive military presence and periodic bombing raids, the embargo has greatly impaired the victims' ability to import the nutrients, medicines and other materials necessary to saving the lives of even their toddlers.

All told, Iraq had a population of about 18 million. The 500,000 kids lost to date thus represent something on the order of 25 percent of their age group. Indisputably, the rest have suffered—are still suffering—a combination of physical debilitation and psychological trauma severe enough to prevent their ever fully recovering. In effect, an entire generation has been obliterated.

The reason for this holocaust was/is rather simple, and stated quite straightforwardly by President George Bush, the 41st 'freedom-loving' father of the freedom-lover currently filling the Oval Office, George the 43rd: "The world must learn that what we say, goes," intoned George the Elder to the enthusiastic applause of freedom-loving Americans everywhere. How Old George conveyed his message was certainly no mystery to the US public. One need only recall the 24-hour-per-day dissemination of bombardment videos on every available TV channel, and the exceedingly high ratings of these telecasts, to gain a sense of how much they knew.

In trying to affix a meaning to such things, we would do well to remember the wave of elation that swept America at reports of what was happening along the so-called Highway of Death; perhaps 100,000 "towel-heads" and "camel jockeys"—or was it "sand niggers" that week?—in full retreat, routed and effectively defenseless, many of them conscripted civilian laborers, slaughtered in a single day by jets firing the most hyper-lethal types of ordnance. It was a performance worthy of the Nazis during the early months of their drive into Russia. And it should be borne in mind that Good Germans gleefully cheered that butchery, too. Indeed, support for Hitler suffered no serious erosion among Germany's "innocent civilians" until the defeat at Stalingrad in 1943.

There may be a real utility to reflecting further, this time upon the fact that it was pious Americans who led the way in assigning the onus of collective guilt to the German people as a whole, not for things they as individuals had done, but for what they had allowed—nay, empowered—their leaders and their soldiers to do in their name.

If the principle was valid then, it remains so now, as applicable to Good Americans as it was the Good Germans. And the price exacted from the Germans for the faultiness of their moral fiber was truly ghastly. Returning now to the children, and to the effects of the post–Gulf War embargo—continued bull force by Bush the Elder's successors in the Clinton administration as a gesture of its 'resolve' to finalize what George himself had dubbed the 'New World Order' of American military/economic domination—it should be noted that not one but two high United Nations officials attempting to coordinate delivery of humanitarian aid to Iraq resigned in succession as protests against US policy.

One of them, former U.N. Assistant Secretary General Denis Halladay, repeatedly denounced what was happening as "a systematic program . . . of deliberate genocide." His statements appeared in the *New York Times* and other papers during the fall of 1998, so it can hardly be contended that the American public was 'unaware' of them. Shortly thereafter, Secretary of State Madeline Albright openly confirmed Halladay's assessment. Asked during the widely-viewed TV program Meet the Press to respond to his 'allegations,' she calmly announced that she'd decided it was 'worth the price' to see that U.S. objectives were achieved.

The Politics of a Perpetrator Population

As a whole, the American public greeted these revelations with yawns. There were, after all, far more pressing things than the unrelenting misery/death of a few hundred thousand Iraqi tikes to be concerned with. Getting 'Jeremy' and 'Ellington' to their weekly soccer game, for instance, or seeing to it that little 'Tiffany' and 'Ashley' had just the right roll-neck sweaters to go with their new cords. And, to be sure, there was the yuppie holy war against ashtrays—for 'our kids,' no less—as an all-absorbing point of political focus.

In fairness, it must be admitted that there was an infinitesimally small segment of the body politic who expressed opposition to what was/is being done to the children of Iraq. It must also be conceded, however, that those involved by-and-large contented themselves with signing petitions and conducting candle-lit prayer vigils, bearing 'moral witness' as vast legions of brown-skinned five-year-olds sat shivering in the dark, wide-eyed in horror, whimpering as they expired in the most agonizing ways imaginable.

Be it said as well, and this is really the crux of it, that the 'resistance' expended the bulk of its time and energy harnessed to the systemically-useful task of trying to ensure, as a 'principle of moral virtue' that nobody went further than waving signs as a means of 'challenging' the patently exterminatory pursuit of Pax Americana. So pure of principle were these 'dissidents,' in fact, that they began literally to supplant the police in protecting corporations profiting by the carnage against suffering such retaliatory 'violence' as having their windows broken by persons less 'enlightened'—or perhaps more outraged—than the self-anointed 'peacekeepers.'

Property before people, it seems—or at least the equation of property to people—is a value by no means restricted to America's boardrooms. And the sanctimony with which such putrid sentiments are enunciated turns out to be nauseatingly similar, whether mouthed by the CEO of Standard Oil or any of the swarm of comfort zone 'pacifists' queuing up to condemn the black block after it ever so slightly disturbed the functioning of business-as-usual in Seattle.

Small wonder, all-in-all, that people elsewhere in the world—the Mideast, for instance—began to wonder where, exactly, aside from the streets of the US itself, one was to find the peace America's purportedly oppositional peacekeepers claimed they were keeping.

The answer, surely, was plain enough to anyone unblended by the kind of delusions engendered by sheer vanity and self-absorption. So, too, were the implications in terms of anything changing, out there, in America's free-fire zones.

Tellingly, it was at precisely this point—with the genocide in Iraq officially admitted and a public response demonstrating beyond a shadow of a doubt that there were virtually no Americans, including most of those professing otherwise, doing anything tangible to stop it—that the combat teams which eventually commandeered the aircraft used on September 11 began to infiltrate the United States.

Meet the 'Terrorists'

Of the men who came, there are a few things demanding to be said in the face of the unending torrent of disinformational drivel unleashed by George Junior and the corporate 'news' media immediately following their successful operation on September 11.

They did not, for starters, 'initiate' a war with the US, much less commit 'the first acts of war of the new millennium.'

A good case could be made that the war in which they were combatants has been waged more-or-less continuously by the 'Christian West'—now proudly emblematized by the United States—against the 'Islamic East' since the time of the First Crusade, about 1,000 years ago. More recently, one could argue that the war began when Lyndon Johnson first lent significant support to Israel's dispassion/displacement of Palestinians during the 1960s, or when George the Elder ordered 'Desert Shield' in 1990, or at any of several points in between. Any way you slice it, however, if what the combat teams did to the WTC and the Pentagon can be understood as acts of war—and they can—then the same is true of every US 'overflight' of Iraqi territory since day one. The first acts of war during the current millennium thus occurred on its very first day, and were carried out by U.S. aviators acting under orders from their then-commander-in-chief, Bill Clinton. The most that can honestly be said of those involved on September 11 is that they finally responded in kind to some of what this country has dispensed to their people as a matter of course.

That they waited so long to do so is, notwithstanding the 1993 action at the WTC, more than anything a testament to their patience and restraint.

They did not license themselves to 'target innocent civilians.'

There is simply no argument to be made that the Pentagon personnel killed on September 11 fill that bill. The building and those inside comprised military targets, pure and simple. As to those in the World Trade Center . . .

Well, really. Let's get a grip there, shall we? True enough they were civilians of a sort. But innocent? Gimme a break. They formed a technocratic corps at the very heart of America's global financial empire—the 'mighty engine of profit' to which the military dimension of U.S. policy has always been enslaved—and they did so both willingly and knowingly—recourse to 'ignorance'—a derivative, after all, of the word 'ignore'—counts as less than an excuse among this relatively well-educated elite. To the extent that any of them were unaware of the costs and consequences to others of what they were involved in—and in many cases excelling at—it was because of their absolute refusal to see. More likely, it was because they were too busy braying, incessantly and self-importantly, into their cell phones, arranging power lunches and stock transactions, each of which translated conveniently out of sight, mind and smelling distance, into the starved and rotting flesh of infants. If there was a better, more effective, or in fact any other way of visiting some penalty befitting their participation upon the little Eichmanns inhabiting the sterile sanctuary of the twin towers, I'd really be interested in hearing about it.

The men who flew the missions against the WTC and Pentagon were not 'cowards.' That distinction properly belongs to the 'firm-jawed lads' who delighted in flying stealth aircraft through the undefended airspace of Baghdad dropping payload after payload of bombs on anyone unfortunate enough to be below—including tens of thousands of genuinely innocent civilians—while themselves incurring all the risk one might expect during a visit to the local video arcade. Still more, the world describes all those 'fighting men and women' who sat in computer consoles aboard ships in the Persian Gulf, enjoying air-conditioned comfort while launching cruise missiles into neighborhoods filled with random human beings. Whatever else can be said of them, the men who struck on September 11 manifested the courage of their convictions, willingly expending their own lives in attaining their objectives.

Nor were they 'fanatics' devoted to 'Islamic fundamentalism.'

One might rightly describe their actions as 'desperate.' Feelings of desperation, however, are a perfectly reasonable—one is tempted to say 'normal'—emotional response among persons confronted by the mass murder of their children, particularly when it appears that nobody else really gives damn (ask a Jewish survivor about this one, or even more poignantly, for all the attention paid them, a Gypsy). That desperate circumstances generate desperate responses is no mysterious or irrational principle, of the sort motivating fanatics. Less is it one peculiar to Islam. Indeed, even the FBI's investigative reports on the combat teams' activities during the months leading up to September 11 make it clear that the members were not fundamentalist Muslims. Rather, it's pretty obvious at this point that they were secular activists—soldiers, really—who, while undoubtedly enjoying cordial relations with the clerics of their countries, were motivated far more by the grisly realities of the U.S. war against them than by a set of religious beliefs.

And still less were they/their acts 'insane.'

Insanity is a condition readily associable with the very American idea that one—or one's country—holds what amounts to a 'divine right' to commit genocide, and thus to forever do so with impunity. The term might also be reasonably applied to anyone suffering genocide without attempting in some material way to bring the process to a halt. Sanity itself, in this frame of reference, might be defined by a willingness to try and destroy the perpetrators and/or the sources of their ability to commit their crimes. (Shall we now discuss the US 'strategic bombing campaign' against Germany during World War II, and the mental health of those involved in it?)

Which takes us to official characterizations of the combat teams as an embodiment of 'evil.'

Evil—for those inclined to embrace the banality of such a concept—was perfectly incarnated in that malignant toad known as Madeline Albright, squatting in her studio chair like Jaba the Hutt, blandly spewing the news that she'd imposed a collective death sentence upon the unoffending youth of Iraq. Evil was to be heard in that great American hero 'Stormin Norman' Schwartzkopf's utterly dehumanizing dismissal of their systematic torture and annihilation as mere 'collateral damage.' Evil, moreover, is a term appropriate to describing the mentality of a public that finds such perspectives and policies attending them acceptable, or even momentarily tolerable.

Had it not been for these evils, the counterattacks of September 11 would never have occurred. And unless 'the world is rid of such evil,' to lift a line from George Junior, September 11 may well end up looking like a lark.

There is no reason, after all, to believe that the teams deployed in the assaults on the WTC and the Pentagon were the only such, that the others are composed of 'Arabic-looking individuals'—America's indiscriminately lethal arrogance and psychotic sense of self-entitlement have long since given the great majority of the world's peoples ample cause to be at war with it—or that they are in any way dependent upon the seizure of civilian airliners to complete their missions.

To the contrary, there is every reason to expect that there are many other teams in place, tasked to employ altogether different tactics in executing operational plans at least as well-crafted as those evident on September 11, and very well equipped for their jobs. This is to say that, since the assaults on the WTC and Pentagon were acts of war—not 'terrorist incidents'—they must be understood as components in a much broader strategy designed to achieve specific results. From this, it can only be adduced that there are plenty of other components ready to go, and that they will be used, should this become necessary in the eyes of the strategists. It also seems a safe bet that each component is calibrated to inflict damage at a level incrementally higher than the one before (during the 1960s, the Johnson administration employed a similar policy against Vietnam, referred to as 'escalation').

Since implementation of the overall plan began with the WTC/Pentagon assaults, it takes no rocket scientist to decipher what is likely to happen next, should the U.S. attempt a response of the inexcusable variety to which it has long entitled itself.

About Those Boys (and Girls) in the Bureau

There's another matter begging for comment at this point. The idea that the FBI's 'counterterrorism task forces' can do a thing to prevent what will happen is yet another dimension of America's delusional pathology. The fact is that, for all its publicly-financed 'image-building' exercises, the Bureau has never shown the least aptitude for anything of the sort.

Oh, yeah, FBI counterintelligence personnel have proven quite adept at framing anarchists, communists and Black Panthers, sometimes murdering them in their beds or the electric chair. The Bureau's SWAT units have displayed their ability to combat child abuse in Waco by burning babies alive, and its vaunted Crime Lab has been shown to pad its 'crime-fighting' statistics by fabricating evidence against many an alleged car thief. But actual 'heavy-duty bad guys' of the sort at issue now—this isn't a Bruce Willis/Chuck Norris/Sly Stallone movie, after all. And J. Edgar Hoover doesn't get to approve either the script or the casting.

The number of spies, saboteurs and bona fide terrorists apprehended, or even detected by the FBI in the course of its long and slimy history, could be counted on one's fingers and toes. On occasion, its agents have even turned out to be the spies, and, in many instances, the terrorists as well.

To be fair once again, if the Bureau functions as at best a carnival of clowns where its 'domestic security responsibilities' are concerned, this is because—regardless of official hype—it has none. It is now, as it's always been, the national political police force, an instrument created and perfected to ensure that all Americans, not just the consenting mass, are 'free' to do exactly as they're told.

The FBI and 'cooperating agencies' can thus be relied upon to set about 'protecting freedom' by destroying whatever rights and liberties were left to U.S. citizens before September 11 (in fact, they've already received authorization to begin). Sheeplike, the great majority of Americans can also be counted upon to bleat their approval, at least in the short run, believing as they always do that the nasty implication of what they're doing will pertain only to others.

Oh Yeah, and 'The Company,' Too

A possibly even sicker joke is the notion, suddenly in vogue, that the CIA will be able to pinpoint 'terrorist threats,' 'rooting out their infrastructure' where it exists and/or 'terminating' it before it can materialize, if only it's allowed to beef up its 'human intelligence gathering capacity' in an unrestrained manner (including full-bore operations inside the U.S., of course).

Yeah, right.

Since America has a collective attention-span of about 15 minutes, a little refresher seems in order: 'The Company' had something like a quarter-million people serving as 'intelligence assets' by feeding it information in Vietnam in 1968, and it couldn't even predict the Tet Offensive. God knows how many spies it was fielding against the USSR at the height of Ronald Reagan's version of the Cold War, and it was still caught flatfooted by the collapse of the Soviet Union. As to destroying 'terrorist infrastructure,' one would do well to remember Operation Phoenix, another product of its open season in Vietnam. In that one, the CIA enlisted elite US units like the Navy Seals and Army Special Forces, as well as those of friendly countries—the south Vietnamese Rangers, for example, and Australian SAS—to run around 'neutralizing' folks targeted by the The Company's legion of snitches as 'guerrillas' (as those now known as 'terrorists' were then called).

Sound familiar?

Upwards of 40,000 people—mostly bystanders, as it turns out—were murdered by Phoenix hit teams before the guerrillas, stronger than ever, ran the US and its collaborators out of their country altogether. And these are the guys who are gonna save the day, if unleashed to do their thing in North America?

The net impact of all this 'counterterrorism' activity upon the combat teams' ability to do what they came to do, of course, will be nil.

Instead, it's likely to make it easier for them to operate (it's worked that way in places like Northern Ireland). And, since denying Americans the luxury of reaping the benefits of genocide in comfort was self-evidently a key objective of the WTC/Pentagon assaults, it can be stated unequivocally that a more overt display of the police state mentality already pervading this country simply confirms the magnitude of their victory.

On Matters of Proportion and Intent

As things stand, including the 1993 detonation of the WTC, 'Arab terrorists' have responded to the massive and sustained American terror bombing of Iraq with a total of four assaults by explosives inside the US. That's about 1% of the 50,000 bombs the Pentagon announced were rained on Baghdad alone during the Gulf War (add Oklahoma City and you'll get something nearer an actual 1%).

They've managed in the process to kill about 5,000 Americans, or roughly 1% of the dead Iraqi children (the percentage is far smaller if you factor in the killing of adult Iraqi civilians, not to mention troops butchered as/after they'd surrendered and/or after the 'war-ending' ceasefire had been announced).

In terms undoubtedly more meaningful to the property/profit-minded American mainstream, they've knocked down a half-dozen buildings—albeit some very well-chosen ones—as opposed to the 'strategic devastation' visited upon the whole of Iraq, and punched a $100 billion hole in the earnings outlook of major corporate shareholders, as opposed to the U.S. obliteration of Iraq's entire economy.

With that, they've given Americans a tiny dose of their own medicine.

This might be seen as merely a matter of 'vengeance' or 'retribution,' and, unquestionably, America has earned it, even if it were to add up only to something so ultimately petty.

The problem is that vengeance is usually framed in terms of 'getting even,' a concept which is plainly inapplicable in this instance. As the above data indicate, it would require another 49,996 detonations killing 495,000 more Americans, for the 'terrorists' to 'break even' for the bombing of Baghdad/extermination of Iraqi children alone. And that's to achieve 'real number' parity. To attain an actual proportional parity of damage—the US is about 15 times as large as Iraq in terms of population, even more in terms of territory—they would, at a minimum, have to blow up about 300,000 more buildings and kill something on the order of 7.5 million people.

Were this the intent of those who've entered the US to wage war against it, it would remain no less true that America and Americans were only receiving the bill for what they'd already done. Payback, as they say, can be a real motherfucker (ask the Germans). There is, however, no reason to believe that retributive parity is necessarily an item on the agenda of those who planned the WTC/Pentagon operation. If it were, given the virtual certainty that they possessed the capacity to have inflicted far more damage than they did, there would be a lot more American bodies lying about right now.

Hence, it can be concluded that ravings carried by the 'news' media since September 11 have contained at least one grain of truth: The peoples of the Mideast 'aren't like' Americans, not least because they don't 'value life' in the same way. By this, it should be understood that Middle-Easterners, unlike Americans, have no history of exterminating others purely for profit or on the basis of racial animus. Thus, we can appreciate the fact that they value life—all lives, not just their own—far more highly than do their U.S. counterparts.

The Makings of a Humanitarian Strategy

In sum one can discern a certain optimism—it might even be called humanitarianism—imbedded in the thinking of those who presided over the very limited actions conducted on September 11.

Their logic seems to have devolved upon the notion that the American people have condoned what has been/is being done in their name—indeed, are to a significant extent actively complicit in it—mainly because they have no idea what it feels like to be on the receiving end.

Now they do.

That was the 'medicinal' aspect of the attacks.

To all appearances, the idea is now to give the tonic a little time to take effect, jolting Americans into the realization that the sort of pain they're now experiencing first-hand is no different from—or the least bit more excruciating than—that which they've been so cavalier in causing others, and thus to respond appropriately.

More bluntly, the hope was—and maybe still is—that Americans, stripped of their presumed immunity from incurring any real consequences for their behavior, would comprehend and act upon a formulation as uncomplicated as 'stop killing our kids, if you want your own to be safe.'

Either way, it's kind of a 'reality therapy' approach, designed to afford the American people a chance to finally 'do the right thing' on their own, without further coaxing.

Were the opportunity acted upon in some reasonable good faith fashion—a sufficiently large number of Americans rising up and doing whatever is necessary to force an immediate lifting of the sanctions on Iraq, for instance, or maybe hanging a few of America's abundant supply of major war criminals (Henry Kissinger comes quickly to mind, as do Madeline Albright, Colin Powell, Bill Clinton and George the Elder)—there is every reason to expect that military operations against the US on its domestic front would be immediately suspended.

Whether they would remain so would of course be contingent upon follow-up. By that, it may be assumed that American acceptance of onsite inspections by international observers to verify destruction of its weapons of mass destruction (as well as dismantlement of all facilities in which more might be manufactured), Nuremberg-style trials in which a few thousand US military/corporate personnel could be properly adjudicated and punished for their Crimes Against Humanity, and payment of reparations to the array of nations/people whose assets the US has plundered over the years, would suffice.

Since they've shown no sign of being unreasonable or vindictive, it may even be anticipated that, after a suitable period of adjustment and reeducation (mainly to allow them to acquire the skills necessary to living within their means), those restored to control over their own destinies by the gallant sacrifices of the combat teams the WTC and Pentagon will eventually (re)admit Americans to the global circle of civilized societies. Stranger things have happened.

In the Alternative

Unfortunately, noble as they may have been, such humanitarian aspirations were always doomed to remain unfulfilled. For it to have been otherwise, a far higher quality of character and intellect would have to prevail among average Americans than is actually the case. Perhaps the strategists underestimated the impact a couple of generations-worth of media indoctrination can produce in terms of demolishing the capacity of human beings to form coherent thoughts. Maybe they forgot to factor in the mind-numbing effects of the indoctrination passed off as education in the US. Then again, it's entirely possible they were aware that a decisive majority of American adults have been reduced by this point to a level much closer to the kind of immediate self-gratification entailed in Pavlovian stimulus/response patterns than anything accessible by appeal to higher loci, and still felt morally obliged to offer the dolts an option to quit while they were ahead.

What the hell? It was worth a try.

But it's becoming increasingly apparent that the dosage of medicine administered was entirely insufficient to accomplish its purpose.

Although there are undoubtedly exceptions, Americans for the most part still don't get it.

Already, they've desecrated the temporary tomb of those killed in the WTC, staging a veritable pep rally atop the mangled remains of those they profess to honor, treating the whole affair as if it were some bizarre breed of contact sport. And, of course, there are the inevitable pom-poms shaped like American flags, school colors worn as little red-white-and-blue ribbons affixed to lapels, sportscasters in the form of 'counterterrorism experts' drooling mindless color commentary during the pregame warm-up.

Refusing the realization that the world has suddenly shifted its axis, and that they are therefore no longer 'in charge,' they have by-and-large reverted instantly to type, working themselves into their usual bloodlust on the now obsolete premise that the bloodletting will 'naturally' occur elsewhere and to someone else.

'Patriotism,' a wise man once observed, 'is the last refuge of scoundrels.'

And the braided, he might of added.

Braided Scoundrel-in-Chief, George Junior, lacking even the sense to be careful what he wished for, has teamed up with a gaggle of fundamentalist Christian clerics like Billy Graham to proclaim a 'New Crusade' called 'Infinite Justice' aimed at 'ridding the world of evil.'

One could easily make light of such rhetoric, remarking upon how unseemly it is for a son to threaten his father in such fashion—or a president to so publicly contemplate the murder/suicide of himself and his cabinet—but the matter is deadly serious.

They are preparing once again to sally forth for the purpose of roasting brown-skinned children by the scores of thousands. Already, the B-1 bombers and the aircraft carriers and the missile frigates are en route, the airborne divisions are gearing to.

To where? Afghanistan?

The Sudan?

Iraq, again (or still)?

How about Grenada (that was fun)?

Any of them or all. It doesn't matter.

The desire to pummel the helpless runs rabid as ever.

Only, this time it's different.

This time the helpless aren't, or at least are not so helpless as they were.

This time, somewhere, perhaps in an Afghani mountain cave, possibly in a Brooklyn basement, maybe another locale altogether—but somewhere, all the same—there's a grim-visaged (wo)man wearing a Clint Eastwood smile.

'Go ahead, punks,' s/he's saying, 'Make my day.'

And when they do, when they launch these airstrikes abroad—or maybe a little later—it will be at a time conforming to the 'terrorists' own schedule, and at a place of their choosing—the next more intensive dose of medicine will be administered here 'at home.'

Of what will it consist this time? Anthrax? Mustard gas? Sarin? A tactical nuclear device?

That, too, is their choice to make.

Looking back, it will seem to future generations inexplicable why Americans were unable on their own and in time to save themselves, to accept a rule of nature so basic that it could be mouthed by an actor, Laurence Fishburne, in a movie, *The Cotton Club*.

'You've got to learn,' the line went, 'that when you push people around, some people push back.'

As they should.

As they should.

As they must.

And as they undoubtedly will.
There is justice in such symmetry.

Source: "'Some People Push Back': On the Justice of Roosting Chickens" (http://www.kersplebedeb.com/mystuff/s11/churchill.html). Ward Churchill has given permission to reprint this essay.

Document 40

Selected Excerpts from the Testimony of FBI Agent Harry Samit in the Zacarias Moussaoui Trial on March 9, 2006

FBI agent Harry Samit was stationed at the FBI's Minneapolis field office at the time when Zacarias Moussaoui was reported to be acting suspiciously. Samit also became suspicious; he suspected that Moussaoui was planning to use an aircraft for a terrorist act. This testimony reveals Samit's actions and the lack of response from FBI headquarters on obtaining a warrant to search Moussaoui's possessions. He tried for both a criminal warrant and a FISA warrant but was turned down on both. His testimony expresses his frustrations in dealing with his superiors in FBI headquarters. The questions in this testimony come from Mr. Novak, a federal prosecutor in the Moussaoui trial, and the answers come from Harry Samit. The trial testimony of Mr. Samit took up 196 pages, so only about a third of his testimony is recorded here, but it covers most of the major points of his testimony.

Q. And could you tell the good folks on what—what kind of assignment do you have as a special agent with the FBI up there in Minneapolis?

A. I'm an investigator assigned to the Joint Terrorism Task Force.

Q. Tell the folks what the Joint Terrorism Task Force is.

A. The Joint Terrorism Task Force is an organization of law enforcement agents and officers who investigate international terrorism under the framework set up by the FBI. It's got personnel from a variety of different law enforcement agencies.

Q. Do you want to list some of the different agencies that work with you on that Joint Terrorism Task Force?

A. Immigration and Naturalization Service, United States Secret Service, local police officers, sheriff's deputies, a variety of different investigators.

Q. Beyond your assignment to the JTFF, can you tell us what else you do there as a special agent up there in Minnesota?

A. At the time in 1999, I was assigned as a pilot with the FBI as well.

Q. We're going to talk about your pilot training in a second, but your squad that you're assigned to is squad what?

A. Squad 5.

Q. And squad 5 up there includes the investigation of what types of crime?

A. In 2001, it included the investigation of international terrorism, domestic terrorism, and foreign counterintelligence.

Q. And would it be fair to say that since your inception into the FBI, your initial assignment up there in Minneapolis, you've basically been working full-time on terrorism investigations?

A. Yes, sir.

Q. Now, could you tell us, have you received any type of specialized training in the world of terrorism?

A. I have. During the FBI academy, the new agent training, there was a terrorism integrated case scenario which I participated in along with my class. I also attended a basic international terrorism in-service after graduating the FBI academy, and then later a double agent and recruitment in-service as well.

Q. Agent Samit, on August the 15th of 2001, were you assigned still as the special agent to the FBI in Minneapolis?

A. I was.

Q. And at that time did you have occasion to get assigned to the investigation of Zacarias Moussaoui?

A. I was.

Q. And at that time who was your supervisor?

A. I had an acting supervisor, Gregory Jones.

Q. And was there a fellow special agent by the name of Dave Rapp that also worked with you?

A. Yes, sir.

Q. Was he relatively new?

A. He was very new, yes, sir.

Q. Do you want to tell us how it is that you—how the investigation into Zacarias Moussaoui began?

A. Special Agent Rapp had complaint duty that day. It is a rotating shift. All the agents in the office have to answer phone calls from the public and other law enforcement agencies. Special Agent Rapp had occasion to take a call from Pan Am, and the person, the caller, Tim Nelson, provided some fairly significant information.

Q. What was the initial information that you-all received there from Pan Am?

A. That they had a student they were training at the flight academy on simulators for 747-400 series aircraft who was very unusual.

Q. Okay. Did they give you the student's name?

A. They did.

Q. And did they tell you why it is that the student was unusual?

A. Yes, sir. They said that he didn't have any ratings, any aviation ratings or licenses.

Q. What does that mean to you as a criminal investigator?

A. It means that for a person to want to do expensive aviation training, typically it is going to lead somewhere, to a job opportunity or to a job enhancement.

Q. And by not pursuing the ratings, that means they are just not doing it for the—benefit themselves financially; is that right?

A. Yes, sir.

Q. Not worth the investment, right?

A. Yes, sir.

Q. Did they tell you whether the student, Mr. Moussaoui, was employed by an airline?

A. They did. They said he was not. He had no affiliation with any airline.

Q. Was that unusual?

A. It was.

Q. Why was that unusual?

A. Because the typical student, as was explained to us, is an airline pilot or is seeking employment with an airline and is already qualified to do so.

Q. Why would that be unusual?

A. Because the airlines typically would pay for the student, or the student would be making an investment in their own training in order to become eligible to be hired by an airline.

Q. Okay. Did they tell you how much the training for Mr. Moussaoui cost?

A. The caller didn't know for sure, but said it was between 8- and 9,000 dollars.

Q. Okay, And what, if any, information did you get about the amount of hours or licensing that Mr. Moussaoui had?

A. It was low. It was less than 60 hours of flight time.

Q. All right. Did you receive information about what type of plane it was that Mr. Moussaoui was pursuing the training on?

A. Yes, sir.

Q. What type of plane was that?

A. 747-400 series airliner.

Q. All right. And could you tell us, are you familiar with the notion of a glass cockpit?

A. Yes, sir.

Q. Could you tell us what the glass cockpit means to you and the investigatory significance of that?

A. What it means to me as a pilot is the way the information is displayed to the pilot in the cockpit is different. Older airplanes, as compared to glass cockpit airplanes, have individual gauges that display the information, critical information that the pilot needs. When an airplane is said to have a glass cockpit, it relies on a much smaller number of multi-function displays, television screens in the cockpit.

Q. What, if any, impact did that have in terms of your thinking about whether criminality was afoot?

A. My initial thought was that it's a simpler interface for a relative novice, so that if someone had illegitimate purposes in mind for wanting to receive the flight training, that would be an ideal type of aircraft, because they wouldn't need as much training and experience if they were to try and fly it.

Q. And what if any impact would the glass cockpit have on the number of—if there was criminality afoot, the number of accomplices that would have to be involved?

A. The other issue would pertain to the number of crew members in the cockpit. Because the glass cockpit airplanes typically have increased automation, they need fewer people in the cockpit. And so in order to take over an airplane, it would be the difference between having to overwhelm one or two people as opposed to three or four.

Q. All right. Now, in addition to that information, did you ask for and receive any additional background information, identifiers or anything like that from the defendant?

A. We were able to get his name, his date of birth, and the fact that he was, said he lived in England and was from France, at least initially.⁖

Q. Now, once you got that information, did you open up a case, an investigation?

A. We did.

Q. Could you explain to the ladies and gentlemen what kind of case that you opened up?

A. Within probably 30 minutes of receiving that telephone call we opened an intelligence investigation.

Q. Back in August of 2001, could you tell us what type of investigatory cases that you could open up?

A. During that time we had the intelligence investigation, which we did actually open on Mr. Moussaoui, and we also had a criminal investigation.

Q. All right. I want to ask you to explain the difference. Starting with the criminal, what is—criminal investigation, what was your goal back in 2001 if you were to open up just a standard criminal investigation?

A. Like any other type of crime that the FBI investigates, the goal of a criminal investigation pertaining to terrorism is to collect evidence of a crime relating to international terrorism.

Q. And would that—with a mind-set towards what?

A. Towards prosecution.

Q. All right. Now, contrast that with opening up an intelligence investigation, what's, what do you do there?

A. An intelligence investigation is designed to generate intelligence, intelligence whose goal would be to safeguard national security.

Q. And by safeguarding national security, what does that mean? What would you try to accomplish towards that goal?

A. We would attempt to use any information derived from a case, an intelligence investigation, to strengthen our ability to deal with threats to national security, whether it be espionage or terrorists, ways to implement countermeasures to deny them their objectives, without necessarily prosecuting anybody, but we would still take steps, countermeasures to prevent them from accomplishing their goals.

Q. Explain to us, if you are not going to arrest somebody, how is it that you could end up protecting national security during your investigation? What are the types of things you can do?

A. We can use that intelligence to deny personnel access to the United States, to certain classified information; we can use that intelligence to implement countermeasures, security countermeasures to make whole sectors safer. Any time information comes of a threat, or intelligence comes regarding a threat, the countermeasures which would counter that.

Q. Okay. Now, what if during the course of an investigation, an intelligence investigation, you decide that you have gathered enough information to charge somebody criminally? Are you allowed to do that?

A. Yes, sir. At the time we could, there was a mechanism by which a criminal investigation and prosecution could occur, but there were a number of steps that needed to be gone through before that could happen.

Q. Could you explain to us what those steps were?

A. There was a term called the wall. And the wall was supposed to be a barrier between intelligence and criminal investigations wherein information developed on the intelligence investigation could not be supplied at the wall to those working the criminal investigation.

Q. What was the purpose of the wall?

A. To prevent abuse, to prevent people in the FBI and law enforcement from utilizing information gathered under the auspices of national security to be used to prosecute someone, without safeguards and checks imposed on that.

Q. Now, we were talking about the wall there. Again, could you explain to us the amount of safeguards that you had to, or oversight that you had to go through, if you were working on the intelligence side versus the criminal side?

A. We could—the system was set up whereby there could be a group of, separate group of agents within the same office who were working criminal investigation against the same subject. It was important, especially for the people working the intelligence case against that person, to be very cognizant that they not share information that was derived directly. Instead what we were required to do during that time period was apply to our headquarters, who would then apply to the Department of Justice for authority to do that.

Q. Okay. And was there a particular unit within the Department of Justice that you needed approval from in order to switch the case from an intelligence to a criminal case?

A. Not to switch, not to switch the cases.

Q. Or share the information.

A. It was the Office of Intelligence Policy Review, OIPR.

Q. In a criminal case, who are the attorneys that you would normally deal with if you were to pursue a criminal investigation?

A. Assistant United States attorneys in the District of Minnesota.

Q. And if you opened an intelligence case, were you able to deal with the assistant United States attorneys that were located there in Minneapolis?

A. No, that would fall under the heading of our needing to go to the Office of Intelligence Policy Review first for authority.

Q. And they would have to approve that before you could share information with them; is that correct?

A. Yes, sir.

Q. Now, in addition to finding out that he was French, did Agent [John] Weess [special agent with the Immigration and Naturalization Service] determine, along with you, what Mr. Moussaoui's status was in terms of being an immigrant into the United States?

A. He did. He was able to determine very quickly that Mr. Moussaoui was out of status.

Q. Well, out of status means what?

A. Out of status means illegally in the United States.

Q. Can you tell us what it is that Mr. [Clancy] Prevost [Moussaoui ground school instructor] told you at that time?

A. Mr. Prevost was able to elaborate on his contact with Mr. Moussaoui, to describe his interest in aviation but his utter lack of experience and knowledge. He discussed the fact that they talked about Mr. Moussaoui was a resident of the U.K., originally from France. When we asked Mr. Prevost what sparked his suspicion that's when he related a story about Mr. Moussaoui's interest in the aircraft doors, the fact that he was surprised to learn that they couldn't be opened in flight, and then that led into the discussion about Mr. Moussaoui's religion.

Q. Okay, Now, after you interviewed Mr. Prevost, could you tell us if you made any decision about how to proceed with your investigation?

A. We did. Special Agent Weess and I consulted and we decided that on the basis of the suspicious behavior discussed, provided to us by the school, that we were going to arrest Mr. Moussaoui.

Q. Okay. And why was that? You were going to arrest him for what?

A. We were going to arrest him on his visa waiver overstay.

Q. But were you focused upon that or were you focused on other concerns?

A. We were obviously focused on learning more about his plans. And we saw that as a way of preventing him from getting any simulator training, any meaningful aircraft training before we had the opportunity to talk to him and sort things out.

Q. Okay. Now, at the time that you arrested him, did you notice if Mr. Moussaoui had any other bags or any other items that were in the hotel room on the left side?

A. He did. The room was full of household goods, of clothing, of bags, backpacks, suitcases, and I noticed a considerable quantity of clothing and other materials like that on the left side of the room.

Q. Okay. And at that time did you search those items?

A. No, we did not.

Q. Okay. Why not?

A. We asked Mr. Moussaoui for permission to search. He became very upset at being informed he was being placed under arrest. He again noted to us that he had expensive flight training, urgent flight training he needed to attend. And I suggested to him that maybe there was a reply to that, that he had received—

Q. Reply to what?

A. To his request to adjust status.

Q. Okay.

A. That there might be other documents which would show that he was, in fact, in status.

Q. And what was his response to that?

A. His response was no, you may not search my things, you can't go through anything else. He was very insistent that we not do that.

Q. Why didn't you search them anyhow?

A. Because we're not allowed to do that under the law. Mr. Moussaoui was in custody. He had been patted down. He was, he was subsequently searched, his person was searched, but under the Fourth Amendment we're not allowed to search his room.

Q. All right. Now, could you tell us on August 17 of 2001, did you make some kind of notification to your headquarters?

A. We did.

Q. And could you tell us—first of all—would you explain to the ladies and gentlemen what ITOS is in the world of FBI?

A. ITOS stands for the International Terrorism Operations Section. It's a group of supervisors and analysts at headquarters . . ., who are assigned to oversee and support investigations in the field, like in Minneapolis.

Q. And within ITOS, are there various units dealing with particular groups of terrorists?

A. There are.

Q. Could you just summarize what some of the units are there that are within the ITOS division of the FBI?

A. Two important ones for this are the Usama Bin Laden Unit that deals with al Qaeda, or UBLU is the acronym, and the Radical Fundamentalist Unit, or RFU.

Q. And what do they deal with?

A. The Usama bin Laden Unit deals with al Qaeda. The Radical Fundamentalist Unit at the time dealt with Sunni extremists who are not al Qaeda, various other groups.

Q. And as a field agent out there, are you supposed to go to the, to the unit that deals with the particular terrorist that you're looking at?

A. Exactly.

Q. And—now, you believed that Mr. Moussaoui was a terrorist, and you've—you confronted him with, as you've testified; is that right?

A. Yes, sir.

Q. Did you know which terrorist organization he was a member of?

A. We did not.

Q. And so how did you know which unit to go to in the ITOS?

A. Well, we didn't originally, and the one that most logically fitted it was the Radical Fundamentalist Unit.

Q. And why is this that you went to the Radical Fundamentalist Unit?

A. We knew that Mr. Moussaoui was a Sunni Muslim, he was an extremist, and we believed he was involved in an ongoing plot. The Radical Fundamentalist Unit was the logical unit.

Q. Okay. And now could you tell us how is it that a field agent communicates with the headquarters? Do you just call them up on the telephone, or do you do something else.

A. Informal communications can be via telephone or e-mail, but in the FBI world, formalized communications were through a document that we call an electronic communication.

Q. Okay.

A. Or an EC is how we abbreviate it.

Q. This EC, did you send it then to the RFU unit?

A. Initially it was sent to the Iran unit and then routed to the RFU unit.

Q. Why did you go to the Iran unit then?

A. Because before speaking with Mr. Moussaoui, FBI database checks indicated that his name might be connected to Iran.

Q. Okay. And what happened when your EC got to Iran? Did you get kicked over to the RFU unit?

A. We did. By then there had been enough of a delay, the interviews had occurred, and we were well aware that it was not under the purview of the Iran unit but in fact the Radical Fundamentalist Unit.

Q. Where you should have been in the first place, all right. Now, could you tell us who was your contact in the RFU unit?

A. The supervisor who was assigned oversight and support responsibilities for Minneapolis was Supervisory Special Agent Mike Maltbie.

Q. Okay. And when you sent that electronic communication to Mr. Maltbie, what was it that your initial request was that you wanted to do?

A. My request to Mr. Maltbie was to apply to the Office of Intelligence Policy Review, to OIPR—

Q. That's in the Department of Justice. You talked about them before, right?

A. Yes, sir, that's correct.

Q. What did you want them—what did you want to occur?

A. I wanted them to grant permission to go to the United States Attorney's Office in the District of Minnesota so that we could pursue criminal charges.

Q. Are you trying to overcome the wall, so to speak?

A. Not overcome it. I'm trying to get permission to release selected information over it. The wall will still exist, and that will still be, certainly in August of 2001 will be a factor, but what I'm trying to do is pass information to criminal investigators so they can begin pursuing that type of investigation.

Q. Okay. And were you given permission to do that?

A. I was not.

Q. Okay. And why is it—were you told why it is you were not given permission?

A. I was told that, that our headquarters, FBI headquarters, Radical Fundamentalist Unit did not believe that sufficient evidence of a crime existed, and also there was a fear that if we were to try and go for a criminal case, to pursue a criminal search initially, and then we had to go back and use techniques under the intelligence world, that it might taint that.

Q. Could you tell us what the—would you describe for us what the process was then for you to go about procuring a FISA [Foreign Intelligence Surveillance Act] warrant back in August of 2001?

A. Once my investigation had convinced myself and supervisors, other agents working the case with me, that probable cause existed to believe that the subject of that warrant—of that search was acting as an agent of a foreign power, then I would prepare an electronic communication, an EC, and supporting documentation that would go to the Radical Fundamentalist Unit, or the FBI headquarters unit that was overseeing that investigation. They would, they would take that information, they would add whatever type—whatever information they could to amplify their request, and then they would take it to a headquarters unit, FBI headquarters unit called the National Security Law Unit, comprised of lawyers whose expertise is in the area of national security law. They would review it to ensure that probable cause did, in fact, exist to establish that that person was acting as an agent of a foreign power. When that was in agreement and the FBI agreed that the application had merit, it would then go to the Department of Justice, OIPR, Office of Intelligence Policy Review, where it would again be reviewed by attorneys, this time in the Department of Justice outside the FBI, and again, when all parties agreed that probable cause existed, it would go forward to the FISA court in the form of a declaration.

Q. Okay.

A. Which a judge would sign or not.

Q. Is the FISA court a local judge then in Minnesota, or is that somewhere else?

A. It's somewhere else.

Q. All right. And is it generally headquartered somewhere in the Washington area, with affiliates around the country?

A. Yes, sir.

Q. And, and even when the application goes to the FISA judge, the FISA judge still has the decision whether to approve it or disapprove it; is that right?

A. That's correct. There's many points along the way where it can be forwarded and not forwarded. The ultimate person who decides is a FISA court judge.

Q. After you were denied the authority to seek a criminal search warrant, did you take steps to try to get a FISA warrant?

A. Yes, sir.

Q. Could you explain what it is that—the steps that you took in order to do so?

A. We, we shifted—I personally shifted gears slightly, because now the nature of the information that I need is different. I no longer need to establish that, in fact, the person is engaged in an ongoing crime, but rather that they're doing any actions on behalf of a foreign power, that they are now acting as an agent of a foreign power, and so the focus changed slightly to that. The substance of the interviews was still useful to some extent and misleading to other extents, but the objective was the same, was the search of those belongings.

Q. Well, and specifically factually, are you trying to connect Mr. Moussaoui to a terrorist organization?

A. Yes, absolutely.

Q. Now, directing your attention to August 23, earlier on in your testimony, you had told us that you had made a request to your—to Jay Abbott, one of the French legats that the FBI has; is that correct?

A. Yes, sir, the assistant legal attaché in the Paris office.

Q. All right. And on August 23, did you get some information back from your French legat?

A. I did.

Q. All right. And did you get information from Mr. Abbott connecting Mr. Moussaoui to a dead Chechen fighter?

A. Yes, sir.

Q. Could you tell the folks what a Chechen fighter is?

A. Yes, sir. There was a conflict then going on in the former Soviet—the former Soviet, now Russian, region of Chechnya. They were seeking independence from the Russian Federation and, in fact, had seen an influx in the late '90s of foreign fighters from various Muslim countries. A number of these soldiers were trained in Afghanistan. They reported into Chechnya and began engaging the Russians in military combat.

Q. Well, let me ask you this: You had told us that al Qaeda was identified on a State Department list as a foreign terrorist organization. Were Chechen rebels identified as a foreign terrorist organization?

A. No, sir, they weren't.

Q. Now, on August 30, did you get additional information back through your French legat?

A. Yes, sir.

Q. And did you get specific information about Mr. Moussaoui's fundamentalism?

A. Yes.

Q. Could you describe what the extent of the information was about his religious views?

A. That he was extreme, that he was—had espoused violence, that he attempted to recruit and convert others to both the extreme view of Islam and to violence, and that he had followed closely the Wahhabi sect of Islam.

Q. And on August 19, did you send a request to the English government asking them to do investigation on your behalf?

A. To our legal attaché in London, yes, sir.

Q. Same type of thing you have in France, you've got one over there in England?

A. Correct.

Q. And what type of information was it that you were trying to gather in England?

A. The same type of information regarding associates, sources of funding. The one that was sent to London to our legal attaché carried particular weight and detail because those are the items not only that Mr. Moussaoui had disclosed to the associate, Ahmed Atif, but he had done so in such a way in the interview that made me believe that that was a person of significance.

Q. Now, on August 22, did you have—receive information from the Central Intelligence Agency?

A. I did.

Q. Well, what information did you get back from—summarizing what you got from the CIA at that time?

A. I received information from them that Mr. Moussaoui's dead associate was connected to the leader of the Chechen rebels by name, and that that—

Q. Who is the—what name did you receive of the leader of the Chechen rebels?

A. Ibn Khattab.

Q. Okay. Did you receive any other information about Ibn Khattab, the leader of the Chechen rebels?

A. From the Central Intelligence Agency I learned that Ibn Khattab and Usama Bin Laden had had a relationship based on their past history.

Q. Okay. Did you receive any information about Mr. Moussaoui being a member of al Qaeda?

A. No.

Q. Now, did you continue to try to accumulate the information that you had gotten through your French legat and from the Central Intelligence Agency in terms of pursuing your FISA warrant?

A. Yes. It was, it was the obsession of our squad, of the Joint Terrorism Task Force, was doing just that.

Q. When you say obsession, could you tell us what do you mean by that?

A. I mean that on the basis of the interviews that Special Agent Weess and myself had done on the 16th and the 17th, we were convinced that Mr. Moussaoui was involved in some type of plot, and so all of our energies were directed at accumulating whatever was required, evidence or intelligence, to get into his belongings and search them for information as to what was going to happen.

Q. Now, at some point, your request to get a FISA search warrant was denied by your headquarters; is that right?

A. Yes, sir.

Q. Okay. Do you know approximately when that was?

A. Approximately August 28.

Q. All right. At the time that your request for a search warrant was denied, could you explain to us what was the extent of the information that you had available that connected you to a terrorist organization?

A. Yes, sir.

Q. Or Mr. Moussaoui, I'm sorry.

A. Yes, sir. We had information from our legat in Paris that Mr. Moussaoui had recruited this fighter for the Chechens who had since been killed in Chechnya, that that fighter, in fact, was connected to Ibn Khattab, who was the leader of the Chechen fighters. The CIA was able to confirm that information and also to provide information that Ibn Khattab and Usama Bin Laden had a relationship.

Q. Let me ask you this: At any point, were you able to satisfy your headquarters' demands as to the proof as to what the foreign power was?

A. No.

Q. All right. Now, after your headquarters denied your efforts to try to get a FISA warrant, did you come up with a different plan in order to try to get a search into Mr. Moussaoui's bags, at least his bags that he had with him?

A. Yes, sir.

Q. And what was that plan?

A. Through consultation with our legal attaché's office in Paris, we learned that the French government had an interest in Mr. Moussaoui and, in fact, that they were willing to accept his being deported there with the provision of French law that his belongings could be searched upon his arrival.

Q. Now, you could lawfully deport him already based upon his overstay in the visa waiver program; is that right?

A. Yes, sir, that's correct.

Q. And through this series of days thereafter, did you set up plans in order to do so?

A. We did. We worked—that became the primary focus. We kept the other options, obviously mindful of the criminal and of the intelligence, the FISA option as well, but our primary focus then became the deportation of Mr. Moussaoui to France in order to allow his goods to be—his property to be—property to be searched.

Q. And when was that finally approved by all parties, that that was—that that could occur?

A. On the afternoon of September 10, 2001.

Q. And, and Mr. Moussaoui obviously as of September 11 had not been sent back to France; is that right?

A. That's correct.

Q. When was that to occur, do you know?

A. In the very near future. We had received authority to begin planning for that on the afternoon of September 10. Obviously, the time difference being what it was, the legal attaché's office in Paris was closed, so that next morning, we were going to set up the logistics, but it was going to be a matter of days.

Q. Now, in addition to taking those precautions, at any point did you ask your headquarters to notify the FAA about the threat that Mr. Moussaoui posed?

A. Yes, sir.

Q. And on August 31, did you send what is known as an LHM to Mr. Maltbie in the RFU unit?

A. I did.

Q. Do you want to tell the folks what an LHM is in the jargon of the FBI?

A. An LHM stands for letterhead memorandum, and a letterhead memorandum is a document authored by someone in the FBI that is intended to be released outside of the FBI, whether it's to another law enforcement agency in the United States, to another member of the intelligence community, or to a friendly foreign government.

Q. And why is that you wanted your headquarters to notify FAA about what was happening with Mr. Moussaoui?

A. Because of the, our investigative theory that he was involved in a plan to hijack a commercial airliner.

Q. And on September 5 of 2001, do you know if your headquarters did, in fact, make that notification?

A. They did. In fact, our headquarters issued a teletype, a message to a number of other government agencies, to include the FAA.

Q. Now, in addition to what you requested your headquarters to do, were you so concerned about the FAA being notified that you took steps on your own as a local guy on the ground out in Minnesota to make sure the FAA knew what was going on with Mr. Moussaoui?

A. Yes, sir, Special Agent Weess and myself on September 5 went to the FAA investigators in the Twin Cities, in Minneapolis-St. Paul, and provided them a personal briefing on the contents of the teletype, as well as case agent perspective on what we believed was actually going on.

Q. And as a result of those attacks [September 11], those crimes occurring, were you then authorized to go get a criminal search warrant?

A. Yes, sir.

Q. And did you go that very day, September 11, to the United States Attorney's Office in Minneapolis and procure a search warrant?

A. Within minutes of our being granted permission, I was on my way to the United States Attorney's Office at full speed, yes, sir.

Q. And did the U.S. Attorney's Office help you and your brother agents to get a search warrant then signed by a United States magistrate judge?

A. Yes, sir.

Q. Now, after you got a search warrant, now you had the legal ability to go in and search Mr. Moussaoui's items; is that right?

A. Yes, sir.

Q. And did you do so?

A. Yes, sir.

Q. Can you tell the folks what it is that you did finally with those bags that he had stored in INS for those three weeks?

A. Special Agent Weess went down to Immigration and was, was responding lights and sirens to bring those bags to the FBI office at full speed. The warrant was signed, and I had an FBI organization within our office call the evidence response team, agents who are specially trained in evidence recovery, standing by. When the goods arrived, when the personal property arrived and the warrant arrived, the evidence response team under my direction immediately began executing the search warrant.

Source: Testimony of FBI Agent Harry Samit in the Zacarias Moussaoui Trial (March 9, 2006): transcript pages 794–795, 802–818, 827–828, 845–846, and 922–952. (http://www.law.umkc.edu/faculty/projects/ftrials/moussaoui/zmsami/).

Document 41

Testimony of the American Red Cross before the Management, Integration, and Oversight Subcommittee of the House Homeland Security (July 12, 2006)

In testimony before the Management, Integration, and Oversight Subcommittee of the House Homeland Security, Leigh A. Bradley, Senior Vice President, Enterprise Risk of the American Red Cross, outlined steps taken by the American Red Cross to assist the victims and their families in the aftermath of September 11.

Chairman Rogers, Congressmen Meek, and Members of the Committee, my name is Leigh Bradley and I am the Senior Vice President for Enterprise Risk at the American Red Cross. I want to thank you for providing me with the opportunity to appear before you today to talk about the American Red Cross response to the attacks of September 11th—work that is ongoing to this very day. I appreciate the opportunity to share with you our lessons learned regarding fraud prevention, detection, and controls.

The attacks on the United States that occurred on September 11, 2001, tested the American Red Cross and America in ways we had not experienced as an organization or as a nation. It is a day that will remain burned into the minds of all who witnessed on national television two of our nation's tallest and proudest buildings fall more than 100 stories, a massive inferno at the Pentagon and a plane crash in a remote field in Shanksville, Pennsylvania. Thousands of innocent people died on September 11, including members of the first response community who put their lives at risk to save others. Since September 11, thousands more have suffered from the physical and emotional stress of responding to these vicious attacks. All who witnessed this day will remember where they were, what they were doing, and will always recount their feelings and emotions as we, as a nation, were overcome with grief.

The American Red Cross had been America's partner in disaster preparedness, prevention and response for nearly 120 years on that fateful day in September. In our long history, we have aided soldiers on the battlefield, supported victims of all disasters, and provided support to first responders.

Our experience in the aftermath of the Oklahoma City Bombings in 1995 helped to prepare us for this day. Almost immediately after the first plane struck the World Trade Center, Red Cross volunteers and personnel were on the scene ready to aid in the response.

I want to acknowledge the work of Alan Goodman, who is with me today. Alan is the Executive Director of the American Red Cross September 11th Recovery Program (SRP). For the past four years, Alan has been at the helm of this program, which has provided longer term recovery to tens of thousands of individuals and families, including families of the deceased, the physically injured rescue and recovery workers and their families, and people who were living or working in the areas of the attacks.

Response to September 11, 2001

One year after the terrorist attacks occurred on 9/11, the American Red Cross issued a report to the American people regarding the activities of the Red Cross, the Liberty Disaster Relief Fund, and the execution of the September 11th Recovery Program. Included in this report was a chronology of our response, which is attached to my testimony. (Appendix I) Before I discuss the Red Cross response to 9/11 and some of the lessons learned, it is important that I briefly share what the Red Cross traditionally does during times of disaster and how this response differed.

The American Red Cross responds to disasters in communities across the nation each and every day. In fact, we respond to more than 70,000 disasters each year. The vast majority of disasters we respond to are single family home fires. We also respond to large-scale disasters, such as hurricanes, floods, tornadoes, and man-made events. There is one constant in all of our response operations and that is to ensure the immediate emergency needs of our clients are met. Individual client assistance has been provided by the American Red Cross for as long as the organization has been in existence. Red Cross individual client assistance includes much more than just financial support. In fact, traditional individual client assistance has been based on a cadre of services to ensure that the health and welfare needs of our clients are met. This includes feeding and sheltering operations, mental health assistance, first aid, and relief and recovery referrals. We partner with other nongovernmental organizations, the for profit community, and with all levels of government to ensure that the emergency needs of disaster victims are met. In each response, our first priority is to ensure that those affected by disaster have a safe shelter and are provided with the basic necessities of life.

The next priority is to assist families in taking the first steps toward recovery. This is the purpose and concern that individual client assistance is designed to serve. It has long been the case that while shelter, feeding and the distribution of critical items are sufficient to stabilize individuals and families, it is not sufficient to meet all short term emergency needs necessary for disaster victims to begin their individual road to recovery. Critical items of assistance such as resources for food, changes of clothing and bedding bridge the gap between mass care activities and the receipt of state and federal recovery assistance. This allows a family a modicum of independence and a flexible resource for the types of essential items mentioned above. Ultimately, within the framework of disaster assistance provided by other agencies, as well as state and federal programs, individual client assistance helps bridge the gap between mass care activities and loans, temporary housing, and other assistance.

The response of the American public in the wake of 9/11 was extraordinary. When thousands of Americans needed help following the attacks, tens of thousands volunteered with the Red Cross, and tens of thousands made financial contributions. The American Red Cross received more than $1 million in contributions. While the Red Cross often provides financial assistance for the immediate emergency needs of our clients, the intent of our donors was to ensure this money was earmarked for the victims of 9/11.

To that end, we created the Liberty Disaster Relief Fund as a distinct and segregated fund for those financial donations and to assist those directly affected by the September 11th attacks. Former Senate Majority Leader George Mitchell was appointed as the independent overseer of the fund. Under the distribution plan, and consistent with the Red Cross mission of providing immediate emergency disaster relief, the majority of funds were to be distributed to the families of those who were killed in the September 11 attacks, those who were seriously injured, and others directly affected by the disaster.

For an organization that is accustomed to providing de minimus amounts of financial assistance—money that is meant to provide for immediate emergency needs such as a change of clothes, toiletries, or diapers for children—this meant providing much larger sums of money. The American Red Cross had two phases of response to the tragic events of September 11. Phase One represents the immediate response to the terrorist attacks, dating from September 11, 2001, through October 1, 2002, and is referred to as the Relief Operation Phase. Phase Two encompasses the long term recovery effort, dating from October 2, 2002, to the present, and is referred to as September 11th Recovery Program (SRP) Relief Operation Phase.

- Family Gift Program #1 (FGP I)—The FGP I provided three months of rent, food, utilities and other ongoing expenses to family members of those missing, deceased, or injured from the World Trade Center (WTC), Pentagon, or Shanksville, Pennsylvania events.
- Family Gift Program #2 (FGP II)—The FGP II began on December 6, 2001, and provided six months of living expenses to family members and injured clients who received FGP I and nine months of expenses to clients who initially sought financial assistance after December 2002.
- Family Gift #3 (FGP III)—FGP I and FGP II met the early financial needs for the victims covered under the Family Gift Program. The first two gifts were designed to cover the first nine months of living expenses and these gifts were all disbursed prior to June 30, 2002. In January 2002, the Red Cross determined that the Family Gift Program should also cover unmet essential living expenses for an entire year through September 11, 2002. The third Family Gift (FGP III) was created to cover expenses for the months ending on September 11, 2002. No funds were distributed for FGP III until

July of 2002. Specifically, FGP III granted expenses, depending on whether or not clients received the previous two gifts, to financially dependent immediate and extended family members of decedents, child guardians, and the 'seriously injured.' The 'seriously injured' were defined as individuals who were in the immediate vicinity of the WTC, the Pentagon or the Pennsylvania crash site on 9/11 and as a result suffered a verifiable, serious physical injury or illness for which they were admitted to a hospital for at least 24 hours between 9/11 and 9/18/01. The FGP III ended on June 15, 2004.

Source: U.S. House of Representatives, Management, Integration, and Oversight Subcommittee of the House Homeland Security, *Reaction of the American Red Cross and Fraud in 9/11 Assistance* (Washington, DC: U.S. Government Printing Office, 2006), pp. 140–146.

Document 42

Confession of Khalid Sheikh Mohammed at the Combatant Status Review Tribunal at Guantánamo Detention Camp (March 10, 2007)

This testimony by Khalid Sheikh Mohammed at the Combatant Status Review Tribunal at Guantánamo Detention Camp on March 10, 2007, answers many questions about the September 11, 2001, attacks. He takes complete responsibility for the planning and implementation for the attacks. In fact, Mohammed almost glorifies his role. He also takes responsibility for a number of other initiatives and operations of al-Qaeda, including some that never materialized. His confession of responsibility for the Bali nightclub bombing and the murder of Daniel Pearl are new bits of information. Mohammed considers his operations to be part of an ongoing war between the Muslim and Western worlds. Earlier in the proceedings Mohammed complains about the use of torture on him. His personal statement is often in broken English, but it is important to read his justification for his actions in his own words.

I hereby admit and affirm without duress to the following:

1. I swore Bayaat (i.e., allegiance) to Sheikh Usama Bin Laden to conduct Jihad of self and money, and also Hijrah (i.e., expatriation to any location in the world where Jihad is required).
2. I was a member of the Al Qaida Council.
3. I was the Media Operations Director for Al-Sahab, or 'The Clouds,' under Dr. Ayman Al-Zawahiri. Al-Sahab is the media outlet that provided Al-Qaida-sponsored information to Al Jazeera.
4. I was the Operation Director for Sheikh Usama Bin Laden for the organizing, planning, follow-up, and execution of the 9/11 Operation under the Military Commander, Sheikh Abu Hafs Al-Masri Subhi Abu Sittah (Mohammad Atef).

5. I was the Military Operational Commander for all foreign operations around the world under the direction of Sheikh Usama Bin Laden and Dr. Ayman Al-Zawahiri.

6. I was directly in charge, after the death of Sheikh Abu Hafs Al-Masri Subhi Abu Sittah, of managing and following up on the Cell for the Production of Biological Weapons, such as anthrax and others, and following up on Dirty Bomb Operations on American soil.

7. I was Emir (i.e., commander) of Beit Al Shuhada (i.e., the Martyrs House) in the state of Kandahar, Afghanistan, which housed the 9/11 hijackers. There I was responsible for their training and readiness for the execution of the 9/11 Operation.

Also, I hereby admit and affirm without duress that I was a responsible participant, principal planner, trainer, financier (via the Military Council Treasury), executor, and/or a personal participant in the following:

1. I was responsible for the 1993 World Trade Center Operation.

2. I was responsible for the 9/11 Operation, from A to Z.

3. I decapitated with my blessed right hand the head of the American Jew, Daniel Pearl, in the city of Karachi, Pakistan. For those who would like to confirm, there are pictures of me on the Internet holding his head.

4. I was responsible for the Shoe Bomber Operation to down two American airplanes.

5. I was responsible for the Filka Island Operation in Kuwait that killed two American soldiers.

6. I was responsible for the bombing of a nightclub in Bali, Indonesia, which was frequented by British and Australian nationals.

7. I was responsible for planning, training, surveying, and financing the New (or Second) Wave attacks against the following skyscrapers after 9/11:
   a. Library Tower, California.
   b. Sears Tower, Chicago.
   c. Plaza Bank, Washington state.
   d. The Empire State Building, New York City.

8. I was responsible for planning, financing, & follow-up of operations to destroy American military vessels and oil tankers in the Straights of Hormuz, the Straights of Gibraltar, and the Port of Singapore.

9. I was responsible for planning, training, surveying, and financing for the Operation to bomb and destroy the Panama Canal.

10. I was responsible for surveying and financing for the assassination of several former American Presidents, including president Carter.

11. I was responsible for surveying, planning, and financing for the bombing of suspension bridges in New York.

12. I was responsible for planning to destroy the Sears Tower by burning a few fuel or oil tanker trucks beneath it or around it.

13. I was responsible for planning, surveying, and financing for the operation to destroy Heathrow Airport, the Canary Wharf Building, and Big Ben on British soil.

14. I was responsible for planning, surveying, and financing for the destruction of many night clubs frequented by American and British citizens on Thailand soil.

15. I was responsible for planning, surveying and financing for the destruction of the New York Stock Exchange and other financial targets after 9/11.

16. I was responsible for planning, financing, and surveying for the destruction of buildings in the Israeli city of Elat by using airplanes leaving from Saudi Arabia.

17. I was responsible for planning, surveying, and financing for the destruction of American embassies in Indonesia, Australia, and Japan.

18. I was responsible for surveying and financing for the destruction of the Israeli embassy in India, Azerbaijan, the Philippines, and Australia.

19. I was responsible for surveying and financing for the destruction of an Israeli 'El-Al' Airlines flight on Thailand soil departing from Bangkok Airport.

20. I was responsible for sending several Mujahadeen into Israel to conduct surveillance to hit several strategic targets deep in Israel.

21. I was responsible for the bombing of the hotel in Mombasa that is frequented by Jewish travelers via El-Al airlines.

22. I was responsible for launching a Russian-made SA-7 surface-to-air missile on El-Al or other Jewish airliner departing from Mombasa.

23. I was responsible for planning and surveying to hit American targets in South Korea, such as American military bases and a few night clubs frequented by American soldiers.

24. I was responsible for financial, excuse me, I was responsible for providing financial support to hit American, Jewish, and British targets in Turkey.

25. I was responsible for surveillance needed to hit nuclear power plants that generate electricity in several U.S. states.

26. I was responsible for planning, surveying, and financing to hit NATO Headquarters in Europe.

27. I was responsible for the planning and surveying needed to execute the Bojinka Operation, which was designed to down twelve American airplanes full of passengers. I personally monitored a round-trip, Manila-to-Seoul, Pan Am flight.

28. I was responsible for the assassination attempt against President Clinton during his visit to the Philippines in 1994 or 1995.

29. I shared responsibility for the assassination attempt against Pope John Paul the second while he was visiting the Philippines.

30. I was responsible for the training and financing for the assassination of Pakistan's President Musharraf.

31. I was responsible for the attempt to destroy an American oil company owned by the Jewish former Secretary of State, Henry Kissinger, on the Island of Sumatra, Indonesia.

Personal Representative: Sir, that concluded the written portion of the Detainee's final statement and as he has alluded to earlier he has some additional comments he would like to make.

President: Alright. Before you proceed, Khalid Sheikh Muhammad, the statement that was just read by the Personal Representative, were those your words?

Khalid Sheik Muhammad: Yes, and I want to add some of this one just for some verification. It like some operations before I join al Qaida. Before I remember al Qaida which is related to Bojinka Operation I went to destination involve to us in 94, 95. Some Operations which means out of al Qaida. It's like beheading Daniel Pearl. It's not related to al Qaida. It was shared in Pakistani, other group, Mujahadeen. The story of Daniel Pearl, because he stated for the Pakistanis group, that he was working with the both. His mission was in Pakistan to track about Richard Reed trip to Israel. Richard Reed, do you have trip? You send it Israel to make set for targets in Israel. His mission in Pakistan from Israeli intelligence, Mosad, to make interview to ask about when he was there. Also, he mention to them he was both. He have relation with CIA people and were the Mosad. But he was not related to al Qaida at all or UBL. It is related to the Pakistan Mujahadeen group. Other operations mostly are some word I'm not accurate in saying. I'm responsible but if you read the heading history. The line there 'Also, hereby admit and affirm without duress that I was a responsible participant, principle planner, trainer, financier.'

In the name of God the most compassionate the most merciful, and if any fail to retaliation by way of charity and . . . I apologize. I will start again. And if any fail to judge by the light of Allah has revealed, they are no better than wrong doers, unbelievers, and the unjust.

For this verse, I not take the oath. Take an oath is part of your Tribunal and I'll not accept it. To be or accept the Tribunal as to be, I'll accept it. That I'm accepting American constitution, American law or whatever you are doing here. This is shy religiously I cannot accept anything you do. Just to explain for this one, does not mean I'm not saying that I'm lying. When I not take oath does not mean I'm lying. You know very well peoples take oath and they will lie. You know the President he did this before he just makes his oath and he lied. So sometimes when I'm not making oath does not mean I'm lying.

Second thing. When I wrote this thing, I mean, the PR he told me that President may stop you at anytime and he don't like big mouth nor you to talk too much. To be within subject. So, I will try to be within the enemy combatant subject.

What I wrote here, is not I'm making myself hero, when I said I was responsible for this or that. But you are military man. You know very well there are language for any war. So, there are, we are when I admitting these things I'm not saying I'm not do it. I did it but this the language of any war. If America they want to invade Iraq they will not send for Saddam roses or kisses they send for a bombardment. This is the best way if I want. If I'm fighting for anybody admit to them I'm American enemies. For sure, I'm American enemies. Usama bin Laden, he did his best press conference in American media. Mr. John Miller he been there when he made declaration against Jihad, against America. And he said it is not no need for me now to make explanation of what he said but mostly he said about military presence in Arabian peninsula and aiding Israel and many things. So when we made any war against America we are jackals fighting in the nights. I consider myself, for what you are doing, a religious thing as you consider us fundamentalist. So, we derive from religious leading that we consider we and George

Washington doing same thing. As consider George Washington as hero, Muslims many of them are considering Usama bin Laden. He is doing same thing. He is just fighting. He needs his independence. Even we think that, or not me only. Many Muslims, that al Qaida or Taliban they are doing. They have been oppressed by America. This is the feeling of the prophet. So when we say we are enemy combatant, that right. We are. But I'm asking you again to be fair with many Detainees which are not enemy combatant. Because many of them have been unjustly arrested. Many, not one or two or three. Cause the definition which you wrote even from my view it is not fair. Because if I was in the first Jihad times Russia. So I have to be Russian enemy. But America supported me in this because I'm their alliances when I was fighting Russia. Same job I'm doing. I'm fighting. I was fighting there Russia now I'm fighting America. So, many people who been in Afghanistan never live. Afghanistan stay in but they not share Taliban or al Qaida. They been Russian time and they cannot go back to their home with their corrupted government. They stayed there when America invaded Afghanistan parliament. They had been arrest. They never have been with Taliban or the others. So many people consider them as enemy but they are not. Because definitions are very wide definition so people they came after October of 2002, 2001. When America invaded Afghanistan, they just arrive in Afghanistan cause they hear there enemy. They don't know what it means al Qaida or Usama bin Laden or Taliban. They don't care about these things. They heard they were enemy in Afghanistan they just arrived. As they heard first time Russian invade Afghanistan. They arrive they fought when back than they came. They don't know what's going on and Taliban they been head of government. You consider me even Taliban even the president of whole government. Many people they join Taliban because they are the government. When Karzai they came they join Karzai when come they join whatever public they don't know what is going on. So, many Taliban fight even then be fighters because they just because public. The government is Taliban then until now CIA don't have exactly definition well who is Taliban, who is al Qaida. Your Tribunal now are discussing he is enemy or not and that is one of your jobs. So this is why you find many Afghanis people, Pakistanis people even, they don't know what is going on they just hear they are fighting and they help Muslim in Afghanistan. Then what. There are some infidels which they came here and they have to help them. But then there weren't any intend to do anything against America. Taliban themselves between Taliban they said Afghanistan which they never again against 9/11 operation. The rejection between senior of Taliban of what al Qaida are doing. Many of Taliban rejected what they are doing. Even many Taliban, they not agree about why we are in Afghanistan. Some of them they have been with us. Taliban never in their life at all before America invade the intend to do anything against America. They never been with al Qaida. Does not mean we are here as American now. They gave political asylum for many countries. They gave for Chinese oppositions or a North Korean but that does not mean they are with them same thing many of Taliban. They harbor us as al Qaida does not mean we are together. So, this is why I'm asking you to be fair with Afghanis and Pakistanis and many Arabs which had been in Afghanistan. Many of them been unjustly. The funny story they been Sunni government they sent some spies to assassinate UBL then we arrested them sent them to Afghanistan/Taliban. Taliban put them into prison. Americans they came and arrest them as enemy combatant.

They brought them here. So, even if they are my enemy but not fair to be there with me. That is what I'm saying. The way of war, you know, very well, any country waging war against their enemy the language of the war are killing. If man and woman they be together as a marriage that is up to the kids, children. But if you and me, two nations, will be together in war the others are victims. This is the way of the language. You know 40 million people were killed in World War One. Ten million kill in World War. You know that two million four hundred thousand be killed in Korean War. So this language of the war. Any people who, when Usama bin Laden say I'm waging war because such reason, now he declared it. But when you said I'm terrorist, I think it is deceiving peoples. Terrorists, enemy combatant. All these definitions as CIA you can make whatever you want. Now, you told me when I ask about the witnesses, I'm not convinced that this related to the matter. It is up you. Maybe I'm convinced you are head and he [gesturing to Personal Representative] is not responsible, the other, because you are head of the committee. So, finally it's your war but the problem is no definitions of many words. It would be widely definite that many people be oppressed. Because war, for sure, there will be victims. When I said I'm not happy that three thousand been killed in America. I feel sorry even. I don't like to kill children and the kids. Never Islam are, give me green light to kill peoples. Killing, as in the Christianity, Jews, and Islam, are prohibited. But there are exception of rule when you are killing people in Iraq. You said we gave have to do it. We don't like Saddam. But this is the way to deal with Saddam. Same thing you are saying. Same language you use, I use. When you are invading two-thirds of Mexican, you call your war manifest destiny. It up to you to call it what you want. But other side are calling you oppressors. If now George Washington. If now we were living in the Revolutionary War and George Washington he being arrested through Britain. For sure he, they would consider him enemy combatant. But American they consider him as hero. This right the any Revolutionary War they will be as George Washington or Britain. So we are considered American Army bases which we have from seventies in Iraq. Also, in Saudi Arabian, Kuwait, Qatar, and Bahrain. This kind of invasion, but I'm not here to convince you. Is not or not but mostly speech is ask you to be fair with people. I'm don't have anything to say that I'm not enemy. This is why the language of any war in the world is killing. I mean the language of the war is victims. I don't like to kill people. I feel very sorry they been killed kids in 9/11. What I will do? This is the language. Sometime I want to make great awakening between American to stop foreign policy in our land. I know American people are torturing us from seventies. I know they talking about human rights. And I know it is against American Constitution, against American laws. But they said every law, they have exceptions, this is your bad luck, you been part of the exception of our laws. They got have something to convince me but we are doing same language. But we are saying we have Sharia law, but we have Koran. What is enemy combatant in my language?

Allah forbids you not with regards to those who fight you not for your faith nor drive you out of your homes from dealing kindly and justly with them. For Allah love those who are just. There is one more sentence. Allah only forbids you with regards to those who fight you for your faith and drive you out of your homes and support others in driving you out from turning to them for friendship and protection. It is such as turn to them in these circumstances that do wrong.

So we are driving from whatever deed we do we ask about Koran or Hadith. We are not making up for us laws. When we need Fatwa from the religious we have to go back to see what they said scholar. To see what they said yes or not. Killing is prohibited in all what you call the people of the book, Jews, Judaism, Christianity, and Islam. You know the Ten Commandments very well. The Ten Commandments are shared between all of us. We all are serving one God. Then now kill you know very well. But war language also we have language for the war. You have to kill. But you have to care if unintentionally or intentionally target if I have if I'm not at the Pentagon. I consider it is okay. If I target now when we target in USA we choose them military target, economical, and political. So, war central victims mostly means economical target. So if now American they know UBL. He is in this house they don't care about his kids and his. They will just bombard it. They will kill all of them and they did it. They kill wife of Dr. Ayman Zawahiri and his two daughters and his son in one bombardment. They receive a report that is his house be. He had not been there. They killed them. They arrested my kids intentionally. They are kids. They been arrested for four months they had been abused. So, for me I have patience. I know I'm not talk about what's come to me. The American have human right. So, enemy combatant itself, it flexible word. So I think God knows that many who have arrested, they been unjustly arrested. Otherwise, military throughout history know very well. They don't war will never stop. War start from Adam when Cain he killed Abel until now. It's never gonna stop killing of people. This is the way of the language. American start the Revolutionary War then they starts the Mexican then Spanish War then World War One, World War Two. You read the history. You know never stopping war. This is life. But if who is enemy combatant and who is not? Finally, I finish statement. I'm asking you to be fair with other people.

Source: Verbatim Transcript of Combatant Status Review Tribunal Hearing for ISN 10024 Homeland Security (can be found at http://www.globalsecurity.org/security/library/report/ 2007/khalid-sheikh-muhammad_transcript. htm/).

Annotated Bibliography

The controversy surrounding the events of September 11, 2001, rivals that of Pearl Harbor and the John F. Kennedy assassination as a source of conflicting views. Besides the usual partisan infighting between the adherents of the Clinton presidency and those of the George W. Bush administration, there is a growing industry of authors eager to cast doubt on the official version. They examine each incident and come up with a conspiracy theory to explain any discrepancies. Some of the most extreme authors have charged that the Bush administration orchestrated 9/11 to erode constitutional liberties. The reader of this encyclopedia needs to approach each book on 9/11 listed in this bibliography with an understanding of the author's concentration and/or bias. Most of the works here are authoritative and objective, but several are efforts to cast doubts on the facts of the September 11 attacks. Consequently, each book listed has an annotation to help the reader understand the background and point of view of the author. It is estimated that there are around 3,000 books that deal with one aspect or another of September 11. This bibliography is selective, as it cannot accommodate all of them.

Ahmed, Nafeez Mosaddeq, *The War on Freedom: How and Why America Was Attacked September 11, 2001* (Joshua Tree, CA: Tree of Life Publications, 2002).
  Nafeez M. Ahmed, a British political scientist and executive director of the Institute for Policy Research and Development in Brighton, England, advances the theory that the U.S. government instigates terrorism as a pretext to justify an aggressive foreign policy. He claims that the Bush administration allowed September 11 to happen so that the American government would have an excuse to invade Afghanistan. The author poses some tantalizing conjectures, but his treatment lacks objectivity.

Atwan, Abdel Bari, *The Secret History of Al Qaeda* (Berkeley, CA: University of California Press, 2006).
  The author is a Palestinian journalist and the editor-in-chief of the influential *Al-Quds al-Arabi* publication. He has lived in London for over thirty years. He suggests that al-Qaeda is becoming bigger and stronger because of current

American foreign policy. There is considerable material in this book that contributes to the understanding of the strategy and tactics of both Osama bin Laden and al-Qaeda.

Ausmus, David W., *In the Midst of Chaos: My 30 Days at Ground Zero* (Victoria, Canada: Trafford, 2004).
The author is a construction safety official who was working at Oak Ridge, Tennessee, when word came that he was needed at the World Trade Center site. He recorded his impression of the site and related safety issues. Although Ausmus spent only thirty days at the World Trade Center site, he was able to record the horrors of the debris pile and the hazards of those working in that environment.

Aust, Stefan, et al., *Inside 9/11: What Really Happened* (New York: St. Martin's Press, 2001).
Nineteen reporters, writers, and editors of the German magazine *Der Spiegel* combined their talents to write a narrative of the events leading to September 11 and the events of the day. Emphasis of the authors is on the human interest aspects of 9/11. This book is an excellent introduction to the state of knowledge in the months following September 11.

Barbash, Tom, *On Top of the World: The Remarkable Story of Howard Lutnick, Cantor Fitzgerald and the Twin Towers Attack* (London: Headline, 2003).
The author, a former newspaper reporter, recounts the story of the brokerage firm Cantor Fitzgerald and its loss of 658 employees on September 11. This company is a huge international brokerage firm that handled most of the bond activity for the New York Stock Exchange. This book tells of its resurrection as a company and its efforts to compensate the families of employees lost on September 11.

Barrett, Jon, *Mark Bingham: Hero of Flight 93* (Los Angeles, CA: Advocate Books, 2002).
This laudatory biography explains the complex personality of Mark Bingham, a passenger on United Airlines Flight 93. His participation in the attempt to overthrow the flight's hijackers placed him on a hero's pedestal.

Barrett, Wayne, and Adam Fifield, *Rudy! An Investigative Biography of Rudolph Giuliani* (New York: Basic Books, 2000).
Wayne Barrett, senior editor at the *Village Voice,* has written a critical biography of Rudolph "Rudy" Giuliani. Although the biography ends before September 11, it gives a critical analysis of his lengthy career as mayor of New York City. This book provides background on one of the leading figures in New York City during and after September 11.

Beamer, Lisa, and Ken Abraham, *Let's Roll! Ordinary People, Extraordinary Courage* (Wheaton, IL: Tyndale Publishing, 2002).
The author is the widow of Todd Beamer, one of the heroes of United Airlines Flight 93. She explains the background of Todd Beamer and why he was one of the leaders of the attempt to regain control of the cockpit on September 11, 2001.

She subscribes to the theory that it was his religious faith and his desire to return to his family that motivated Todd Beamer to do what he did.

Bell, J. Bowyer, *Murders on the Nile: The World Trade Center and Global Terror* (San Francisco: Encounters Books, 2003).
J. Bowyer Bell, an adjunct professor at the School of International and Public Affairs at Columbia University and a member of the Council on Foreign Relations, has used his lifetime of research on terrorism to examine the origins of Jihadi terrorism that led to September 11. It is his thesis that the origin of Jihadi terrorism was in Egypt, and the expansion to the rest of the Middle East has been led by Egyptians such as Sayyid Qutb, Sheikh Omar Abdel Rahman, and Ayman al-Zawahiri. This book is a good introductory source on the personalities and events surrounding the September 11 attacks.

Benjamin, Daniel, and Steven Simon, *The Age of Sacred Terror* (New York: Random House, 2004).
Two former Clinton administration officials in Richard Clarke's National Security Council's Directorate of Transnational Threats have written this book on the terrorist threat to the United States before September 11. As key members of Clarke's staff they participated in most of the decisions regarding counterterrorist operations. This book is a good source for actions taken by the Clinton administration.

Bergen, Peter L., *The Osama bin Laden I Know: An Oral History of Al Qaeda's Leader* (New York: Free Press, 2006).
The author is CNN's terrorism analyst and an adjunct professor at the School of Advanced International Studies at Johns Hopkins University. He has used his extensive contacts in the Middle East to produce an oral history of the career of Osama bin Laden. Bergen interviewed bin Laden once, but the strength of the book is the interviews with the associates of bin Laden. This book is a gold mine of information about bin Laden and how he is viewed by Muslims both inside and outside of al-Qaeda.

Bernstein, Richard, *Out of the Blue: The Story of September 11 2001, From Jihad to Ground Zero* (New York: Times Books, 2002).
The author, a journalist with the *New York Times*, has, with the help of the staff of the *Times*, produced this history of the conspirators of September 11 and the impact of the attack on the lives of Americans. He followed the lives of heroes, victims, and terrorists in considerable detail. This survey is strong on human interest stories that give perspective to the tragedy of September 11.

Bin Laden, Osama, *Messages to the World: The Statements of Osama bin Laden* (London: Verso, 2005).
An American professor at Duke University, Bruce Lawrence, and a British specialist on Arab affairs and language, James Howarth, united to compile a book on the messages, writings, and interviews of Osama bin Laden, the head of al-Qaeda. In this work all of bin Laden's principal messages appear, including the famous August 23, 1996, *Declaration of Jihad* and the equally famous February 23, 1998,

The World Islam Front. This book is an indispensable tool for the understanding of Osama bin Laden and his worldview.

Breitweiser, Kristen, *Wake-Up Call: The Political Education of a 9/11 Widow* (New York: Warner Books, 2006).
    Kristen Breitweiser lost her husband on September 11, 2001, in the North Tower of the World Trade Center. She allied with three other New Jersey widows to form the Jersey Girls, whose mission was to find out what happened on September 11 and hold people accountable. To do this Breitweiser and her allies joined the Family Steering Committee to help form and guide the 9/11 Commission.

Bull, Chris, and Sam Erman (eds.), *At Ground Zero: 25 Stories from Young Reporters Who Were There* (New York: Thunder's Mouth Press, 2002).
    The editors have compiled the stories from reporters and photographers who were active at the World Trade Center complex on September 11, 2001, and afterward. Most of the accounts came from young news professionals fresh to the field of journalism and concern how they coped with the disaster. Each of them attests to the fact that they experienced a range of emotions from anger and excitement to terror and depression covering September 11 and the victims' families.

Burnett, Deena, and Anthony Giombetti, *Fighting Back: Living Life beyond Ourselves* (Altamonte Springs, FL: Advantage Books, 2006).
    The widow of Tom Burnett, a passenger on United Airlines Flight 93 on September 11, 2001, recounts her life with her husband and the events of September 11. He was one of those who fought for control of the cockpit on that fateful day. She recounts her cell phone conversations with her husband until the moment when he participated with the other passengers to regain control of the airliner.

Butler, Gregory A., *Lost Towers: Inside the World Trade Center Cleanup* (New York: iUniverse, 2006).
    Gregory Butler is a carpenter in New York City, and in this book he has compiled his impressions about the cleanup at Ground Zero. His tidbits of information give a somewhat different perspective on the cleanup. Butler's insights on work at Ground Zero make this book a valuable resource on the aftermath of September 11.

Calhoun, Craig, Paul Price, and Ashley Timmer (eds.), *Understanding September 11* (New York: New Press, 2002).
    Three editors with support from the Social Science Research Council, New York, have united a host of experts on terrorism and international security to produce a book that attempts to understand why September 11 happened. The authors of the articles tackle such topics as Islamic radicalism, globalism, and terrorism as part of their analysis. This book's value is in the quality of the contributions by experts in the field.

Caran, Peter, *The 1993 World Trade Center Bombing: Foresight and Warning* (London: Janus Publishing, 2001).
    Peter Caran had been a detective and antiterrorist officer with the Port Authority of New York and New Jersey at the World Trade Center complex until 1998.

Caran was one of the investigators at the 1993 World Trade Center Bombing, and he was critical of the lack of security that allowed terrorists to plant a bomb at the World Trade Center complex so easily. It was his thesis before September 11, 2001, that the terrorists had bungled the first bombing, and they were going to come back for another try.

Chomsky, Noam, *9-11* (New York: Seven Stories Press, 2001).
In a series of questions and answers, the noted critic of the U.S. government and its policies Noam Chomsky gives his views on the events surrounding the September 11 attacks. He believes the U.S. government view on al-Qaeda's responsibility for the attacks is correct, but in his eyes the attacks are also a product of American support for repressive Middle Eastern regimes, which has allowed al-Qaeda to constitute a danger to the United States. This book shows his fear that the Bush administration would take advantage of the desire for revenge to worsen the situation in the Middle East by invading Iraq.

Clarke, Richard A., *Against All Enemies: Inside America's War on Terror* (New York: Free Press, 2004).
The author was the counterterrorism expert in both the Clinton and Bush administrations before and after September 11, and in this post he could evaluate each administration's efforts against Osama bin Laden and al-Qaeda. Although a lifetime Republican, Clarke is more critical of the Bush administration's counterterrorism actions than those of the Clinton administration. He also maintains that the Iraq War has emboldened terrorists because most of the leadership of al-Qaeda and the Taliban remain at large to exploit the chaos of war.

Clinton, Bill, *My Life* (New York: Vintage Books, 2005).
President Bill Clinton (1993–2001) presents in this memoir his version of the events in his life and his presidency. He chronicles his efforts to fight terrorism before September 11, including his clashes with a Republican Congress and his rocky relationship with the FBI.

Cole, David, and James X. Dempsey, *Terrorism and the Constitution: Sacrificing Civil Liberties in the Name of National Security* (New York: New Press, 2002).
David Cole, a professor of law at Georgetown University, and James X. Dempsey, deputy director at the Center for Democracy and Technology, have collaborated on a book that shows how the war on terrorism threatens civil liberties. They are critical of how the FBI has acted in the past and present in dealing with those suspected of terrorism. Their thesis is that even after September 11 curtailing civil liberties does not enhance security.

Coll, Steve, *Ghost Wars: The Secret History of the CIA, Afghanistan, and Bin Laden, from the Soviet Invasion to September 10, 2001* (New York: Penguin Books, 2004).
The author won the 2005 Pulitzer Prize for this balanced treatment of the history of the CIA's war against Osama bin Laden and al-Qaeda. He starts his story with the 1979 Soviet invasion of Afghanistan and ends with the assassination of Ahmed Shah Massoud on September 10, 2001. This book is the best source

available for understanding the complexities of dealing with terrorism in the modern world.

Corbin, Jane, *Al-Qaeda: The Terror Network That Threatens the World* (New York: Thunder's Mouth Press, 2002).
Jane Corbin, a senior reporter for the BBC's (British Broadcasting Corporation) current affairs program Panorama, traveled around the Middle East interviewing former associates of Osama bin Laden and other al-Qaeda operatives in an attempt to understand how al-Qaeda operates. Besides these interviews, she depended heavily on the testimony of former al-Qaeda member Jamal al-Fadl. This book gives an excellent background treatment of al-Qaeda's role in the September 11 attacks.

Danieli, Yael, and Robert L. Dingman (eds.), *On the Ground after September 11: Mental Health Responses and Practical Knowledge Gained* (New York: Haworth Maltreatment and Trauma Press, 2005).
The editors, one a clinical psychologist and the other a retired professor of counseling at Marshall University, have compiled a book that contains the experiences of medical and health professionals who worked at the various sites of the September 11 attacks. These responses show the intensity of feeling and the stress felt even from health professionals. This book fills a necessary void in understanding the psychological impact of September 11.

Davis, Mike, *Buda's Wagon: A Brief History of the Car Bomb* (London: Verso, 2007).
Mike Davis, a freelance writer of numerous nonfiction titles, turns his attention to the use of car bombings as a terrorist weapon. He begins with the bombing by an Italian anarchist in 1920 and continues to the use of car bombs in Iraq. His treatment of Ramzi Yousef's truck bomb at the World Trade Center Complex in 1993, and al-Qaeda's 1998 African Embassy bombings, makes this book a valuable resource on how al-Qaeda conducted operations before September 11, 2001.

Drumheller, Tyler, and Elaine Monaghan, *On the Brink: An Insider's Account of How the White House Compromised American Intelligence* (New York: Carroll and Graf, 2006).
Tyler Drumheller was a senior CIA operations officer for more than twenty-five years before retiring in 2005. He uses this book to defend the CIA's intelligence-gathering efforts and criticize how the intelligence information was misused by the Bush administration. Although much of the material in the book covers the post–September 11 era, there are valuable insights into intelligence-gathering problems in the CIA that led up to the September 11 attacks.

Dudziak, Mary L. (ed.), *September 11 in History: A Watershed Moment* (Durham, NC: Duke University Press, 2003).
The editor has recruited a group of cross-disciplinary scholars to examine the question of whether the September 11, 2001, attacks have changed American politics and society as a seminal event in history. They question this assumption in various ways, and they conclude that there is more continuity than change.

This book is a good counterweight against much current political opinion about September 11.

Dunbar, David, and Brad Reagan, *Debunking 9/11 Myths: Why Conspiracy Theories Can't Stand Up to the Facts* (New York: Hearst Books, 2006).
The investigative staff of the magazine *Popular Mechanics*, under the two editors, tackle the myths coming out of the 9/11 conspiracy movement. They consulted more than 300 experts in aviation and scientific fields before publishing this book. This book is the best source available to counter some of the wild theories coming out the conspiracy theorists.

Dwyer, Jim, and Kevin Flynn, *102 Minutes: The Untold Story of the Fight to Survive inside the Twin Towers* (New York: Times Books, 2005).
Jim Dwyer and Kevin Flynn are both reporters for the *New York Times*, and they spent four years researching the story of what happened between the time the first commercial aircraft hit the North Tower of the World Trade Center and the collapse of the twin towers. They give a personalized picture of the dilemmas facing the 14,000 or so workers faced with the chaos of an unfolding disaster. This book also discusses New York City's institutions and their handling of the emergency.

Emerson, Steven, *American Jihad: The Terrorists Living among Us* (New York: Free Press, 2002).
The author is an investigative journalist and executive director of the Investigative Project, which specializes in the study of Islamic militants. In this book Emerson traces the control of the mosques in the United States by partisans of militant Islamist groups—Abu Sayyaf, Algerian Armed Islamic Group, Hamas, Hezbollah, Islamic Jihad, and al-Qaeda. He warns that these terrorists living in the United States constitute a constant danger because they consider the United States to be the enemy, and September 11, 2001, is an example of what they want to do.

Farren, Mick, *CIA: Secrets of "The Company"* (New York: Barnes and Noble, 2004).
This book is an expose of the history of the Central Intelligence Agency (CIA). It has a chapter on how the CIA was hampered in the 1990s by poor leadership, low morale, and the departure of key personnel with experience in intelligence. It is critical of intelligence chiefs in the organization who, it asserts, did not properly heed early warnings about al-Qaeda and terrorist threats.

Fink, Mitchell, and Louis Mathias, *Never Forget: An Oral History of September 11, 2001* (New York: ReganBooks, 2002).
A husband and wife team from New York City conducted a series of nearly eighty interviews of survivors of the events of September 11. These interviews began just days after September 11, and each story gives a different personal perspective of what happened on that day. This book gives a view of September 11 that most books only attempt to do.

Fouda, Yosri, and Nick Fielding, *Masterminds of Terror: The Truth behind the Most Devastating Terrorist Attack the World Has Ever Seen* (New York: Arcade Publishing, 2003).

Yosri Fouda, a journalist with the Arab television service al-Jazeera, and Nick Fielding, a journalist with the British newspaper *The Sunday Times*, combined to write a book on the operational heads of the September 11 attacks in the United States: Khalid Sheikh Mohammed and Ramzi Bin al-Shibh. In a series of interviews in Pakistan in 2002, Mohammed and Bin al-Shibh confessed to their role as planners of the attacks. This is an important book because of Fouda's interviews with Mohammed and Bin al-Shibh.

Freeh, Louis J., and Howard Means, *My FBI: Bringing Down the Mafia, Investigating Bill Clinton, and Fighting the War on Terror* (New York: St. Martin's Press, 2005).
Louis Freeh, the head of the FBI during the Clinton administration and the early Bush administration, gives his interpretation of the events during his tour of duty. He recounts his successes and offers his own explanation for the failures of the FBI before September 11. His blaming of Congress for the FBI's outdated computer system is only one of the symptoms of the FBI's malaise in the years before September 11.

Gerges, Fawaz A., *The Far Enemy: Why Jihad Went Global* (Cambridge, UK: Cambridge University Press, 2005).
Fawaz Gerges, a professor of international affairs and Middle Eastern studies at Sarah Lawrence College, uses his contacts among followers of jihad to explain why al-Qaeda declared war on the West. It is his thesis that there are two competing jihadist schools: those that want to overthrow Arab regimes and those that want to expand the war against the West. In this excellent and informative book, the author concludes that al-Qaeda's attack on September 11 was not universally approved of by the jihadists who want to overthrow Arab regimes and are fearful of a war with the United States.

Gertz, Bill, *Breakdown: The Failure of American Intelligence to Defeat Global Terror*, rev. ed. (New York: Plume Book, 2003).
The author is the defense and national security reporter for the *Washington Times*. In this book Gertz uses his inside connections in the American intelligence community to back his thesis that American security was compromised by failures of the American bureaucracies and by political blunders. He traces what he perceives to be past failures and argues that unless significant reforms take place, another September 11–type of terrorist event will take place.

Gohari, M. J., *The Taliban: Ascent to Power* (Oxford: Oxford University Press, 1999).
M. J. Gohari teaches Islam and Middle Eastern cultures at Oxford University. In this book, Gohari traces the ascendancy to power of the Taliban in Afghanistan. Particularly important is his treatment of Osama bin Laden's relationship with the Taliban, and the negotiations between the United States and the Taliban over bin Laden before September 11.

Goldberg, Alfred, et al., *Pentagon 9/11* (Washington, DC: Historical Office, Office of the Secretary of Defense, 2007).

This book is the official U.S. government version of what happened in the attack on the Pentagon on September 11, 2001. A team of historians interviewed 1,300 survivors and had access to government sources to write the definitive account on what happened on that day.

Graham, Bob, *Intelligence Matters: The CIA, the FBI, Saudi Arabia, and the Failure of America's War on Terror* (New York: Random House, 2004).

Former Senator Robert Graham (D–FL) was the chair of the Senate's Committee on Intelligence, and he was instrumental in the setting up of the Senate-House Joint Inquiry on Intelligence that studied American intelligence failures leading up to September 11. It remains his thesis that systemic failure in the U.S. government contributed to the intelligence failures. He also criticizes the Bush administration for trying to evade responsibility for September 11 and for taking the United States into the Iraq War before wiping out al-Qaeda.

Griffin, David Ray, *The 9/11 Commission Report: Omissions and Distortions* (Northampton, MA: Olive Branch Press, 2005).

Dr. Griffin, a retired and respected postmodernist theology professor, has gathered a number of so-called experts to challenge the official treatment of the events surrounding September 11. It is their contention that the U.S. government, rather than hijackers, planned and implemented the attacks on September 11. This book, much as other works by conspiracy theorists, is of limited value except to study the thought processes of conspiracy advocates.

Gunaratna, Rohan, *Inside Al Qaeda: Global Network of Terror* (New York: Columbia University Press, 2002).

Rohan Gunaratna, a terrorist scholar who has contacts with both the United Nations and several scholarly institutions, spent five years in the field researching the al-Qaeda organization from its beginnings in 1989 to September 11, 2001. This book covers information from al-Qaeda's financial infrastructure to how it trains its soldiers and operatives. Although the research in this book predates September 11, it is an indispensable source in understanding how al-Qaeda operated in the decade before September 11.

Habeck, Mary, *Knowing the Enemy: Jihadist Ideology and the War on Terror* (New Haven, CT: Yale University Press, 2006).

Habeck, a professor at the School of Advanced International Studies at Johns Hopkins University, gives an analysis of the jihadist political thought that led to the September 11 attacks. The jihadists around al-Qaeda and other Islamist groups are the extremist wing of the Islamist movement, but they constitute a danger to the West. She maintains that it is necessary to understand jihadist ideology to be able to fight it.

Hagen, Susan, and Mary Carouba, *Women at Ground Zero: Stories of Courage and Compassion* (New York: Alpha Books, 2002).

The authors, who have backgrounds in professional writing and investigative social work, rushed to New York to interview women who had worked at Ground Zero in the aftermath of the September 11 attacks. They interviewed thirty women from different organizations. At the end of the book, the authors pay tribute to the three women who lost their lives on September 11 while performing their duties: Captain Kathy Mazza, Yamel Merino, and Moira Smith.

Halberstam, David, *Firehouse* (New York: Hyperion, 2002).
David Halberstam, a Pulitzer Prize–winning journalist-author, wrote this study of the firefighters of Fire House 40/35 in mid-Manhattan. This Fire House became famous for the loss of twelve out of thirteen of its firefighters sent to the World Trade Center on September 11, and a serious injury to the thirteenth. This book is full of human interest, and how the loss of these men affected their families and others.

Hayes, Stephen F., *The Connection: How al Qaeda's Collaboration with Saddam Hussein Has Endangered America* (New York: HarperCollins, 2004).
Stephen Hayes, a staff writer for the *Weekly Standard* and a frequent commentator on CNN, Fox News, and The McLaughlin Group, has compiled information to support his argument that Saddam Hussein and al-Qaeda collaborated to attack American interests. He asserts that the Saddam Hussein regime had no role in the September 11, 2001, attacks in the United States, but that there had been contact between the Hussein regime and al-Qaeda over training and others issues.

Henshall, Ian, and Rowland Morgan, *9/11 Revealed: Challenging the Facts behind the War on Terror* (London: Robinson, 2005).
Two British journalists question both the official version of the September 11, 2001, attacks, and the report from the 9/11 Commission. They believe that certain facts do not make sense, and they wonder why no one has been held accountable for misjudgments. This book does not fall into the realm of the 9/11 conspiracy movement, but it gives considerable ammunition to the conspiracy theorists for often unsupported theories and theses.

Hersh, Seymour M., *Chain of Command: The Road From 9/11 to Abu Ghraib* (New York: HarperCollins, 2004).
Seymour M. Hersh is a Pulitzer Prize–winning author for *The New Yorker*, and this book is his treatment of the decision-making processes in the Bush administration. In his eyes the Bush administration has been so blinded by neoconservative ideology that it has made a series of blunders. Hersh argues that it took political momentum from the September 11 attacks to pursue policies that have made the United States more vulnerable to terrorism, rather than less.

Jacquard, Roland, *In the Name of Osama bin Laden: Global Terrorism and the Bin Laden Brotherhood* (Durham, NC: Duke University Press, 2002).
In a book that has been updated since it made its appearance the week before September 11, Roland Jacquard, terrorist expert and president of the Paris-based International Observatory on Terrorism, gives an assessment of Osama bin Laden and al-Qaeda. He presents evidence that bin Laden has been interested in acquiring biological, chemical, and nuclear weapons, making him and his organization an ongoing danger to the Western world. Jacquard has collected forty key documents, including a British intelligence report on extremist base camps in Afghanistan in 2000.

Jefferson, Lisa, and Felicia Middlebrooks, *Called: "Hello, My Name Is Mrs. Jefferson. I Understand Your Plane Is Being Hijacked?"—9:45 AM, Flight 93. September 11, 2001* (Chicago: Northfield Publishing, 2006).

Lisa Jefferson was the Verizon Airfone supervisor whom Todd Beamer talked to during the last twenty minutes of his life on September 11, 2001. It gave Beamer an opportunity to tell authorities what was going on during the hijacking but also to pass on his love for his family. The author also spends a considerable amount of the book explaining what an impact this conversation had on her life and religious beliefs.

Joint Inquiry into Intelligence Community Activities before and after the Terrorist Attacks of September 11, 2001, *Hearings before the Select Committee on Intelligence U.S. Senate and the Permanent Select Committee on Intelligence House of Representatives*, 2 volumes (Washington, DC: U.S. Government Printing Office, 2004).

The reports of the Joint Inquiry into Intelligence Community Activities before and after the Terrorist Attacks of September 11, 2001, provide the best source for understanding the actions and, in some cases, perceived failure of American intelligence agencies before September 11. These reports and the testimony of leaders of the intelligence community show that the most serious deficiency was the failure of the various intelligence agencies to communicate with each other.

Kashurba, Glenn J., *Quiet Courage: The Definitive Account of Flight 93 and Its Aftermath* (Somerset, PA: SAJ Publishing, 2006).

The author is a Board Certified Child and Adolescent Psychiatrist who wrote this book to bring closure to the families of the victims of the hijacking of United Airlines Flight 93 on September 11, 2001. He counseled and interviewed the families of the victims and the inhabitants of Somerset County, where the plane crashed. His goal is to establish an accurate picture of the events of that day and to build a lasting memorial to those who lost their lives on that fateful day.

Kean, Thomas H., Lee H. Hamilton, and Benjamin Rhodes, *Without Precedent: The Inside Story of the 9/11 Commission* (New York: Knopf, 2006).

The co-chairs of the 9/11 Commission, Thomas Kean and Lee Hamilton, recount their trials and tribulations during the start, middle, and end of the life of the 9/11 Commission. From the beginning of the 9/11 Commission, they believed that the commission had been set up to fail. Kean and Hamilton refused to allow the 9/11 Commission to fail, but it was a long, hard struggle that is told in this book.

Keegan, William Jr., and Bart Davis, *Closure: The Untold Story of the Ground Zero Recovery Mission* (New York: Touchstone Books, 2006).

William Keegan is a lieutenant in the Port Authority police department, and he served as the night swing supervisor at Ground Zero for nine months. He recounts in depth the search and recovery efforts at the World Trade Center site during those months. His treatment is balanced, but he does display some resentment over how the Port Authority police were ignored in the early days of the cleanup.

Kepel, Gilles, *The War for Muslim Minds: Islam and the West* (Cambridge, MA: Belknap Press, 2004).

Gilles Kepel, professor at the Institute for Political Studies in Paris and an eminent scholar on Middle East politics, gives his assessment of the motivation of the planners of September 11. In his eyes they considered it the initial blow in an ongoing battle, leading ultimately to the West's submission to Islam. Kepel is one of the leading authorities in the West on Islamist studies, and his work is an indispensable source for understanding the jihadist Muslim mind.

Kessler, Ronald, *The CIA at War: Inside the Secret Campaign against Terror* (New York: St. Martin's Griffin, 2003).

The author, a former *Washington Post* and *Wall Street Journal* investigative reporter now affiliated with the *New York Times,* has compiled a book that is a defense of the Central Intelligence Agency (CIA) in its war against terrorism. He is critical of the Clinton administration for its inaction against Osama bin Laden and al-Qaeda but has nothing but praise for the actions of the Bush administration in its attempts to combat terrorism. The author also expresses criticism of the FBI.

Kushner Harvey, and Bart Davis, *Holy War on the Home Front: The Secret Islamic Terror Network in the United States* (New York: Sentinel, 2004).

Harvey Kushner, an academic and chairman of a university department of criminal justice, uses his expertise as a scholar of terrorism to survey secret Islamic terrorist activities in the United States. Little of the material in this book refers directly to the conspiracy of September 11, but it does show the motivations of those who consider martyrdom missions. This book has value in that it traces many of the organizations in the United State that sponsor terrorist activities.

Lance, Peter, *1000 Years for Revenge: International Terrorism and the FBI—the Untold Story* (New York: ReganBooks, 2003).

Lance is an award-winning investigative reporter who has intertwined the careers of FBI agent Nancy Floyd, New York City Fire Department fire marshal Ronnie Bucca, and the terrorist Ramzi Yousef to tell the story of the events leading up to September 11, 2001. The author presents Floyd's and Bucca's attempts to warn authorities about the dangers of terrorism. This book is well researched and is well worth reading for anyone interested in the history of September 11.

Langewiesche, William, *American Ground: Unbuilding the World Trade Center* (New York: North Point Press, 2002).

William Langewiesche, a writer for the *Atlantic Monthly* and author of several nonfiction books, has written a detailed story of his six months covering the cleanup of the World Trade Center site. An accurate and objective treatment, his account of all of the ups and downs of the cleanup nonetheless caused some controversy among those involved.

Ledeen, Michael A., *The War against the Terror Masters: Why It Happened, Where We Are Now, How We'll Win* (New York: Truman Talley Books, 2002).

The author is a member of the American Enterprise Institute, a conservative think tank. He has written his version of why something like September 11 happened. In his treatment, the Clinton administration was at fault for the events of September 11.

Longman, Jere, *Among the Heroes: United Flight 93 and the Passengers and Crew Who Fought Back* (New York: HarperCollins, 2002).
The author is a journalist at the *New York Times* who conducted hundreds of interviews in an attempt to re-create the events on United Airlines Flight 93 on September 11, 2001. His thesis is that the reaction of the passengers was a heroic act that saved lives in the long run. The strength of the book is that it covers the human side of the story.

Markham, Ian, and Ibrahim M. Abu-Rabi (eds.), *11 September: Religious Perspectives on the Causes and Consequences* (Oxford: One World, 2002).
Religious leaders attempt in this book to bring together the moral and religious aspects of September 11. This book of readings by religious scholars gives insight into the moral dimension of September 11 but offers no conclusions regarding the events of the day. This book is for those looking at how the events of September 11 fit into a moral and religious context.

Marrs, Jim, *The Terror Conspiracy: Deception, 9/11, and the Loss of Liberty* (New York: Disinformation, 2006).
Jim Marrs, a former investigative journalist and now a freelance writer, is a veteran conspiracy theorist going back to the John F. Kennedy assassination conspiracy. Much as in his other books, Marrs believes that there was a U.S. government conspiracy leading to September 11. This book has marginal value except as an example of how conspiracy advocates look for any discrepancies to prove their points.

McCole, John, *The Second Tower's Down* (London: Robson Books, 2002).
John McCole, a lieutenant in the Fire Department of New York, recounts his experience at the World Trade Center complex beginning on September 11 and for the six months afterward. He tells of the emotional toll on the firefighters with the loss of 343 of their colleagues. This book is another of the personal accounts of the aftermath of September 11 that should be read to understand the impact of September 11.

McDermott, Terry, *Perfect Soldiers: The 9/11 Hijackers: Who They Were, Why They Did It* (New York: Harper, 2005).
Terry McDermott, a journalist for the *Los Angeles Times*, has compiled extensive information about the conspirators of the September 11, 2001, attacks. He conducted interviews in twenty countries in the course of writing this book. This book is the best source available on the backgrounds of the al-Qaeda conspirators leading up to September 11.

Miller, John, Michael Stone, and Chris Mitchell, *The Cell: Inside the 9/11 Plot, and Why the FBI and CIA Failed to Stop It* (New York: Hyperion, 2002).
Three veteran journalists produced this book as an explanation for the failure of the American intelligence community to stop the 9/11 plot. Their explanation is that it was a combination of risk-averse bosses and a bureaucratic structure that

prevented information from being shared and coordinated. They cover the 9/11 plot from its conception to its execution.

Mohamedou, Mohammad-Mahmoud Ould, *Understanding Al Qaeda: The Transformation of War* (London: Pluto Press, 2007).
Mohammad-Mahmoud Ould Mohamedou, the associate director of the Program on Humanitarian Policy and Conflict Research at Harvard University, traces the development of al-Qaeda from its beginnings. It is his contention that from the beginning the leaders of al-Qaeda have had a plan to challenge the West but that the West has been slow to understand. The attacks on September 11, 2001, were only one stage of this plan to confront the West.

Moussaoui, Abd Samad, and Florence Bouquillat, *Zacarias, My Brother: The Making of a Terrorist* (New York Seven Stories Press, 2003).
The author is the brother of the al-Qaeda operative Zacarias Moussaoui, and in this book he traces the change of a French-born Moroccan secularist into an Islamist extremist. Abd Samad Moussaoui is a moderate Muslim, and he has difficulty in understanding how his younger brother could make this transition into an extremist, but he tries. This book is an excellent source for understanding why young Muslims are attracted to extremist causes.

Murphy, Dean E., *September 11: An Oral History* (New York: Doubleday, 2002).
Dean Murphy has compiled a lengthy list of oral histories from the survivors of September 11. These oral histories help give context to the events of that day. This book is an invaluable source to understand how some survived while others did not, and the serendipity of survival.

Murphy, Tom, *Reclaiming the Sky: 9/11 and the Untold Story of the Men and Women Who Kept America Flying* (New York: AMACOM, 2007).
The author, an aviation trainer for the Port Authority of New York and New Jersey's aviation division, recounts the impact on aviation caused by the September 11 attacks. He describes what happened at the airports and on the airliners that day, and how members of the aviation industry responded to the tragedy. This book provides a valuable insight into how the aviation industry dealt with the aftermath of September 11.

Naftali, Timothy, *Blind Spot: The Secret History of American Counterterrorism* (New York: Basic Books, 2005).
The author, a professor at the University of Virginia's Miller Center of Public Affairs and a contractor for the 9/11 Commission, has written a survey of American counterterrorism efforts since 1945. He traces his assertion that American counterterrorism policy has lurched from one crisis to another as American presidents have failed to recognize the dangers of terrorism. This book is a strong source for the study of American counterterrorism.

Office of Inspector General, *EPA's Response to the World Trade Center Collapse: Challenges, Successes, and Areas for Improvement: Evaluation Report* (Washington, DC: Government Printing Office, 2003).

A team from the Office of Inspector General investigated the successes and failures of the Environmental Protection Agency (EPA) during its supervision of the cleanup of the World Trade Center complex site and the Pentagon. This team concluded that the press statements issued by the EPA to reassure the cleanup crew and the public were misleading because at the time the air-monitoring data were lacking for several pollutants of concern, especially for particulate matter and polychlorinated biphenyls (PCBs). This report is also critical of the influence of the White House Council on Environmental Quality on statements issued by the EPA.

Picciotto, Richard, *Last Man Down: A Firefighter's Story of Survival and Escape from the World Trade Center* (New York: Berkley Books, 2002).
The author was a Battalion Commander of FDNY 11 in New York City on September 11, 2001. Responding to the aircraft crash into the North Tower of the World Trade Center, he was busy leading the evacuation when the tower began to show signs that it was about to come down. His miraculous escape allowed the death toll for the New York Fire Department to stay at 343.

Posner, Gerald, *Why America Slept: The Failure to Prevent 9/11* (New York: Ballantine Books, 2003).
Gerald Posner, a former Wall Street lawyer who is now a freelance journalist, gives his assessment why American agencies and government failed to prevent the September 11 attacks. He is critical of all the agencies, and in particular the Clinton administration, but is kinder to the Bush administration. This book presents the material in a rapid-fire fashion, and some of its instant assessments have been overtaken by further research.

Powers, Richard Gid, *Broken: The Troubled Past and Uncertain Future of the FBI* (New York: Free Press, 2004).
Richard Gid Powers, a professor of history at CUNY Graduate Center and the College of Staten Island, and an acknowledged expert on the FBI, writes a history of the FBI from its beginnings until September 11, 2001. He posits the question of whether the FBI can handle the intelligence burden of combating terrorism when its entire culture has been reactive to solving crimes rather than proactive in preventing them. The section on the FBI during the Freeh administration is particularly valuable.

Randal, Jonathan, *Osama: The Making of a Terrorist* (New York: Knopf, 2004).
The author, a former correspondent for the *Washington Post*, used his extensive contacts in the Middle East to write this biography/analysis of Osama bin Laden. Bin Laden has been able to build a legend in the Muslim world mostly because of the ineptness of the Americans. He concludes that even the capture or death of bin Laden will not end terrorism from al-Qaeda or similar organizations.

Reuters, *After September 11: New York and the World* (New York: Prentice Hall, 2003).
Reuters, the international wire service, commissioned members of its staff to produce this combination of text and photography. It chronicles the weeks and months of the recovery in New York City through commentary and photos.

Although this work adds little to the information surrounding September 11, it does add visual evidence to show the recovery following September 11.

Ridgeway, James, *The 5 Unanswered Questions about 9/11: What the 9/11 Commission Report Failed to Tell Us* (New York: Seven Stories Press, 2005).
    James Ridgeway, Washington correspondent for the *Village Voice* and a prolific writer in newspapers, magazines, and books, posed five key questions that he believes were not covered adequately by the 9/11 Commission. These questions are fundamental to answering the ultimate question of accountability for failure to uncover and stop the September 11 plot.

Risen, James, *State of War: The Secret History of the CIA and the Bush Administration* (New York: Free Press, 2006).
    James Risen, a journalist specializing in national security for the *New York Times*, has investigated the relationship between the Bush administration and the CIA. He argues that the Bush administration pressured the CIA to comply with the administration's agenda. A valuable feature of the book is its discussion of the activities of the National Security Administration (NSA).

Robinson, Adam, *Bin Laden: Behind the Mask of the Terrorist* (New York: Arcade Publishing, 2001).
    This biography of Osama bin Laden appeared shortly after September 11, 2001, but the author, a veteran Middle East journalist, had been working on this book for over a year at that time. Because he had already concluded that bin Laden was an imminent danger to the United States, the events of September 11 did not surprise him. This book is an important look at bin Laden and his ambitions, but the author is sometimes a little sloppy with his facts.

Rubin, Barry, and Judith Colp Rubin (eds.), *Anti-American Terrorism and the Middle East: A Documentary Reader* (New York: Oxford University Press, 2002).
    Barry Rubin, the director of the Global Research in International Affairs Center and editor of *Middle East Review of International Affairs*, and Judith Colp Rubin, a journalist specializing in the Middle East, compiled a documentary reader that covers the variety of anti-American opinion in the Middle East. The editors filled this book with primary documents, many of which were hard to find, that scholars studying Middle East studies will find useful. Several of these are part of the September 11 story, and they need to be read for understanding September 11.

Ruthven, Malise, *A Fury for God: The Islamist Attack on America* (London: Granta Books, 2002).
    The author, a PhD from Cambridge University with extensive teaching and writing experience on Islamic subjects, has written this book to explain the motivation in the Islamic world for September 11. He believes that the lack of democracy in the Middle East has made the United States a convenient target for Islamist militants as they are unable to overturn the regimes of their own countries. This book is a balanced assessment from a scholar with expertise on Muslim culture and society.

Saar, Erik, and Viveca Novak, *Inside the Wire: A Military Intelligence Soldier's Eye-witness Account of Life at Guantánamo* (New York: Penguin Press, 2005).
Erik Saar, an enlisted linguist specialist in the U.S. Army, tells about his stay at the Guantánamo Bay Detention Camp as an Arab linguist dealing with detainees there. He documents tensions between the Military Police and the linguists, and he discusses what he perceived as problems in the handling of detainees.

Sageman, Marc, *Understanding Terror Networks* (Philadelphia: University of Pennsylvania Press, 2004).
The author, a former Foreign Service officer and forensic psychiatrist, traces the terrorist network of al-Qaeda and how it operated in carrying out the September 11 attacks. He concludes that the Hamburg Cell was part of a cluster of four terrorist cells—Central Staff Cluster Cell (Osama bin Laden and al-Qaeda central command), Core Arab Cluster Cell (Hamburg Cell and other Arab groups), Southeastern Asian Cluster Cell (Jemaah Islamiyya in Indonesia), and the Maghreb Arab Cluster Cell (North African groups). This book is an invaluable study in the type of terrorist networking that produced September 11.

Scheuer, Michael, *Imperial Hubris: Why the West Is Losing the War on Terror* (Washington, D.C.: Brassey's, 2004).
Michael Scheuer continued his assessment of the American war on terror in this book written after he left the CIA. His thesis is that the U.S. government needs to change its foreign policy to undercut the appeal that Osama bin Laden and al-Qaeda have in the Muslim world. Unless it does so, there is the possibility that the United States will lose its war on terrorism.

Scheuer, Michael, *Through Our Enemies' Eyes: Osama Bin Laden, Radical Islam, and the Future of America* (Washington, DC: Brassey's, 2002).
The author was the former head of the CIA's Alec Station, a unit charged with capturing or assassinating Osama bin Laden. In this CIA-vetted book Scheuer tries to inform the American public how bin Laden and the leaders of al-Qaeda view the United States and the West. This book became so controversial that the CIA revamped its policy on CIA officials writing books.

Simpson, David, *9/11: The Culture of Commemoration* (Chicago: University of Chicago Press, 2006).
David Simpson, a professor of English at the University of California–Davis, examines the way America commemorated the dead on and after September 11, 2001. He puts the process of commemorating the dead into a historical context of how the dead have been handled in previous wars and catastrophes. His thesis is that the 9/11 commemorations have been overtaken by ideas of revenge.

Smith, Ennis, *Report from Ground Zero: The Story of the Rescue Efforts at the World Trade Center* (New York: Viking, 2002).
Dennis Smith, a former firefighter and founder of *Firehouse Magazine*, gives his insight on what the New York Fire Department's (NYFD) firefighters went through on September 11. As an eighteen-year veteran of the NYFD, he had access to information that the firefighters were reluctant to share with outsiders.

This book gives a good picture of the firefighters on September 11 and later, and it is recommended reading.

Stewart, James B., *Heart of a Soldier: A Story of Love, Heroism, and September 11th* (New York: Simon & Schuster, 2002).
The author, a Pulitzer Prize–winning journalist, has written a biography of Rick Rescorla from his birth in Hayle, Cornwall, England, to his death on September 11, 2001, in the World Trade Center complex. Rescorla was a heavily decorated Vietnam veteran of the 2nd Battalion, 7th Cavalry, but he was also a writer and security specialist with a law degree. He died heroically, evacuating people from the South Tower, and his body was never found.

Stout, Glenn, Charles Vitchers, and Robert Gray, *Nine Months at Ground Zero: The Story of the Brotherhood of Workers Who Took on a Job Like No Other* (New York: Scribner, 2006).
A journalist and two construction workers compiled this book from their experiences working at Ground Zero of the World Trade Center. In the months that Vitchers and Gray worked there, they developed a close working relationship with the New York City Fire Department. At the end they considered the nine months spent at Ground Zero working seven twelve-hour days per week "the most precious and most painful time of their lives."

Suskind, Ron, *The One Percent Doctrine: Deep Inside America's Pursuit of Its Enemies since 9/11* (New York: Simon and Schuster, 2007).
Ron Suskind is a former Pulitzer Prize–winning journalist who uses his contacts in the Washington, D.C., area to write about the war between the U.S. government and the terrorists in the aftermath of 9/11. The title of the book comes from Vice President Dick Cheney's remark that, if there is a 1 percent chance of a threat to the security of the United States, then it is necessary to take action against that threat.

Sweet, Christopher (ed.), *Above Hallowed Ground: A Photographic Record of September 11, 2001* (New York: Viking Studio, 2002).
The photographers of the New York City Police Department took photos of the World Trade Center complex from minutes after the first aircraft hit the North Tower until the last steel beam was removed in May 2002. These never-before-published photos give a sense of reality about what happened on September 11 and its aftermath. It is a tribute to the loss of twenty-three members of the New York City Police Department and to all the others who died that day.

Sylvester, Judith, and Suzanne Huffman, *Women Journalists at Ground Zero: Covering Crisis* (Lanham, MD: Rowman and Littlefield, 2002).
Two journalism professors, Sylvester at Louisiana State University and Huffman at Texas Christian University, were intrigued at how many women journalists risked their lives over the September 11, 2001, story. They decided to interview twenty-four women journalists ranging from TV reporters to newspaper journalists. These journalists recorded their horror at the loss of life and the devastation, but they believed that they were just doing their jobs.

Tenet, George, and Bill Harlow, *At the Center of the Storm: My Years at the CIA* (New York: HarperCollins, 2007).

George Tenet, the head of the CIA for most of the Clinton and Bush administrations, uses this book to counter what he considers misrepresentations of how the CIA operated during his years in command. Although Tenet admits mistakes on the part of the CIA and himself, he maintains that the CIA has been used as a scapegoat by the Bush administration. Though there has been debate over some of the details, this is a must-read for anybody interested in how the CIA operated and its limitations in the period before September 11.

Thomas, R. Andrew, *Aviation Insecurity: The New Challenges of Air Travel* (Amherst, NY: Prometheus Books 2003).

Thomas, a global business expert and an aviation security analyst, uses his expertise on aviation matters to expose the inadequacies of commercial airline security. It is his thesis that the FAA's weaknesses in regulating security compliance by the commercial airline industry contributed to what happened on September 11. This book is an invaluable resource on security issues before and after September 11.

Thompson, Paul, *The Terror Timeline: Chronicle of the Road to 9/11—And America's Response* (New York: ReganBooks, 2004).

Paul Thompson, a political activist and the founder of the Center for Cooperative Research, has combed newspapers and reports on events before and after September 11. His analysis of more than five thousand articles and reports points out the contradictions in the media. This book is also the most detailed chronology of the events surrounding September 11, and it is marred only by the author's acceptance of sometimes dubious sources.

Trento, Susan B., and Joseph J. Trento, *Unsafe at Any Altitude: Failed Terrorism Investigations, Scapegoating 9/11, and the Shocking Truth about Aviation Security Today* (Hanover, NH: Steerforth Press, 2006).

This husband and wife team with experience in investigative journalism has produced a book on commercial airline security before and after September 11. The authors assert that the airline industry and other lobbyists worked against improved airline security before September 11, and that private security companies have since been used as scapegoats.

Von Essen, Thomas, with Matt Murray, *Strong of Heart: Life and Death in the Fire Department of New York* (New York: ReganBooks, 2002).

Thomas Von Essen was the Commissioner of the Fire Department of New York (FDNY) on September 11. As a former firefighter and firefighter union official, he traces the events of September 11 and how the loss of 343 firefighters impacted the FDNY. Von Essen's viewpoint and his close association with Mayor Giuliani make this book a valuable source.

Weiss, Murray, *The Man Who Warned America: The Life and Death of John O'Neill, the FBI's Embattled Counterterror Warrior* (New York: ReganBooks, 2003).

The author traces the colorful career of FBI counterterrorism expert John O'Neill through its ups and downs. Weiss traces O'Neill's clashes with the upper levels of the FBI hierarchy and his position as head of security at the World Trade Center complex.

Woodward, Bob, *Bush at War* (New York: Simon and Schuster, 2002).
Bob Woodward has been a longtime investigative journalist for the *Washington Post* and the author of many books on American politics. In this book he examines the reaction to September 11 by President George W. Bush and the Bush administration. It covers the period from September 11 through the overthrow of the Taliban to the eve of the invasion of Iraq.

Wright, Lawrence, *The Looming Tower: Al-Qaeda and the Road to 9/11* (New York: Knopf, 2006).
The author is a freelance journalist with extensive contacts in the Middle East that he used to write this book, which traces the origins of the September 11 conspiracy. The strength of the book is the numerous interviews of people close to the leaders of al-Qaeda. This book is an excellent treatment of al-Qaeda's role in the conspiracy, and it won the 2007 Pulitzer Prize for General Nonfiction.

Index

Note: Page entries printed in **bold** font refer to main entries.

1975 Church Committee, 123
1996 Reauthorization Act, 102
9/11, 210
9/11 Commission: Able Danger and, 6–8; aviation security, 106, 493–500; Clinton administration, 74; creation and results, 96, 97–98, 100–101, 164–66, **205–8**; Freeh, Louis, 130; Goss, Porter J., 140, 141; Hamilton, Lee H., 152–54; Kean, Thomas Howard, 174–75; Kerik, Bernard Bailey, 177; New York City Police Department, 212; NORAD, 216–17; Saudi financial support for al-Qaeda, 504–6; testimony of Richard A. Clarke, 474–79
9/11 Commission Report: Family Steering Committee, 101; Griffin, David Ray, 144; Hamilton, Lee H., 153; Jersey Girls, 165; *The Path to 9/11,* 231; *United 93,* 289
911: Press for Truth, 165
9-11: The Big Lie, 188

A&E Network, 289
ABC, 231
Abdel Rahman, Sheikh Omar: career as radical Islamist, **3–5**, 10, 167; Islamist extremists and, 26, 192, 193, 321; New York City landmarks bombing conspiracy, 122, 210, 211; World Trade Center bombing (1993), 8, 9, 313
Abdullah, Abdullah Ahmed, 10

Able Danger: 9/11 Commission, 153, 207–8; intelligence program, **5–8**; Weldon, Curtis "Curt," 302–3, 507–10
Abouhalima, Mahmud, **8–9**, 309, 312, 313
Abu Nidal Handbook, The, 76
Abu Nidal Organization (ANO), 76
Abu Sayyaf, 227, 242–43, 313, 315
Abu Sitta, Sobhi. *See* Atef, Mohammad
Afghan Northern Alliance. *See* Northern Alliance
African embassy bombings: Alec Station, 13; Clinton administration and, 73; Fadl, Jamal al-, 93; Hage, Wadih el-, 148, 149; Mohamed, Ali Abdel Saoud, 193–94; Qaeda, al-, **9–12**, 245
Against All Enemies: Inside America's War on Terror, 67
Agiza, Ahmed, 250
Ahmed, Mehmood, 140, 142
Ahmed, Mustafa Mahmoud Said, 11
Ahmed the German, 10–11
Aircraft Communications and Reporting System (ACARS), 284
airline industry: economic impact, 90; Federal Aviation Administration (FAA), 102–6; pilot training, 237; security, 20, 356–57; TIPOFF, 280–81; Transportation Security Administration, 281–82, 283; Victims' Compensation Fund, 293; World Trade Center attack, 307–8

air marshals. *See* federal marshals

Air Transportation Safety and System Sta-
bilization Act, 106

Ajaj, Ahmed, 313

Albright, Madeleine, 10, 231

Alec Station, **12–14**, 59, 263, 264. *See
also* bin Laden Unit

Algeria, 243

Ali, Ibrahim Siddig, 210

Allbaugh, Joe M., 109, 407–9

al-Qaeda, **242–46**

"Al-Qaeda's Instruction on Living in the
Western World While on a
Mission," 345–47

"Al-Qaeda Training Camps in Afghanistan
in 2000," 340–44

Alvarez, Victor, 211

Amec Construction Management, 68–69,
82, 83

American Airlines, 24, 90, 294

American Airlines Flight 11: Atta,
Mohamed el-Amir Awad el-Sayed,
25; hijacking of, **14–16**, 213, 214;
Lewin, Daniel M., 183; NORAD,
216; Ogonowski, John, 221–22;
Ong, Betty Ann, 226–27; World
Trade Center, 304, 307

American Airlines Flight 77: Argenbright
Security Company, 20; Burlingame,
Charles Frank "Chic" III, 44–45;
DCA members and, 81–82; hijack-
ing of, **16–17**, 213, 214; NORAD,
216, 217; Olsen, Barbara, 222–24;
Pentagon attack, 233; September
11 hijackers, 154–56, 189–91

American Association of University Professors (AAUP), 65

American Civil Liberties Union (ACLU),
64, 291–92

American Conservative Union (ACU),
291–92

American Film Renaissance, 95

American Library Assocation, 292

American Red Cross, 98, 535–38

American Society of Civil Engineers
(ASCE), **18–19**, 428–34

American Special Forces, 324

Anderson, Ted, 385–90

Ansar, al-, 246

anti-Americanism: Atta, Mohamed el-
Amir Awad el-Sayed, 24; Clinton
administration and, 72; *Fahrenheit
9/11*, 95; Meyssan, Theirry, 74, 188

Antiterrorism and Effective Death Penalty
Act of 1996, 72

Aqsa Martyrs' Brigade, al-, 173

Arar, Maher, 251

Arce, David, 115

Argenbright Security Company, 16,
20–21, 47, 284

Ariana Afghan airline, 73

Arlington County Fire Department, 234

Armed Islamic Group (GIA), 243, 255

Arriza, John, 279

Ashcroft, John, 48, 50, 201, 290

Ashley, Carol, 100

Asia. *See* South Asia

"Assessment of the FBI on Pre-9/11
Intelligence (August 18, 2004),"
485–87

Associated Press, 227

Assuna Annabawiyah Mosque, 254

Atef, Mohammad: career as Islamist
extremist, **21–22**; coconspirators,
41, 196; Predator and, 240, 246;
September 11 hijackers and, 23,
163, 270–71

At the Center of the Storm, 279

Atta, Mohamed el-Amir Awad el-Sayed:
Able Danger and, 5–8; career as
Islamist extremist, **22–25**, 247;
coconspirators, 22, 28, 41, 197;
Hamburg Cell, 149–50, 198; letter
of advice for hijackers, 362–66;
pilot training, 237–38; Qaeda, al-,
244, 319, 324; September 11
hijackers and, 15, 163, 190, 269,
270–71; September 11 hijackings
and, 212, 213

Attas, Hussein al-, 200

Aum Shinrikyo, 72

Aviation and Transportation Security Act
(ATSA), 281

Aviation Emergency Preparedness Working Group (AEPWG), 220

aviation industry. *See* airline industry

aviation security: Federal Aviation Administration (FAA), 102–6, 356–57;
prescreening, 104; September 11
attacks, 493–500; Sullivan, Brian,
353–55, 360–61, 501–3;
Transportation Security Administration, 281–83

Awad, Hamden Khalif Allah, 10–11

Ayyad, Nidal, 309

Azhar University, al-, 26

Azzam, Sheikh Abdullah Yussuf: bin Laden, Osama, 34, 35; career as Islamist extremist, **25–27**; Kifah Refugee Center, al-, 178–79; Qaeda, al-, 242, 243; radical islamists and, 3, 4, 21, 218, 321

Baccus, Rick, 146
Backo, Bill, 310
Baer, Robert, 145
Bahaji, Said, **28–29**, 42f, 149
Bahrain, 73
Bald, Gary, 109f
Balkh (Mazar-e-Sharif) training camps, 343
Bamyan Province training camps, 343–44
Bandar, Prince, 129
Bangkok, 315
Banihammad, Fayez Rashid, 213, 214f, 287
Bank of Nova Scotia, 120
Banna, Hassan al-, 312
Banshiri, Abu Ubaidah al-, 10, 21, 92
Barrett-Arjune, Renee, 53
Barrett, Wayne, 137
Barsky, Robert F., 62
Battle of the Lion's Den, 35
Bayoumi, Omar al-, 190
Beamer, Lisa, 30
Beamer, Todd Morgan, **29–30**, 285, 289
Bear (the dog), 87, 134
Beirut, 76, 249
Belfas, Mohammad, 149
Bellevue Hospital, 57
Bello, Maria, 308
Benjamin, Daniel, 160
Bennett, Ronan, 151
Ben-Veniste, Richard, 175, 206
Benyaer, Michael, 231
Berez, Maurice, 160, 161
Bergen, Peter L., 35
Bergeron, Kayla, 380
Berloff, Andrea, 308
Bernton, Hal, 255
Betrayal of Palestine, 36
Bevin, Kimi, 294
Bhutto, Benazir, 203, 314
Biggart, William, **31**
bin-Abdul-Aziz, Prince Ahmed bin Salman, 324, 325
bin al-Shibh, Ramzi: Bahaji, Said, 28; career as Islamist extremist, **40–43**; coconspirators, 22, 197, 261; Kuala Lumpur meeting, 180; September 11 hijackers and, 23, 162, 270, 271
bin Atash, Khallad, 180
Bingham, Mark Kendall, **32–33**, 285, 289
"Bin Laden Determined to Strike in United States," 78
Bin Laden family, 98, 206
bin Laden, Osama: African embassy bombings, 9–10; Alec Station, 12–14; Bucca, Ronald, 44; Bush administration, 48–51; career as Islamist extremist, **34–40**; Central Intelligence Agency (CIA), 59–60; Clarke, Richard A., 66–67; Clinton administration and, 71, 72, 73; Counterterrorism Center, 77, 78; *Dawn* Interview, 415–17; Declaration of Jihad, 331–34; economic impact of attacks, 90; Federal Aviation Administration (FAA), 103; Hamburg Cell, 150; interview, 402–3; O'Neill, John, 224; Operation Bojinka, 228; pilot training, 237; Predator, 240; Presidential Daily Briefing (August 6, 2001)," 358–59; Scheuer, Michael, 263, 264; September 11 hijackers, 418–24; Taliban, 274, 275, 276; Tenet, George, 277, 278
"Bin Laden's Homage to the Nineteen Students (December 26, 2001)," 418–24
bin Laden Unit: Federal Bureau of Investigation (FBI), 107; Moussaoui, Zacarias, 261; Phoenix Memo, 235, 236; Scheuer, Michael, 263, 264. *See also* Alec Station
biological weapons, 42, 246, 278–79. *See also* weapons of mass destruction
biometrics, 282–83
Bird, Antonia, 151
Black, J. Cofer, 77
Bloomberg, Michael R., 97, 125, 182
Bodine, Barbara, 225, 231
Borelli, Joseph, 219
Boren, David, 278
Bosnia, 155, 190, 195, 240, 319
Bosnian Muslims, 322
Bovis Company, 68–69, 82, 83
Boyle, Mike, 115
Bracher, Barbara Kay, 17, **222–24**
Bradley, Leigh A., 535–38
Bradshaw, Sandy, 285

Braman, Chris, 387–89
Breitweiser, Kristen, 97f, 100, 164
"Brian Sullivan's E-mail to Michael Cana-
van, FAA Associate Administrator
for Civil Aviation Security about
Aviation Security (August 16,
2001)," 360–61
Brigham Young University, 75, 168–69,
266
Bright Lights, 79
Britain, 38, 151, 246
British Intelligence, 340–44
Brittiochi, Antonio, 304
Brown, Maureen, 57
Bruguiere, Jean-Louis, 256
Bucca, Ronald, **43–44**
Buchanan, Pat, 299
Buckley, William, 76
Burlingame, Charles Frank "Chic" III, 16,
44–45, 81
Burlingame, Debra, 45
Burnett, Deena, 47, 391–96
Burnett, Thomas Edward, **46–48**, 285,
391–96
Burns, Donald, 369
Burton, Michael, 82–84, 120–21
Bush administration: 9/11 Commission,
175, 205, 207; Central Intelligence
Agency (CIA), 59–60; Clarke,
Richard A., 65, 66–67; counterter-
rorism, 48–49, **50–51**; Counterter-
rorism Center, 78; families of
victims, 45, 95–96, 97–98, 100,
164–65; Foreign Intelligence
Surveillance Act of 1978 (FISA),
124; Guantánamo Bay Detainment
Camp, 145–46, 147; Joint Inquiry
committee, 143, 268; Kerik,
Bernard Bailey, 177; National Security Agency (NSA), 209; Predator,
240; rendition, 250; Scheuer,
Michael, 264; September 11
conspirators, 43, 197; Swift Project,
273; theorists, 62, 113–14, 145
Bush, George W.: 9/11 Commission,
174, 205–6; address to the nation
(September 11, 2001), 400–401;
airline industry, 106; Central Intelligence Agency (CIA), 59, 60, 78,
140, 278, 279; counterterrorism,
48–50; *Fahrenheit 9/11*, 93–95;
Foreign Intelligence Surveillance

Act of 1978, 124–25; Kerik,
Bernard Bailey, 177; National Secu-
rity Agency (NSA), 209; rendition,
249; Transportation Security
Administration, 21, 281; USA
PATRIOT Act, 290, 291f
Bushnell, Prudence, 10

Cable News Network (CNN), 268
Cairo, 23, 26
Cairo University, 23
Caliphate, 26
Callahan, Frank, 114
Canada, 94, 191, 251, 254–55
Canadian Security and Intelligence Service
(CSIS), 255–56
Canavan, Michael, 356–57, 360–61
Cannistraro, Vincent, 227
Cantor Fitzgerald, **53–54**, 100, 164, 305
Card, Andrew H. Jr., 49
Casazza, Patty, 100, 164
Casey, William J., 76
Cashman, William, 285
Castro government, 145
casualties: New York City Police Depart-
ment, 212; Pentagon attack, 234,
235; World Trade Center attack,
55–58, 306, 307; World Trade
Center bombing (1993), 309–10
Catholic Church, 69
CBS, 151, 210
CBS News, 265
Centennial Olympic Park bombing, 128
Central Intelligence Agency (CIA): Alec
Station, 12–14, 263–65; Bush
administration, 48, 49, 51; Clinton
administration, 72, 73; counterter-
rorism, **58–60**, 239–41; Countert-
errorism Center, 75–79;
Guantánamo Bay Detainment
Camp, 146–47; Joint Inquiry com-
mittee, 139–41, 143, 267, 268–69;
Joint Terrorism Task Force (JTTF),
167; Mohamed, Ali Abdel Saoud,
192; rendition, 249–51; September
11 terrorists, 150, 180, 190, 196,
358–59; Swift Project, 273; Tenet,
George, 276–79; watch lists, 103,
279–80, 281; Zubaydah, Abu, 325
Chain of Command, 59
Charlebois, David, 16, 81
Chechen rebels, 150, 156, 190, 201

Chechnya, 124, 156, 190
chemical weapons, 11, 42, 93, 191, 246
Cheney, Dick, 49, 60, 216, 268
Childs, David, 125
Chomsky, Noam, **61–62**, 65
Christians, 4, 38, 172, 191
Churchill, Ward, **62–65**, 511–21
Cirri, Robert D., 186
Citadel Prison, 3
Civil Aviation Security. *See* aviation security
Claremont University, 144
Clarke, Richard A.: Bush administration and, 51, 350–52; Clinton administration and, 73, 74; counterterrorism, 12, **65–67**; Federal Bureau of Investigation (FBI), 108, 224; *The Path to 9/11*, 231; testimony, 474–79
Clarridge, Duane R. "Dewey," 76
cleanup operations: firefighter riot, 119–21, 159; Fresh Kills Landfill, 130–32; Ground Zero, **68–71**, 82–84; Occupational Safety and Health Agency (OSHA), 228–30; Pentagon attack, 235; Zadroga, James, 317–18
Cleland, Max, 206
Clinton administration: 9/11 Commission, 205, 207, 263; Alec Station, 12, 13; Bush administration and, 50, 51; Central Intelligence Agency (CIA), 59, 277; "Communiqué of the World Islamic Front," 338–39; Counterterrorism Center, 78; Freeh, Louis, 128–29; *The Path to 9/11*, 231; rendition, 250; terrorism and, **71–74**; *Wag the Dog*, 299–300; Wall, the, 301; Weldon, Curtis "Curt," 302
Clinton, Bill: African embassy bombings, 11; Bush administration and, 48; Central Intelligence Agency (CIA), 59, 276–77; Clarke, Richard A., 66; Commission on Aviation Safety and Security, 104; Counterterrorism Center, 77; Freeh, Louis, 128–29, 130; Predator, 240; rendition, 249; *Wag the Dog*, 299–300; Yousef, Ramzi Ahmed, 315
Clinton, Hillary, 318
Code of the Firefighters, 117

Cohen, Joel, 256f
Cohen, William, 51, 300
Coll, Steve, 277
Combatant Status Review Tribunal, 325, 539–45. *See also* prisoners of war
"Comments of Representative Maxine Waters (D-CA) on Saudi Financial Support for Al-Qaeda before the House of Representatives' Financial Services Committee (August 22, 2004)," 504–6
commercial airline industry. *See* airline industry
Commission on Aviation Safety and Security, 104
committee of twenty-six representatives, 69, 70
"Common Strategy," 105. *See also* aviation security
communication systems: Giuliani, Rudolph, 136, 295–96; New York City Police Department, 176, 177, 211–12; New York Fire Department (NYFD), 116, 117; Office of Emergency Management (OEM), 220–21; Port Authority of New York and New Jersey, 239, 306
"Communiqué of the World Islamic Front," 338–39
Computer-Assisted Passenger Prescreening System (CAPPS), 104, 284
computer systems, 107–8, 129, 209, 259
"Confession of Khalid Sheikh Muhammad at the Combatant Status Review Tribunal at Guantánamo Detention Camp (March 10, 2007)," 539–45
Congress: 9/11 Commission, 95–98, 100, 101, 164, 205–7; airline industry, 106; aviation security, 21, 102, 103, 281; families of victims, 45, 84, 111, 293; Joint Committee on Intelligence, 143; warrants, 208, 290
conspiracy theorists: Fetzer, James H., 112–14; Griffin, David Ray, 144–45; Jones, Steven E., 168–69; Marrs, Jim, 184–85; Meyssan, Thierry, 187–89; Scholars for 9/11 Truth, 265–66; September 11 attacks, **74–75**, 217
construction workers, 68–69, 83, 119, 120

Container Camp, 41
Contras, 76
Coordinated Interagency Partnership Regulating International Students (CIPRIS), 160–61
Corcoran, Marty, 83
Corley, Dr. W. Gene, 18, 428–34
Correa, Victor, 233
Coughenour, John, 256
Coulter, Ann, 165–66
Counterterrorism Center, 59, **75–79**, 261, 278
Counterterrorism Division, 108, 235
Counterterrorism Security Group, 66
Critical Incident Stress Management (CISM), 110
cruise missile attack, 73
Cuba, 145–47
Cunningham, David L., 231
Cunningham, Randy "Duke," 141
"Curt Weldon's Testimony about Able Danger (September 20, 2005)," 507–10
Czech Republic, 232

Dahab, Khalid, 193
Dahl, Jason Matthew, **80–81**, 93, 156–57, 284
Dahoumane, Abdelmajid, 255
Daily News, 272
Damascus, Zammar, 320
Dar es Salaam, 10–11, 73, 93, 245
Darkanza, Mamoun, 150
Darunta training camp, 255
Daschle, Tom, 205–6
Dasquie, Guillaume, 189
D'Auria, Michael, 115
"*Dawn* Interview with Osama bin Laden (November 10, 2001)," 415–17
Dawson, Mark, 397–99
DCA Gathering Place, **81–82**
Dean, Diana, 191, 255
death certificates, 57, 86, 99
"Declaration of the World Islamic Front," 335–37
Defense Intelligence Agency (DIA), 7
Delta airlines, 103
Democratic party: 9/11 Commission, 153, 165, 205, 207; Freeh, Louis, 128; Joint Inquiry committee, 140
Department of Defense (DOD), 6, 7–8, 74, 240

Department of Design and Construction (DDC), 69, 70, **82–84**, 120
Department of Justice: counterterrorism and, 48, 160; Guantánamo Bay Detainment Camp, 145; Moussaoui, Zacarias, 201; Wall, the, 300–301; warrants, 124, 290
Department of Transportation (DOT), 281, 282, 283
DeStefano, Phil, 65
detainees. *See* prisoners of war
Deutch, John, 58–59, 72
DeVona, Al, 305
Dewdney, A. K., 74–75
Dhahran, 10, 36, 245
DiFrancesco, Donald, 181–82
DiGiovanni, John, 310
Dinkins, David N., 220
Director of National Intelligence (DNI): 9/11 Commission, 207; Goss, Porter J., 140, 141; Joint Inquiry committee, 143, 269
Disaster Mortuary Operation Response Team (DMORT), **84–86**
DNA analysis, 57–58, 84, 85, 118, 286
"Dog Handlers at Ground Zero," 397–99
dog teams (search and rescue), **86–88**, 110, 235
Doha, Abu, 255
Downey, Raymond Matthew, **88–89**, 266, 296
Dubai, 73
Dulles International Airport, 16, 20, 81, 163
Dunbar, Carson, 122, 123
Dunlavey, Michael, 146
Dunne, Joe, 306

Eckert, Beverly, 96, 100
economic impact, **90–91**, 95, 98, 110, 307–8
Egypt: bin Laden, Osama, 39; Qaeda, al-, 243, 320, 321–22; radical Islamists, 3, 4, 9, 21, 26; rendition, 249, 250, 251; September 11 hijackers, 23
Egyptian Islamic Jihad: Atef, Mohammad, 21; Mohamed, Ali Abdel Saoud, 192; Qaeda, al-, 243; Zawahiri, Ayman al-, 320, 321, 322; Zubaydah, Abu, 323, 324
Eiffel Tower, 38
Eisner, Michael, 94

emergency medical technicians (EMT), 56, 116, 151, 186–87
Emery Roth and Sons, 304
enemy combatants. *See* prisoners of war
Environmental Protection Agency (EPA), 68, 317, 404–6
Essabor, Zakariya, 149
"Essay by Ward Churchill (September 11, 2001)," 511–21
Europe, 246
evacuation, 55, 221, 235, 305–6
explosives detection systems (EDA), 282. *See also* aviation security

Fadl, Jamal al-, **92–93**
Fahrenheit 9/11, **93–95**
Faisal, Prince Turki al-, 36, 190
Falk, Richard, 65
Families of 9/11 Movement, 125
Families of September 11 (FOS11), 96, 206
families of victims: 9/11 Commission, 100–101, 205–8; assistance for, 98–99, 106, 110–11, 293–94; Ferer, Christine Ann, 182; Giuliani, Rudolph, 120–21, 135–36; *Hamburg Cell* TV movie, 151; Ielpi, Lee, 158–59; September 11 attacks, **95–98**; testimony of Mary Fetchet, 480–84
Families of Victims of 9/11, 96
Family Assistance Act, 84
Family Assistance Center, **98–99**
Family Steering Committee, 98, **100–101**, 175, 206
Far Falastin Detention Center, 320
Farooq Mosque, al-, 9, 218
Fatah, al-, 173
Fazazi, Mohammed al-, 247
Fazil, Haroun, 10, 149
federal aid. *See* financial assistance
Federal Aviation Administration (FAA): 9/11 Commission, 153, 175, 207; aviation security, 20, 281, 353–55, 356–57, 360–61; civil aviation and, **102–6**; hijackers, 24, 155, 238; NORAD, 215, 216, 217; Samit, Harry, 261; TIPOFF, 280–81
Federal Bureau of Investigation (FBI): Able Danger and, 6; Bush administration, 50; Central Intelligence Agency (CIA) and, 13, 58, 72, 263;

clean up operations, 69, 286; Clinton administration, 73; Counterterrorism Center, 76, 77, 78, 79; Family Assistance Center, 98; Freeh, Louis, 127–30; hijackers, 190; informants, 93, 122–23, 193–94; Joint Inquiry committee, 140, 143, 267, 268–69; Joint Terrorism Task Force (JTTF), 166–67; Moussaoui, Zacarias, 201, 257–59, 260–61, 468–73; O'Neill, John, 224–25; Phoenix Memo, 235–36, 454–67; pre-9/11 intelligence, 485–87; radical Islamists, 196, 197, 203–4, 218–19, 324; rendition, 249; terrorism, 48, 49, **107–9**; TIPOFF, 280; Wall, the, 300–301, 450–53; warrants, 123–25, 290–92; World Trade Center bombing (1993), 9, 310, 315
Federal Emergency Management Agency (FEMA), 18, 85, 98, **109–11**, 407–14
federal marshals, 103, 105, 282
Feehan, Bill, **111–12**, 118, 133, 134, 296
Feinberg, Kenneth, 293, 294
Fellowship Adventure Group, 94
Fensome, Terry, 238
Feret, Christy, 97
Fetchet, Mary, 96, 97f, 100, 480–84
Fetzer, James H., 75, **112–14**, 169, 265–66
Fielding, Fred F., 206
financial assistance: airline industry, 90, 106; Family Assistance Center, 98–99; Federal Emergency Management Agency (FEMA), 110–11; Giuliani, Rudolph, 135; Victims' Compensation Fund, 293–94
financial impact. *See* economic impact
financing of terrorists: 9/11 Commission, 488–92; Clinton administration 73; Saudi financial support, 504–6; sources, 245; Swift project, 273; USA Patriot Act, 291, 292
firefighters (New York). *See* New York Fire Department (NYFD)
firefighters (Pentagon attack), 234
firefighters riot, **119–21**, 135, 158–59, 298
Flight 93, 289
Florida, 24

Florida Flight Training Center, 163
Floyd, Nancy, **122–23**, 231
Foggo, Kyle Dustin "Dusty," 141
Foreign Affairs, 51
Foreign Intelligence Surveillance Act
  (FISA): Moussaoui, Zacarias, 201,
  257, 260–61; Wall, the, 107;
  warrants, **123–25**, 208, 209, 292
Foreign Intelligence Surveillance Court
  (FISC), 123, 124–25, 209, 301
foreign students, 160–61, 237, 238
Fouda, Yosri, 197
Four Feathers, 200
FOX News, 54
France: bin Laden, Osama, 38; conspiracy
  theories, 74, 188; Moussaoui,
  Zacarias, 124, 201; Ressam,
  Ahmed, 254
Frasca, David, 257
Freedom Tower, 97, **125–27**, 159
Freeh, Louis, 13, 109f, **127–30**, 301
Fresh Kills Landfill, 69, **130–32**

Gabrielle, Monica, 100
Gama'a Islamiyya, al-. *See* Islamic Group
Ganci, Peter J. "Pete," 87, 112, **133–34**,
  136f, 296
Garvey, Jane, 104
Gary, Bruce, 114–15
Geneva Convention, 145. *See also* prison-
  ers of war
Germany: Central Intelligence Agency
  (CIA), 58; Hamburg Cell, 28,
  40–41, 42, 149, 150, 198; Qaeda,
  al-, 246, 319; Quds Mosque, al-,
  247; rendition, 251; September 11
  hijackers, 23, 162, 270
Ghamdi, Ahmed al-, 213, 287
Ghamdi, Hamza al-, 213, 214f, 287
Ghamdi, Saeed al-, 213, 214f, 284
Ghor Province training camp, 344
Gintly, John, 115
Giuliani, Rudolph William Louis "Rudy"
  III: Department of Design and
  Construction (DDC), 82–83; Fam-
  ily Assistance Center, 98–99;
  firefighters riot, 118, 119, 120,
  121; Office of Emergency Manage-
  ment (OEM), 220, 221; September
  11 attacks, **134–36**, 176, 177
Giuliani Time, **137**
Glick, Jeremy, **137–38**, 285, 289
Global Terrorism Analysis, 265

Globe Security, 15
Glynn, Martin, 377–79
Gonzales, Nydia, 226
Goodrich, Donald W., 96
Gorbachev, Mikhail, 218
Gore Commission, 104
Gorton, Slade, 206, 485–87
Goss, Porter J.: Bush administration and,
  279; Central Intelligence Agency,
  60, **139–41**; Joint Inquiry commit-
  tee, 143, 267, 268
Graham, Daniel Robert "Bob," 141f,
  142–43, 267, 268
Grancolas, Lauren, 289
Grand Mosque, 34
Greenbelt Theater, 227
Greene, Donald, 285, 289
Greengrass, Paul, 289
Griffin, David Ray, 75, **144–45**
Gronlund, Linda, 285
Ground Zero. *See* cleanup operations;
  World Trade Center complex
Group Islamique Armé (GIA), 38
Guadago, Rich, 285
Guantánamo Bay Detainment Camp: con-
  fession of Khalid Sheikh
  Muhammad, 539–45; creation and
  use, **145–47**; terrorists held, 43,
  160, 197, 325
Guisnel, Jean, 189
Gunaratna, Rohan, 243
Guzman, Abimael, 76

Hada Family, 180
Hage, Wadih el-, 10, 11–12, 93,
  148–49
Hamas, 26, 173, 243, 324
Hambali, Riduan Isamuddin, 273
Hamburg Cell: Central Intelligence
  Agency (CIA), 58; creation and
  actions of, **149–50**; Moussaoui,
  Zacarias, 124; Qaeda, al-, 23,
  28–29, 40–42, 198, 319; Quds
  Mosque, al-, 247; September 11
  hijackers, 22, 269, 270; suicide mis-
  sions, 173;
Hamburg Cell, **151**
Hamdani, Mohammad Salman, **151–52**
Hamilton, Lee: 9/11 commission,
  152–54, 174, 175, 206–8; Able
  Danger and, 7; testimony, 488–92,
  505–6
Hampton-El, Clement R., 211

Hanjour, Hani Saleh Husan: career as Islamist extremist, **154–55**; Phoenix Memo, 235; pilot training, 238; September 11 hijacking, 16, 24, 45, 213, 233

Hanlon, James, 210

Hannachi, Abderraouf, 255

Hanson, Peter, 287

Haouari, Mohktar, 255

Harazi, Muhammad Omar al, 180

Harithi, Abu Ali al-, 240

Haruki Ikegami, 227, 315

Harvey, Bill, 100

Hassan ibn Sabbah sect, 172

Hatch, Orrin, 291f

Hauer, Jerome M., 221

Hayden, Michael, 79, 208, 209, 268

Hayden, Peter, 88

Hazmi, Bandar al-, 155

Hazmi, Nawaf bin Muhammad Salim al-: American Airlines Flight 77, 16, 233; career as Islamist extremist, **155–56**; intelligence community and, 167, 301, 440–49; Kuala Lumpur meeting, 180; September 11 hijackers, 24, 190, 213

Hazmi, Salem al-: American Airlines Flight 77, 16, 233; Kuala Lumpur meeting, 180; September 11 hijackers, 156, 213, 214f

Haznawi, Ahmed al-, 163, 213, 214f, 284

Hazouri, Cathryn, 64

health problems: cleanup operations, 68, 70, 71, 87; Environmental Protection Agency, 404–6; New York Fire Department (NYFD), 117, 118; Zadroga, James, 317–18

Heidenberger, Michelle, 81, 82

Hekmatyar, Gulbuddin, 35

Herman, Neil, 166

Hersh, Seymour, 59, 299

Hezbollah, 76, 173, 243

Hezbollah al-Hijaz, 10

hijackers: Atta's letter of advice for, 362–66; bin Laden's homage, 418–24; Immigration and Naturalization Services (INS), 159–61; pilot training, 237–38; September 11 attacks, **212–15**. See also individual hijackers

hijacking policy, 105, 106, 215, 282

Hijazi, Ahmed, 240

Hill, Dan, 252, 253

Hill, Eleanor: FBI Investigation of Zacarias Moussaoui, 468–73; intelligence prior to September 11, 435–39, 440–49; Joint Inquiry committee, 267–68; Phoenix electronic communication, 454–67

Holden, Kenneth, 82–84, 120

holy war. See jihad

Homeland Security Department, 161

Homer, LeRoy Wilton Jr., 80, **156–57**, 284

Horrocks, Michael, 175, 262, 287

House Homeland Security Committee, 535–38

House of Representatives, 72, 140, 290, 302

House Permanent Select Committee on Intelligence Joint Inquiry into the Terrorist Attacks of September 11. See Joint Inquiry committee

Huczko, Stephen, 186

Huffman Aviation, 24, 237–38

Huntleigh USA, 287

Husayn, Zayn al-Abidin Mohamed, 324

Hussein, Saddam: bin Laden, Osama, 36; Bush administration, 50, 51, 66, 67; Central Intelligence Agency (CIA), 14, 60; Chomsky, Noam, 62

Ibn Khalid, Abdullah, 196

ibn Walid, Khalid, 92

identifying victims. See DNA analysis

Ielpi, Jonathon, 158–59

Ielpi, Lee, **158–59**

IFC Films, 94

Immigration and Naturalization Service (INS): pilot training, 237; September 11 conspirators, 25, **159–61**, 201; Yousef, Ramzi Ahmed, 313

Imperial Hubris: Why the West is Losing the War on Terror, 264

Indonesia, 39, 243

Indonesian Islamist terrorist group, 195

Infante, Anthony, 239

informants, 58–59, 92–93

Intelligence Matters: The CIA, the FBI, Saudi Arabia, and the Failure of America's War on Terror, 143

International Islamic Front for Jihad against Jews and Crudaders, 38

International Islamic University, 26

interrogations: Bright Lights, 78–79;
    Guantánamo Bay Detainment
    Camp, 146–47; rendition and, 249,
    250, 251; Zammar, Muhammad
    Heydar, 319–20; Zubaydah, Abu,
    325
Inter-Services Intelligence (ISI), 73
"Interview with Mullah Umar
    Muhammad (September 21,
    2001)," 402–3
Iran, 76, 129, 245, 315
Iran-Contra scandal, 76
Iraq: bin Laden, Osama, 36; Bush admin-
    istration, 49–50, 51, 66, 67;
    Central Intelligence Agency (CIA),
    14, 60; Chomsky, Noam, 62; con-
    spiracy theorists, 113; *Fahrenheit
    9/11*, 94; Kerik, Bernard Bailey,
    177; Predator, 240–41; Qaeda, al-,
    246; Scheuer, Michael, 264; Tenet,
    George, 278–79
Iraq Embassy of Beirut, 173
Iraq Study Group (ISG), 135
Islamabad, 26, 77
Islamic Cultural Center of New York, 152
Islamic Group, 4, 195, 243, 273
Islamic Jurisprudence. *See* Jurisprudence
Ismaeli Assassins, 172
Israel: bin Laden, Osama, 36, 38; jihad
    and, 172, 173; Yousef, Ramzi
    Ahmed, 313, 316; Zawahiri, Ayman
    al-, 322
Israeli Embassy, 315
Israeli-Palestinian conflict, 60
Italy, 251

Jamestown Foundation, 265
Janjalani, Abdurajak, 313
Jarrah, Ziad Samir: career as Islamist
    extremist, **162–64**; coconspirators
    and, 22, 23, 270; Hamburg Cell,
    149, 150; Qaeda, al-, 244, 319;
    United Airlines Flight 93, 33, 47,
    80, 81, 284, 285
Jawzjan Province training camps, 343
Jeddah, Zawahiri, 321
Jefferson, Lisa, 30
Jersey Girls, 98, 100, **164–66**, 294
Jews, 23, 38, 313. *See also* Israel
jihad: Azzam, Sheikh Abdullah Yussaf, 25,
    26; bin al-Shibh, Ramzi, 41; bin
    Laden, Osama, 34, 35, 36, 38; bin

Laden's declaration of, 10, 331–34;
    instructions on, 345–47; Kifah
    Refugee Center, al-, 179; Quds
    Mosque, al-, 247; suicide missions
    and, 172
Jimeno, 308
John Paul II (pope), 195, 315
Joint Inquiry committee: 9/11 Commis-
    sion, 164, 205; Federal Bureau of
    Investigation (FBI), 108, 450–53,
    468–73; Goss, Porter J., 140, 141;
    Graham, Daniel Robert "Bob,"
    142, 143; Phoenix Memo, 236,
    454–67; reports on intelligence by
    Eleanor Hill, 435–39, 440–49; Sep-
    tember 11 attacks, **267–69**; Tenet,
    George, 276–77
Joint Terrorism Task Force (JTTF):
    Argenbright Security Company, 20;
    creation and focus, **166–67**; Ham-
    dani, Mohammad Salman, 151,
    152; Moussaoui, Zacarias, 201;
    New York City Landmarks bombing
    conspiracy, 211; Nosair, El Sayyid,
    218–19; O'Neill, John, 224–25;
    Phoenix Memo, 236; Samit, Harry,
    260
Jones Aviation Flying Service, 237–38
Jones, Greg, 260
Jones, Steven E., 75, 113, **168–69**, 266
Jordan, 26, 39, 191, 324
Journal of 9/11 Studies, 169
Judge, Mychal, **169–71**, 210, 296
jurisprudence, 3, 26, 415
Justice Department. *See* Department of
    Justice

Kabul, 22, 275, 343
Kahane, Rabbi Meir, 9, 166, 193, 217,
    218–19
Kallafal, Fares, 210
Kandahar, 23, 150, 198–99, 270, 275,
    276
Kandhar Province training camps, 344
Kappes, Steve, 141
Karim, Abdul Basit Mahmud Abdul-, 312
Karling, Walter, 232
Kasi, Mir Amal, 77
Katani, Mohamed al-, 160
Kean, Thomas Howard: 9/11
    Commission, 153, 154f, **174–75**,
    206–8, 501–3; Family Steering

Committee, 100–101, 164, 165;
    Ong, Betty Ann, 226; *The Path to
    9/11,* 231
Keating, Kevin, 137
Keegan, William, Jr., 56
Keinberg, Mindy, 100, 164
Kelly, Edmond, 152
Kelly, Thomas, 136f
Kemal, Fateh, 255
Kennedy International airport, 138
Kennifer Memorial Garden, 82
Kenya, 9–12, 93, 148, 149, 193–94, 245
Kerekes, Tibor, 376
Kerik, Bernard Bailey, 135, **176–78**, 212,
    373–77
Kerrey, Bob, 206
Kerry, John, 353–55
Khaldan training camp, 23, 200, 255,
    270, 324
Khalifa, Mohammed Jamal, 227
Khartoum, 9, 11, 13, 36
Khobar, 10, 36, 129, 224, 245
Khost training camps, 11, 340–41
Kifah Mosque, al-, 193
Kifah Refugee Center, al-: Joint Terrorism
    Task Force (JTTF), 166; militant
    Islamists and, 9, 148, **178–79**, 218,
    313; New York City Landmarks
    bombing conspiracy, 122, 210
Kifah Refugee Services Office, 92
King Abdul Aziz University, 26, 34
Kirkpatrick, Bob, 310
Kissenger, Henry, 98, 164, 205–6
Knapp, Steve, 310
Knights Under the Prophet's Banner, 322
Koran, 172, 275
Kosovo War, 322
Kuala Lumpur meeting, 41, **180**, 190
Kunar Province training camps, 342–43
Kunstler, William, 219
Kuwait, 36, 73

Lakar-e-Toiba, 324
Lake, Tony, 12
Lawless, Joe, 105
Leahy, Patrick, 291f
Lebanon: Counterterrorism Center, 76;
    Hezbollah, 173, 243; international
    money-laundering laws, 73; rendi-
    tion, 249
Leder, Robert, 371–73
Lee, Lorraine, 97

Lehman, John F., 177, 206
Lemack, Carie, 96, 100
*Let's Roll!: Ordinary People, Extraordinary
    Courage,* 30
"Letter from Brian F. Sullivan to Thomas
    Kean, Chairman of the National
    Commission on Terrorist Attacks
    Upon the United States," 501–3
"Letter from Brian F. Sullivan, Retired
    FAA Special Agent to U.S. Senator
    John Kerry (May 7, 2001),"
    353–55
"Letter from Michael Canavan, Associate
    Administrator for Civil Aviation
    Security to FAA Federal Security
    Managers (May 30, 2001),"
    356–57
"Letter Justifying the Bombing of the
    World Trade Center (February 7,
    1993)," 329–30
Levin, Neil David, **181–82**, 239
Lewin, Daniel M., 11, 15, **182–83**, 226
Lewinsky, Monica, 59, 299
Lewis, Ken and Jennifer, 81, 82
Libeskind, Daniel, 125
LiBrizzi, Marcus, 75
Libya, 76, 103
Lim, David, 382
Lions Gate Entertainment Corporation, 94
lobbyists: Antiterrorism and Effective
    Death Penalty Act of 1996, 72;
    colleges and universities, 160–61;
    families of victims, 95–98,
    100–101, 125, 206, 294; Federal
    Aviation Administration (FAA),
    103, 106
Logan International Airport, 15, 24, 25,
    104–105, 287
Logar Province training camps, 342
Los Angeles International Airport, 191,
    254, 255
Lower Manhattan Development Corpora-
    tion, 125
Loy, James, 282
Lucci, Patty, 228
Lutnick, Howard, 53–54
Lynch, Michael, 115

Magaw, John, W., 281–82
Maisel, Todd, 114
Maktab al-Khidanet (MAK). *See*
    Mujahideen Services Bureau

Malaysia, 180, 190
Maltbie, Michael, 257
Manila, 197, 227, 228, 315
Manila Airport, 315
Manley, Sarah, 100
Maoist terrorist group, 76
Marrone, Fred, 239
Marrs, Jim, 75, **184–85**
martyrdom. *See* suicide missions
Martyr's Blood," 348–49
Masada Training Camp, 243
Masri, Khalid el-, 251
Massachusetts Port Authority (Massport),
    105
Massoud, Ahmad Shah, 27, 35, 37, 66,
    78, 275
Matar Training Complex, al-, 197
May, Renee, 17, 81, 82
Mazza, Kathy, **185–86**, 239
McCain, John, 205
McDermott, Terry, 313
McGuinness, Thomas, 14
McLaughlin, John, 141, 308
McVeigh, Timothy, 72
Melendez-Perez, Jose, 160
"Memorandum from Richard A. Clarke
    for Condoleezza Rice Informing
    Her about the Al-Qaeda Network
    (January 25, 2001)," 350–52
memorial. *See* Freedom Tower
Mendoza, Rodolfo, 203
Mercado, Steve, 115
Mercado, Wilfredo, 310
Merino, Yamel, **186–87**
Mes Aynak, Mihdhar, 190
Meskini, Abdelghani, 255
Metropolitan Transportation Authority,
    125
Metzinger, Jeffrey L., 411–14
Meyssan, Thierry, 74, **187–89**
Michael Moore Hates America, 95
Mihdhar, Khalid al-: intelligence prior to
    September 11, 167, 301, 440–49;
    radical Islamists and, 155, 156, 180;
    September 11 hijacking, 16,
    189–91, 213, 233
Milan, 251
Military Affairs Committee, 242
*Military Studies in the Jihad against the
    Tyrants*, 193
Miller, Geoffrey, 146
Miller, John, 231

Miller, Nicole, 289
Minter, Vanessa, 226
Mir, Ali, 325
Miramax Films, 94
Mitchell, Chris, 231
Mitchell, George, 205–6
Mohamed, Ali Abdel Saoud, 9–10,
    192–94, 218
"Mohamed Atta's Letter of Advice for
    Hijackers (September 2001),"
    362–66
Mohamed, Khalfan Khamis, 10–12
Mohammed, Khalid Sheikh: career as
    Islamist extremist, **194–98**; cocon-
    spirators, 22, 38; confession,
    539–45; Guantánamo Bay Detain-
    ment Camp, 147; millennium plots,
    191; Operation Bojinka, 227, 228;
    The Path to 9/11, 231; September
    11 hijackers, 24, 25, 155; World
    Trade Center bombing (1993),
    309, 313; Yousef, Ramzi Ahmed,
    314, 315, 316
Monroe, Amy, 56
Moore, Michael, 93–95
Moqued, Majed, 16, 213, 233
Morell, Mike, 278
Morello, Vince, 115
Morgan Stanley, 252, 253
Morin, Terry, 17
Morocco, 39, 247, 319
Moro Islamic Liberation Front, 243
Morrone, Fred V., 182
Motah-Hary, Morteza, 348–49
Motassadeq, Mounir el-, 28, 149,
    198–99
Moussaoui, Abd Samad, 200
Moussaoui, Zacarias: FBI Investigation of,
    257–59, 260, 468–73, 522–34;
    Foreign Intelligence Surveillance
    Act of 1978 (FISA), 124; Joint
    Inquiry committee, 143, 267–68,
    269; radical Islamists and, 42,
    199–202, 255
Mubarak, Hosni, 4, 167, 245, 321–22
Mueller, Robert, 49, 109f, 129
Mueller, Rowley, 259
mujahideen: Atef, Mohammad, 21;
    Azzam, Sheikh Abdullah Yussaf, 26;
    bin Laden, Osama, 36; Mohammed,
    Khalid Sheikh, 195; Omar,
    Mohammed, 274

Mujahideen Services Bureau (MSB), 26, 35, 242

Murad, Abdul Hakim Ali Hashim: career as Islamist extremist, **203–4**; commercial airplanes and, 195, 227, 228; Yousef, Ramzi Ahmed, 312, 315–16

Murray, Patrick, 141

Muslim Brotherhood, 34, 194, 312–13, 320

Muslim world, 39, 172, 213–14, 219, 244

Muslim World League, 148

Mzoudi, Abdelghani, 149

Na'ami, Ahmed al-, 213, 214f, 284

NAFSA: Association of International Educators, 161

Nairobi: African embassy bombings, 9–12; Clinton administration and, 73; Fadl, Jamal al-, 93; Hage, Wadih el-, 148, 149; Qaeda, al-, 245

Nangharar Provinces training camps, 342

Nasr, Hassan Osama, 250–51

Nasser, Gamal Abdel, 3

National Air Transportation Association (NATS), 237

National Commission on Terrorist Attacks Upon the United States. *See* 9/11 Commission

National Institute of Standards and Technology (NIST), 169

National Military Command Center (NMCC), 105, 215, 216

National Security Agency (NSA): electronic spy service, **208–9**; Joint Inquiry committee, 268–69; Kuala Lumpur meeting, 180; Predator, 240; warrantless searches, 124; Zubaydah, Abu, 324

National Security Council, 65, 66

National Security Law Unit (NSLU), 123–24

National Terrorist Asset Tracking Center, 51

National Transportation Safety Board (NTSB), 286

NATO, 246

Naudet, Jules and Gédéon, **209–10**

Neda, Al-, 246

Negroponte, John, 60, 141

Nelson, Ed, 20

neoconservatives, 49, 51, 60

Newark International Airport, 138, 284

New York City Joint Terrorism Task Force. *See* Joint Terrorism Task Force

New York City landmarks plot, 5, 122, **210–11**

New York City Police Department (NYPD): casualties, 55, 56–57; cleanup operations, 68, 130f; firefighters riot, 119, 120; Freedom Tower, 125, 126; Hamdani, Mohammad Salman, 151–52; Joint Terrorism Task Force (JTTF), 166–67; Kerik, Bernard Bailey, 176–78; other emergency personnel and, 116, 220, 239; September 11 attacks, **211–12**; Smith, Moira, 271–72; World Trade Center bombing (1993), 310

New Yorker, 299

New York Fire Department (NYFD): Bucca, Ronald, 43–44; casualties, 55, 56, 57; Downey, Ray Matthew, 88–89; family assistance, 99; Feehan, William M. "Bill," 111–12; Fire House 40/35, **114–15**; Ganci, Peter J. "Pete," 133–34; Giuliani, Rudolph, 135–36; Ground Zero, 68, 69, **115–19**, 305; Judge, Mychal, 169–71; Naudet documentary, 209; other emergency personnel and, 211, 220, 239; riot, 84, **119–21**; Seven World Trade Center, 19; World Trade Center bombing (1993), 310

New York Post, 152

New York Stock Exchange. *See* stock market

New York Times, 232

New York Times Review of Books, 65

Nidal, Abu, 76

Nigeria, 39

nineteen martyrs. *See* hijackers

NORAD, 105–6, 153, 207, **215–17**

Nordenson, Guy, 126–27

Northeast Air Defense Sector (NEADS), 216

Northern Alliance: Bush, George W., 49; Central Intelligence Agency (CIA), 59; Clarke, Richard A., 66; hijackers and, 156, 190; Qaeda, al-, 37, 39, 246; Taliban, 274, 275–76

North, Oliver, 76
Nosair, El Sayyid, 9, 166, 193, 211, **217–19**
Nowrasteh, Cyrus, 231
nuclear weapons, 12, 42, 246. *See also* weapons of mass destruction
Nunn, Sam, 267

O'Brien, Steve, 233
Occupational Safety and Health Agency (OSHA), 70, **228–30**
O'Connell, Geoff, 77
Odeh, Mohamed Saddiq, 10, 11–12
Office of Emergency Management (OEM), 136, **220–21**
Ogonowski, John, 14, 15, **221–22**, 227
Oklahoma City bombing, 72, 88
Olson, Barbara K., 17, **222–24**
Omar, Abu, 250–51
Omar, Mohammed, 37, 274–75, 376, 402–3
Omari, Abdul Aziz al-, 15, 25, 214f
Omnibus Counter-Terrorism Act of 1995, 72
O'Neill, John, 13, 129, **224–26**, 231, 263
O'Neill, Paul, 51
One Percent Doctrine, 325
Ong, Betty Ann, 15, 183, **226–27**
Operation Bojinka, 195, 203, **227–28**
"Operation Pearl," 74
"Oral Testimony from Survivors of the World Trade Center," 367–84
O'Reilly, Bill, 54
Orlando International Airport, 160
"Osama bin Laden's Declaration of Jihad (August 23, 1996)," 10, 331–34
Osama bin Laden Unit. *See* bin Laden Unit
Owens, Bill, 64
Owhali, Mohamed Rashed Daoud al-, 10, 11–12

Pakhtia Provinces training camps, 341–42
Pakistan: bin Laden, Osama, 13, 35, 36, 39, 40; Kifah Refugee Center, al-, 179; money-laundering laws, 73; Qaeda, al-, 11, 243, 246, 324; September 11 conspirators, 42, 195, 197; Taliban, 50, 275, 276; Yousef, Ramzi Ahmed, 313, 314–15, 316

Pakistani Inter-Services Intelligence (ISI), 275
Palestine, 26, 200, 218, 243, 313
Palestine Liberation Organization (PLO), 26
Palestinian Islamic Jihad, 173
Palmer, Oriole, 44
Pan American Airlines, 103
Pan Am International Flight Academy, 201, 257, 260
paramedics. *See* emergency medical technicians
Paramount Pictures, 308
Parham, James W., 186
Parker, Istaique, 316
Pashtuns, 275
passports. *See* visas
Pataki, George, 97, 125, 126, 181–82, 318
Path to 9/11, The, 175, **231**
Patriot Act. *See* USA Patriot Act
Patriotic Americans Boycotting Anti-American Hollywood (PABAAH), 95
Pavel Hlava, **232**
Pearl, Daniel, 147, 198
Pennsylvania State Police, 286
Pentagon: 9/11 Commission, 175; Able Danger and, 6, 303f; Clinton administration and, 73; Guantánamo Bay Detainment Camp, 145; hijacking and, **233–35**, 385–90
Perl, Richard, 49
Persian Gulf War, 36, 66
Peru, 76
Peru's Shining Path, 76
Peshawar, 312
Pfeifer, Joseph, 210, 367–71
Philippines: Mohammed, Khalid Sheikh, 195; Murad, Abdul Hakim Ali Hashim, 203–4; Operation Bojinka, 227, 228; Qaeda, al-, 243; Yousef, Ramzi Ahmed, 312, 313, 315
Philippines Airline Flight 434, 227
Philpott, Scott, 6, 7
Phoenix Memo: Federal Bureau of Investigation (FBI), 108, **235–36**; Joint Inquiry committee, 143, 267–68, 269, 454–67; Rowley, Coleen, 257–58
Phucas, Keith, 6

Pickard, Thomas J., 236
pilot training, **237–38**
Plaugher, Edward P., 409–11
Port Authority of New York and New Jersey: casualties, 55, 56–57; cleanup operations, 68, 70, 119; Freedom Tower, 125; Levin, Neil David, 181–82; Mazza, Kathy, 185–86; Rescorla, Cyril Richard (Rick), 253; roof exits, 116; September 11 attack, **238–39**, 305–6; *World Trade Center,* 308
Posse Comitatus Act, 6
Powell, Colin, 49, 278–79
Predator, 51, 66, **239–41**, 246
"President George W. Bush's Address to the Nation (September 11, 2001)," 400–401
"Presidential Daily Briefing (August 6, 2001)," 358–59
Presidential Decision Directive 62, 66
Press, Bill, 299
Priesser, Dr. Eileen, 6
prisoners of war, 145, 146–47, 197–98, 425–27
Project Bojinka. *See* Operation Bojinka
Prospect, 62
Provost, Clancy, 260
Puerto Rican nationalists, 166
Push, Stephen, 97f

Qaeda, al-, **242–46**
Qatada, Abu, 200
Qatari officials, 196
Quds Mosque, al-: Hamburg Cell, 149, **247**; September 11 coconspirators, 28, 41, 198, 319; September 11 hijackers, 23, 162, 269, 270
Quinn, Ricardo J., 118
Qutb, Muhammad, 34
Qutb, Sayyid, 34, 320

Rabbani, Burhanuddin, 35
Radical Fundamentalist Unit (RFU), 107, 124, 235, 236
Ray, April, 148
Reagan administration, 249
Reagan National Airport, 111
Reagan, Ronald, 6
Red Book, 160
Red Cross, 98, 535–38
Reddy, Moira. *See* Smith, Moira

Regenhard, Sally, 100
Reid, Harry, 291f
rendition, **249–51**
Reno, Janet, 77, 129, 301
"Report by Eleanor from the Joint Inquiry Staff on the Intelligence Community's Knowlede of the September 11 Hijackers Prior to September 11, 2001 (September 20, 2002)," 440–49
"Report by Eleanor Hill from the Joint Inquiry Staff Statement on the Intelligence on the Possible Terrorist Use of Airplanes (September 18, 2002)," 435–39
"Report of the Joint Inquiry Staff by Eleanor Hill on the FBI Investigation of Zacarias Moussaoui (September 24, 2002)," 468–73
"Report of the Joint Inquiry Staff by Eleanor Hill on the FBI's Handling of the Phoenix Electronic Communication (September 24, 2002)," 454–67
Republican Party: 9/11 Commission, 100, 101, 174, 205, 207; aviation security, 21, 103; Clinton administration and, 72, 73, 299; families of victims, 45, 165; Freeh, Louis, 128; Giuliani, Rudolph, 135, 136; Joint Inquiry committee, 140, 143
Rescorla, Cyril Richard (Rick), **252–54**
rescue and recovery. *See* cleanup operations
respirators, 228, 230
respiratory illness. *See* health problems
Ressam, Ahmed, 191, **254–56**
Rice, Condoleezza, 49, 51, 165, 209, 350–52
Riley, Patricia, 97
riots. *See* firefighters riot
Risen, James, 208
Riyadh, 36
Robbins, James S., 189
Rodriguez, Bert, 163
Rodriguez-Smith, Monica, 310
Roemer, Timothy J., 206
Rolince, Michael, 236
Romito, James A., 186, 239
Roosevelt, Franklin Delano, 145
Roosevelt, Theodore, 145
Ross-Lyles, CeeCee, 285

Rowe, Karl, 49

Rowley, Coleen, 143, **257–59**

Royal Mounted Canadian Police (RMCP), 251

Rule 6E, 107, 300, 301

Rumsfeld, Donald, 50–51

Russell, Mark, 299

Russia, 124, 150, 190

Sadat, Anwar, 4, 192, 320–21

Said, Prince Sultan bin Faisal bin Turki al-, 325

Salah, Mohammed, 210

Salem, Abdel Emad: Floyd, Nancy, 122–23; Joint Terrorism Task Force (JTTF), 166, 167; Kifah Refugee Center, al-, 179; New York City Landmarks bombing conspiracy, 210, 211; *The Path to 9/11*, 231

Salameh, Mohammed, 309, 310

Salou, 24

Samit, Harry, 201, 257, **260–61**, 522–34

Santiago, Hector, 373–76

Saracini, Victor J., **262–63**, 287

Saudi Arabia: 9/11 Commission, 98, 206; Abouhalima, Mahmud, 9; bin Laden, Osama, 34, 36, 193, 331–34; express visa program, 160; *Fahrenheit 9/11*, 94; financial support for Al-Qaeda, 273, 275, 504–6; Joint Inquiry committee, 268; Khobar Towers, 10, 245; radical islamists, 3, 129, 321, 324–25; September 11 hijackers, 190, 212, 213

Saudi Binladen Group, (SBG), 34

Sayyaf, Abdul Rasool, 35

Scheuer, Michael, 12–14, 249, 250, **263–65**

Scholars for 9/11 Truth: conspiracy theories, 75, **265–66**; Fetzer and, 112, 113; Griffin and, 144; Jones and, 169; Marrs and, 185

Scholars for 9/11 Truth and Justice, 75, 169

Schwartz, John, 107–8

Scotiabank, 70

search and recovery. *See* cleanup operations

search warrants. *See* warrants

Secretary of Homeland Security, 177

Secret Service Agents, 69

Securicor, 20

security. *See* aviation security

"Selected Excerpts from the Testimony of FBI Agent Harry Samit in the Zacarias Moussaoui Trial on March 9, 2006," 522–34

Senate: Burlingame, Charles Frank "Chic" III, 45; Goss, Porter J., 140; Jersey Girls, 164; USA PATRIOT Act, 290, 292

Senate Ethics Committee, 206

Senate Judiciary Committee, 259, 485–87, 507–10

Senate Select Committee on Intelligence. *See* Joint Inquiry committee

Sengün, Aysel, 162, 163

September 11 Inquiry: Questions to Be Answered, 206

Seven World Trade Center: American Society of Civil Engineers (ASCE), 19; conspiracy theories, 168–69; Office of Emergency Management (OEM), 220, 221; Von Essen, Thomas, 296; Zadroga, James, 317

Shaffer, Anthony, 6, 7, 208, 303f

Shahi Kowt, 246

Shah, Wali Khan Amin, 227

Shaikh, Abdussattar, 190

Shalabi, Mustafa, 4, 92, 178–79

Sharia College of Damascus, 26

Shea, Kevin, 114

Shehhi, Marwan Yousef Muhammed Rashid Lekrab al-: career as Islamist extremist, **269–71**; coconspirators, 22, 41, 319; Hamburg Cell, 149, 150, 247; pilot training, 237–38; Qaeda, al-, 244; September 11 hijackers, 24, 25, 163; September 11 hijacking, 18, 213, 214f, 262, 287

Shehri, Mohammad al-, 213, 214f

Shehri, Mohand al-, 287

Shehri, Wail al-, 15, 213, 214f

Shehri, Waleed al-, 15, 213, 214f

Shelby, Richard C., 143, 267, 268, 301

Shelton, Hugh, 5–6

Shields, Scott, 87

Shifa pharmaceutical plant, al-, 11, 13, 73

Shiite Amal organization, 173

Shiites, 246, 315

Shura (Consulting) Council, 92

Silverstein, Larry, 125, 239

Simon, Steven, 160

Six Day War, 26

skyjackers. *See* hijackers
Skyscraper Safety Campaign, 206
Slahi, Mohamedou Ould, 150
Smith, James, 271, 272
Smith, J.D., 7
Smith, Moira, **271–72**, 377, 378–79
Snider, L. Britt, 267
Soba, 36
Social Security Administration, 98
Society for Worldwide Interbank Financial
    Telecommunication (SWIFT). *See*
    Swift project
Somalia, 36, 322
Sorbi, Fred, 190
South Asia, 39, 180, 312, 313
Soviet-Afghan War: bin Laden, Osama,
    34–35; radical Islamists and, 4, 8,
    21, 26, 92, 193, 195, 218, 312
Spain, 24, 247
Stark, John, 136f
Star-Ledger, 175
State Department, 10, 74, 103, 279
"Statement of a Special Agent of the Fed-
    eral Bureau of Investigation
    (September 20, 2002)," 450–53
"Statements by Federal Emergency Man-
    agement Agency on Its Response to
    the Terrorist Attacks on the World
    Trade Center in New York City and
    the Pentagon before the United
    States Senate's Committee on Envi-
    ronment and Public Works (Octo-
    ber 16, 2001)," 407–14
Staten Island, 69, 130
State of Denial, 51
Steinberg, Jim, 6
stock market, 53, 54, 91
Stone, Michael, 231
Stone, Oliver, 308
Sudan: African embassy bombings, 9, 11;
    bin Laden, Osama, 36–37, 77, 93;
    Clinton administration and, 73;
    Qaeda, al-, 245; radical Islamists, 4,
    148, 321, 322
Sufaat, Yazid, 180
Suhr, Daniel, 170
suicide missions: hijacking policy and,
    105, 106, 215, 217; intelligence on
    use of airplanes, 435–39; Qaeda,
    al-, 243, 244, 245; radical islamists,
    203, 247; September 11 hijackers
    and, 163–64, 197, 213–14, 270;
    use of, **172–73**, 348–49

Sulick, Michael, 141
Sullivan, Brian F., 353–55, 360–61,
    501–3
Sunnis, 172, 246
Suqami, Satam al-, 15, 183, 213, 214f
Suraghi, Hasan Abd-Rabbuh al-, 243
surveillance. *See* warrants
survivors, 86, 367–84
Suskind, Ron, 325
Sweden, 250
Sweeney, Brian, 287
Sweeney, Madeleine, 15
Sweeny, Amy, 183
Swift Project, **273**. *See also* financing of
    terrorists
Syria, 250, 251, 319–20

Tabligh, 319
Taibi, 34
Taliban: bin Laden, Osama, 37, 39;
    Bush administration, 49, 50, 51,
    67; Central Intelligence Agency
    (CIA), 59, 78; Clinton administra-
    tion and, 73; creation and rule,
    274–76; detainees, 425–27;
    Muhammad, Mohammed, 402–3;
    Predator, 240; Qaeda, al-,
    245–46; September 11 hijackers,
    156, 190
Tamil Tigers, 173
Tanzania, 10–11, 93, 245
Tardio, Dennis, 371
Tarnak Farm compound, 13, 66
Technical University of Hamburg-
    Harburg (TUHH), 23, 28, 198,
    270
Tenet, George: Alec Station, 12, 13–14;
    Bush administration, 48, 49, 51,
    78; Central Intelligence Agency
    (CIA), 59, 60, **276–79**; Clinton
    administration and, 73; Joint
    Inquiry committee, 268; National
    Security Agency (NSA), 209; Reno,
    Janet, 77; Rice, Condoleezza, 51;
    Samit, Harry, 261
Terrible Lie, The, 189
"terrorist surveillance program," 209
"Testimony by Lee Hamilton, Vice Chair-
    man of the 9/11 Commission,
    before the House of
    Representatives' Financial Services
    Committee (August 22, 2004),"
    488–92

"Testimony of Dr. W. Gene Corley on
   Behalf of the American Society of
   Civil Engineers before the Subcom-
   mittee on Environment,
   Technology, and Standards and
   Subcommittee on Research of the
   U.S. House of Representatives
   Committee on Science (May 1,
   2002)," 428–34
"Testimony of Mary Fetchet, Founding
   Director, Voices of September 11th,
   on the Need for Reform in a Hear-
   ing of the Senate's Committee on
   Government Affairs (August 17,
   2004)," 480–84
"Testimony of Richard A. Clarke before
   the National Commission on Ter-
   rorist Attacks upon the United
   States (March 24, 2004),"
   474–79
"Testimony of the American Red Cross
   before the Management,
   Integration, and Oversight
   Committee of the House
   Homeland Security (July 12,
   2006)," 535–38
Thailand, 39, 315
"The Aviation Security System and the
   9/11 Attacks (2004)," 493–500
the Wall, 300–301, 450–53
Thomas, Andrew R., 282
Thompson, James R., 206
Thornton-Tomasetti, 83
*Through Our Enemies Eyes: Osama bin
   Laden, Radical Islam, and the
   Future of the
United States,* 264
Time magazine, 135
Times Herald, 6
TIPOFF, **279–81**, *See also* watchlists
Tokyo, 72
Tomasetti, Richard, 83
Tora Bora, 39, 196, 246
torture: rendition and, 250, 251;
   Zammar, Muhammad Heydar, 320;
   Zawahiri, Ayman al-, 321;
   Zubaydah, Abu, 325
Toth, John, 382
training camps: Islamist extremists and,
   23, 92, 150, 198–199, 270; special-
   ties of camps, 340–44; suicide mis-
   sions and 173

Transportation Security Administration
   (TSA), 21, 106, **281–83**
Trans World Airlines, 103
Trevor, Greg, 379–84
Trusted Traveler Program, 283
Tully Construction Company, 68–69, 82,
   83
Turabi, Husan al-, 36
Turco, Fred, 76
Turner Construction Company, 68–69,
   82, 83
TWA Flight 800, 170
Twin Towers. *See* World Trade Center
   complex

Unabomber, 128
Union officials, 120
United 93, **289**
United Airlines, 16, 24, 47, 90
United Airlines Flight 93: Beamer, Todd
   Morgan, 29, 30; Bingham, Mark
   Kendall, 32, 33; Burnett, Thomas
   Edward, 46–48; Dahl, Jason
   Matthew, 80–81; Disaster Mortuary
   Operation Response Team
   (DMORT), 84, 85, 86; Glick,
   Jeremy, 137–38; Homer, LeRoy
   Wilton Jr., 156–57; Jarrah, Ziad
   Samir, 162, 163–64; NORAD,
   216–17; Pentagon attack, 235; Sep-
   tember 11 hijacking, 213, 214,
   284–86; "United Airlines Flight
   93," 391–96
United Airlines Flight 175: Saracini, Vic-
   tor J., 262–63; September 11
   hijacking, 213, 214, **287–88**; She-
   hhi, Marwan Yousef Muhammed
   Rashid Lekrab al-, 269–70, 271;
   World Trade Center attack, 306–7
United Airlines Flight 800, 167, 225
United Arab Emirates, 13, 73
United Nations, 49
Universal Pictures, 289
University of al-Azhar, 3
University of Colorado, 62–65
University of Maine, 75
University of Minnesota, 75, 113
University of Montpellier, 200
University of Waterloo, 74
unlawful detainees. *See* prisoners of war
Urduni, Abu Turab al-, 197
U.S. Air Force, 239–41

Usama Bin Laden Unit. See bin Laden Unit
USA PATRIOT Act, **290–92**, 301
U.S. Customs Service, 70
U.S. Department of Defense. *See* Department of Defense
U.S. Department of State. *See* State Department
U.S. Institute of Peace, 135
USS Cole: Counterterrorism Center, 78; Kuala Lumpur meeting, 180; O'Neill, John, 225; Predator, 240; Qaeda, al-, 242, 245; Zubaydah, Abu, 324
USS *The Sullivans,* 191–92
U.S. Supreme Court, 124
U.S. Treasury Department, 273

Van Auken, Lorie, 100, 164
Van Essen, Thomas, 177
Victim's Compensation Fund, 164, **293–94**
Visa Express Program, 160, 191
visas, 160–61, 213, 237, 279
Voices of September 11, 96, 206
Volz, Thomas, 150
Von Essen, Thomas: firefighter riot, 120; Ganci, Peter J. "Pete," 133; Giuliani, Rudolph, 135, 136f; September 11 attacks, **294–98**; testimony from survivors, 376

Wag the Dog, 11, **299–300**
Wahhabi strain of Islam, 200
Wainio, Honor Elizabeth, 289
Wall Street Journal, 130
Wall, the, **300–301**, 450–53
Walt Disney Company, 94, 231
war on terrorism, 125, 140, 292
warrants, 123–25, 208, 290, 522–34
Washington Times, 208, 268
watch lists, 192, 279–81
Waters, Maxine, 504–6
Watson, Dale, 108, 109f, 236
weapons of mass destruction, 60, 93, 278–79
Webster, William, 76
Weeks Marine, 83
Weiner, Robin, 100
Weinstein, Harvey, 94
Weldon, Curtis "Curt," 6–8, 207–8, **302–3**, 507–10

whistle-blower protection, 259
Whitaker, Anthony, 305–6
White House: 9/11 Commission, 205–7; Clarke, Richard A., 66, 67; Counterterrorism Center, 78; families of victims, 97, 100, 164–65; Guantánamo Bay Detainment Camp, 145; Joint Inquiry committee, 140, 143, 267, 268, 269; USA PATRIOT Act, 290
"White House Declaration on the Human Treatment of al Qaeda and Taliban Detainees (February 7, 2002)," 425–27
Whitman, Christie, 318, 404–6
Wiley, Winston, 77
Williams, Kenneth, 235
Wilson, Garret, 167
Wilson, Michael, 95
Without Precedent: The Inside Story of the 9/11 Commission, 153
Witness Protection Program, 93
Wolfowitz, Paul, 49
Woods, James, 24
Woodward, Bob, 48, 51
Woolsey, James, 72
World Islamic Front, 338–39, 335–37
World Trade Center, **308–9**
World Trade Center Bombing (1993): Counterterrorism Center, 77; Downey, Ray Matthew, 88, 89; New York Fire Department (NYFD), 116, 305; *The Path to 9/11,* 231; plan and implementation **309–10**; radical Islamists, 3, 4–5, 8, 9, 195, 198; Salem, Emad, 122, 166–67; Yousef, Ramzi Ahmed, 312, 314, 315, 316, 329–30
World Trade Center complex: American Society of Civil Engineers (ASCE), 18–19, 428–34; building of, **303–4**; casualties, 55–58; cleanup operations, 68–71, 82–84; September 11 attacks and, **304–8**
World Trade Center United Family Group, 96
Worthington, Skilling, Helle, and Jackson firm, 304
WTC United, 96

Yamasaki, Minoru, 303–4
Yasin, Abdul Rahman, 179, 218, 309

Yemen: bin Laden, Osama, 36; National
    Security Agency (NSA), 208; Preda-
    tor, 240; Qaeda, al-, 245, USS *Cole*,
    191–92, 225
Your Father's Voice, 138
Yousef, Ramzi Ahmed: career as Islamist
    extremist, **312–16**; Counterterror-
    ism Center and, 77; Operation
    Bojinka, 203, 227–28; radical
    Islamists and, 5, 179, 195; rendition,
    249; World Trade Center bombing
    (1993), 8, 9, 309–10, 329–30
Yugoslavia, 322
Yunis, Fawaz, 249

Zadroga, James, 71, **317–18**
Zadroga, Linda and Joseph, 318f
Zammar, Muhammad Heydar, 23,
    319–20
Zawahiri, Ayman al-: bin Laden, Osama,
    35, 37f; career as Islamist extremist,
    320–23; Qaeda, al-, 246; radical
    islamists and, 21, 27, 192, 193,
    323
Zawhar Kili training camp, 73
Zelikov, Philip, 7
Zelikow, Philip D., 100, 175, 206, 208
Zery, Muhammed al-, 250
Zubaydah, Abu, 22, 255, **323–25**

About the Author

STEPHEN E. ATKINS is the Dorothy G. Whitley Professor and Curator for French Collections at Texas A&M University. He also teaches a course on extremism and terrorism in the Texas A&M History Department. His numerous published works include *Encyclopedia of Modern Worldwide Extremists and Extremist Groups* (Greenwood, 2004), *Encyclopedia of Modern American Extremists and Extremist Groups* (Greenwood, 2002), *Historical Encyclopedia of Atomic Energy* (Greenwood, 2000), which was awarded a Booklist Editor's Choice Award for 2000, and *Terrorism: A Reference Handbook* (ABC-CLIO, 1992).